Xunzi

*A Translation and Study
of the Complete Works*

VOLUME I
BOOKS 1-6

Aonao kosa akitoa hana lawama.
Who finds a mistake and removes it is not to be blamed.

From the Swahili poem *Wajiwaji*

Xunzi

*A Translation and Study
of the Complete Works*

VOLUME I

BOOKS 1–6

John Knoblock

STANFORD UNIVERSITY PRESS
Stanford, California

Stanford University Press
Stanford, California
© 1988 by the Board of Trustees of the
Leland Stanford Junior University
Printed in the United States of America

CIP data appear at the end of the book

To
J. Owen Knoblock
and
Anne V. Knoblock

who inspired in me in childhood
a love of learning

Preface

Though scarcely known in the West, Xunzi 荀子 occupies a place of importance in classical Chinese philosophy comparable to that of Aristotle in Greek thought. Standing near the end of a great tradition of philosophy, he is a systematic figure whose works sum up, criticize, and extend the traditional analysis of the perennial problems of Chinese philosophy. His works encompass virtually the whole range of topics discussed by Chinese scholars.

Like Aristotle, he molded successive ages. During the Han dynasty, his philosophy shaped learning and scholarship not only because of the pervasive influence of his thought but also because of his remarkable successes as a teacher. Xunzi taught a whole generation of scholars whose traditions of learning dominated the intellectual world of the Han dynasty. Through the filiation of master and student, he determined the Han interpretation of ritual and its role in government, of the Classic of Poetry, of the role of music, of the nature of education, and of the lessons of history. More important still, the classical texts, understood within the framework of his philosophy, were the source of inspiration for countless thinkers, government officials, and scholars. Thus, his thought was absorbed into the whole Weltanschauung that then shaped the Chinese world, and through its incorporation into the structure of Han dynasty institutions, it persisted for many centuries thereafter.

His influence first began to decline when Buddhism introduced alien patterns of thinking to the Chinese world and added dimensions of thought undeveloped during the classical period. Later in the Song dynasty, the reemergence of Mencius as a major thinker caused Xunzi's reputation to suffer an eclipse. Interest in him revived only during the florescence of scholarship during the Qing dynasty. With the advent of the modern period, and especially since the Communist Revolution, he has again been recognized as a thinker of great importance.

The world of Xunzi, like that of Aristotle, was undergoing a rapid and radical transformation. Aristotle witnessed irrevocable changes in the fundamental character of the ancient world—Greek, Egyptian, and Persian—wrought by the conquests of his student Alexander. Xunzi saw the end of the Zhou dynasty that had ruled for more than 700 years. He observed the annihilation of the feudal states and the unification of the Chinese world by the invincible military power of the First Emperor of Qin 秦始皇帝. Finally, he witnessed the emergence of a new world order crafted by his brilliant student Li Si 李斯.

Xunzi was deeply affected by these events. They made impossible the optimistic and idealistic views advocated by Mencius, and they molded his philosophy in ways later generations of Chinese would find unattractive. At the end of his life, Xunzi believed that the collapse of the world he had known had resulted in the renunciation of all the values he thought fundamental to civilized life. He concluded that left to follow its course, man's nature would inevitably lead to conflict and evil and that only through man's conscious effort is good possible. Idealists of later centuries abhorred this doctrine and excoriated Xunzi for advocating it. They never considered seriously the hope that his doctrine nonetheless permitted and did not notice that he himself had never despaired that the vision of society he shared with Confucius and Mencius could be realized.

Xunzi's works have generally been neglected in the West. They never enjoyed imperial patronage like the *Analects* and *Mencius*. They contain no doctrines that could be construed to anticipate Christian doctrines like Mo Di's 墨翟 "universal love." They were not written in fluent and evocative language like the *Daode jing* 道德經 and *Zhuangzi* 莊子. The *Xunzi* has accordingly not proved attractive to translators. Xunzi's earnest intensity and careful precision in argumentation led to a clear but unattractive style. To the lay reader, his thought seems insufficiently "Chinese." It does not intrigue with esoteric mysteries known only in the inscrutable Orient, and it is too systematic and rigorous to allow boundless speculations on the ultimate.

In English, there are at present only the partial translations of H. H. Dubs and Burton Watson, which present the text with only the barest of discussion. Both are inadequate for scholarly research. More recently, Herman Köster translated Xunzi's complete works, again with only brief discussion, into German. My translation attempts to rectify this by examining virtually every available critical study in Chinese and Japanese and taking into account recent developments in the study of Chinese philosophy both on the mainland and in the West. My aim has been to produce a literate English translation that conveys the full meaning of Xunzi's philosophical arguments. My translation differs from most recent efforts in several respects.

1. It includes substantial explanatory material identifying technical terms, persons, and events so that the English reader is provided the same level of information routinely provided in such Chinese and Japanese editions of the text as Fujii Sen'ei 藤井專英, the Beijing University student edition, and Liang Qixiong 梁啓雄, for audiences much better informed about China than are Americans.

2. It provides a detailed introduction to each book that summarizes the philosophical points made and their relation to the thought of other philosophers.

3. It indicates in extensive annotations, with characters when desirable, the basis of my renderings when alternatives exist either in the textual tradition or when the text is variously emended by important scholars.

To present Xunzi in a fashion that is easily understood and provides all the material necessary to grasp his argument, I have provided a general introduction with chapters devoted to: (1) the biography of Xunzi set in the history of his times, particularly as it directly affected his works; (2) the influence he had on later times through his thought, his students, and the institutional structure of learning in ancient China; (3) the intellectual world in which Xunzi lived and the controversies and figures that then thrived; and (4) the basic terms that the Chinese use to discuss the structure and pattern of nature and the origins and ideal nature of society.

Much of this is obvious to sinologists, but these facts are quite unknown even to the educated, who find themselves confronted with an impossible task in trying to locate a convenient explanation of some mystery. Such information would doubtless be superfluous in a work on Greek philosophy since there are standard references in English and other European languages that address virtually every problem that might be encountered in Greek philosophic texts. This is not true of philosophy or of any other discipline in China. My aim in doing this is to present an edition useful to scholars without requiring constant reference to the Chinese original, but providing the necessary apparatus to do so when desired, and a translation accessible to a general, educated public interested in Chinese philosophy.

I provide extensive historical information so that the reader will have some sense of the setting of philosophical controversies and the historical background they assumed. Whereas the translator of Aristotle can assume that an educated reader knows that Alexander came after Perikles or that the Trojan War was described in the *Iliad*, the educated public recognizes only two ancient Chinese names: Confucius and Mencius. More recently the First Emperor has become known, but it is the rare

Western reader who can place these figures in their correct chronological order.

The reader's task is greatly complicated by the confusion created by different systems of romanization. Distinguishing between the older Wade-Giles system and the newer *pinyin* makes every name problematic even for a devoted reader. I have chosen to adopt the *pinyin* because it eliminates the constant problem posed by the apostrophes of the Wade-Giles system, it allows people to pronounce correctly many important names and concepts, and it is quite likely that it will become universal during the next decade.

Xunzi's works can be divided into four groups. Books 1–6 discuss self-cultivation, learning, and education. Books 7–16 discuss political theory, ethics, the ideal man (the *junzi* 君子 or "gentleman"), and the lessons to be drawn from history. Books 17–24 discuss problems of knowledge, language, and logic, the fundamental nature of the world, the significance of music and ritual, and the nature of man. Books 25–32 contain Xunzi's poetry, short passages collected together in one book, and various anecdotes about historical events and persons. Some of these last books have often been regarded as compilations made by his students. I present these materials in three volumes: (1) General Introduction and Books 1–6; (2) Books 7–16; and (3) Books 17–32. Materials specific to each book and to each volume can be found in the introductions to each book and to each volume. Thus, materials on Xunzi's interpretation of history and his political philosophy are in the introductory materials to Volume 2, and those on logic, epistemology, and language are in Volume 3. Each volume contains an appendix dealing with the problems of composition of each book, as well as a glossary defining the more important technical terms that Xunzi uses.

This translation is based on the texts of Wang Xianqian 王先謙 (1842–1918) and Kubo Ai 久保愛 (1759–1832) with reference to the basic scholarship published since. The speculations of commentators are sometimes very tedious, and I have accordingly omitted most of them, but I occasionally cite specific examples to give the reader a feel for the intellect of the commentator and a basis for independent judgment. By observing how a commentator's understanding of a variety of passages differs from mine, the reader can determine whether there is some merit to another interpretation of certain critical passages. Although it is possible to check a Chinese edition of the text, unfortunately no edition, Chinese or Japanese, contains all the commentaries that I consulted and that are cited in the notes. The most comprehensive are those of Wang Xianqian and Kubo Ai, but they reflect only nineteenth-century scholarship. The work of twentieth-century scholars is scattered in articles (many in obscure periodicals), collected works, and a few editions of the *Xunzi* prepared for the general public during this century. For this reason, I sometimes cite important divergent opinions of commentators even when I reject their conclusions. To facilitate location of the Chinese text for a particular passage, I include tables correlating each paragraph with the pagination of Wang Xianqian's *Xunzi jijie* and the Harvard-Yenching Index line numbers.

I have adopted the convention of calling each *pian* 篇 a "book" since each has a title. Within each book I have divided the text into paragraphs. The books are numbered according to Yang Liang's order, with the major divisions being numbered within each book, thus 1.1, 1.2, ... Where a paragraph is extremely long or where there is a natural division within it, such as a later passage explicating an earlier passage, I have made subdivisions indicated by letters (15.1a, 15.1b). In matters of paragraph divisions, I have generally followed Fujii Sen'ei, who in turn based his divisions on Lu Wenchao 盧文弨, Kubo Ai, and Wang Xianqian. Most of these divisions date to Song times and possibly earlier. These matters are discussed in the introductory chapter entitled "History and Authenticity of the *Xunzi*."

Throughout this work, all dates are B.C. unless otherwise indicated. In the notes to the translation, I cite only the authority, but do not give the pagination since this varies between editions and printings. In the commentaries, the practice is to cite the text passage under consideration in the order of the *Xunzi* text before the commentary itself. This makes for easy location. Translations within the text and notes are my own, though I have consulted the standard translations of most works. I cite a particular translator when his rendering provides a difference in meaning that would affect the argument or when it makes additional points that cannot be made by a single version of the Chinese original in English.

I have benefited from the generous support of the University of Miami over the long period I have worked on this project. This includes two sabbatical leaves, three Orovitz Summer fellowships, travel grants, and research support grants.

I am indebted to the National Endowment for the Humanities for a one-year fellowship that enabled me to examine rare editions of the text in Japan and Taiwan.

Much of the bibliographic research for these volumes was undertaken at the Libraries of the Hoover Institute, Stanford University, and the East Asiatic Library, University of California, Berkeley. I am indebted to the staffs of both libraries for their unfailing assistance to a visiting scholar.

Without the help and guidance of friends, colleagues, and librarians, this study could never have been undertaken or completed. To the many individuals who have been so generous with their time, information, advice, and wisdom, I offer my sincere gratitude: to my old friends and colleagues Dr. Jeffrey Riegel and Dr. Richard Williams, with whom over the years I think I must have discussed every sentence and who have contributed to this work in countless ways; to the anonymous Stanford University Press reader for his constructive criticism and intelligent suggestions, which have greatly improved this work; to Mr. Raymond Hsu 徐振寰, bibliographer at the Richter Library, University of Miami, for his assistance in many matters; to my assistants, Mr. Zhu Xiaorong 朱小榮 and Ms. Liu Quanxin 劉全心, for their help in inserting the characters and in proofing the *pinyin*; to my editor, Ms. Helen Tartar, for her help and encouragement through the long process of preparing the final form of the manuscript; and to those who have helped me in preparing this work and who are best served by anonymity. The errors and misapprehensions that remain are my own.

J.K.

Contents

Abbreviations

The following acronyms are used in the text, the Notes, and the Bibliography:

ACRONYM	TITLE	EDITION
BIHP	*Bulletin of the Institute of History and Philosophy*, Academia Sinica	
BMFEA	*Bulletin of the Museum of Far Eastern Antiquities*, Stockholm	
BTSC	*Beitang shuchao*	Dai Hai
DDJ	*Daode jing*	SBBY
DDLJ	*Da Dai Liji*	SBCK
DLZZ	*Dalu zazhi*	
FSTY	*Fengsu tongyi*	SBBY
GSB	*Gushibian*	
HFZ	*Hanfeizi*	SBBY
HNZ	*Huainanzi*	SBBY
HS	*Hanshu*	SBBY
HSBZ	*Hanshu buzhu*	Yiwen
HSWZ	*Hanshi waizhuan*	SBCK
JAOS	*Journal of the American Oriental Society*	
KZJY	*Kongzi jiayu*	SBBY
LSCQ	*Lüshi chunqiu*	SBBY
LY	*Lunyu*	SBBY
QSZY	*Qunshu zhiyao*	Yiwen
SBBY	Sibu beiyao Collection	
SBCK	Sibu congkan Collection	
SFGW	Shifan Daxue *Guowen yanjiusuo jikan*	
SJ	*Shiki kaichū kōshō*	
SY	*Shuoyuan*	SBBY

TP	*T'oung Pao*	
TPYL	*Taiping yulan*	
TZ	Taizhou edition of the *Xunzi*	
WX	*Wenxuan*	Guang Da
YWLJ	*Yiwen leiju*	Zhonghua
ZGC	*Zhanguo ce*	SBBY
ZT	*Zuantu huzhu* edition of the *Xunzi*	

In addition, the following editorial conventions are used in the notes to the *Xunzi*:

GE (Graphic Error). A character misread and miscopied for another character that it resembles in some identifiable script form. Some such errors are systematic. A problematic emendation, generally rejected except where context confirms the word or where the error is systematic in the *Xunzi* or in related texts.

GL (Gloss). Reference is to the sequentially numbered glosses in Bernhard Karlgren, "Glosses on the *Book of Odes*," *BMFEA* 14 (1942), 16 (1944), 18 (1946); and "Glosses on the *Book of Documents*," *BMFEA* 20 (1948), 21 (1949). The separately numbered glosses to the *Zuo zhuan* and *Liji* in Karlgren, "Glosses on the *Tso Chuan*," *BMFEA* 41 (1969), 1–158, and "Glosses on the *Li Ki*," *BMFEA* 43 (1971), 1–65, are distinguished by *Tso* GL and *Li* GL.

GV (Graphic Variant). A character that is an orthographical variant of another character normalized with another "signific" or, in rare instances, another "phonetic" in the later development of the script; confirmed by regular variation in the *Xunzi* or in other contemporary texts.

LC (Loan Character). A character to be read as a substitution for another of similar or identical pronunciation. These have been examined by Bernhard Karlgren, "Loan Characters in Pre-Han Chinese," *BMFEA* 35 (1963), 1–128, 36 (1964), 1–105, 37 (1965), 1–136, 38 (1966), 1–82, 39 (1967), 1–51, and by Zhang Heng, whose opinions I have generally followed.

SF (Short Form). A character consisting only of a "phonetic" and lacking the "signific" that was normalized for the word in later developments of the script.

UR (Urtext). A reading inferred as the original reading of the text on the basis of variants between editions, parallel texts, or quotations in Tang works predating the Yang Liang commentary. Indicated by an asterisk (*) preceding the romanization or reconstructed character.

GENERAL INTRODUCTION
■■

I

Biography: The Early Years

For most ancient Chinese philosophers, we know little more than that they once visited a particular king, which supplies a rough dating of their life and work. The sources for Xunzi's life permit not only a reconstruction of the outlines of his career but also an understanding of his intellectual development. Sima Qian 司馬遷 wrote a biography of Xunzi,[1] which was later expanded by Liu Xiang 劉向, who edited and compiled Xunzi's works to create the *Xunzi*.[2] Together with what we can deduce from the *Xunzi* itself and from other sources, we have an uncommonly complete and detailed picture of his career. Like most Chinese, Xunzi was deeply versed in the ancient lore that was then thought to be the true record of history. In common with the practice of the time, he used the mirror of history to judge the present. By combining our rich historical knowledge of Xunzi's times with the material in his books, we can not only understand the development of his thought through his long career but also see the probable effects historical events had on it. Thus, in developing Xunzi's biography and in dating his various works, we will examine the major events of the day when their effect can be seen in his thought.

STUDENTSHIP AT THE JIXIA ACADEMY

Xunzi was born about 310 in the state of Zhao 趙.[3] His name was Xun Kuang 荀況, but he was generally known as Xun Qing 荀卿, Minister Xun, after the office he once held. The age in which he lived is known as the Warring States period because of the incessant, internecine conflicts that consumed all the rulers of the time. The Warring States period began in 453 with the partition of the ancient state of Jin 晉 into the states of Wei 魏, Han 韓, and Xunzi's native Zhao. The partition sparked an ever-more violent series of confrontations between the various states of ancient China, first for domination and then to become the universally recognized successor to the moribund Zhou 周 dynasty. Many eminent families in Jin had been destroyed during the internal struggle leading up to the partition, two branches of the Xun family among them. Xunzi was perhaps a descendant of this noble family. But we know nothing of his background, and we cannot relate the development of his thought to any of the historical events affecting either Zhao or the Xun family.

We do know that he was precocious and traveled from his native Zhao to Qi 齊 when only fifteen to pursue his studies in the intellectual center of ancient China, the Jixia 稷下 Academy.[4] In his studentship and apprenticeship as a young scholar, Xunzi lived in a world that delighted in skill, virtuosity, and cleverness. He was obliged to master the doctrines of the many schools, the forms of argumentation, and the techniques of rhetoric at which the Jixia scholars excelled. It was the custom of the day for scholars to offer advice to rulers in the form of a reasoned argument that showed the utility of the plan presented, appealed to historical precedent, and showed the futility of other lines of action. These formal arguments were called *shuo* 說, or "persuasions," since their intent was to persuade a high minister or ruler to adopt a course of action. His studies complete, Xunzi first enters history with a persuasion addressed to the prime minister of Qi, Tian Wen 田文, Lord of Mengchang 孟嘗君 and Duke of Xue 薛公, a famous patron of learning.[5] He was at the height of his power and influence in the very years when Xunzi was in Qi, and it was natural that Xunzi should seek Tian Wen out to offer his talents and philosophy. But since Xunzi would be bitterly disappointed by his failure to influence Tian Wen and since that disappointment is evident in many of his books, it is important that we understand the basis of his judgments of men and of the lessons of history.

Tian Wen was the scion of a cadet branch of the ruling family of Qi. His career spanned the years 299–279. Because Tian Wen welcomed scholars from other states and treated them as his equals, his retainers came to number in the thousands. For this reason, he attracted scholars whose talents could "overthrow the empire" (*SJ*, 75.6). On the death of his father, Tian Wen succeeded to the fief of Xue (*SJ*, 75.4–6). Early in his career, he was invited to Qin 秦, where he was made prime minister, but since he was from Qi, his loyalty was suspect, and he was later forced to flee (*SJ*, 75.8–10). His cousin King Min of Qi 齊湣王 (r. 300–284) regretted that out of jealousy he had sent Tian Wen away and recalled him, putting him in charge of the government (*SJ*, 75.10). Subsequently, however, Tian Wen was slandered to King Min and was forced to take refuge in the security of his own fief, Xue (*SJ*, 75.12). After the conquest of Song in 286, King Min wanted to destroy Tian Wen; Tian Wen fled to Wei, where King Zhao 魏昭王 made him prime minister.[6]

It is evident that this is the immediate context of Xunzi's persuasion since he warns of the excesses of Qi's policies, of the resentments it has aroused, and of the inevitable doom that awaits it if it persists. He cites the traditional examples of Jie 桀 and Zhou Xin 紂辛, the ill-fated last rulers of the Xia 夏 and Shang 商 dynasties, who for all their power and prestige lost everything to the conquering Kings Tang 湯 and Wu 武, who founded the succeeding Shang and Zhou dynasties. He warns Tian Wen that though Jie and Zhou Xin had every advantage that power and position could offer and held spiritual authority over the empire, the whole world abandoned them because "Jie and Zhou Xin were adept at what men hate, whereas Tang and Wu were accomplished at what men like." Anyone, warns Xunzi, who pursues policies that men hate will be annihilated. But the persuasion did not succeed. Xunzi believed that Tian Wen exploited the flawed character of King Min to his own advantage. Both came to symbolize for him the wicked kings and unscrupulous ministers of his own day whose conduct was marked by "expediency and opportunism" ("Qiangguo" 強國, 16.4; "Wangba" 王霸, 11.1d).

King Min was a megalomaniac. Ambitious and ruthless, he alienated the other states, his own family, and his people. By alluding to the losses Chu 楚 and Qin suffered at the hands of King Min, Xunzi conveys the growing alienation that King Min was creating. King Min's annexation of Song 宋 in 286 made Zhao and Wei covetous of the rich territory that he had obtained. The hostility between Tian Wen and the king crystallized the opposition against the king. Tian Wen used his diplomatic skills to form a coalition against King Min. To Xunzi, this indicated that Tian Wen was a man utterly without scruples who schemed in behalf of his private interests by deceiving his king ("Chendao" 臣道, 13.1). So dangerous had the situation become that Xunzi seems to speak from the conviction that it was only necessary to await the proper moment when internal dissension made the time ripe for the coup de grace.

This happened in 284, when, at the head of the combined armies of Yan 燕, Qin, Wei, and Zhao, General Yue Yi 樂毅 invaded Qi and crushed the army led by Viscount Xiang 向子, who escaped in a single chariot (*ZGC*, 4.50b). King Min was forced to flee, first to Wey 衛, then to Zou 鄒 and Lu 魯, where his overweening pride and arrogance caused the inhabitants to bar his entrance. Blocked everywhere, he turned back to Qi and took refuge in Ju 莒, a small city-state then belonging to Qi near its border with Chu. The king of Chu sent General Nao Chi 淖齒 to rescue Qi (*SJ*, 46.41–42), but Nao Chi also became disaffected with King Min and bitterly indicted him for his crimes (*ZGC*, 4.50b–51a). He then incarcerated King Min, had his tendons drawn, and left him hanging from the beams of the Eastern Ancestral Temple overnight until he died.[7] During the chaos that ensued, the scholars of the Jixia Academy scattered. Some had left before, finding their criticism to no avail. "Shen Dao 慎到 and Master Jie 捷子 disappeared. Tian Pian 田駢 went to Xue. Xun Qing proceeded to Chu. Not a single good minister remained in the country" (*Yantie lun* 鹽鐵論, 2.10b–11a).

We can date a number of Xunzi's works to this period. The task is made more difficult by the fact that Xunzi did not compose the works in the form we have them today. The form of the present text is the result of Liu Xiang, who collected those of Xunzi's works that existed in the Han dynasty, edited and collated them, and arranged them to form the work we now know as the *Xunzi*. We do not know the original state of the materials that Liu Xiang collected or whether they were written by Xunzi himself or were compiled from the notes of his students or from fragments actually written by Xunzi. But however originally compiled, some books are today, through transmission if not original compilation, composite and heterogeneous entities. Some books, such as "On Strengthening the State," which contains Xunzi's persuasions of Tian Wen (dating 286–284) and of Fan Sui 范雎, Marquis of Ying 應侯 (dating 265–260), clearly contain parts that must be dated over a broad span of time. This testifies to their compilation from smaller units that once had an independent existence. Scholars have expressed the opinion that various passages or books were not by Xunzi because of apparent contradictions or other factors, but many of the objections can be removed if we merely assume that the works we now possess reflect the development of Xunzi's thought over time and as affected by the historical events of his day. We will defer to later examination of specific passages that appear to be interpolations into genuine texts. For now, we will treat each of his works as though the whole had been composed at one time by Xunzi.

While still in Qi, Xunzi probably wrote three of his books in addition to delivering the persuasion to the prime minister of Qi: the "Jiebi" 解蔽, "Dispelling Blindness"; the "Zhenglun" 正論, "Rectifying Theses," which offers his first criticism of the Jixia scholars; and the "Zhongni" 仲尼, "On Confucius." In these books, Xunzi criticizes and refutes doctrines known to have been associated with Shen Buhai 申不害, Shen Dao, Zhuang Zhou 莊周, Hui Shi 惠施, Mo Di 墨翟, and Song Xing 宋銒. In "Dispelling Blindness," Xunzi contends that such men were blinded by their obsession with a single aspect of the truth. "Rectifying Theses" records Xunzi's reply to various propositions advanced by the dialecticians of the day. Both books demonstrate the subtlety of his reasoning. We can date these books to early in his career because of his criticism of Zhuang Zhou and Shen Buhai, who are not mentioned in his later books, and because he calls attention to the recent demise of Song (in 286) and to Tang Yang 唐鞅, who was "so blinded by his desire for power that he expelled Master Dai" 戴子 ("Jiebi," 21.3). These two books reflect the same intellectual milieu as the persuasion for Tian Wen, where Xunzi had warned that a state must treasure its scholars, but his warnings did nothing to avert the blindness of Qi, which shortly would precipitate its near destruction.

"On Confucius," which states Xunzi's early political doctrines through the standard contrast made by the Ru 儒, as the adherents of Confucius styled themselves, between the way of kings 王 and that of the lords-protector 霸. His rigid, even doctrinaire, criticism of the lords-protector in favor of the founding kings of the Zhou dynasty bespeaks his early dependence on the traditional formulas of Ru political doctrine. His characterization of Guan Zhong 管仲 and of Duke Huan of Qi 齊桓公 is at odds with his later positions.

These three works, and the persuasion, present Xunzi as a fully mature scholar, accomplished in debate, master of the Ru tradition, and anxious to show wherein conflicting views go wrong.

AT THE COURT OF CHU

Leaving Qi, Xunzi traveled to the southern state of Chu. Whereas we have detailed knowledge of the major intellectual figures at the Jixia Academy, we know little of those at the cultivated and wealthy court of Chu, whose rulers had long patronized learning. We may presume that Xunzi knew of the poet Qu Yuan 屈原, who committed suicide shortly before Xunzi arrived. His acquaintance with the story of Shentu Di 申徒狄 (mentioned in "Bugou" 不苟, 3.1), who also committed suicide, may derive from this period, as almost certainly does his knowledge of poetry in the *fu* 賦 or rhyme-prose style first mastered by Qu Yuan. Xunzi himself became so skilled in writing rhyme-prose poems that his book of poems maintained an independent existence as a work of literature for some centuries.

Xunzi's visit corresponded to a brief period when Chu enjoyed a respite from constant attacks by Qin. Yet there he would witness the dismaying spectacle of a great and extensive country constantly forced to do Qin's bidding, demoralized by decades of bad government and weak and ineffective rulers, and slowly being devoured. Xunzi would later recall the events he had witnessed there in a conversation with his famous disciple Li Si 李斯: "Consider the circumstances of the death of the Father of the House of Chu, or when Qin overran the whole country so that Chu had to physically remove the ancestral temples of three kings, or finally its being forced to remove its capital to the region of the old states of Chen 陳 and Cai 蔡." [8]

Before Xunzi arrived, the king of Qin had inflicted defeat after defeat on Chu, taking thousands of heads and seizing and annexing its cities. During this time, King Huai of Chu 楚懷王, called the "Father of the House of Chu" after his treacherous capture by Qin, escaped his confinement and tried to flee home, but he was recaptured, having been refused sanctuary by his fellow lords. In 295, "King Huai died in Qin, which returned his body for burial in Chu. The people of Chu wept for him as though they were mourning the loss of a close relative" (SJ, 40.67–69, 5.66–67).

After this remarkable episode, Qin's attention was occupied elsewhere, and Chu enjoyed a decade of recovery. Near the end of this period, in about 283, Xunzi arrived. But in 280, before he had been there long, Qin forced Chu to cede the territories of Hanbei and Shangyong (SJ, 40.77). Two years later, in 278, General Bo Qi 白起 launched a major offensive against Chu, forced the capitulation of Ying, and desecrated by fire the Chu royal tombs at Yiling (SJ, 15.98). The position of the king of Chu was utterly destroyed, and the king quit Ying, fleeing eastward to reestablish himself at Chen.[9] His troops had been so badly routed that they could not reform for an orderly retreat and withdrawal. The next year, in 277, Zhang Ruo 張若, administrator of the lands conquered from Chu, attacked Chu and took the Wu Commandery as well as Jiangnan (SJ, 5.72–73). By this series of campaigns, the old heartland of Chu was lost, and the country reduced to the area of Chen and Cai, which it had conquered centuries earlier.[10] Xunzi observed that as a consequence of these events: "When Qin orders Chu to move to the left, it feels constrained to move left, and when Qin orders it to move right, it is constrained to move right. To such an extent has Qin made a lackey of its former adversary" ("Qiangguo," 16.5).

The following year, in 276, about the time Xunzi would leave Chu to return to Qi, the people by their independent action offered hope when ruler and ministers could offer none. The population on the Chu side of the Yangtze that Qin had just conquered revolted against its rule (SJ, 5.75, 15.99). Thereupon King Qingxiang of Chu 楚頃襄王 gathered an army of more than 100,000 men from his eastern territories and marched back to the west, where he succeeded in recovering all the territories that had been surrendered up to the bank of the Yangtze, some fifteen cities in all. From this reconquered territory, a commandery was created that it was hoped would block any further advance by Qin (SJ, 40.78).

From all these events, Xunzi drew important lessons for his political philosophy. They convinced him that Qin was in a position to conquer all of China. They showed him that "when the techniques of power," which he had witnessed Qin practice, "have reached their end, one must put into practice the arts of justice," that "one should moderate the over-emphasis on overawing others and should turn back to an emphasis on civilian matters," and that "the use of gentlemen who are correct, sincere, trustworthy, and complete is required to govern the whole world." Finally, the besting of Qin by the people of a conquered territory showed Xunzi that "for our present generation, augmenting territory is not as important as increasing the attention we devote to becoming trustworthy" ("Qiangguo," 16.5).

It seems probable that it was during this visit to Chu that Xunzi first became acquainted with the logical doctrines of the Mohists 墨家, who were particularly active in the south. They had been associated with Chu prominently since Mo Di himself had visited Chu during the reign of King Hui 楚惠王 (488–432)[11] and since Meng Sheng 孟勝, head of the Mohist Order, died in the defense of Yangcheng in 381.[12] The Mohists had made great progress in the two decades before Xunzi's visit to Chu in formalizing the discipline of logical argumentation and in defining the basic abstract concepts of logic.[13] In works attributable to this period, Xunzi mentions several logical problems that they analyzed: "hardness and whiteness," "similarity and difference," and "dimension and dimensionless." Xunzi rejects discussion of these problems because they are like "attempting to exhaust the inexhaustible and pursue the boundless." Rather, the gentleman will undertake "only what has an end."

We may presume that Xunzi's philosophy underwent considerable development in this milieu, though there is little in his works that, at present, can be directly dated to this period. Since Xunzi was considered an eminent scholar on his return to Qi, he must have first established his reputation by works produced in Chu. On varying grounds, we can associate the following works with Xunzi's stay in Chu:

1. "Quanxue" 勸學, "Exhortation to Learning";
2. "Xiushen" 修身, "On Self-Cultivation";
3. "Fuguo" 富國, "Enriching the State";
4. "Lilun" 禮論, "Discourse on Ritual Principles"; and
5. "Junzi" 君子, "On the Gentleman."

These books concern traditional Ru topics. As a group, they occupy an intermediate position between that illustrated in such early works as "Dispelling Blindness" and later works directly datable to his return to Qi. The "Exhortation to Learning" stresses the effects that education produces through the process of gradual accumulation. Education intensifies and permanently alters one's basic, inborn nature, like the blue dye that is bluer than the indigo plant from which it comes or like the wood steamed into the shape of a wheel rim that will not straighten out again as it dries. Education permits man to "borrow" the good qualities of other things. What distinguishes the gentleman is that he is good at making use of external things. The curriculum that makes this possible is the study of the classics, which are revivified by a teacher.

In the "Exhortation," in "On Self-Cultivation," and in the "Discourse on Ritual Principles," the central importance of ritual principles is stressed. For Xunzi, even more than for other Ru philosophers, ritual was fundamental to life. Everything depends on it—success, a fine reputation, even survival. "On Self-Cultivation" stresses that even such techniques as "control of the vital breath" and "nurturing life" must be based on ritual principles, since only then will good order penetrate everywhere. The "Discourse" explains that this occurs because the ancient kings, loathing the disorder produced by desires that observed no measure and no limit, "established the regulations of ritual and moral principles to apportion things, to nurture and train the desires of men, and to supply the means for their satisfaction" ("Lilun," 19.1). These three works form a piece, each related in concept and theme to the other. Xunzi clearly identifies himself with the Ru heritage and attempts to adapt Ru teachings to the issues of his day. Thus, during his stay in Chu, Xunzi's mature philosophy begins to emerge. Generally, after his visit to Chu, Xunzi makes use of its shortcomings as cautionary examples to other states similarly disposed.

During the time that Xunzi was in Chu, General Yue Yi of Yan conquered one city of Qi after another, sacked the capital, Linzi, and shipped its wealth back to Yan (SJ, 46.41). Since many of the royal family had fled to Anping, Yue Yi attacked it and took it by storm. In the ensuing melee, most of the royal family was captured, the relatives of Tian Dan 田單 alone escaping (SJ, 82.2). Yue Yi captured some 70 cities; only Jimo and Ju held out (ZGC, 4.50b). Knowing that King Min was in Ju, the Yan army attacked in force, but General Nao Chi stubbornly held the city, even after the execution of King Min (SJ, 82.2). After several years of siege, Nao Chi and Yan reached an accommodation, divided the territory that Qi had appropriated, and expropriated its famous saltworks (SJ, 46.42). The army of Yan then turned its attention to Jimo, but before Yue Yi could take it, King Zhao of Yan 燕昭王 died (279), and King Hui 惠王 ascended the throne. He had an aversion to Yue Yi that was aggravated by a secret agent from Qi. Sensing that his life was in danger, Yue Yi returned home to Zhao (ZGC, 9.34a).

The soldiers of Yan were indignant that Yue Yi had been relieved of his command. Tian Dan took advantage of the situation to give the appearance that divine power was in favor of Qi and that Yan could not take its last redoubt. By trickery, he took the Yan army by complete surprise and routed it. The Qi soldiers captured Yan's commanding gen-

eral, Qi Jie 騎劫, whom they executed. The Yan army then fled in confusion, pursued by the Qi soldiers. His ranks swelled with every fresh
victory, Tian Dan easily defeated the troops of Yan, reconquered the 70
cities, and then invited Min's son Fazhang 法章 to return from his exile in
Ju to Linzi to take the throne. Fazhang, known as King Xiang 襄王, subsequently enfeoffed Tian Dan as Lord of Anping 安平君 in recognition of
his services (*SJ*, 82.4–6).

We do not know how long the process of liberation lasted or when
King Xiang actually began to rule from Linzi.[14] Presumably after a short
interval, the king attempted to restore the Jixia Academy to its former
prestige, granting the title "distinguished grand officer" to the scholars
he attracted. Since Xunzi was at the time the "most eminent elder
scholar," King Xiang had him "thrice make the sacrifice of wine" (*SJ*,
74.13–14). It was ritual practice that in the feasting accompanying sacrifices to the ancestors, the most honored member of the party officiated
at the ceremony. Thus, Xunzi was three times selected to hold the place
of preeminence among the distinguished grand officers. This possibly
means that Xunzi was head of the Academy during this period.

AT THE JIXIA ACADEMY

We may assume that Xunzi arrived in Qi sometime after 275 when
he would have been in his mid-thirties. His prestige must have been significant, considering the honors paid him by the king. We are familiar
with the most important figures of the day who, like Xunzi, were associated with the Academy. Tian Pian and Shen Dao were probably dead,
but their ideas must have been well defended by their followers.[15] Huan
Yuan 環淵, Yin Wen 尹文, and Chen Zhong 陳仲 were presumably still
active there and must have been his principal rivals.[16] Near the end of his
tenure, Zou Yan 鄒衍 and Zou Shi 鄒奭 had perhaps arrived.[17] Quite
likely this is the period when the work known as the *Daode jing* 道德經,
the *Way and Its Power*, associated with Laozi 老子, the "Old Master,"
came into general circulation. Xunzi's mature philosophy is to be found
in five works that probably date from this period:

1. "Rongru" 榮辱, "Of Honor and Disgrace";
2. "Wangba" 王霸, "Of Kings and Lords-Protector";
3. "Tianlun" 天論, "Discourse on Nature";
4. "Yuelun" 樂論, "Discourse on Music"; and
5. "Xing'e" 性惡, "Man's Nature Is Evil."

The demise of Song wrought by King Min and the subsequent destruction of Qi because of his unwise policies and those of Tian Wen
forced Xunzi to rethink his earlier position. He concluded: "Though

[Qi's] strength was sufficient to break Chu in the south, to subjugate Qin in the west, defeat Yan in the north, and confiscate the territory of Song in the middle, it still led to Yan's and Zhao's rising up to attack Qi. As easily as shaking dead leaves from a tree, King Min was murdered and his country lost. He suffered the greatest disgrace in the world. When later generations teach about evil, they must examine his case" ("Wangba," 11.1).

Tian Wen, who had helped engineer the destruction of King Min, managed to get independence for his fief Xue, but it came to nought; after his death in 279, his sons fought over the succession to his position. Qi and Wei collaborated in absorbing his lands; no one succeeded to the title of Duke of Xue, and the line of Tian Wen was cut short. The "expediency and opportunism" that marked "each day" of the careers of both Tian Wen and King Min so imperiled their countries that they "could not escape danger and destruction until ultimately they perished." "Their fate was the result of no other cause than that they proceeded not from a basis of ritual principles and moral duty but rather from the dictates of expediency and opportunism" ("Wangba," 11.1).

Xunzi held that the "state is the greatest structure in the world" and as such "it involves heavy responsibilities" that are not easily met. The ruler and his ministers must keep in mind the model of government bequeathed from antiquity by the sage kings, who founded the great dynasties of the past. Xunzi continued to believe "the theory that a territory of 100 square *li* could be used to take the empire." History taught that this was the case with King Tang of Shang and Kings Wen 周文王 and Wu of Zhou. Thus, the theory could not be dismissed as "mere empty rhetoric." The "difficulty lies in getting the lords of men to know it" ("Wangba," 11.6).

To contrast with the negative examples of the Duke of Xue and King Min, Xunzi develops the positive, though imperfect, example of the Five Lords-Protector 五霸, "all of whom were of despised and backward countries," yet who "held majestic sway over the world and whose might held peril for all the Central States." Xunzi reiterates ("Wangba," 11.1) the same criticism he had made of them in "On Confucius" (7.1): "They were not a source for the fundamentals of instruction in the art of government"; they did not attain to "what is highest and most noble"; they provided no "standard of good form" or any "principle of order"; and they were unable "to win over the hearts and minds of mankind." But he now notes that their success "resulted from no other cause than that they were in the main trustworthy." In his early work "On Confucius," Xunzi had criticized Duke Huan of Qi, the first and most important of the Five Lords-Protector, as merely a "hero for ordinary men." There Xunzi thought the duke's conduct had been so "treacherous, vile, lecherous, and excessive" that it was inconceivable that "he could ever truly deserve to be praised by the school of the Great Gentleman," as Confucius was known to the Ru. All of this had been written in Qi, where the institution of lord-protector was highly regarded since it had been founded by their greatest ruler.

Having seen Qi destroyed through the misinformed policies of King Min and Tian Wen and having just observed in Chu the servile and demeaning captivity of that state at the hands of Qin, Xunzi reconsidered as he wrote "Of Kings and Lords-Protector." He was now prepared to recommend that if a ruler might not aspire to the example of the sage kings, he might at least protect his state with the lessons of the lords-protector. Xunzi, who previously was willing only to discuss those "who possess it [the Way] in pure form" and who could become kings, would now discuss those "who possess it in mixed form" and could become lords-protector, which was much better than those "who lack any [knowledge of the Way] at all and are annihilated" ("Wangba," 11.2).

Xunzi continues to regard the doctrines of Mo Di and Shen Buhai as invidious to good government. He still finds the influence of Shen Dao and Song Xing strong, and for the first time we find that the doctrines associated with Laozi have become so important that Xunzi expresses his criticism of them. Now he was powerfully influenced by the concept of a constant Nature, one that did not respond to good government with auspicious signs or to bad government with omens. "The course of Nature is constant: it does not survive because of the actions of a Yao; it does not perish by the actions of a Jie.... Accordingly, flood and drought cannot cause famines; cold and heat cannot cause sickness; inauspicious and weird events cannot cause misfortune" ("Tianlun," 17.1). This constancy of Nature is of the utmost importance since it means that the gentleman too must be constant: "Heaven possesses a constant Way 道, Earth has an invariable size; the gentleman has a constant character" (17.5).

Because Nature is constant, order and chaos result not from Nature, but from man. Unusual events such as stars falling or trees groaning occur "because of a modification of the relation of Heaven and Earth or a transmutation of the Yin 陰 and Yang 陽.... We may marvel at them, but we should not fear them" (17.7). Though we may pray for rain and it does rain, there is "no special relationship—as when you do not pray for rain and there is rain" (17.8). Thus, for the gentleman, the ceremonies and rites are "embellishments," whereas the petty man considers them to be "supernatural": "To consider them embellishments is fortunate; to consider them supernatural is unfortunate" (17.8). Ritual principles are markers that the enlightened ruler uses to show the people the Way so that the "pitfalls that entrap the people can be avoided" (17.11).

In "Of Honor and Disgrace," Xunzi observes that the inborn nature of man is certainly that of the ordinary man (4.10). All men possess the same fundamental characteristics (4.9). The gentleman and the petty man do not differ as to their inborn nature: "In natural talent, inborn nature, awareness, and capability, the gentleman and the petty man are one. In cherishing honor and detesting disgrace, in loving benefit and hating harm, the gentleman and the petty man are one. Rather, it appears that the Way they employ to make their choices produces the difference" (4.8). Differences between men are created by the effect of differences in their aspirations and by the habituation of their customs. The gentleman, though he knows that behaving with humanity, justice, and virtue may involve peril, follows their dictates because he is led by the normal, whereas the petty man is led by the exceptional (4.8). These doctrines are given their full development in "Man's Nature Is Evil." Xunzi builds on the earlier development of his ideas in "Exhortation to Learning," "On Self-Cultivation," and the "Discourse on Ritual Principles" together with the ideas on inborn nature found in "Of Honor and Disgrace."

Xunzi argues that "inborn nature" consists only in "what is spontaneous from Nature, what cannot be learned, and what requires no application to master, ... like the clear sight of the eye and the acute hearing of the ear" ("Xing'e," 23.1c). Mencius and others err in imagining that man's inborn nature is good. Goodness is the result of conscious effort. "The sage by transforming his original nature gives rise to his acquired nature" (23.2a). This change is produced in the sage, as in the ordinary individual, by the "transforming influence of a teacher and the model" and through "the guidance of ritual principles and a sense of moral duty" (23.1a). These are like the press-frame that straightens crooked wood or the whetstone that sharpens dull metal (23.1b). The process by which this is accomplished is accumulation. "The sage accumulates his thoughts and ideas. He masters through practice the skills of his acquired nature in order to produce ritual principles and moral duty and to set up the model and objective measures" (23.2a).

A sage like Yu 禹 possesses no special talents. His inborn nature is identical to that of the common mass of men. He has no special talents that exceed those of the ordinary man. What makes him "different from them" is acquired nature, and wherever "he exceeds them, it is his acquired nature" (23.3a). The ancient saying that "a man in the street can become a Yu" means that "every man has the capacity to know and the full ability to put into practice" what is required to become a Yu. "What made Yu a Yu was his use of the principle of humanity, of justness, the model, and rectitude" (23.5a). If the man in the street were to "cleave to these methods and to engage in study," were he "to ponder these principles, examine them, and thoroughly investigate every aspect of them," were he "to add each day to his accomplishments over a long period of time," and were he "to accumulate what is good without slacking off," then he could become a sage himself. "The sage is a man who has reached this high state through the process of gradual accumulation" (23.5a).

In his "Discourse on Music," Xunzi argues that music is the necessary and inescapable natural expression of man's essential nature. Musical performances of the *Odes* 雅 and *Hymns* 頌 broaden and deepen our experience. They give cultivated expression to our delight and to our anger, containing both within their perfected form. Since music transforms man, the ancient kings were assiduous in creating proper forms. Music allows the emotions of love and hate to find expression in feelings of joy and anger. Music contains the whole gamut of emotion— sadness, dignity, obedience, joy—but also arousal and dissipation. Mindful of this, the ancient kings took care that no disorder should be produced ("Yuelun," 20.1). Because of the immediate response it evokes in men (20.2), "music is the most perfect method of bringing order to man" (20.3). Here, as elsewhere in his works, Xunzi is responding to arguments of Mo Di, who condemned as wasteful the elaborate ritual in funerals and elaborate musical performances in court that the Ru advocated. "What benefits men, the man of humane principles will carry out; what does not benefit them, he will leave alone," argued Mo Di (*Mozi*, 32 "Fei yue" 非樂, I 上, 8.21a). "Sounding great bells, striking drums, strumming zithers, blowing pipes, and waving shields and axes in the war dance," observed Mo Di, "do nothing to feed the people when they are hungry, clothe them when they are cold, or give them rest when they are weary" (32 "Fei yue," I, 8.22b). But to Xunzi, Mo Di's understanding of music was shallow. He failed to grasp its essential place: "Music embodies harmonies that may never be altered, just as ritual embodies principles of natural order that may never be changed. Music joins together what is alike; ritual separates what is different. The guiding principles of ritual and music are the pitchpipe for the mind of man" (20.3). Because of the havoc Mozi's doctrine of condemning music would cause with the government of the sages, one would have expected Mozi to meet with some kind of punishment. That Mo Di did not could only be because in his time "all the enlightened kings had already died and there was no one to put things aright" (20.3).

In his years as the "most eminent elder scholar" at the Jixia Academy, Xunzi established the reputation that would ultimately bring him such talented students as Han Fei 韓非 and Li Si. We do not know how long

Xunzi remained in Qi at the Academy, but eventually he was slandered and began to entertain invitations from other feudal lords. The likely time for this to have happened is at the end of 265 when King Xiang died and King Jian 齊建王 succeeded him.

Xunzi would now be in his mid-forties, having established a solid reputation, having written significant books, and having thrice been libationer at the Jixia Academy. He had not yet been entrusted with any office but was consigned only to debate and deliberate what should be done. It was the lot of philosophers, good and bad, to be "traveling persuaders" who went from court to court and from patron to patron. They always hoped to attract the attention of some powerful official who would present them to the ruler or the powerful lord who held the actual reins of power. Xunzi must have hoped that his eminence in Qi would result in office, but it did not. Now, at mid-life, he faced the prospect of joining the ranks of the unemployed scholars who traveled from court to court.

2

Biography: The Later Years

Xunzi's eminence at the Jixia Academy probably enabled him to receive invitations to visit the courts of other rulers. We know no details of these invitations, but it is apparent from his works that he visited at least Qin and Zhao. From Qi, the sources tell us that Xunzi went to Qin.[1] His journey to Qin presented both an opportunity and a challenge: the opportunity to convert the king of the most powerful country to the practice of True Kingship and thereby to establish the new dynasty to succeed the decrepit Zhou; and the challenge to make Ru doctrines attractive to the king of Qin, who was wedded to the practical, strict philosophy of government created by Shang Yang 商鞅. Although the effects of his reforms were well known in the Chinese world, no philosopher mentions Shang Yang's ideas as constituting a philosophy of government. Both the Mohist *Canons* and the *Zhuangzi*, which antedate Xunzi's visit to Qin, ignore Shang Yang.[2] Even Xunzi mentions him only as a general and then only in his debate with the Lord of Linwu 臨武君 on military affairs ("Yibing" 議兵, 15.1d). It is first in the *Hanfeizi* 韓非子 that Shang Yang is reckoned a philosopher of government.[3]

Wey 衛 Yang, the Lord of Shang 商君, is known to history as Shang Yang, taking the name of his fief Shang as his surname, as was the custom. He was the descendant by a concubine of the ducal family of Lesser Wey, a noble and ancient state that had been reduced to utter insignificance. Being fond of the doctrine of performance and office,[4] Shang Yang attached himself to Prince Zuo 公叔座 of the state of Wei, who realized his immense talents. But before Prince Zuo could present Shang Yang to the court, the prince fell ill. When King Hui 魏惠王 came to see him, Prince Zuo recommended Shang Yang. The king listened but did not respond.

[Prince Zuo] asked that everyone leave and said to the king: "If your majesty will not heed my advice to employ Shang Yang, then you must put him to death and not allow him to leave the country." The king agreed and departed.

Prince Zuo summoned Yang and said to him with regret: "Today, the king asked me who should be made prime minister, and I said that it should be you. From the king's appearance, he did not agree with my recommendation. At that time, because I put the interests of the king first and that of his subjects second, I advised that if you were not to be employed, you should be executed. The king assented to my request. You should depart as soon as possible or you will be arrested."

King Hui attributed the advice of Prince Zuo to the effects of his illness and ignored it (*SJ*, 68.2–3).

In 361, just as Prince Zuo died, Duke Xiao 秦孝公 came to the throne of Qin. Long before this, under Duke Mu 穆公 (r. 659–621), Qin had been so powerful that its duke was made lord-protector (*Zuo*, Huan 3; *SJ*, 5.36). Duke Mu had forced mighty Jin to yield substantial territories west of the Yellow River, but these had been lost under his successors (*SJ*, 5.27). Duke Xiao was anxious to restore this lost grandeur, and he sought out capable men from throughout the Central States with promises of wealth and power (*SJ*, 5.49–50). Shang Yang, learning of the invitation, traveled west to seek audience with the duke. Relying on the standard prescriptions of the way of the ancient kings and emperors, Shang Yang merely bored the duke. Finally he discussed the way of the lords-protector, which proved to interest the duke. So intense did their conversation become, the duke did not notice that in his enthusiasm Shang Yang violated ritual protocol by allowing his knees to advance onto the duke's mat. They talked continuously for several days without the duke tiring (*SJ*, 68.3–4).

Finally employed, Shang Yang proposed in 359 to reform the laws, but the duke feared disapproval from the rest of the world. Shang Yang responded:

He who is hesitant to act will acquire no fame. He who falters once the course of action is begun will accomplish nothing. Further, those who act so as to exceed what others can accomplish will, as a matter of course, be condemned by their age. Those who have thoughts of independent knowledge are certain to be mocked by the people.

The stupid hear only of what is already accomplished, but the wise man sees what is to come before it has begun.[5]

The people are incapable of participating in the beginning, but they can share in the joy of its completion.

One who aims in his discourse to analyze the highest virtue is not in harmony with the customs of his time. One who intends to perfect a great achievement does not take counsel with the masses.[6]

It is for these reasons that the sage, if he is to be able to strengthen his country, does not model himself after ancient traditions, nor can the sage, if he is to benefit his people, adhere to established ritual practices.[7]

This speech expresses most of the radical views of Shang Yang, ideas that would become increasingly influential in the last half of the third century and would win over Xunzi's most famous pupils: Li Si and Han Fei.

The sage aspires to "independent knowledge" that does not derive from what he has "heard" from his teachers since then he would know only "what has already been accomplished"; rather, he aims "to see what is to come before it has begun." That others condemn and mock him is to be taken for granted since the stupid cannot be expected to understand anything great when it has just begun. They can share only the joy of its completion. Ancient traditions and established ritual practices are as nothing to the man who aspires to the highest virtue and the greatest accomplishment.

Other ministers at the Qin court predictably opposed Shang Yang's suggestions. They argued, in full accord with the Ru tradition, that "the sage teaches without changing the people. The wise govern without changing the laws. One who teaches his people in accord with established custom perfects his achievements without effort" (*SJ*, 68.6). Shang Yang dismissed such opinions as the pedestrian views of the man in the street. History teaches something quite different: "The Three Dynasties established their royal dominion with different ritual practices. The Five Lords-Protector attained their hegemony with different laws. The wise create laws; the stupid are governed by them. The worthy man alters ritual practices; the talentless man is enslaved by them" (*SJ*, 68.7).

Gaining the duke's assent, Shang Yang began the general reform of Qin's laws and thereby transformed the whole character of Qin society (*SJ*, 68.7-9). A crisis occurred when the crown prince broke the law. Shang Yang insisted that the laws be applied. Since the crown prince could not be executed, his guardian and his teacher were punished instead. After this, the laws were obeyed, and when ten years had passed, the people were content with the new order. Sima Qian, probably quoting an earlier account, describes the result in utopian language: "Things lost on the road were not picked up and pocketed. In the mountains there were no brigands or robbers. Families had enough to support their members. The people fought bravely in war, but were timid in private feuds. Great order prevailed in the countryside and towns" (*SJ*, 68.10).[8]

A few years later, Shang Yang built a new capital and inaugurated a second set of reforms as radical as the first. He abolished the old land system, introduced new and regular tax measures, and standardized weights, scales, and measures of quantity and length (*SJ*, 68.11).[9] Despite his great success in reforming the country and making it a powerful state,[10] he succeeded in alienating most of the nobility and insisted that the crown prince, who had once again disobeyed the laws, be punished (*SJ*, 68.11). When the duke died and the crown prince became king, Shang Yang met his doom, but the transformation he had made in Qin remained (*SJ*, 68.20).

AT THE QIN COURT

When Xunzi came to Qin, he had an audience with Fan Sui, the Marquis of Ying, who was the prime minister ("Qiangguo," 16.6). Xunzi may have met Fan Sui some years before when Fan Sui had been part of a diplomatic mission from Wei to King Xiang of Qi.[11] At that time, Fan Sui attracted King Xiang's attention as a gifted practitioner of the art of philosophical debate. Their association perhaps renewed, the Marquis of Ying asked Xunzi what he had observed since he first entered the borders of Qin. Xunzi's response, though couched in the polite and deferential language required when addressing the chief minister of a powerful state, showed how impressed he was with what he had seen. He had become aware that the geographical position of the state gave it great power, that "its topographical features are inherently advantageous," and that its manifold natural resources gave it remarkable inherent strength. Its people were unspoiled and exceedingly deferential; its officers unfailingly respectful, earnest, reverential, loyal, and trustworthy; and its high officials public-spirited, intelligent, and assiduous in the execution of the duties of their position. Its courts and bureaus functioned without delays and with such smoothness that it was as if there were no government at all. In all these respects, generally conceded to be the result of Shang Yang's philosophy, the government of Qin was like that of antiquity.

Even allowing for the customary exaggeration that good form required, this is a remarkable description, coming as it does from an inhabitant of an eastern state, who would as a matter of course regard everything in Qin as barbaric, and from a person of the Ru persuasion, who would be naturally inclined to be suspicious of and to deprecate the elevation of positive, created law that characterized Qin. All of this, concluded Xunzi, shows that it was the result not of chance good fortune but of method and calculation that Qin for four consecutive generations had been victorious over all its opponents. Still, noted Xunzi, "the vast extent to which it fails to reach the ideal of True Kingship" is manifest in the fact that it is "filled with trepidation" that its neighbors will unite to destroy it. The reason was simple: "It is dangerously lacking in Ru scholars" ("Qiangguo," 16.6).

When Xunzi subsequently had an audience with King Zhaoxiang of Qin 秦昭襄王 (r. 306–251), he pursued the point that Ru are necessary to the attainment of True Kingship ("Ruxiao" 儒效, 8.2). Though all the rulers of the day called themselves "king," they had no right to the title since they could not and did not claim to have received any Mandate from Heaven such as justified the Zhou dynasty and before it the Xia and Shang. Their title was an empty pretension without recognized authority. A True King was universal, he ruled with the assent of the people and not through force of arms, and he received a Mandate from Heaven that entitled him to rule. His government was based on *de* 德, an inner power or moral force, the prestige of which attracted others to him. When he gave commands, the people obeyed. Compulsion was unnecessary since they were anxious to please and wanted, even sought out, his rule. He had no cause for fear because none could oppose his *de* moral power. But since Qin followed the doctrines of Shang Yang, it required armies and was fearful. It thus needed further reform, and the agent of that reform must be the Ru scholar, who alone possessed the authentic traditions that enabled Xia and Shang to rule over "all under heaven."

The king was unsympathetic to such views. Qin was a backward state where scholarship had no place and where learning was not admired. The contrast between rustic Qin and the sophisticated and learned court of Qi was complete. Qin had succeeded in attracting an unbroken succession of brilliant and able ministers following Shang Yang by offering them unparalleled opportunity and by not placing impediments of birth or background in the way of their advancement. Skill and success alone counted. Some twenty years later, when Lü Buwei 呂不韋, himself only a merchant, became prime minister, the climate of opinion had so changed that Lü thought it necessary to invite scholars to Qin to give it the prestige and polish required for a universal state. King Zhaoxiang, however, was unaffected by such sentiments and bluntly demanded of Xunzi: "Are the Ru scholars of no real benefit to the state?"

Xunzi answered that they are "a real treasure to the lord of a state" and "true ministers to its altars of soil and grain," and that "in them the Way is in truth preserved." They are all these because "they esteem to the utmost their superiors," because "they are clear as to the great principles to be employed," and because "they are totally acquainted with the classical standards and ordering norms" that enable them "to control and complete the myriad things and to nourish the Hundred Clans." Xunzi cites the example of Confucius, who, during his tenure as director of crime 司寇 in Lu, altered the behavior of the people because the transforming influence of "his cultivation of personal rectitude" so affected them. Even children "apportioned the catch of their nets so those who had parents took more because his cultivation of filial piety so transformed them."

Naive and conventional though it may now seem, the argument interested the king enough to make him inquire what happens when a man of the Ru persuasion becomes a ruler. Xunzi noted:

Such a lord acts with justice and faithfulness toward the people. When news of him travels to the limits of the four seas, the whole world will respond to him with shouts of joy. Why is this? Because whenever his noble reputation is clearly made known, the world becomes well ordered. Hence those who are near him sing his praises and rejoice in him, while those who are far away stumble and fall over each other in their rush to be near him. All within the four seas are as of one family, for wherever his reputation penetrates, no one fails to follow him and submit to him. ("Ruxiao," 8.2)

Though the king responded with the customary "well argued," he did not see fit to follow Xunzi's advice or to give him any office.

When Xunzi came to Qin, he was an orthodox, though sophisticated, Ru scholar. His merit consisted in his ability to answer the arguments of the Jixia scholars while retaining traditional Ru values. His thought was broader, more complex, and more systematic than that of his predecessors. Had he undergone no further change, he might be remembered as a pessimistic Mencius because of his doctrine that man's nature is evil. His stay in Qin changed all that. His orthodox and glib adherence to the model of antiquity, his faith in the Ancient Kings, his stress on ritual, and his distrust of created, positive law would all be challenged by the example of Qin. It had all the appearances of a well-ordered state. Even the example of Confucius in Lu hardly exceeded it. Yet it possessed none of the values transmitted from the Ancient Kings. How could such order have been produced? It was a question that required Xunzi to reexamine his whole philosophy. The visit to Qin and the events he witnessed on his return to his native Zhao shattered the world that, even after King Min's demise, still permitted the comfortable Ru confidence that moral suasion alone could transform the age. When Xunzi left Qin, he was about 50. He had not held even a minor office. He had never had an opportunity to test his views. His successes were all as a gifted scholar. He still had been allowed only to deliberate, but never to govern.

AT THE COURT OF THE LORD OF PINGYUAN

Xunzi left Qin at a critical juncture. Qin had begun a major campaign against his native Zhao. By 261, when we must surmise Xunzi was still there, Qin had so extended its domains that it had an effective border with Qi and, having seized Weijin, was within 40 miles of the Wei capital, Daliang. The threat such an expansion posed was clear to all, since these moves were the deliberate policy of Fan Sui.

Years before, Wei Qi 魏齊, a prince of the ruling family who served as prime minister of Wei, had ordered Fan Sui killed, but Fan had escaped to Qin (*SJ*, 79.3). In 271, Fan Sui managed to get the ear of King Zhaoxiang (*SJ*, 79.6). He advanced his plan of action, citing the examples of the disasters associated with Tian Wen and King Min of Qi (*SJ*, 79.10–19). After his advice had yielded success, Fan Sui was in a position to challenge the authority of the king's relatives, who held the most important posts of government, particularly the Marquis of Rang 穰侯. He triumphed by 265 when he had become the Marquis of Ying and had assumed the office of prime minister (*SJ*, 79.23–24). It was then that Xunzi arrived.

Now in a position to repay Wei for its treatment of him, Fan Sui launched an attack that routed the army of Wei, allowing the Qin army to lay siege to the capital Daliang (*SJ*, 77.2). The king of Wei sent Xu Jia 須賈, who had been responsible for Fan Sui's bad treatment in Wei, to plead for peace from Qin. Since Fan Sui had assumed another identity when he fled to Qin, Wei had not anticipated the effect of Xu Jia's arrival (*SJ*, 79.24). Vindicated, Fan Sui demanded the head of Wei Qi (*SJ*, 79.24–28). The revenge against Wei was but the first stage of a broader campaign.

During Xunzi's stay in Qin, General Bo Qi had begun a series of brilliant campaigns that were decimating the Three Jin, as Han, Zhao, and Wei were collectively known. In 264, he attacked the Xing fortress in Han, forcing the surrender of five cities and taking 50,000 heads (*SJ*, 5.76, 15.104, 45.22). The following year, he attacked Nanyang in Han and cut off Han's line of communication across the Taihang mountains (*SJ*, 73.4, 5.76, 15.104, 45.22). In 262, he attacked Yewang, which surrendered, severing Han's line of communication with the rich region of Shangdang (*SJ*, 73.4). That year, faced with the Qin threat, the people of Shangdang proposed an alliance with Zhao, which King Xiaocheng 趙孝成王 (r. 265–245) deliberated with the Lords of Pingyang 平陽君 and Pingyuan 平原君 before accepting (*SJ*, 43.84–88, 73.4–5). The next year, Qin attacked Han again, forcing the capitulation of two cities (*SJ*, 73.5).

This put Qin in a position to seize Shangdang and attack Zhao. In 260, when Qin began its campaign against Shangdang, the Zhao army took up positions at Changping in order to calm the people of Shangdang. After months of skirmishes, Qin gained the advantage and forced the surrender of the entire army, some 400,000 soldiers, who were buried alive except for 240 of the smallest, who were allowed to return to Zhao (*SJ*, 73.5–8, 15.105, 5.76). The defeat was devastating to Zhao, which was left defenseless and unable to raise another army. Its demise seemed inevitable, awaiting only Qin's pacification of Shangdang.

This, of course, gave urgency to considerations of the principles of warfare. We may presume that Xunzi arrived in Zhao sometime about 260, just as these events were reaching their denouement. There he had a debate on the principles of warfare with the Lord of Linwu before King Xiaocheng. Xunzi warned against expediency and opportunism. He had seen these fail Tian Wen and King Min. He rejected recourse to sudden attacks, incursions, shifts in tactics, and dissimulation because these are unworthy of the humane man ("Yibing," 15.1b). He stressed that it was a general principle of the way of the ancients that unification of the people was the fundamental requirement that had to be met before the army could engage in attacks and campaigns (15.1a). Xunzi's advice seemed too vague to the Lord of Linwu, who pressed for the tactics deemed permissible for the warfare of a True King. Xunzi dismissed such matters as "secondary considerations left to marshals and generals." He advised that scholars are needed, just as he had advised the king of Qin. He suggested that the ordinances and edicts of the government must be trustworthy and the people must be coordinated (15.1a). This was a traditional notion, but one he had learned afresh from Shang Yang's successes in Qin. Incentives must be generous, and punishments must inspire awe (15.1c). This again was a policy inaugurated by Shang Yang. He continued with a detailed analysis of the skill of the various armies: the soldiers of Qi, who stress hand-to-hand combat; those of Wei, who are well trained to meet the demands of campaigning with heavy provisions and armaments; and those of Qin, who perform obligatory services that are stern and harsh (15.1d). He pointed out that of these three, Qin is best for maintaining over the long run a strong and populous country with vast territories yielding taxation. This is precisely why "there have been four consecutive generations of victories" in Qin (15.1d). Xunzi concluded with a review of the practices of the sage kings of antiquity.

That Xunzi still mentioned here, as he had in his audience with Fan Sui, Qin's four generations of victories, means that the debate took place before 257, when Qin was defeated at the siege of Handan, the Zhao capital. Xunzi discussed, in the aftermath of the debate, the recent unsuccessful attempt of Zhao to annex Shangdang (261–259). This suggests that the debate must have taken place between the tenth month of 259, when Shangdang had been secured by Qin (*SJ*, 73.8), and the first month of 258, when the first attacks on Handan were made (*SJ*, 73.10).

Xunzi's book "Yibing," "Debate on the Principles of Warfare," is distinctive in treating warfare, which is usually unmentioned, or even avoided, in the books of Ru scholars. Nonetheless, it was a traditional part of ritual, and possibly Xunzi is merely continuing to regard the matter of warfare within this context. Or perhaps he is departing from the usual Ru practice because of the extraordinary threat that Qin then posed to his own state. A second book, "Chendao," "On the Way of Ministers," can be dated to the siege of Handan. In it, he discusses the skill of the Lord of Pingyuan, who was able "to assemble the wise and to collect the strong together" and to secure the aid of "strong and martial lords," so that even though the king of Zhao was insecure, incapable, and would not listen, the Lord of Pingyuan still was able "to rescue the state from the greatest of calamities and to deliver it from danger of the greatest injury." That in the end the actions of the Lord of Pingyuan caused "his lord to be shown deference and his country to be made secure" was for Xunzi "the true meaning of 'assistance.'" Similarly the exceptional course that the Lord of Xinling 信陵君 took in obstructing the mandate of his lord, in acting without permission in matters of overwhelming importance to his lord, and in contravening what his lord had decreed "in order to secure the state against danger and to deliver the lord from disgrace, resulting in accomplishments and military achievements sufficient to consummate the greatest benefits for the state is the true meaning of 'opposition'" ("Chendao," 13.2). Xunzi concludes that their actions in the crisis surrounding the rescue of Handan and the salvation of Zhao from impending annihilation show that the conduct of the Lord of Pingyuan may be called "true assistance" and that of the Lord of Xinling may be called "loyal opposition": "One should follow the Way and not follow the lord" (13.2).

Zhao Sheng 趙勝, the Lord of Pingyuan, was a member of the ruling family of Zhao and by common consent the ablest of the nobles. He was a patron of learning and supported several thousand scholar-retainers (*SJ*, 76.2). He served as prime minister under both King Huiwen 趙惠文王 (r. 298–266) and King Xiaocheng (*SJ*, 15.90, 15.103). When Qin laid siege to Handan, the Lord of Pingyuan was sent on a secret mission to Chu to secure its aid in the struggle against Qin (*SJ*, 76.4). He was successful in securing the aid he requested, but by the time he returned, the situation in Handan had become desperate, and the city was on the verge of capitulation (*SJ*, 76.6–7). "The people of Handan are in such straits that they are exchanging their sons, eating their flesh, and using their bones as kindling. . . . The people don't have even enough sackcloth to cover their backs or enough chaff and husks to fill their bellies. Exhausted and left with no weapons, they are reduced to sharpening sticks to serve as bows and arrows" (*SJ*, 76.8–9). Following the advice of his retainers, Lord Pingyuan distributed all his supplies and had the ladies of his harem assist his troops. Assembling 3,000 men who were prepared to risk their lives, he made a desperate charge against the entrenched Qin troops, who were forced back some ten miles (*SJ*, 76.9).

Wei Wuji 魏無忌, the Lord of Xinling, was the brother-in-law of the Lord of Pingyuan (*SJ*, 77.6) and the younger brother of King Anxi of Wei 魏安釐王 (r. 276–243; *SJ*, 77.2). Having a reputation for a kindly and unassuming manner, the Lord of Xinling attracted several thousand followers, who kept him informed of all that happened in every court of China (*SJ*, 77.2–3). The Lord of Pingyuan asked for aid against Qin, and Wei dispatched 100,000 men to rescue Zhao. But before the troops reached the border, the king of Qin sternly warned that Zhao was about to fall and Qin would attack any state coming to its aid. King Anxi of Wei was utterly terrified. He ordered his troops to halt at the border. Despite repeated pleas from the Lord of Xinling and the constant entreaties of the Lord of Pingyuan, the king would not send aid to Zhao. Finally, the Lord of Xinling resolved to go to Zhao's aid himself and set out with 100 men (*SJ*, 77.7). After a retainer contrived a scheme that enabled him to seize command of the Wei army (*SJ*, 77.8), the Lord of Xinling sent home fathers whose sons were serving in the army and the elder of brothers. With 80,000 troops remaining, he proceeded to Zhao. He arrived just as the Lord of Pingyuan's troops had made their successful charge against the Qin troops (*SJ*, 77.10). At the same time, troops under the command of Huang Xie 黃歇, the Lord of Chunshen 春申君, arrived from Chu (*SJ*, 78.15). The three armies united, attacked the Qin army, routed it, and lifted the siege. This success delayed by some 30 years the ultimate conquest of all China by Qin. It was the most celebrated event of the century, and the reputations of Pingyuan, Xinling, and Chunshen were made there.

The "loyal opposition" of the Lord of Xinling caused Xunzi to rethink the role of the loyal minister. Such men were in his view the "true ministers of the altars of soil and grain and real treasures to their lord. To an intelligent lord they deserve the deference and generosity he shows them, but to a benighted lord they seem to be a threat. Thus, those whom the intelligent lord rewards, the benighted lord punishes; those whom the benighted lord rewards, the intelligent lord punishes" ("Chendao," 13.2).

The actions of the Lord of Xinling constitute true obedience deriving from "a comprehensive understanding of loyalty." It is to be contrasted with the "blind adherence to instructions that hold the potential for calamity and anarchy" (13.9). To the examples of the Lords of Xinling and Pingyuan, Xunzi adds that of Wu Zixu 伍子胥, who several centuries earlier had offered good advice only to be killed by his king, who would not heed it. Xunzi realized that any advice that was useful to his own age would have to deal with the fact that there were no sage rulers nor, it seemed, any who aspired to sagehood. Rather, there were mediocre rules, who had little ability, no strong principles, and no inclination to self-restraint. With them, one faced the problem of being loyal and trustworthy without toadying to their desires and the problem of remonstrating and wrangling without engaging in flattery. Worse than the weak and inept ruler was the cruel and violent lord who aspired to accomplishment and power. Here the problem was to be conciliatory without compromising principles, flexible without causing distortion, and tolerant without causing anarchy. Faced with service of such a lord, "one proceeds as though one were driving unbroken horses, or caring for an infant, or feeding a starving man. Thus, one should avail oneself of his fears to modify his excesses, use his distress to discriminate its causation, depend on his pleasures to gain entrance into his way, and avail oneself of his wrath to gain protection from rancor" (13.4).

In addition to the "Debate on the Principles of Warfare" and "On the Way of Ministers," it seems probable that Xunzi completed his "Wangzhi" 王制, "On the Regulations of a King," and his "Zhishi" 致仕, "On Attracting Scholars," both of which he probably had begun in Qin. The most important of his works to be associated with his stay in Qin and Zhao is "Fei shier zi" 非十二子, "Contra Twelve Philosophers," which reflects the intellectual milieu that Xunzi found in the court of the Lord of Pingyuan. Below we will examine the many figures active at the court of the Lord of Pingyuan. All of them were scholars who, except perhaps Zou Yan, would have become well known to Xunzi during his stay in Zhao. Except for Yu Qing 虞卿, their ideas were opposed to Xunzi's fundamental beliefs. He criticized their views and castigated those who debased the Ru heritage by allowing such ideas to be associated with the name of Confucius. His stay in Zhao represents the transition to his late philosophy.

MAGISTRATE OF LANLING

Just after the siege of Handan was lifted, Xunzi had his first and only opportunity to implement his policies. Huang Xie, the Lord of Chunshen, impressed with his abilities, offered Xunzi the position of magistrate of Lanling (SJ, 74.14, 78.15; Liu Xiang, Preface). Xunzi may have come to the attention of Huang Xie when Huang was a diplomat from Chu in Qin at the same time as Xunzi's visit there (SJ, 78.2), but more probably they became acquainted in the aftermath of the siege when both were in Handan. His appointment as magistrate is the only firm date in Xunzi's life; it occurred in 255 (SJ, 78.15).[12] It would appear that from 255 to 246 Xunzi passed his life uneventfully in Lanling teaching his students (SJ, 74.14). But sometime between 246 and 240, a retainer persuaded Chunshen to dismiss Xunzi: "Tang started with Bo, King Wen with Hao, neither exceeding 100 li in size, yet these fiefs were enough for them to gain the whole world. At present, Xunzi is one of the worthiest men in the world, yet my lord would give him a fief of 100 li for his maintenance. Your servant ventures to suggest that this may prove inconvenient to my lord. Is this not so?" (ZGC, 5.38b). The retainer alluded to the theory, then accepted as historical fact, that the great founding kings of the Shang and Zhou dynasties had started their campaigns to conquer the world with tiny and insignificant fiefs. The success of their efforts gave testimony to the justness of their cause since they could not have succeeded without the action of Heaven, which had given them a mandate to rule in recognition of their moral worth. As Xunzi was similarly worthy, would not Chunshen be creating his own destruction by giving him a fief sufficient to conquer the world? Chunshen accepted this argument and sent an envoy to thank Xunzi for his services.

During the time he held no position in Chu, Xunzi traveled to Zhao, where he was made a senior minister, and possibly to Qin as well (Liu Xiang, Preface; FSTY, 7.2a). Wang Xianqian 王先謙, after a thorough review of the evidence, surmises that his dismissal and subsequent invitation to return to his post at Lanling are connected with the events of 240 when Chunshen was blamed for the failure of an alliance against Qin that he had been charged with managing.[13] Another retainer persuaded the Lord of Chunshen: "When Yi Yin 伊尹 left Xia and went to Yin 殷, Yin came to rule and Xia perished. When Guan Zhong left Lu and went to Qi, Lu grew weak and Qi grew strong. Indeed, wherever there is a worthy man, the lord is always honored, and the state always flourishes. At present, Xunzi is one of the worthiest men in the world, so why has my lord declined his services?" Chunshen accepted this argument and sent an envoy to request that Xunzi return to his post (*ZGC*, 5.38b). Invited to return, Xunzi declined in a famous letter harshly critical of Chunshen:[14]

"Even a leper pities a king." The words of this saying are disrespectful; nonetheless, it is important that we examine their meaning more deeply. They refer to rulers who have been robbed and murdered or who died in ruin. If a ruler who is young in years wants to depend on his own abilities but lacks any model or method through which to recognize treachery, then his great ministers will usurp his rule. They will decide affairs of state according to their own private interests so as to prevent themselves from being punished. For this reason, they will murder older, worthier rulers to set up immature weaklings in their stead, and they will degrade the legitimate heir to install one who is not. The "Spring and Autumn Annals" warns against this, saying:[15]

Prince Wei of Chu 楚王子圍 had left on a goodwill mission to Zheng, when, before he reached the border, he heard that the king had fallen ill. He turned back to inquire about the king's disease, used the opportunity to strangle the king with the tassel of his cap, and in the course of events had himself placed on the throne.

Duke Zhuang of Qi 齊莊公 committed adultery with the wife of Cui Zhu 崔杼, who was quite beautiful. Cui Zhu led his partisans in an attack on the duke. The duke requested that he be permitted to divide his dukedom with Cui. Cui would not permit it. He next begged that he be permitted to put himself to the knife in his ancestral temple. But again Cui would not allow it. Then the duke tried to flee and, while climbing over the outer wall, was shot in the rump. The duke having been murdered, his younger brother Duke Jing 景公 was installed in the position.

In our own time, we have witnessed Li Dui 李兌, who, when he administered Zhao, starved the "Father of the Ruler" 主父 in the Sand Dune palace, where after 100 days he died. Further, there was Nao Chi, who, when he administered Qi, had the tendons of King Min drawn and let him hang from the beams of his ancestral temple overnight until he died.

So, though a leper endures ulcerations, swelling, and disease, this is better than, as in earlier times, being strangled with a tassel or shot in the rump, or, as in recent times, having one's tendons drawn or being starved to death. Certainly the ruler who is robbed and murdered or who dies in ruin is agonized in mind and suffers in body far more than does the leper. From this point of view, it can be seen how "a leper pities a king."

At the end of this letter Xunzi composed the "Rhyme-prose Poem for the Lord of Chunshen," which is now to be found in his collection ("Fu" 賦, 26.8), and cited, as was customary, appropriate verses from the *Odes*.

His letter outraged the powerful lord, but Chunshen nonetheless again summoned Xunzi to return to Lanling. "Because he could not avoid it" (*FSTY*, 7.2a), Xunzi resumed his post, which he kept until the assassination of Chunshen in 238, when he was again dismissed (*SJ*, 74.14; Liu Xiang, *Preface*).

Xunzi no doubt believed that if given a chance to implement his philosophy, he would be able to make significant changes. It was a cardinal belief of the Ru scholars, which Xunzi firmly held, that in three years major changes could be wrought. He had told the king of Qin of the extraordinary changes produced by Confucius in just three years as director of crime. He had personally witnessed the remarkable changes accomplished by the New Laws of Shang Yang in Qin. These laws did not follow the model, yet were impressive. How much more might be done following the correct model bequeathed from the sages! Though Lanling might be small, it was large enough. Indeed, it was approximately the same area as the dominions of Tang of Shang and King Wen of Zhou before they became universal kings. Though Xunzi was then in his mid-sixties and no longer in his prime, he was at last afforded an opportunity to demonstrate the effectiveness of his teachings. We have no indications of his successes as magistrate. Liu Xiang thought that had Xunzi been made a high officer, his lord might have become a universal king (*Preface*).

Four of Xunzi's books probably date to this period:

1. "Bugou" 不苟, "Nothing Indecorous";
2. "Fei xiang" 非相, "Contra Physiognomy";
3. "Zhengming" 正名, "On the Correct Use of Names"; and
4. "Fu" 賦, "Rhyme-prose Poems."

Two of these contain direct evidence of their dating. "Contra Physiognomy" mentions the physiognomist Tang Ju 唐舉, who gained fame for predicting the career of Cai Ze 蔡澤, who, like Xunzi, lived into the reign of the First Emperor 秦始皇帝. Tang Ju's prediction came true in 255 when Cai Ze replaced Fan Sui as prime minister of Qin (*SJ*, 79.34–35). It is possible that Xunzi's criticism of the view that "since the circumstances of the past and present are quite different," the way by which the past and the present are to be governed "must be different" is aimed at the views of his pupils Li Si and Han Fei ("Fei xiang," 5.5). Li Si is known to have left Xunzi in 247 to seek office in Qin, and Han Fei perhaps left shortly thereafter (*SJ*, 87.2–4). The rhyme-prose poem that Xunzi composed declining Chunshen's offer of reinstatement must date to approximately 240 ("Fu," 26.8). "Nothing Indecorous" and "On the Correct Use of Names" contain Xunzi's final attack on the sophisms of the logicians and the confusion they bring to thinking. "On the Correct

Use of Names" makes use of the whole range of logical analysis developed by the Mohists and such logicians as Hui Shi and Gongsun Long 公孫龍 and refutes their positions with a coherent defense of the Ru positions. To many readers, it is his most impressive book, and it shows his considerable debt to the Mohists.

RETIREMENT IN LANLING

The Lord of Chunshen was assassinated in 238. Chunshen had been prime minister of Chu for more than twenty years. During most of that time, he had been the de facto king. When the old titular king became ill, Chunshen was presented with an opportunity to become regent as had Yi Yin and the Duke of Zhou of old. Zhu Ying 朱英, however, warned him that Li Yuan 李園 was plotting a palace coup to seize the government. Chunshen chose to ignore the counsel, dismissing Li Yuan as a weak and ineffective man. Zhu Ying, realizing that disaster was imminent, fled. Seventeen days later the king died; Li Yuan sprang his coup, sent a suicide squad to ambush Chunshen, killed him, and wiped out his whole family (*SJ*, 78.21). "Early in his career, when Chunshen persuaded King Zhao of Qin and risked his own life to secure the safe return of Chu's crown prince, what brilliance and perspicacity he showed! Later when he allowed himself to be manipulated by Li Yuan, he had become old and senile" (*SJ*, 78.22).

The Lords of Pingyuan, Xinling, and Chunshen had by their joint action at the siege of Handan, given the Central States twenty years of relative peace from the depredations of Qin. When in 247 Qin invaded Wei, Xinling, in command of the combined armies of five states, crushed the Qin army and pursued it as far as Hangu Pass, which guarded entry into Qin proper (*SJ*, 44.48, 77.14). But by the expedient of simple bribery, Qin was successful in getting Xinling removed from his command (*SJ*, 77.15). He died in 244 (*SJ*, 44.49, 77.15). Now with the assassination of Chunshen, not a single great minister remained to oppose Qin. The end only awaited its action.

Xunzi was devastated and demoralized by Chunshen's assassination. He was instantly dismissed from office, but far worse he realized that the last hope was gone. His thoughts are expressed in a collection of poetic laments based on a working-song meter, "Working Songs."

> The ruination of our generation:
> stupid and benighted, stupid and benighted, bringing to
>   naught the worthy and virtuous,
> these rulers of men who have no worthy ministers

> are like the blind without their assistants.
> How aimlessly they wander about!
>
> ("Chengxiang" 成相, 25.1)

The spectacle of the age, with its worthless rulers, filled with suspicion, unwilling to listen to criticism, stupid yet willful, could only be the harbinger of tragedy.

> Slanderers advance to prominence,
> worthy and able men flee and hide so their nation is torn apart;
> the stupid are used to give importance to the stupid,
> the benighted importance to the benighted.
>
> (25.6)

The age condemned itself by despising worthy knights. Great men are killed like Wu Zixu or banished like Boli Xi 百里奚. If only one ruler could realize that worthy ministers like these could make him powerful, even great.

> The stupidity of this age
> is its hatred of the great Ru.
> They are opposed, rebuffed, and made unsuccessful,
>   like Confucius being seized.
> Zhan Qin 展禽 was thrice degraded.
> The way of Chunshen was cut short,
> and its realization brought down.
>
> (25.11)

Xunzi saw that "the chariots in the van have already overturned." Zhou no longer existed, and Han and Wei had been reduced to vassals of Qin. Yet the "rear-guard" states—Chu, Zhao, Qi, and Yan—"still do not realize the necessity of altering their course. When will they wake up?" (25.35).

At this late date, in his mid-seventies, Xunzi saw the principal opponents of the Ru tradition to be Shen Dao, Mo Di, and Hui Shi. He had opposed their views his whole life but had not been able to defeat them. To these names, he adds the philosopher Ji 季子, a shadowy figure perhaps to be identified with the Ji Liang 季梁 of the Liezi 列子. His solution was a return to the "way of the Later Kings" (25.14). Du Guoxiang first noticed that in this work we have a different conception of the workings of society.[16] The classical standards of order are to be found in "ritual associated with punishments" (25.18). Xunzi now begins to stress "methods" and "law." He speaks of "when penal sanctions fit what has been set forth," of "when punishments and chastisements have fixed standards," of a time "when none will succeed in making them lighter or more severe" (25.50), and of when the people "devote themselves to the fundamental occupations" and "moderate expenditures" so that "resources should be without limit" (25.46). These ideas are related to the doctrines of the "Legalists" who reformed the laws in Qin and anticipate the doctrines of his student Han Fei.

Yet for all the changes we can see in his ideas, in his own mind Xunzi remained dedicated to Ru ideals.

> The way to good government
> is a thing of beauty that does not grow old.
>
> (25.21)

The gentleman cherishes it, devotes himself to it, and proceeds along this Way.

> His thoughts are refined to the essence,
> the flowering of his purpose.
> Cherish it, unify it, so the spirit is made complete.
>
> (25.20)

The gentleman dwells in it, steadfastly and earnestly. He keeps it deep within himself. He stores it up. He finds his authentic and genuine self in it. He becomes able to reach the furthest truths by pondering it.

> When essence and spirit revert to one another,
> when they are one and not two,
> he becomes a sage.
>
> (25.20)

The gentleman cultivates his inner power. He refines himself with music and ritual. All that he may do is keep in good repair the model transmitted from the Later Kings:

> So the nation will become orderly
> and the four seas tranquil.
>
> (25.18)

The gentleman cleaves to the Ru ideals "as though his mind were tied to them." Xunzi has no final doubts:

> Let us be as shepherds to its foundations;
> let those who are worthy ponder it;
> let Yao, who belongs to 10,000 generations, be visible in ours.
>
> (25.12)

The last stage of Qin's conquest of all China was about to begin. A major figure in its rise was the merchant-prince Lü Buwei, who used his

wealth to advance the career of a minor prince of Qin. Prince Chu 公子楚,
sent as a hostage to Zhao, made the acquaintance of Lü in Handan.
Lü used his persuasive powers and the influence of his money to have
the prince made crown prince (SJ, 85.2–4). His scheme worked. He
was able to persuade Lord Anguo 安國君 and Lady Huayang 華陽夫人,
who were childless, to adopt the prince and to designate him the rightful
heir to the throne when Lord Anguo, then himself crown prince, should
become king (SJ, 85.6). Unfortunately, Prince Chu and Lü found themselves in Handan during the siege. As the situation grew desperate, the
people of Handan wanted to kill Prince Chu. Lü used much of his
money to ransom the prince, and they fled to Qin, leaving behind Prince
Chu's wife and young son (SJ, 85.8). When Lord Anguo became king of
Qin, Zhao released his heir's wife and young son. Lord Anguo ruled but
one year. When Prince Chu became king, he made Lü his prime minister
and enfeoffed him as the Marquis of Wenxin 文信侯. Prince Chu ruled
only three years, leaving the throne to his young son. Lü became regent
(SJ, 85.9).

At Handan, Lü had seen how great lords like Xinling, Pingyuan,
and Chunshen were willing to humble themselves to attract worthy
followers. He believed that if Qin were ever to be accepted for the
powerful state it had become, it had to attract scholars who would add
intellectual brilliance and a veneer of culture to its court. He decided to
attract gentlemen to his service with offers of generous stipends and respectful treatment. In time, he gathered about him some 3,000 followers,
whom he supported from his own resources.

This was the time when there were many debaters in the courts of the feudal
lords, men such as Xun Qing, who wrote books that they circulated throughout
the world. Lü Buwei accordingly ordered that each of his retainers should record
what he had been taught. He collected these disquisitions, which were arranged
into eight encyclopedic surveys, six analytical discussions, and twelve records,
totaling more than 200,000 characters. He intended that they should encompass
all the affairs of Heaven and Earth, of all the myriad things, and of the past and
present. The work was entitled the Spring and Autumn of Mr. Lü 呂氏春秋.

(SJ, 85.10)

This work survives largely intact. It encompasses virtually the whole
range of classical Chinese thinking and provides us with an encyclopedic
view of the intellectual concerns of the 240's. The names of the retainers
who wrote the various books contained in the collection are not recorded,
but among his retainers was Xunzi's student Li Si, who in 247 had left
Lanling to heed Lü's call and seek his fortune (SJ, 87.3).

Lü allowed himself to be trapped in a palace intrigue and was exiled
in 237 (SJ, 85.14). There was a xenophobic reaction to all the eastern

intellectuals that Lü had attracted. A decree was promulgated expelling all aliens from Qin, but was annulled through the argument Li Si presented in a famous memorial (*SJ*, 87.6). Xunzi's student Han Fei went to Qin to present his views to its king and died there in 233 (*SJ*, 63.14, 27–28). During the next decade, Qin began its final conquest. Han was absorbed in 230, Zhao conquered in 228, Wei absorbed in 224, Chu absorbed in 223, Yan conquered in 222, and Qi conquered in 221. All the important states had been taken. For the first time, all of China was united in a single empire. The king of Qin was proclaimed the First Emperor. A new age dawned. Li Si participated in these events, constantly rising in power and influence until ultimately he became a high minister before 219 and chancellor before 213.[17]

Remembering his old teacher, now in his nineties, Li Si offered him a nominal position, but "prescient that he would fall into unfathomable disasters," Xunzi "would not take office under Li Si" (*Yantie lun*, 4.5b). Later, in 211, at the height of his career, during a banquet in his honor, Li Si suddenly speculated about his final end, recalling the advice given him by his teacher:

Alas! I heard Xun Qing say: "Prevent things from flourishing too much." I was then but an ordinary villager from Shangcai. My superior was unaware that his nag is inferior, and so I have been promoted to this position. Today, among all his servants, there is none who holds a higher position. This may truly be called the summit of wealth and honor. "When things reach their zenith, they begin their decline." I do not yet know where I shall be unharnessed.   (*SJ*, 87.14)

Sometime during these years Xunzi died a very old man, in his late nineties or possibly a hundred years old.

3

The Influence of Xunzi's Thought

Xunzi exercised a major influence on the Chinese world through the brilliance of his thought and the comprehensive nature of his writings, the exceptional talents of his disciples, and the role his tradition of scholarship played in the transmission of classical learning. Though he never met with any political success, Xunzi did have remarkable success as a teacher. Names survive of only a few of the students he attracted, but among them are several eminent figures: Han Fei, Li Si, Fouqiu Bo 浮邱伯, Zhang Cang 張蒼, Mao Heng 毛亨, and Chen Xiao 陳囂.[1]

XUNZI'S STUDENTS

Han Fei

Han Fei was the last great philosopher of the Warring States period and a gifted stylist. Burdened with a stutter that made it difficult for him to participate in persuasions and discriminations at court audiences, he polished his writings, which attracted him considerable attention (*SJ*, 63.14). When the king of Qin read his "Solitary Indignation" 孤憤 and "Five Vermin" 五蠹, he wanted to meet the man (*SJ*, 63.27). A scion of the ruling family of the state of Han (*SJ*, 63.14), Han Fei saw his country dwindling and weakening under the leadership of an impotent king who never attempted to reform the laws, never made use of the majesty of his position, never tried to strengthen his army, never sought to enrich his state, and never chose worthy and capable ministers. Instead, he elevated worthless vermin and frivolous beauties and supported arrogant literati who brought confusion to the laws. Han Fei devoted himself to writing books that warned against the king's policies and the impending doom of his country, but the ruler proved incapable of following his counsels (*SJ*, 63.15–16). Faced with disaster, the king of Han finally sent

Han Fei to Qin, where he made a good impression on that country's king (*SJ*, 45.23, 6.15, 63.28). But before he could gain his confidence, a court intrigue, perhaps involving Li Si, resulted in his death in 233.[2]

Li Si

Li Si is one of the two or three most important figures in Chinese history. He was largely responsible for the creation of those institutions that made the Qin dynasty the first universal state in Chinese history. He unified the laws, governmental ordinances, and weights and measures. He caused chariots and carts to be made of uniform gauge. He standardized the characters used in writing. By creating such universal institutions, he facilitated the cultural unification of China. He laid out imperial highways and inaugurated imperial tours of inspection to further the sense of unity. He created a government based solely on merit, so that in the empire sons and younger brothers in the imperial clan were not ennobled, but meritorious ministers were. He pacified the frontier regions by subduing the barbarians to the north and south. He had the weapons of the feudal states brought to the capital, Xianyang, where they were melted and cast into musical bells and huge statues of human figures. He relaxed the draconian punishments inherited from Shang Yang and reduced the taxes.[3] In all this, he acted from a vision of a universal empire. No one before him had so clear an idea of one world comprising all Chinese, bringing with universal dominion universal peace.

Finally, he is associated with two of the most remarkable episodes of the reign of the First Emperor, the building of the Great Wall (*SJ*, 87.15) and the burning of the books. He has been castigated ever since for the loss of ancient literature in the "burning of the books." The effect has been grossly exaggerated. Not all books were burned, but the histories of Qin's rivals were destroyed, and the *Odes* and *Documents* so often quoted by the Ru literati were suppressed. Books thought to contain practical knowledge were expressly exempted. Philosophical works seem not to have been included, and works in the possession of "scholars of wide learning," the Erudites, were excluded. The aim was quite specific—to silence those who "use the past to criticize the present" (*SJ*, 87.12–13, 6.49–52). That Xunzi was the teacher of both Han Fei and Li Si greatly damaged his reputation in later centuries when they were officially anathematized. But today the Qin dynasty seems a great watershed in Chinese history and worthy of admiration. That two of Xunzi's students were a part of it is testimony in his favor.

Fouqiu Bo

Fouqiu Bo, unlike Li Si and Han Fei, was never a famous figure. He has always remained on the fringe of history, a footnote in the traditions of scholarship. He was known for teaching famous scholars such as Shen Pei 申培 and Liu Jiao 劉交 and for transmitting Xunzi's teachings to scholars of the Han dynasty. Then, when traditions concerning him were fresh, his life was contrasted with that of Li Si.

Both Li Si and Fouqiu Bo sat at the feet of Xun Qing. His studies complete, Li Si entered the service of Qin, where he rose to the rank of one of the Three Dukes. He possessed the power of a feudal lord with 10,000 chariots. He held sway over the realm within the seas. In achievement he equaled Yi Yin and Lü Wang 呂望, and in fame he excelled Mount Tai. But Fouqiu never advanced beyond the broken jar of his thatched hovel. His fate was like that of frogs that prosper mightily during a flood year but are destined eventually to die in some drain or ditch.... Fouqiu, who lived on wild cabbage growing among the hemp, cultivated the Way beneath a plain whitewashed roof, was happy in his aspirations, and more content than he would have been in a spacious mansion eating meat. Though he never enjoyed the resplendent circumstances [of Li Si's success], he never had the least sorrow or pity over his sad condition.[4]

Fouqiu Bo taught Shen Pei the interpretation of the *Odes*. Master Shen lived to an advanced age and was responsible for the Lu 魯 School, whose interpretation now survives only in fragments. Han sources mention that the disciples of Xunzi compiled books using the works of the Spring and Autumn period and that Shen Pei and Liu Jiao studied under Fouqiu Bo. Shen Pei also transmitted the *Guliang Commentary* to the *Spring and Autumn Annals*, which he received from Fouqiu Bo. In addition, Fouqiu had two other students of some reputation in the Han dynasty, a Master Bo 白生 and a Master Mu of Lu 穆生.[5]

Zhang Cang

Zhang Cang studied under Xunzi as a youth, held office in the Qin court, became a follower of Liu Bang 劉邦, who conquered Qin and founded the Han dynasty, attained the office of chancellor under Emperor Wen 漢文帝 in 176, and died at more than 100 years old in 162. He loved books, was learned in literature, was broadly acquainted with the various documents and registers of the empire, was skilled in matters of calculation, pitchpipes, and calendrics, and was one of the most eminent ministers of the Han.[6] Zhang is famous for having transmitted our most important source for the early history of China, the *Zuo zhuan* or "Tradition of Master Zuo." This work had been received, the traditional account says, by Xunzi from Yu Qing, whom he had known when in Zhao. Having received it from Xunzi, Zhang transmitted it to Han scholars.[7]

Mao Heng

Mao Heng studied the *Odes* under Xunzi and taught his explanations to his son Mao Chang 毛萇. From the two Mao comes the current text and the orthodox interpretation of the *Odes* during the imperial period. Although some discrepancies exist between the Mao text and that contained in Xunzi's quotations, there is a close affinity between the interpretations of the Mao commentary and the lessons drawn by Xunzi in his quotations of the *Odes*.[8]

The Influence of Xunzi's Teaching at Lanling

Xunzi, through his own teaching and that of his disciples, concentrated in his own person the treasury of national learning for the early Han dynasty. Two centuries later, Liu Xiang, writing the *Preface* to the collected works of Xunzi, notes that Lanling still had a reputation for producing fine scholars because of the influence of Xunzi. We know the names of several such scholars: Wang Zang 王臧, who was appointed junior tutor to the future Emperor Wu 漢武帝 by Emperor Jing 漢景帝; Master Miao 繆生, who was clerk of the capital at Changsha; Meng Qing 孟卿, who studied the *Annals*; his son Meng Xi 孟喜, who studied the *Changes*; Hou Cang 後蒼, a student of Meng Qing's and a scholar of the *Annals*; and Shu Guang 疏廣, also a student of Meng Qing's and a scholar of the *Annals*.[9]

Shen Pei, who taught during the first 50 years of the Han dynasty, between the reigns of the founder Gaozu 漢高祖 and Emperor Wu, trained more than 100 students who held official positions and no less than ten scholars who subsequently became Erudites in the Classics.[10] All of these scholars were renown for their love of learning. Two of them, Kong Anguo 孔安國 and Zhou Ba 周霸, were particularly famous for their knowledge of the *Documents* (*SJ*, 121.22). With many of the students of his students or their students occupying important government positions, Xunzi reached the peak of his influence during the reign of Emperor Jing (156–141), when Dong Zhongshu 董仲舒, the greatest scholar of his time, wrote a letter praising Xun Qing (Liu Xiang, *Preface*).

The System of Erudites

Xunzi's influence was powerful in part because of the development of institutions of learning during the Han dynasty. This institutionalization was undoubtedly based on the practices of the Jixia Academy in Qi. Its basic pattern was created by the Qin dynasty, which instituted the title Erudite (*boshi* 博士) and established 70 Erudites, among them Fu Sheng 伏生, who transmitted the New Script 今文 text of the *Documents* to the Han dynasty (*HSBZ*, 88.11a). The institution of Erudites survived the collapse of the Qin dynasty. Chen Sheng 陳勝, who raised the first rebellion, was illiterate, but he advanced a descendant of Confucius, Kong Fu 孔鮒, as his Erudite (*HSBZ*, 88.14b). During the early Han dynasty, though individual scholars achieved high position, like Zhang Cang and Jia Yi 賈誼, the Ru scholars did not dominate the government. Though the early Han emperors were sympathetic to the Legalist philosophies that had helped Qin conquer, there were scholars who adhered to the Ru learning among the advisers of Shusun Tong 叔孫通, who organized the Han dynasty court ceremonies. Emperor Wen 漢文帝 adopted the Qin practice of establishing 70 Erudites. It seems that all the major philosophies were represented among them, though the emperor was personally interested in Legalist philosophies. We know that he did make the Ru scholars Jia Yi and Shen Pei Erudites (*HSBZ*, 36.2a), and that among the 70, he "established one Erudite each for the *Analects* of Confucius, the *Classic of Filial Piety*, the *Mencius*, and the *Erya* Lexicon."[11]

His successor, Emperor Jing, was dominated by his mother, who disliked the Ru scholars and supported Daoist adepts (*SJ*, 28.45). Though Ru scholars held office, they were not given the opportunity to offer counsel to the emperor. We know that in 141, at the beginning of Emperor Wu's reign, there were Erudites in the philosophies of Shen Buhai, Shang Yang, Han Fei, Su Qin 蘇秦, and Zhang Yi 張儀 since Wey Wan 衛綰 asked that all persons who were expert in their philosophies be dismissed. The intention of his memorial was to eliminate the influence of all philosophies that conflicted with the teachings of Confucius (*HSBZ*, 6.1b, 6.39a).

Under Emperor Wu the literary and historical treasures of China, particularly the Classics, were especially studied and expounded by the [Ru] Confucians and a definite canon formed.... Emperor Wu was a highly educated man and was greatly interested in literature. His poems and edicts show genuine literary ability. He was consequently attracted to Confucianism because of its literary and historical scholarship. He was the first ruler to select for his highest official a man who was primarily an outstanding scholar.[12]

This man was Gongsun Hong 公孫弘, a noted authority on the interpretation of the *Annals*. Emperor Wu selected men whose scholarship was "universal," which in the context of the day meant eclectic. It was during this period that the amalgamation of independent schools became prevalent. The emperor wanted men of scholarship and ability who could read the Old Script 古文, who held high ideals, who loved refinement and correctness in literary pursuits. In 136, the emperor appointed Erudites for the Five Classics: the *Changes*, the *Documents*, the *Odes*, the *Rituals*, and the *Spring and Autumn Annals* in the interpretation of the *Gongyang Commentary*.[13] In 124, Gongsun Hong proposed that they be given 50 disciples, who were to be exempted from military service and taxes. The idea of an imperial university had been proposed by Dong Zhongshu, and now was the time to establish it. The grand master of ceremonies was to select eighteen persons each year to be disciples, and high-ranking officials were to nominate suitable persons. Students who became well-versed in one classic would be given official positions. Those with greater skill might become "gentlemen of the palace." Persons of extraordinary ability might be recommended by the emperor himself. In the reign of Emperor Zhao 漢昭帝 (86–74), the number of disciples was increased to 100, and in 49 Emperor Xuan 漢宣帝 (r. 73–49) increased the number of Erudites to twelve and the number of disciples to 200. In the reign of Emperor Ping 漢平帝 (A.D. 1–5), the students at the imperial university were increased to 3,000 since Confucius was said to have had that number of disciples![14]

Through these actions, the court gradually became filled with scholars who embraced a wide variety of doctrines in the eclectic spirit of the time, but who found personal inspiration in the literary pursuits that characterized the Ru in Xunzi's time. Gradually the Ru tradition inherited from Xunzi was transformed into the state cult of Confucius. A vivid expression of this change can be seen in the remarkable positions offered as pious gestures to distant descendants of Confucius.[15] The organization of the Erudites was connected to Xunzi's own career in the Jixia Academy. In Qin times, the Erudites selected one of their number to be their supervisor, but in Han times, the grand master of ceremonies selected the outstanding individual and had him make the sacrifice of wine. This became his title, libationer, which symbolized that he was the general supervisor and head of the Erudites at the university.

XUNZI'S INFLUENCE ON HAN LEARNING

Xunzi's concept of the "classics" was dominant in the emergence of these texts as the focus of learning and thought during the whole imperial period. In "Exhortation to Learning," Xunzi argued that learning began with the recitation of the classics and concluded with reading the ritual texts. The first purpose of learning is scholarship, but its ultimate task is creation of the sage. His curriculum was the *Documents*, *Odes*, *Rituals*, *Music*, and *Annals*. But as these texts are not easily understood, a teacher is necessary. "The *Rituals* and *Music* present models but do not offer explanation; the *Odes* and *Documents* present matters of antiquity but are not always apposite; the *Annals* are laconic, and their import is not quickly grasped. It is just on these occasions that the man of learning repeats the explanations of the gentleman. Thus, he is honored for his comprehensive and catholic acquaintance with the affairs of the world" ("Quanxue," 1.10).

We know that by Xunzi's time centuries of citation and study had settled on certain works that were considered canonical. Though these works carry familiar titles, they had not yet assumed the form of the surviving works we now know by those same titles. Pre-Confucian statesmen and thinkers, Mohists and Ru philosophers, rhetoricians and sophists, all cited classical works. Not all thinkers embraced every work, but there was a common heritage in which differences were more matters of the relative importance of one work over another than the inclusion or exclusion of a particular work.

THE CLASSICS

The *Odes* and *Documents* held classical status even before the time of Confucius. The *Changes* held a similarly important place, but the *Appendixes*, which contain much of the philosophy, date from Confucius' own time or later. Judging from his discussions and those of Mo Di, there were important texts on ritual and music that held classical status, especially a *Ritual of Zhou*. Xunzi's curriculum is thus traditional. His own contribution consists in the interpretation he gave these works and in the texts of them that he transmitted.

The Documents

The *Documents* 書 were thought to contain records from highest antiquity that portrayed in the very words of the time the events, actions, and justifications of men acting at critical moments of antiquity, just those junctures that posed the worst threats and yet presented the greatest opportunities. All scholars, whatever their intellectual persuasion, used them and treasured their words as hoary wisdom that proved their own arguments. We do not know how these documents were actually composed or how far they are indeed actual records of the past. But whatever their authenticity, they were thought to contain the true record of history since, in Chinese, history literally means what is recorded. As a whole, the *Documents* encompassed a wide variety of materials, some known today only through quotations in ancient writings, others surviving genuine documents of the ancient period they describe, yet others imaginative scholarly reconstructions of an idealized past—but all works circulating in the educated community of late Warring States China.

The *Documents* were specifically prohibited during the Qin dynasty, with the result that they survive in a fragmentary state, transmitted entirely through Fu Sheng, who had been an Erudite during the Qin dynasty. Because it was recorded in the new script inaugurated by the Qin dynasty, the text of Fu Sheng is called the New Script text. We can be sure that Fu Sheng interpreted the *Documents* contrary to Xunzi's understanding since in "Contra Twelve Philosophers" Xunzi specifically criticizes views that Fu Sheng included in his commentary.

Xunzi quotes from the *Documents* twelve times in his works, but from these quotations and more numerous allusions we cannot develop a "school" of interpretation to be associated with him. Yet his influence may have been of some consequence through his disciples. In the middle of the Han dynasty, other copies of various *Documents* were found preserved in the archaic script, which became known as the Old Script text to distinguish them from the texts of Fu Sheng. Kong Anguo and Zhou Ba, who studied under Shen Pei, were largely responsible for the decipherment of the Old Script text and its interpretation. There is some reason to believe that the Old Script school opposed the interpretations of Fu Sheng in many important respects and that their opposition was related to Xunzi's views. Unfortunately, however, the Old Script version did not survive the Han dynasty, and the present Old Text *Documents* are artful forgeries, probably by Mei Ze 梅賾, who presented them to the throne in the reign of Emperor Yuan 元帝 (A.D. 317–22).[16]

The Odes

The *Odes* 詩 held an elevated place in Ru education. Confucius himself had recommended their study to his son, suggesting that true education was impossible without them (*LY*, 16.13). The Ru constantly referred to them. An inability to cite an apt verse or to respond with a suitable quotation or a failure to recognize an allusion suggested a lack of learning so grave as to make worthless any argument one might advance. Though today many of the *Odes* are regarded as originating in folk songs, they were then conceived as wonderful allegories containing the most sublime thoughts on the art of government, on the practice of self-cultivation, and on the nature of the Way and its Power.

As they survive today, the *Odes* consist of three types of poems, the *Airs* 風, which are thought to have been composed in the centuries immediately before Confucius; the *Odes* 雅, which date from a century or so earlier; and the *Hymns* 頌, which are the most ancient part, dating from the beginning of the Zhou period. It is clear that in the Zhou period there was no standard collection since the poems are often cited quite variously from the present text, with lines in different order and with stanzas in different poems. The legend that Confucius culled from 3,000 poems 300 that he approved is without foundation, and we may be confident that most of the ancient poems survive in the present collection.[17]

Xunzi's influence is nowhere more important than in the transmission of the *Odes*. In the Han dynasty, there were four versions of the *Odes*— the Lu 魯, Qi 齊, Han 韓, and Mao 毛 schools—differing as to the correct text of the poems and in the right interpretation of their meaning. We have seen that Xunzi directly influenced the Lu school through Shen Pei, who founded that school of interpretation and who had studied the *Odes* under Fouqiu Bo. The Qi school's origins are obscure, and there is no evidence of influence from Xunzi. The texts and interpretations of the Lu and Qi schools are known only through occasional quotations, and those fragments that survive are subject to learned controversy. The Han school was founded by Han Ying 韓嬰, who flourished about 150. Since the book used as a text by the school survives, we can easily see the enormous influence of Xunzi in the numerous quotations from his various books, including significant portions of some books. The *Hanshi waizhuan* 韓詩外傳 has passages in common with 18 of the 32 books of the *Xunzi* and quotes the work in 54 of its 304 paragraphs.[18]

It is through his student Mao Heng and Mao's son Mao Chang that Xunzi's ideas dominated study of the *Odes*. Their text, and with it Xunzi's interpretation, became the standard text of the *Odes*, influencing Chinese thinking through 2,000 years of scholarly discussion of the *Odes*. It is hard for us to appreciate the pervasive influence of the *Odes* without thinking of the universal influence that Latin poets such as Vergil once had in European education. But in China the *Odes* held a scriptural authority denied Greek and Latin works. With the development of commentaries on the Mao interpretation and then of subcommentaries on those, the influence of Xunzi attenuated. Yet every reform movement that returned afresh to the Mao commentary once again reconsidered Xunzi's ideas and often revived them as part of its reform by a return to true antiquity.

The Changes

The *Changes* 易經 play no important role in the main corpus of the *Xunzi*. From it we would have no indication that he was concerned with the Yin-Yang dualism of the *Changes*. Yet Liu Xiang, who compiled the present *Xunzi* corpus from independent books he found in the Imperial Library, says that Xunzi was expert in the *Changes* (Liu Xiang, *Preface*).

The "Dalue" 大略, or "The Great Compendium" (27.38, 27.49, 27.81), of the *Xunzi* contains three paragraphs explicating the *Changes*, which may reflect an interest that Xunzi developed late in life. Further, Meng Xi, who was of the Xunzi tradition in the Han dynasty, was an expert in the *Changes* and may have transmitted his views (*SJ*, 121.15). More than that we cannot presently say, but a great role for the *Changes* in Xunzi's thought would alter rather considerably our understanding of certain aspects of his philosophy.

The Music

The *Music* 樂 is the most problematic of the classics. Since we have no surviving text on music, we cannot be certain whether it was a theoretical work on music or a general philosophical discussion of the significance of music. Both types of works existed in ancient China. The significance of music in Xunzi's thought is made clear in his "Discourse on Music." For educated men, music was the expression of inner states in a form that inhibited what was unhealthy and undesirable and ornamented and developed what was healthy and desirable. Music could restrain, yet urge on. Beyond any effects it had on man, music expressed the cosmic harmony. It could influence the fundamental processes of the world. To disrupt music not only brought social anarchy, but might produce natural disasters.

From Han times onward, the principal sources on music have been three related texts: the *Yueji* 樂記 or "Record of Music," now included in the *Liji* 禮記 or "Record on Ritual" but then apparently an independent work; the "Treatise on Music" in the *Shiji* 史記 of Sima Qian; and the "Discourse on Music" of Xunzi. Although it is clear that the three texts are related, it is not certain what their relation is. The commonality of the three texts, however, assured that Xunzi's views would be consulted whenever a point in any of them was to be understood and developed. Xunzi's philosophy provided the intellectual framework that made music significant to the cultivated man, to society and to the state.

The Rituals

Ritual was central to Xunzi's thought. It is discussed repeatedly throughout his works and one of his most important books, the "Lilun" or "Discourse on Ritual Principles," is devoted to it. By the end of the Han dynasty, there were three collections of ritual texts:

1. The *Zhou li* 周禮 or "Ritual of Zhou," which was thought to be an authentic record of ritual employed at the beginning of the Zhou dynasty and to have been composed by the Duke of Zhou 周公 himself.

2. The *Yili* 儀禮 or "Book of Etiquette and Ceremonial," which was also thought to be ancient and possibly by the Duke of Zhou and which contains minutely detailed descriptions of the ceremonies associated with marriages, funerals, sacrifices, banquets, and other matters of interest to aristocratic society.

3. The *Liji* or "Record on Ritual" and the *Da Dai liji* 大戴禮記 or "Record on Ritual of the Elder Dai," which were Han dynasty compilations made from heterogeneous sources.

None of the three is descended from a known pre-Han tradition of scholarship, which has resulted in claims that one or another was a "forgery" by this or that scholar. The scholarly battles that the claims of forgery buttressed or undermined are no longer of interest. It is now clear that substantial parts of the texts of both the *Zhou li* and *Yili* circulated in Xunzi's time and before. There were texts with the name *Zhou li* that are ancestral to the current *Zhou li*. What is unclear, and still the subject of much dispute, is when the text reached its current form and how far it reflects either actual Western or Eastern Zhou institutions and practices or early Zhou notions of how such institutions ought ideally to function.[19] The details of the *Yili* are attested in so many works that it is certain that some such manual existed even in Confucius' day.

It is clear that Xunzi was familiar with texts ancestral to both the *Yili* and the *Zhou li*. It is apparent that he accepted some of the governmental theories to be found in the *Zhou li*. But there is no evidence to suggest that he or his students had any significant role in the formation of the canon of either text. Meng Qing, who belongs to Xunzi's tradition, is prominently associated with the general formation of a canon of ritual texts that developed during the Han dynasty (*HSBZ*, 88.20b–21a). This may account for the substantial overlap of contents between Xunzi's writings on rituals and the contents of the two large collections of ritual texts, the *Liji* and the *Da Dai liji*. Traditionally, these texts were compiled by Dai De 戴德 and Dai Sheng 戴聖 during the first century B.C. from materials that dated from several centuries earlier. Both works are compendiums of heterogeneous materials, dating from the time of Mo Di to the first decades of the Han dynasty, some of it not of Ru origin or compatible with pre-Qin Ru notions. It is now thought that these works, though perhaps descended from the work of the two Dai, reached their present form only in the Later Han period.[20]

Both collections contain extended quotations from Xunzi's works. If the filiation of masters responsible for the corpus of ritual texts in these works is accurate, both works must closely resemble the books on ritual texts that Xunzi used with his students. Beyond any textual influence that Xunzi may have exerted through his students, a more pervasive influence arose from his conception of the role and nature of ritual, which was accepted during the Han period and followed thereafter. This influence is also to be seen in the incorporation of his views, by extended direct quotation of his "Discourse on Ritual Principles," in the "Document on Rites" in the *Shiji*. Whether written by Sima Qian or some centuries later by an interpolator,[21] the extended quotation from Xunzi's "Discourse" circulated his explanation of ritual principles and incorporated the rationale he gave of their purpose. Xunzi transformed the concepts of ritual from an aristocratic code of conduct, a kind of *courtoisie* that distinguished gentlemen from ordinary men, into universal principles that underlay society and just government. Man's nature, which Xunzi believed to produce evil results if left undeveloped, made it necessary to have ritual principles. The desires must be satisfied, but if men observed no limits, there would be constant strife and conflict resulting in chaos. Ritual principles apportion things. They train the desires and cause them to be satisfied. Thus, they are the fundamental basis of all social order. Rites enhance life. They provide ornament and beauty. They give visible order with perfect and proper form to what is without shape or shadow. "Rites trim what is too long, stretch out what is too short, eliminate excess, and remedy deficiency" ("Lilun," 19.5). These concepts pervaded later generations and were among Xunzi's most important and enduring legacies.

The Annals

The last of the Classics was the *Annals* 春秋. Xunzi observed that the *Annals* were "laconic and their import not quickly grasped," which is why the learning of a teacher is required. The *Annals* occupied a very special place in the philosophies of the Ru. Since they argued that their doctrines represented the true teachings of the sages transmitted to Confucius and handed down since his time from master to student to their own times, an accurate record of antiquity and its institutions was indispensable. History records the accomplishments of the great and the misdeeds of the wicked. Historians from Confucius' own time and before showed great courage in stating, as a warning for posterity, what wicked rulers had done.[22] Mencius suggests that the *Annals* came to be written in the various feudal states, when at the end of the Western Zhou songs ceased to be collected and presented to the royal court. He names several such works: the *Carriage* or *Sheng* 乘 of Jin, the *Block* or *Taowu* 檮杌 of Chu, and the *Spring and Autumn* 春秋 of Lu. These works recorded in the narrative style of official histories the events of the feudal lords such as Duke Huan of Qi and Duke Wen of Jin 晉文公 (*Mengzi*, 4B.21).

Mencius tells us that Confucius, who never held the office of court historian, privately composed the *Annals*. Though doing so was a breach of propriety since this was a prerogative of the Son of Heaven, Confucius felt justified because he feared the outcome of the declining morality of his age: "Those who understand me will do so through the *Spring and Autumn Annals*, as will those who condemn me." When his task was completed, continues Mencius, rebellious subjects and unfilial sons were struck with terror. Confucius thus believed that he was carrying on the tradition represented in the collection of *Odes* by officials during the golden age of the Zhou dynasty. He felt that his work drew the morals that could be learned from history (*Mengzi*, 3B.9).

What this work of Confucius was is unknown. But in the early Han dynasty, there were two works that purported to be traditions of interpretation of the original *Annals* that Confucius had written and his disciple Zixia 子夏 had transmitted. Both professed to find in the variations of language of each entry the praise or blame that represented the moral drawn by Confucius. The kings of Wu and Chu, for instance, are censured because the *Annals* call them "viscounts."

The Gongyang Commentary

One of these commentaries was the *Gongyang zhuan* 公羊傳, which was orally handed down from Gongyang Gao 公羊高 and stayed in the Gongyang family for some 300 years until it was recorded on silk, probably under the direction of Erudite Master Huwu 胡毋生, in the reign of Han Emperor Jing. Because of the influence of Dong Zhongshu and Gongsun Hong, this work was recognized as the standard interpretation during the reign of Han Emperor Wu (*HSBZ*, 88.21b–23a).

The Guliang Commentary

The second commentary was the *Guliang zhuan* 穀梁傳. This work is traced back to Guliang Chi 穀梁赤, who received it from Zixia. The transmission of the text following him is unknown until the time of Xunzi, who received it and transmitted it to Shen Pei. This work became ascendant during the reign of Han Emperor Xuan, when it was championed by such scholars as Cai Qianqiu 蔡千秋, Liu Xiang, and Xiao Bing 蕭秉 (*HSBZ*, 88.23a–25a). Though neither the *Gongyang* nor the *Guliang* can be judged books of any great significance if they do not represent the judgments of Confucius, as modern scholars unanimously agree they do not, the *Guliang* does contain a number of theories that are also to be found in the *Xunzi*, and it is probably correctly associated with him. This does not suggest that Xunzi had any important role in the development of the text, however, since it is clear that these texts are interdependent.[23]

The Zuo zhuan

Far more important than either of these texts is the *Zuo zhuan* 左傳, which was transmitted by Xunzi's student Zhang Cang.[24] This text provides a detailed picture of the period it covers, in contrast to the laconic entries of the *Annals*. It cannot be considered a "commentary" on the *Annals*, in the fashion of the *Gongyang* or the *Guliang*, nor does the "praise and blame" theory play a significant role in it. It does contain occasional judgments of Confucius that present him in quite a different light than do the *Analects*, and it provides the conclusions that the "gentleman" would draw from some of the events described. It seems probable that these judgments represent authentic pre-Han traditions.[25] The material concentrates on the state of Jin to the neglect of other important states such as Qi except when Jin is involved. Without this work and the related *Guoyu* 國語 materials, we should be uninformed about the Spring and Autumn period. Attempts to read into the *Zuo zhuan* esoteric meaning containing Confucius' judgments make much of traditional scholarship on the book worthless. Nonetheless, it is certainly the most important source of historical material available. It seems clear that Xunzi used it, that it helped shape his views, and that transmission of it to his students constituted an important source of his influence on Han dynasty and later scholarship.

THE DECLINE OF XUNZI'S INFLUENCE

Xunzi's influence on Han dynasty intellectual life was strong at the beginning of the dynasty and increased as the dynasty's traditions of scholarship were established, reaching its apogee in the reign of Emperor Jing. Thereafter, it markedly declined, especially in the reign of Emperor Wu when the intellectual atmosphere was at odds with Xunzi's basic views. By the time of Liu Xiang, his work had no fixed corpus, there was no tradition of scholarship associated with it, and there was no longer much interest in the attitudes he represented. So striking is this contrast that Bernhard Karlgren has suggested that compendiums such as the *Da Dai liji* and *Liji* were a kind of "salvage work" on his texts, among others, which were "by way of being forgotten."[26] There is, for instance, little evidence of remaining influence of his ideas or of knowledge of him in the *Shiji*. This suggests that by 100 his direct influence had come to an end and his work was being forgotten, though the fact that he was given a biography in the *Shiji* testifies to a recognition of his importance.

4

The World of Thought

So numerous were the philosophers and their schools during the period from the sixth to the third centuries that the Chinese called them the "Hundred Schools." During the Han dynasty, historians of philosophy attempted to group these philosophers together into schools. Sima Tan 司馬談 (d. 110) produced the first and most influential classification of the philosophers into six main groups (*SJ*, "Postface," 126.7–9). The great scholar Liu Xin 劉歆 (46 B.C.–A.D. 23) produced a more elaborate but overlapping classification that attempted to account for the origins of the schools.[1] Because originally there had been no difference between a teacher and an officer, officers being responsible for teaching their subordinates, he believed that each of the schools originated within the major ministries of the government, though in its later development each school became independent. Both scholars agreed on six fundamental schools.

1. The Yin-Yang 陰陽家 philosophers, who studied the nature of the cosmos and attempted to account for all its changes in terms of two fundamental principles, the Yin and the Yang. This philosophy was thought to have originated with scholars in the departments concerned with astronomy, calendrics, and meteorology.

2. The Ru 儒家 scholars, who derived inspiration from Confucius. These philosophers were concerned with education and ritual in the various offices concerned with teaching and instruction. By the time of Xunzi, the Ru philosophers were divided into several groups, one of them headed by Xunzi.

3. The Mohist 墨家 philosophers, who emphasized frugality, utility, and economy in all things. They were exceptionally conservative in following traditional religious notions and were thought to have originated in offices concerned with temples and sacrifices.

4. The Logicians 名家, who dealt with the relation of names to reali-

ties. They were thought to have emerged from officers concerned with ranks and positions in the court and with the ceremonies to which such rank and position entitled an officer.

5. The Legalist 法家 philosophers, who emphasized the importance of legislation over tradition and custom as embodied in ritual and social practice. Liu Xin thought they had emerged from among officers concerned with the application of penal sanctions.

6. The school of the Dao or Way 道家, which attempted to understand the ultimate principles of reality and to offer a fundamentally different concept of social organization. Liu Xin thought that the archivists who studied the success and failure of various activities had given rise to this school.

To these six schools, Liu Xin added two more of importance.

7. The Agronomists 農家, who emphasized the importance of the basic occupations—farming and sericulture—and who offered a thorough critique of contemporary society in Xunzi's day.

8. The theorists of diplomatic strategies 縱橫家, who gained great importance during Xunzi's lifetime with their development of rhetoric and formal debates known as persuasions.

Modern scholars tend to follow in general terms the division of the early philosophers into schools such as these, but usually reject the account of their origins from different government offices. Scholars during the 1920's and 1930's demonstrated that there were important social differences between the schools. More recent scholarship indicates that ethnic and cultural as well as social differences were involved. Below, I discuss some of these differences and the controversies between the schools in the context of Xunzi's philosophy.

THE BACKGROUND TO XUNZI'S THOUGHT

Xunzi and Mencius are considered the greatest philosophers of the Confucian tradition. Xunzi mentions Mencius only to criticize him, but like Mencius he venerated Confucius, though his concept of the sage's teachings was quite different. In common with his contemporaries (see, for example, *Mengzi*, 6B.6), Xunzi believed that Confucius held high office in his native state of Lu, even if only briefly, and that while in office he accomplished remarkable changes, some of which Xunzi cites (see "Ruxiao," 8.3). Confucius is rarely mentioned or quoted in the main body of Xunzi's works, though extended anecdotes about him comprise the substance of the last books in the arrangement of Xunzi's commentator Yang Liang. This is not surprising since it was the corpus of the classics that were the substance of Confucius' teachings and not sayings of his own. The Master himself had said that "I have transmitted what was taught to me without creating anything of my own" (LY, 7.1).[2]

We tend to misstate the relation of Mencius and Xunzi to Confucius by calling them "Confucians." The term they used was Ru, which apparently originally meant "weakling."[3] It was adopted by those who pursued learning as the proper path of the shi 士 or "knight" class. So general was this change that even by Xunzi's day the term shi had come to mean "scholar" except in archaic usages, where it might still mean "knight." The convention of translating ru as "Confucian" and rujia as "Confucian school" is unfortunate since it does not reflect the Chinese, but the practice is so pervasive that it can hardly be avoided. In ancient China there was no "school" of Confucius. Nor was there any other school except that of Mo Di, whose followers called themselves Mohists.

The intellectuals who termed themselves Ru regarded Confucius as the founder of their movement, as the Mohists regarded Mo Di as the founder of their movement. But unlike the Mohists, they held few doctrines in common, apart from a reverence of rituals, an allegiance to traditional values, a passion for knowledge of antiquity, and an admiration of the traditions of the early Zhou period. They shared a veneration of Dan 旦, the Duke of Zhou, who had saved the Zhou dynasty and founded the state of Lu. They believed, with Confucius, that they must faithfully carry on his teachings and follow his example. Even these beliefs were not professed by all Ru. More often they engaged in bitter quarrels with each other; such controversies began even among Confucius' own disciples. Han Fei observed that by Xunzi's time there were eight different groups who called themselves Ru, indicating not only the wide appeal of Confucius as a hero but also the lack of any real agreement among them.[4]

It is apparent that Xunzi does not mean by Ru any coherent body of thinkers. In his "Contra Twelve Philosophers," he lists three groups of Ru—those who folow the disciples Zizhang 子張, Zixia 子夏, and Ziyou 子游, respectively—whom he condemns as "base Ru," "untutored Ru," "corrupt Ru," "lesser Ru," and "vulgar Ru" in contrast to "cultivated" and "great Ru." He also condemns those Ru who claimed falsely to follow Zisi 子思, the grandson of Confucius, and Mencius, who was Zisi's disciple (Xunzi, 1.11, 5.6, 8.12, 8.10, 6.7). All of these he criticized and chastised. He believed he shared with them few essential doctrines, and even these he interpreted quite differently. Worse still, such individuals corrupted the genuine heritage of Confucius, which was truly transmitted only by the disciple Zigong 子弓.

The followers of Zengzi 曾子 together with the three groups of Ru Xunzi singles out for condemnation—the followers of Zizhang, Zixia, and Ziyou—are commonly credited with the compilation of the *Lunyu* 論語 or *Analects*.[5] Today the *Analects* is our basic source of materials concerning Confucius; then it was but one of several competing collections of Confucian sayings. Mencius twice mentions together the three disciples condemned by Xunzi as though they were a party or group (*Mengzi*, 1A.1, 3A.4). Thus, for our concept of the personality of Confucius and for our knowledge of his fundamental teachings, we depend on a collection deriving from traditions that Xunzi expressly rejected. This can only mean that our views must differ in important, but presently indefinable, ways from what Xunzi believed to be the authentic tradition.

The Disciple Zigong

The Zigong 子弓 (not to be confused with the better-known disciple Zigong 子貢) whom Xunzi regards as the authentic source is something of an enigma since none of the disciples known today has that name. Scholars today generally consider that Xunzi must mean Ran Yong 冉雍, who was styled Zhonggong 仲弓.[6] Unfortunately, very little is known of this disciple, and we do not know why Xunzi esteemed him so highly. Ran Yong is said to have belonged to the same family as the disciple Ran Boniu 冉伯牛 and to have been 29 years younger than Confucius (*SJ*, 67.8; *KZJY*, 9.1a). His father seems to have been of base origins, which might have caused Zhonggong to be "passed over" by those who "felt he was not good enough to be used." Despite his origins, the Master thought he "could be given the seat facing south" since he embodied moral force in his conduct (*LY*, 6.6, 6.1, 13.2; *SJ*, 67.9).

Xunzi makes it clear that Zigong alone transmitted the true doctrines of the Master. The teachings of the sages, Confucius and the Duke of Zhou, are carried on by the real Ru, who alone are able to follow the model of the Later Kings, who exalt ritual principles and moral duty, who are careful to fulfill their roles as ministers and sons properly, and who esteem their superiors to the utmost ("Ruxiao," 8.2).

Confucius sought out the rulers of his day to lead them to the way of True Kingship, but he never succeeded. His disciples, following his example, sought their fortunes in the courts of the ruling lords of their day. They hoped to attract the attention of an enlightened ruler whom they could persuade to follow the Way and hence to attain universal rule. Some had moderate success, but none became sufficiently influential to reform the government and establish True Kingship. But from Con-

fucius' time onward, the development of scholarship and philosophy was
to be dependent on the patronage of the ruling princes of the day.

Wei's Patronage of Scholarship

The tradition of rulers honoring scholars with high titles and providing them with generous stipends was almost two centuries old in Xunzi's
day. The tradition can be traced to the beginning of the Warring States
period. Since Wei's emergence as an independent state, its rulers had
supported many eminent scholars. Marquis Wen 魏文侯, the grandfather
of King Hui, patronized the Confucian disciple Zixia as well as Li Kui
李悝, who first introduced statistical methods into statecraft.[7] Marquis
Wu 武侯 continued the tradition and built a powerful state partly as a
result of the good advice given by his counselors. His son, King Hui, was
the heir to a tradition of patronage and also to a patrimony of considerable wealth and power, which he squandered on ill-conceived military
adventures: "As you know, in power the state of Wei was once second
to none in the whole world. But in my own time, we have suffered defeat in the east by Qi, where my eldest son died, and we have lost territory
700 *li* in extent to Qin in the west, while to the south we have been
humiliated by Chu. I am deeply ashamed of this and wish, in what little
time is left me in this life, to wash away all this shame" (*Mengzi*, 1A.5).

To do this, King Hui lavishly patronized scholars who might offer
some way to recover his honor and restore the prestige of his state. He
collected at his capital of Daliang a large group of scholars who were
justly famous for their learning, making Daliang a great center of learning and thought. Among the more important figures were the logician
Hui Shi, the rhetorician Shunyu (also rendered Chunyu) Kun 淳於髡,
Mencius, and possibly Zhuang Zhou as well.[8] But his successor, King
Xiang 魏襄王, was unimpressive. "When I saw him at a distance," observed the philosopher Mencius, "he did not look like a ruler of men,
and when I went close, I saw nothing that commanded respect" (*Mengzi*,
1A.6). The scholars attracted by his father scattered, many like Mencius
traveling to Qi to seek out King Xuan 齊宣王.

The Jixia Academy

The intellectual center of ancient China at this time was the Jixia
Academy—named after the Ji Gate, the western gate in the wall of
the capital of Qi, beneath which scholars gathered.[9] Xu Gan says that
patronage of scholarship began with Tian Wu 田午, known as Duke Huan
田桓公 (375-358), who "established a bureau at the Jixia, inaugurated the

practice of bestowing the title of grand officer, and extended his welcome to wise men whom he honored and esteemed."[10] The Academy itself seems to have been founded by his son, King Wei of Qi 齊威王 (357–320), who brought together from all over China the outstanding minds of the day. Under the influence of his prime minister, Zou Ji 鄒忌, King Wei patronized some 72 scholars in the Academy, who "took delight in deliberating the affairs of government," but who "treated Zou Ji disrespectfully whenever they had occasion to associate with him."[11]

King Xuan (319–301) founded a Scholars Hall outside the Ji Gate (Liu Xiang, *Bielu*, apud *TPYL*, 18). During this period, the Academy reached its zenith. The king was fond of scholars who were accomplished in learning and who were gifted virtuosos at rhetoric. Seventy-six such men were associated with the Academy, were given ranks and honors, and made senior grand officers, not to participate in the government but to deliberate and propound learned theories. For this reason, "the scholars beneath the Ji Gate enjoyed a renaissance, coming to number in the hundreds and thousands" (*SJ*, 46.31). Mencius says of King Xuan that the "heart behind his actions was sufficient to enable him to become a true king" and that despite his inordinate fondness for acts of valor, money, sex, and musical performances, he might have become great but for his refusal to act in the proper fashion (*Mengzi*, 1B.1, 3, 5; 1A.7).

The Jixia scholars seem to have been free to debate with one another without any of the responsibilities of high office, though they were accorded its honors and emoluments. Freed from having to put their theories into action, the Jixia scholars seem to have delighted in displays of skill in argumentation. A few, such as Shunyu Kun, abjured the holding of office as a matter of principle (*SJ*, 74.11), but most seem to have hungered for the power to act that office alone provided. We know very little more about the Jixia Academy and how its scholars debated one another.

Attacks on Ru Doctrines

Mencius complained that in his time "scholars who held no official responsibilities were utterly uninhibited in the expression of their views" (*Mengzi*, 3B.9).[12] The doctrines of "Yang Zhu 楊朱 and Mo Di filled the whole world," so that everyone was "either of the school of Yang or of the school of Mo" (*Mengzi*, 3B.9). A generation later when Xunzi arrived, the school of Yang Zhu seems to have faded into relative insignificance, but the Mohist school was still influential. Mencius felt that if the ways of Yang and Mo did not subside and if "the way of Confucius is not proclaimed, then the people will be deceived" by such aberrant views. Morality will be lost: "We will be showing animals the way to devour men, and ultimately it will result in men devouring men" (*Mengzi*, 3B.9).

Ru scholars such as Mencius represented in their own view the middle ground between the excessive puritanism and conservatism of the Mohists and the self-indulgence preached by Yang Zhu and his followers. Both tendencies of thought can be seen among thinkers of Confucius' time and before. The predecessors and successors of Yang Zhu were generally individualists. Antecedents of Mohism can be seen in the lives of ascetics and hermits, particularly in Chu, and in the careers of certain ministers like Yan Ying 晏嬰, an older contemporary of Confucius' (*SJ*, 62.7). To Mencius, the adherents of Yang Zhu seemed to represent an attack from the left that undermined the state's authority with their individualism, destroying conventional values with their egoism and attacking social constraints with their self-indulgence. The Mohists attacked from the right, ridiculing Ru skepticism of traditional religious belief, condemning the Ru emphasis on court rituals and entertainments, and attacking their adherence to the doctrine of Fate.

The old age of Mencius saw a new series of attacks. Even before Confucius, some statesmen had seen the need for new forms of social regulation. New conditions required new ideas. Guan Zhong reformed the government of the state of Qi (*SJ*, 62.4, 129.7), Prince Chan 公子產 that of Zheng 鄭 (*Zuo*, Xiang 30, Zhao 7),[13] Wu Qi 吳起 that of Chu (*SJ*, 65.18), and Li Kui that of Wei (*SJ*, 30.46, 74.16). Each achieved signal successes widely admired by their ages. Though to Confucius, as also to Mencius, such willingness to alter the teachings of the past were scandalous, later statesmen would continue the work of these early reformers. Gradually there developed the corpus of theory of statecraft that came to be known as Legalism. This represented a new attack on basic Ru doctrines, one that Xunzi had to face and one that persuaded his student Han Fei to abandon Ru doctrines altogether.

Yet other thinkers disdained both the Mohist and Ru emphasis on political theory. They argued for a return to a primitive society in which differences of rank and status did not exist, in which gradations of wealth were unknown. Such utopian thinkers came, in Xunzi's time, to have great appeal as the political conditions of his day deteriorated. These thinkers attacked conventional knowledge, conventional society, and conventional values. Such thinkers formed no coherent schools, but everyone felt their influence. The views of these men were articulated by the scholars of the Jixia Academy toward the end of Mencius' life and during the whole of Xunzi's career.

THE HUNDRED SCHOOLS

Just after the time of King Xuan, when the Academy had reached its zenith and Qi was at the height of its power and prestige, Xunzi came there to study. The great and famous teachers who were still there or who had taught there a few years before include many of the most famous men of Chinese philosophy: Shunyu Kun, Peng Meng 彭蒙, Shen Dao, Huan Yuan, Tian Pian, Zou Shi, Song Xing, Master Jie, Mencius, and Yin Wen (SJ, 74.10, 46.31). In addition, the works of Shen Buhai, Yang Zhu, Hui Shi, and Zhuang Zhou, none of them members of the Academy, were well known there. The only major philosophy apparently not represented at the Jixia was that of Mo Di, but his ideas were generally known there. It is hard to imagine a more vibrant and exciting intellectual environment. This is the milieu that shaped Xunzi's development. His philosophy was formed against the background of arguments at the Jixia and in reaction to the positions of these famous men. In consequence, Xunzi is much broader than Mencius, for example, and shows both knowledge of and indebtedness to the arguments of philosophers outside the Ru tradition.

Mo Di

No philosopher was more important in Warring States China than Mo Di. In many respects, his influence was then greater than that of any other man, including Confucius. Alone among the ancient philosophers, Mo Di founded a personal school that transmitted and developed his doctrines. His followers were certainly the best-organized group and were in many regards the most innovative of all the philosophers of ancient China. The Mohists attracted considerable attention because of their expertise in defensive warfare, which made them indispensable to beleaguered rulers, and their skill in dialectics, which allowed them to triumph in the formal debates, known as "discriminations," that characterized the feudal courts. No school or thinker was immune to the influence of their ideas. Both Mencius and Xunzi vigorously attacked aspects of the Mohist doctrines, but both, especially Xunzi, were influenced by Mohist views on the goals and aims of government.

Mo Di lived during the last half of the fifth century and into the opening decade of the fourth.[14] He is said to have come from Lu (or the neighboring state of Song) and was perhaps of humble origins.[15] He received his education from the learned teachers of his day, who were probably disciples of Confucius or their disciples.[16] His works are filled with quotations from the *Odes* and *Documents*, abound in details of the government and actions of the early sage kings, and exhibit a wide variety of knowledge. His works contain the earliest prose essays on a single topic. "Being fond of study, Mo Di was broadly learned, but would not tolerate differences of opinion" (*Zhuangzi*, 33 "Tianxia" 天下 10.14b). Despite his common ground with the early Ru, he came to regard their ritualistic and ceremonial pursuits as sterile and injurious to the welfare of the people (*HNZ*, 21.6b).

The distinctive doctrines of Mo Di were expressed in his famous Ten Theses:

1. "Elevating the worthy"—rulers should honor the worthy and employ the able rather than advance relatives and favorites;

2. "Conforming to superiors"—the people must be of one mind with their superiors so that unity is maintained;

3. "Universal love"—it is only by an ungraded love that allows no special treatment for one's own kin that a secure society can be constructed;

4. "Condemnation of aggression"—warfare is always unprofitable, and if rulers could be taught this simple truth, there would be peace;

5. "Moderation in expenditures"—the state should expend its resources only on those things that benefit the people;

6. "Moderation in funerals"—the sages had simple funerals, and the Ru doctrines advocating elaborate funerals and extended periods of mourning are falsifications of antiquity;

7. "The will of Heaven" or "honoring Heaven"—the clearest standard in the world, which Mo Di would use as his square and compass;

8. "Explaining the spirits" or "serving the spirits"—a defense of the traditional belief in spirits and a refutation of Ru skepticism;

9. "Condemnation of music"—a refutation of Ru doctrines advocating elaborate musical performances as instruments of state ceremony;

10. "Condemnation of fate"—a refutation of the fatalistic doctrines of certain Ru.

The Mohists' doctrines combined political revolution with religious conservatism. They attacked basic views of the Ru and departed radically from the traditional views of aristocratic society. Their conflicts with the Ru were expressly stated in Mo Di's books, "Contra the Ru Scholars."

Mo Di was motivated by a conviction that only ungraded love, which recognized no special distinctions for one's own kin, would protect society from the evils of greed, partiality, and warfare. He stressed the need for consideration of the efficacy and utility of a project before it was undertaken and for due regard for the ultimate benefit of every action to the people. He rejected the aristocratic order and the system of preferences and privilege for which it stood and which the Ru protected. It was on this point that the most bitter exchanges focused. Part of the animosity may have been based on a difference in social standing between the aristocratic Ru and the Mohists, who were craftsmen.[17] Mo Di is called a commoner, to be ranked with clients and the ordinary populace, and was refused a royal interview because of his base origins. Mencius would not receive his followers, and Xunzi characterizes his teachings as those of a menial.[18] Yet, for all their opposition to his doctrines, thinkers had to admit the nobility of his ideals and the selflessness of his personal actions. A passage in the *Zhuangzi* (33 "Tianxia,"10.16a) best characterizes him: "Mo Di genuinely loved the whole world. Though he became worn and withered from lack of rest, he could not attain all that he sought. But he was indeed a scholar of real worth!"

Song Xing

In Xunzi's time, the most prominent Mohists seem to have lived in the state of Chu. A thinker akin to the Mohist school, and in later times counted among them, was Song Xing, who figures prominently in several of Xunzi's books. A member of the Jixia Academy, Song Xing is usually associated with Yin Wen in the literature. A contemporary of Mencius, who criticizes him, Song was a pacifist who once set out for Chu to dissuade its king from making war by showing him that it was unprofitable to do so. Mencius was horrified that Song did not tell the king that it was immoral (*Mengzi*, 6B.4). Song taught that there was no need to fight since it was no disgrace to suffer insult, that war and aggression were wrong and unprofitable (he instead urged disarmament), and that one must hold fast to an inner ideal, unaffected by popular fashions. He believed that the essential human desires were few and that if men could be shown this, conflict would disappear. He stressed tolerance, equality, affection, the need for peace, and the preservation of life. He held that one should seek only what is needed to keep one alive and ask for no more. Song "traveled about the whole world, persuading the upper classes and preaching to the lower." He "energetically and noisily pressed his views, never relenting." His influence was sufficient to cause Xunzi, early in his career, to think it necessary to make a careful refutation of Song's doctrines. It is unfortunate that we know so little of his views and that what we do know is from unsympathetic sources. It is said that he "discussed the states of the mind that were called the 'behavior of the mind.'"[19] If this was a psychological examination of the mind, it would be unique since we do not find any other until the coming of Buddhism.

Despite the debt he owed both Song and the Mohists, Xunzi rejected their views because they attacked the hierarchical principle of government and the natural inequality of men and things, which must be recognized in society as in Nature. The nobility of their views, their manifest good-will and selflessness, and the intense commitment they exhibited made them particularly dangerous in his view because they seduced men into thinking that such a society could work when in fact it was contrary to man's inborn nature and to Nature itself.

Hui Shi

Another philosopher of immense influence, not for his ideas, but for the mode of his argumentation, was Hui Shi, an older contemporary of Mencius. A prime minister of the state of Wei, Hui Shi is remembered for his brilliance in argumentation.[20] He astonished the world with his bold and startling propositions. He inspired a host of imitators who turned to creating and defending, against all sense, paradoxes meant to confound ordinary men. Hui Shi's aim was not merely to confound, though it seemed so to his contemporaries, but to advocate such theses as pacifism, universal love, and abolition of positions of honor.[21] His close friendship with Zhuang Zhou betokens an interest in Daoist notions only occasionally indicated in his surviving fragments.[22] Though the *Zhuangzi* has several dialogues between Zhuang Zhou and Hui Shi, they cannot be considered true reflections of his views. What little we know of him is to be found in the last book of the *Zhuangzi* (33 "Tianxia," 10.20a–23b), where his accomplishments and doctrines are summarized at some length, giving us a small picture of his many ideas that then were said to "fill five carriages" with manuscripts:

Day by day, Hui Shi employed all his knowledge in dialectical contests with others, where he created astonishing propositions for the dialecticians of the world. This was his most fundamental characteristic....He made everything everywhere the subject of his discourse. Once he began to talk, he could not desist, but would enlarge on the subject endlessly, and just when he might be considered resourceless, he would add on his most astonishing propositions. Whatever opposed the common sense of men, he considered truth, and he desired to gain his reputation by overwhelming their common sense.

It was, of course, this characteristic that Xunzi condemned, but Hui Shi's brilliance in argumentation convinced Xunzi that in order to succeed in gaining the ear of the rulers of the day, the gentleman had to become adept in formal argumentation. Though he profited from the rigorous standards Hui Shi and his followers introduced into intellectual inquiry, Xunzi believed that Hui Shi was concerned only with words and argument and not with reality, with the effect he made and not with the truth, with his reputation and not with the advancement of knowledge.

Shen Dao

A fourth philosopher who influenced Xunzi was Shen Dao, an active participant in the academy when Xunzi was a student there. A thinker of wide interests and great brilliance, Shen Dao's writings once comprised 42 books. Today we have an abridgment of five of these, with scattered quotations from the remainder.[23] Han Fei admired his ideas and employed them along with those of Shen Buhai and Shang Yang in his synthesis of Legalist thought; for this reason Shen Dao is often called a Legalist thinker (*HFZ*, 40 "Nanshi" 難勢, 17.1ab). His true affinities, however, are with the Daoists (*SJ*, 74.12), and the variety of his thought was much broader and more complex than the narrow concept of statecraft found in the writings attributed to Shang Yang, embracing as they do many new and innovative ideas. Xunzi objected to his emphasis on a model rooted in created, legislated, positive law rather than one based on traditional customary usages incorporated in ritual principles. He also distrusted Shen Dao's willingness to engage in innovation, always suspect in the minds of the Ru.

Shunyu Kun and Tian Pian

Two figures perfectly exemplified the urbane, facile, fluent minds admired by the age. Shunyu Kun was famed for his ability to defend any proposition. Once he is said to have constructed an argument advocating a particular strategy of statecraft so brilliant that the court speculated that no one could have argued against it. When Shunyu Kun heard this, though he had already set out on a diplomatic mission to execute the plan, he returned to court and presented an argument for the opposite strategy that convinced the king, who thereafter distrusted his counsel. Tian Pian was not an original thinker, but he was a gifted conversationalist who defended the doctrines of his master, Peng Meng. He was called "Pian with the divine tongue" by the people of Qi because he so loved conversation and could never be exhausted. "It was as if his tongue were in the service of Heaven" (Liu Xin, *Qilue*, apud *SJ*, 74.10).

THE COURT OF THE LORD OF PINGYUAN

The figures discussed above influenced Xunzi's youth and his middle period. Later, when Xunzi returned to his native Zhao about 260, different figures were of importance. Through the efforts of the Lord of

Pingyuan, who was a patron of learning, the court of Zhao was a major intellectual center. Pingyuan thought himself a good judge of men and numbered more than 1,000 scholars among his retainers. The accomplishment of Mao Sui 毛遂 in securing the aid of Chu made Pingyuan realize that the tongue of a gifted scholar is "mightier than an army of a million men" (*SJ*, 76.8). Pingyuan numbered among his many followers three celebrated figures: Yu Qing, Gongsun Long, and Zou Yan.

Yu Qing

Yu Qing was an important minister in Zhao. Though he attained high honors and considerable wealth, he abandoned it all for the sake of his friend Wei Qi 魏齊. Disillusioned after the death of Wei Qi, he wrote a number of books selecting episodes of antiquity from the *Annals* and more recent events based on his personal observations. In all, his writings filled eight volumes, comprising "The Restraints of Duty," "Titles and Privileges," "Searches and Explorations," and "Statecraft and Diplomacy." Since these books contained trenchant and sardonic observations on the successes and failures of nations, it came to be known as the "Spring and Autumn of Master Yu." "What an artist of shrewd judgments of affairs and searching examinations of circumstances was Master Yu in the way he laid out a strategy to meet Zhao's situation!" (*SJ*, 76.22.) Yu Qing's works are now lost, but he is said to have been among those who transmitted the most important work of ancient history, the *Zuo zhuan*. Tradition says that he entrusted the book to Xunzi, through whose students it survived into the Han dynasty.

Gongsun Long

Lord Pingyuan was a generous patron of the philosopher Gongsun Long, who was notorious for his proposition that "a white horse is not a horse" and for his discriminations on the problems of "hardness and whiteness" and "similarity and difference." Such problems of logical inquiry begin perhaps as an outgrowth of the publication of law codes and the consequent need for careful definition of legal matters. In Xunzi's time, the name of the famous Zheng lawyer, Deng Xi 鄧析, was associated with hair-splitting legal arguments. Later Hui Shi transformed the whole character of argumentation with his brilliantly defended theses. In the Jixia Academy, Yin Wen, who was the teacher of Gongsun Long, developed concepts of the logical relationship of names and objects. In Chu the Mohists inquired extensively into the problems of argument. All these wrote books. The works of the Mohists survive in a mutilated form. Those of Hui Shi are lost. Works attributed to Deng Xi and Yin Wen survive, but they are of doubtful authenticity.

Besides Gongsun Long, there were among the retainers of the Lord of Pingyuan several other prominent figures interested in logic. They include Kong Chuan 孔穿, said to be a sixth-generation descendant of Confucius, who wanted to study under Gongsun Long. A book attributed to him survives and includes a dialogue with Gongsun Long.[24] A second was Master Qiwu 綦毋子, a disciple of Gongsun Long.[25] A third was Mao Gong 毛公, who wrote a work on logical inquiry that was said to have discussed the problems of "hardness and whiteness" and "similarity and difference" to make possible real government of the empire. His works are now lost (*HSBZ*, 30.42b). Of those active in the retinue of Pingyuan, only the works of Gongsun Long survive to represent the thinking of these logicians. From a much more extensive corpus, only five works of Gongsun Long remain: "Discourse on the White Horse," "Discourse on Meanings and Things," "Discourse on Understanding Change," "Discourse on Hardness and Whiteness," and "Discourse on Names and Actualities." Versions of these survive, along with a dialogue with Kong Chuan and a brief biography, but unfortunately several of them are of doubtful authenticity.[26]

Problems of logical analysis were especially associated with the Mohists. Hui Shi and Yin Wen are known to have held some positions in common with the Mohists. Lu Sheng 魯勝, who wrote a now-lost commentary on the logical works of the Mohists about A.D. 300, says that both Hui Shi and Gongsun Long continued the Mohist traditions of correcting forms and names.[27] Gongsun Long visited both Kings Zhao of Yan and Hui of Zhao 趙惠王 in an effort to get them to give up offensive warfare and adopt instead policies of disarmament and demobilization, which he believed derive from a heart that universally loves the whole world. Such universal love is not just an "empty name" but must be a reality.[28]

Wei Mou

Gongsun Long continued to enjoy the patronage of Pingyuan until Zou Yan arrived to discuss the "Ultimate Way," whereupon Gongsun Long was instantly dismissed and apparently went to Prince Mou of Wei 魏公子牟, a scion of the royal family and a famous hedonist. Prince Mou apparently belonged to a cadet branch of the family since he is associated with Zhongshan 中山, a state given as an appanage to the younger princes of the royal house. In Han times, he was considered a Daoist. His works comprised four books, which survived only into the Han dynasty. The *Liezi* comments that Prince Mou was the worthiest of the princes, that he was fond of associating with the talented scholars who traveled from state to state, that he took no interest in the governmental affairs of his country, and that he delighted in the arguments of Gongsun Long, whose disciple he became.[29] Wei Mou once advised Fan Sui, the Marquis of Ying, that those who hold high position are certain to become wealthy and to be corrupted by that wealth, and through that corruption, they will surely come to their own death and destruction (*ZGC*, 6.73a). Later he pointed out to King Xiaocheng of Zhao that though the king was unwilling to entrust fine cloth to any but a skilled tailor, he willingly entrusted his state "not to the skilled but to the pretty" even though his state altars were visibly "crumbling and deserted" (*ZGC*, 6.74b). It is clear that Prince Mou traveled to the same courts and had audience with the same people as Xunzi.

Zou Yan

Zou Yan, who bested Gongsun Long with his discussions of the Ultimate Way, dominated the intellectual debate in the middle of the third century. A member of the Jixia Academy when Xunzi was there, his theory of the Five Processes 五行 and their influence on history established his reputation.

When kings, dukes, and important men first became acquainted with his methods, they were awestruck and took care to make transformations, but their successors were incapable of acting accordingly. For this, Master Zou was highly prized in Qi. When he went to Liang, the king went out into the suburbs to welcome him, attending to all the proper ceremonies between host and guest. When he went to Zhao, the Lord of Pingyuan walked alongside his carriage and dusted off his mat. When he proceeded to Yan, King Zhao swept the way, acted as his herald, and requested that he be permitted to take a seat in the ranks of his disciples to receive instruction. He built the Jieshi Palace as a residence for Zou Yan and went there himself to listen to his teachings. Here Zou Yan wrote the *Zhuyun* 主運, "On the Control of the Cycles." Whenever he traveled among the feudal lords, he received such honors and ceremonies.   (*SJ*, 74.8)[30]

This is the way Ru philosophers like Mencius had expected that feudal lords *should* treat scholars and teachers (*Mengzi*, 5B), but neither Mencius nor Xunzi ever received such treatment. It must surely have seemed incredible to Xunzi.

Though Zhou's works, which once numbered more than 100,000 words, are now lost except for a few quotations, Sima Qian provides us with a summary of their remarkable contents:

Zou Yan observed that those who possessed states were [in his time] increasingly given to debauchery and extravagance and that they were incapable of exalting virtue, as the "Da Ya" Odes say, first by putting aright their own selves and then by acting to extend it to the black-headed masses. So he examined deeply the [rhythm of] increase and decrease of the Yin and Yang. He wrote books on their strange and far-reaching permutations, on ends and beginnings, on the Great Sage [era], totaling more than 100,000 words. His discourses were vast, grand, and unclassical.

He first inspected small things, from which he drew conclusions that he then enlarged until he reached what was without limit. He would begin by putting in order [the events of] recent times in order to reach back to the time of Huang Di, to all that had been recounted by scholars, and to periods of florescence and decay as well. Toward this end, he recorded the signs and omens, their rules and laws, drew conclusions from them and extended these back to the time when Heaven and Earth had not yet been formed, into the shrouded and obscure times that were impossible to investigate and determine their origins. He started by cataloging the famous mountains, major rivers, and connecting valleys of China, the birds and beasts, the waters and earths that were productive, and the various types of things that were valuable, and, basing himself on this, he drew conclusions that he extended to what lay beyond the seas and to what men were incapable of observing. From the time when the heavens and earth were separated down to the present, he stated in detail the revolutions and transmutations of the Five Powers 五德, putting each of them in its proper place in sequence, and confirmed that by the responses being what they should be. (*SJ*, 74.5–6)

Zou Yan held that each Power was succeeded by the Power that it could not conquer. The new Power dominated an age. Its dominance had direct and immediate political consequences. Each ruling house came to power through the natural succession of these Powers, which were expressed in the activities of a Process. This Process and Power would in turn be replaced by another that it could not conquer, making the decline of a dynasty inevitable. Since it was obvious that the Zhou dynasty was nearing its end, the burning issue of political speculation was who would succeed. Zou Yan taught that it would be by the Process associated with water and that there would be omens indicating its impending conquest. But how these could be anticipated and identified was uncertain. Nonetheless, most believed that the theory was true. So when Qin did conquer the empire, the First Emperor proclaimed "black," the color of water, his heraldic color, and affairs of government were modeled after water (*SJ*, 28.23–24).

An idea of the astonishing activity of philosophers during the classical age can be seem in the catalogue of the Imperial Library that Liu Xin prepared. He classified among the Ru 53 thinkers, who had written a total of 836 volumes. Many of these survive intact. Confucius is represented by several collections of his sayings, the most important being the *Analects*. Mencius' works are the best preserved of any ancient philosopher. Xunzi is represented by 32 books. The Daoist school consisted of

37 thinkers represented by 993 volumes. The *Daode jing*, popularly attributed to Laozi, survives intact, though subjected to many changes. Zhuang Zhou is represented by several books, and the works of several other thinkers are included in the present book that bears his name. The works of most of the others are now lost or survive only in fragments. The Yin-Yang school comprised 21 individuals represented by 369 volumes, now almost entirely lost. The Legalist school included 10 thinkers represented by 237 volumes. Two of the most important, the corpus of both Shang Yang and Han Fei, survive. But the important work of Shen Dao survives only in fragments, and the works of Shen Buhai and Li Kui are entirely lost except for a few quotations. The works of the logicians were represented by 7 thinkers comprising 36 volumes, most now lost. The works of the Mohists consisted of only six titles constituting 86 volumes, of which only the *Mozi* collection survives. The works of the various other schools consisted of the writings of 64 thinkers, comprising 2,004 volumes, only a tiny fragment of which survives.[31]

We are fortunate that, despite the many losses, Chinese philosophy is more fully preserved than any other ancient tradition. Nothing in ancient Athens or Alexandria, in medieval Paris or Oxford, or in modern Cambridge or Heidelberg exceeded the prodigious energy of the classical age in China. The number of individuals, the astonishing variety of their interests, the depth of their understanding, the breadth of their scholarship, and the genius of their thought make Xunzi's age without parallel in Chinese history and unsurpassed in world history.

5

Man and Nature

The term that the Chinese use to refer to Nature is *tian* 天. The word has several important meanings best translated by different English words to reflect the differences in meaning. Its simplest meaning is that of sky or the heavens that contain the various celestial bodies.

> Swiftly swooped that hawk
> straight up into the sky.
>
> (*Shi*, Mao 178)

In common with many ancient peoples, the Chinese called the god of the sky and the heavens by the same name. The ancient belief was that an anthropomorphic sky god, or Heaven, directed the affairs of the world and listened to the prayers of men. It was a directive moral force. This Heaven might "send down" illness, death, destruction, floods, or droughts in response to what men, particularly rulers, might do. Xunzi occasionally uses the term in this older sense.

The belief in Heaven as a moral force is clearly reflected in the important political doctrine that a legitimate dynasty ruled by a Mandate from this Heaven.

> Heaven looked down upon the world below,
> its Mandate lighted on him.
> When King Wen started his initiative,
> Heaven made for him a mate.
>
> (*Shi*, Mao 236)

A more philosophical analysis understood that in "granting a Mandate" Heaven did no more than listen to the people; thus, the acquiescence of the people was proof that the dynasty did possess a mandate. Though the early Chinese believed that Heaven gave various signs such as eclipses that warned dynasties that misconduct might lead to loss of their Mandate, they never made the concept of Heaven as an intelligent force for good an important part of their philosophy. There was never a sense that Heaven was a person or personal god like Father Zeus, such as characterized thinkers in the West. Nor was there any concept such as Anaximander's notion of the Assessment of Time wherein wrongs were always righted in time. Such anthropomorphic qualities as are evident in the *Odes* soon disappeared, and though the ancient Chinese possessed a rich mythological tradition, now only dimly known, it was quickly euhemerized into history.

Beyond these notions, there developed the concept of *tian* as an abstract, impersonal Nature operating by knowable processes and principles that were certain and constant. Xunzi devotes his book "Discourse on Nature" to the development and defense of this thesis. His concept of Nature owes much to the thinking of Zhuang Zhou, whom Xunzi criticizes for stressing nature while neglecting man and missing the essential nature of the myriad things ("Tianlun," 17.10).

The Chinese had long been aware that celestial events could be predicted and that there were great recurrent periods such as the twelve-year cycle of Jupiter and other, longer cosmic cycles. The rhythms of the night and day and of the seasons constituted only the most obvious of the regularities of nature (*Yijing*, "Xici" 繫辭, 8.9b–10a). Xunzi makes the same point ("Tianlun," 17.2): "The fixed stars follow their revolutions; the sun and moon alternately shine; the four seasons present themselves in succession; the Yin and Yang enlarge and transform; and the wind and rain spread out everywhere. Each of the myriad things must obtain its harmonious ambience in order to grow, and each must obtain its proper nurture in order to become complete."

Xunzi argues that the course of Nature is constant. It does not respond to good government, nor does it perish because of misgovernment. "The sun and moon, the stars and celestial markpoints, the auspicious stars mark off the divisions of time, and the asterisms that calculate the calendar were the same in the time of Yu as in the time of Jie. Since Yu achieved order while Jie brought chaos, order and chaos are not brought about by Heaven" (17.4).

Floods and droughts are natural phenomena. They are not sent down by Nature to punish. They are a modification of the natural processes that also produce the normal pattern of weather on which all life depends. What counts is that we understand the course of Nature and respond to it intelligently. If we act foolishly, then there will be famine and sickness; "even when inauspicious and weird events never occur, there will be misfortune." Though the seasons come the same in a disorderly age as they do in an orderly age, the catastrophes and calamities are of a different order. Yet there is no cause to curse Nature (17.1). Nature does not suspend the winter because men dislike cold weather. It does not respond to our prayers: "If you pray for rain and there is rain, what of that? I say there is no special relationship—as when you do not pray for rain and there is rain" (17.8).

Heaven does not send down omens and signs. Unusual events and strange happenings are part of the course of Nature. Such events occur because of a modification of the relation of Heaven and Earth or because of a transmutation of the Yin and Yang. There is no age in which they do not occasionally occur. "When stars fall or trees groan, the whole state is terrified. They ask what caused this to happen. I reply that there was no specific reason" (17.7). Such things are to be marveled at, but they are not to be feared. Xunzi developed an impersonal, neutral Nature. It did not respond to man or to his good or bad conduct. Man's government must respond to the constancy of nature, taking precautions against its normal variations. Those who thought that Nature responded to the actions of men were deceived.

HEAVEN AND EARTH

Philosophical doctrine distinguished between two pairs of primary elements in cosmology: Heaven 天 and Earth 地 and the Yin and Yang principles, each of which plays a role in the creation and sustenance of life. The Yin and Yang principally account for change in Nature, whereas Heaven and Earth are the materials of which life is composed. "Heaven and Earth are the beginning of life" ("Wangzhi," 9.15). Heaven covers and begets everything; Earth sustains and nourishes everything. "The sky before us is only a bright shining area, but when viewed in its inexhaustible extent, then the sun, moon, stars, and constellations are suspended in it, and all things are overspread by it. The earth before us seems only a handful of soil, but when regarded in its true breadth and thickness, it sustains mountains like Hua and Yue, without feeling their weight, and contains the seas and rivers, without their leaking away" (*Zhongyong* 中庸, 26).

There developed various schools of thinking as to how one must respond to Heaven and Earth. One of the most important contended that Heaven and Earth are indifferent to mankind. Shen Dao held that "Heaven possesses light; it is not distressed by the darkness in which men live. Earth possesses riches; it is not distressed by the poverty in which men live" (*Shenzi*, fragment 1 [Thompson ed.]). In the words of the *Daode jing* (5), "Heaven and Earth are ruthless. They treat the myriad things as so many straw dogs used in sacrifices." Xunzi believed that since Heaven and Earth are the source of all life, they "give birth to the gentleman, and the gentleman provides the organizing principle for Heaven and Earth" ("Wangzhi," 9.15).

What is important is to understand that Heaven and Earth are subject to the thought of the sage and the gentleman, who provide the rational principles of order that enable man to survive despite the adversities visited on him by Heaven and Earth and to prosper when, in the normal course of events, they produce abundance. Man evens out the effects of Nature through philosophy and its translation into social order and government.

THE TRIAD OF HEAVEN, EARTH, AND MAN

These considerations led Xunzi to his doctrine of the Triad 参, a balance between Man, Heaven, and Earth. The doctrine of the Triad antedates Xunzi by some time, though its origins are obscure.[1] It is mentioned by Fan Sui in a persuasion and by General Nao Chi in his indictment of King Min of Qi. Shen Dao makes use of the concept in his philosophy of government. This shows that the idea was generally known, and commonly accepted, in the first part of Xunzi's career at the Jixia Academy. Xunzi makes the doctrine of the Triad a central theme: "The gentleman is the triadic partner of Heaven and Earth, the summation of the myriad things, and the father and mother of the people. If there were no gentleman, Heaven and Earth would lack any principle of order, and ritual and moral principles would have no guidelines" ("Wangzhi," 9.15).

Man must not "contest over the work of Nature," in which nothing is done yet there is completion and in which nothing is sought yet all is obtained. "Heaven has its seasons; Earth its resources; man his government. This, of course, is why it is said that they 'can form a Triad.' When man abandons what he should use to form the Triad yet longs for the rest of the Triad, he has become deluded" ("Tianlun," 17.2).

THE DAO, THE WAY

Within Nature there is a constant principle, the Dao 道, usually translated the Way. The common meaning of the word, even in modern Chinese, is "way" in the sense of a path or road leading somewhere. It is thus the path to something, as to becoming a gentleman, a sage, or a True King, and it is also the path or way that the universe follows in all its processes and movements. A dao or way consists in the methods, principles, and doctrines that constituted the path to the goal. In the thinking of most Ru philosophers, the Dao rarely means more than the methods, principles, and doctrines that lead to the ideal order of society, which was followed by the ancient kings, and the right way of life within human society, which the gentleman observes. But in a few works, principally the *Daode jing*, attributed to Laozi, and the *Zhuangzi*, the Dao is elevated into the principle by which the whole of Nature operates, and this idea was adopted by Xunzi in discussing Nature. The *Daode jing* says (51):

> The Dao gave birth to them;
> Its Power 德 reared them;
> Each thing is embodied in its own form;
> Its special circumstances bring it to maturity.

Thus, everything worships the Dao and does homage to its Power. Yet there was never any "Mandate" 命 that the Dao should be worshipped, and none that homage should be done to its Power.[2] "This was always and ever free and spontaneous." The Dao bears all that exists. "The Dao gave birth to the One; the One gave birth successively to two things, three things, up to the myriad things" (*DDJ*, 42; Waley, *Way and Its Power*, p. 195). The Power of the Dao rears all, makes all grow, fosters all, harbors all, doctors all, nourishes all, and shelters all. The lesson for the philosopher is that the Dao

> Rears all, but lays no claim to them,
> Controls all, but never expects gratitude from them,
> Is chief among them, but exercises no authority over them;
> This is called the Foremost Power 元德.
>
> (*DDJ*, 51).[3]

The Dao as a way or path that could be followed seems like a concrete thing rather than an abstract principle underlying all. Philosophers were thus at pains to point out that although it was a path that could be followed and trusted in, and although it had an essential nature that gave it identity, it was indefinite and unshaped. Although the Dao rears all, bears all, and accomplishes all, it does not act and is not seen.

It can be transmitted to us, but we cannot take it as our own. It can be grasped, but it cannot be seen. It is its own root and its own trunk; since before there was a Heaven and an Earth, it was inherently what it was from of old. It hallows the ghosts and the Di Ancestors. It gives birth to Heaven and to Earth. It is farther than the ultimate zenith, but it is not reckoned a high place. It is beneath the Six Directions, but it is not considered low like a marsh. Though it was before Heaven and Earth were born, it is not reckoned long-lasting. Though more senior than the supremely ancient, it is not considered old.

(*Zhuangzi*, 6 "Dazongshi" 大宗師, 3.5b–6a)[4]

In a famous conversation, Confucius is made to ask the Old Master Laozi what the Ultimate Dao is. The Old Master responds:

The Way is elusive and profound. It is difficult to describe, but I will give you a general outline in words:

> The brightly glowing is born of the darkly obscure.
> What has structured order is born of the unshaped.
> The seminal and divine essence is born of the Way.
> The shape and the root are born of the seminal essence.

For the myriad things use it to shape themselves according to their own kind.

(Zhuangzi, "Zhibeiyou" 知北遊, 7.24b)[5]

The Dao is constant, unvarying, and eternal. It fills what is greatest and is not absent from what is least. It is complete in all things; it is diffused in all things; it is universal in its comprehensiveness (*Zhuangzi*, 13 "Tiandao" 天道, 5.17b). The Dao is One: "Therefore the Sage embraces Oneness and becomes the testing instrument for the world" (*DDJ*, 22; Lau, *Lao Tzu*, p. 79; Waley, *Way and Its Power*, p. 171). The Dao is silent, empty, sufficient unto itself, unchanging, all-pervading, and never exhausted (*DDJ*, 25).

> The Dao is like an empty vessel
> That yet may be drawn from
> Without ever needing to be filled.
> It is bottomless, the very progenitor of all things.

(DDJ, 4; Waley, Way and Its Power, p. 146)

The Dao is calm, quiet, peaceful, tranquil, and we must hold fast to such stillness:

> All the teeming creatures
> Return to their separate roots.
> This returning to the root is known as stillness.
> It is called "reverting to the Mandate."

(DDJ, 16)[6]

These ideas flourished in the Jixia Academy both when Xunzi was a student and later when he was libationer there. The doctrine of the Dao as a universal principle of the cosmos, of a Dao that was constant and could not be "named," was a major attack on the traditional views of the Ru scholars. To judge from the essays advocating such views in the *Guanzi* and *Lüshi chunqiu* compendiums, many scholars accepted this doctrine. The *Daode jing* says explicitly:

> Banish "learning," and there will no longer be sorrow.
> Banish "sageliness," discard "wisdom,"
> and the people will benefit a hundredfold.

> Banish "humanity," discard "morality,"
> and they will once again be filial and compassionate.
> Banish skill, discard profit,
> and there will be thieves and robbers no more.
>
> (*DDJ*, 20, 19)[7]

The same disdain for Ru knowledge is to be seen in the doctrine of Shen Dao that "a clod of earth does not miss the Dao" (*Zhuangzi*, 33 "Tianxia," 10.18a). The *Zhuangzi* dismisses the ideas of the Ru scholars as "vestiges left by former kings," learning and thinking that are so utterly "commonplace" that from the standpoint of the Dao they are quite meaningless (14 "Tianyun" 天運, 5.23b; 16 "Shanxing" 繕性, 6.3a).

> Common people fuss and fret
> but the Sage is a dullard and a sluggard....

While we dream we do not know that we are dreaming. In the midst of our dreaming, we may even interpret a dream. Not until we awake do we realize that we were dreaming. Only at the ultimate awakening shall we realize that this is the ultimate dream. Yet fools think that they awake, so confident are they that they know what they are: princes! herdsmen! Incorrigible they are! You and Confucius are both dreams.

> (*Zhuangzi*, 2 "Qiwulun" 齊物論, 1.23ab; Graham, *Chuang-tzu*, pp. 59–60)

The apparent unanimity of opinion in the Jixia Academy embraced two very different groups of scholars. One represented by Zhuang Zhou and his followers opposed and satirized the logical conundrums of the logicians such as Hui Shi and the dialecticians. They also disdained the narrowness of the Ru and Mohists, who were preoccupied with minutiae of questions of right and wrong and proper burials.

A different line of argument was represented in the *Daode jing* (18), which contends that it was only

> When the Great Dao fell into disuse
> that there was "humanity" and "morality."
> It was when "intelligence" and "wisdom" arose
> that there was the Great Pretense.

The fundamental values of the Ru and Mohist schools were thus expressly rejected in the *Daode jing*. In governing the people, the true sage rules (*DDJ*, 3)

> by emptying their mind
> and filling their bellies,
> by weakening their will
> and strengthening their bones.

> always causing the people to have no knowledge
> and no desires.

Regulations, laws, humanity, morality, filial piety, loyalty, and all the other virtues of the Ru scholars are worthless. Rites are but the husk of vanishing loyalty and good faith (*DDJ*, 38). Filial piety arises when true harmony and kinship have been lost (*DDJ*, 18).

Though Xunzi rejects the critique of "knowledge," "humanity," and "morality," he accepts this view of the nature of the Dao. Two of his most important books are devoted to reinterpreting these doctrines to fit the mold of Ru thinking. Xunzi contends that the True Dao of which he speaks "is not the way of Heaven or the way of Earth, but rather the Way that guides the actions of mankind and is embodied in the conduct of the gentleman" ("Ruxiao," 8.3).

In "Dispelling Blindness," Xunzi contends that the sage uses the Dao as his "suspended balance" to test all the myriad things. The sage and even the ordinary man can know the Dao because of the mind. The mind can know the Dao because it shares the essential qualities of the Dao: emptiness, unity, and stillness. "The mind never stops storing; nonetheless, it possesses the quality of emptiness. The mind never lacks diversity; nonetheless, it possesses the quality of unity. The mind never stops moving; nonetheless, it possesses the quality of stillness" ("Jiebi," 21.5d). Xunzi notes that from birth men are aware, and because of this awareness, they possess a memory. Though the mind constantly stores new memories, it is never full; thus, like the Dao, it is "an empty vessel." This "emptiness" enables the mind to keep what was previously stored in it from interfering with what is being received through awareness. For Xunzi, awareness consists of the perception of differences. In order to distinguish things, the mind must be aware of them all at the same time. The unity of the mind enables men to do this. Whether awake or sleeping, the mind constantly moves of its own accord, sometimes dreaming, sometimes relaxing, sometimes planning. That we can do all these things without one bringing disorder to the other is because of the stillness of the mind.

Xunzi further argues that when we choose between things, we must weigh and balance the alternatives. The Dao is the "balance" we must use. "If one abandons the Dao and rather selects on the basis of private considerations, then he will not know what involves misfortune and what involves fortune" ("Zhengming," 22.6b). Using the Dao is like exchanging one thing for two of the same kind—everyone knows that this is to gain. "No man acts so as to exchange two for one because he understands how to count.... To abandon the Dao and select on the basis of private considerations is like exchanging two for one. How could there be gain!" (22.6a) The Dao for Xunzi is thus not merely the right way to conduct oneself, nor is it just the way by which the ancient sages organized human society; rather, it is a cosmic principle that operates according to certain invariable principles that can be grasped by the mind since the mind shares the fundamental qualities of the Dao.

YIN AND YANG

The Dao is constant, invisible, and one. The diversity of Nature derives from the interaction of two fundamental contrasting, but complementary principles: the Yin and the Yang. The "Great Appendix" to the *Changes* ("Xici," 7.11a–12a; Legge, pp. 355–56) asserts: "One phase of Yin and one phase of Yang constitute what is known as the Dao. What they perpetuate is good." The Yin is the quiescent, cold, dark, humid, soft, female, represented by water and earth. The Yang is the active, hot, light, dry, hard, masculine, represented by air and sun. The character *yang* 陽 shows the sun with its slanting rays, in the traditional analysis, or a person holding an ancient astronomical instrument, a perforated disk of jade. The character *yin* 陰 is formed of elements representing clouds and the shadows of hills. In their most primitive meaning, *yang* refers to the sunny side of something, the south side of a mountain, the north side of a valley, or a north river bank, the *yin* to the shady side opposite (Needham, 2:227, 273; 3:328–29).

The origin of the philosophical meaning of the words has been the subject of considerable debate. They are found clearly used in their philosophical meanings in the "Great Appendix" to the *Changes*; when it was generally believed that this was written in high antiquity, the ideas were thought to be primordial.[8] Modern scholars have generally agreed that these ideas must have developed much later, though hardly as late as some scholars would date the text.[9] Recent evidence, however, shows that milfoil divination dates back to the middle Shang period. Its general use even then is indicated by the appearance of the hexagrams in widely scattered texts. Further investigations may well demonstrate that the ideas have great antiquity.[10]

The "Great Appendix" argues that the Yin and Yang are responsible for the phenomena of Heaven and Earth ("Xici," 8.15ab; Legge, p. 395). They are complementary, not conflicting. Their interaction is the source of all creation. The model is that of male-female, which, though opposites, must contain each other and interact since they cannot stand alone. Dualism in China was thus much different from the dualism of Greece or Persia, which was based on light and dark, which exclude each other.

In such thinking, the one force must necessarily defeat the other, or it cannot exist. Thus, their dualism became one of good versus bad. Chinese Yin-Yang dualism could not sustain such an interpretation. The exclusion or domination of the one by the other only produces disaster, natural or human. As Zhuang Zhou (6 "Dazongshi," 3.9b; Graham, *Chuangtzu*, p. 88) says, "For man the Yin and Yang are more than father and mother."

The Yang was, however, superior to the Yin, just as the Heavens are superior to the Earth. Thus, the male was superior to the female. The way of Heaven was the way of the male. "Though the *yin* has its beauties, it keeps them under restraint in its service of the king and does not claim success for itself. This is the way of Earth, of a wife, of a subject. The way of Earth is not to claim the merit of achievement, but on another's behalf to bring things to their proper issue" (*Yijing* 1.27a; Legge, p. 420). The hierarchical society that differentiated ruler and subject, father and son, husband and wife, elder and younger, was a natural reflection of a cosmic principle embodied in the Yin and Yang.

It is apparent that by the time of Mo Di the concept of abstract principles of Yin and Yang had been developed. But it is already fully developed in the *Jiran* 計然, attributed to Fan Li 范蠡 (also called Ji Nizi 計倪子) and now surviving only in short fragments (Needham, 2:275). Fan Li was an adviser to King Goujian of Yue 越王句踐, which makes him contemporary with Confucius. Fan counsels the king, who wanted to prepare to invade Wu, "to observe the *qi* 氣 vapors of Heaven and Earth, to seek out the source in the action of the Yin and Yang, and to elucidate the operations of the *guxu* 孤虛 [the gate of Heaven and door of Earth] and judge carefully survival and death." [11] Fan Li explains that the vapors of Heaven and Earth are responsible for the birth and death of things; that by seeking out the source in the action of the Yin and Yang, things become noble or base; that by elucidating the operations of the *guxu*, one knows how to act in concert with others and to maintain cordial relations; and that by judging carefully in matters of survival and ruin one can distinguish between what is authentic and what is mere artifice. The king responds by "looking up to observe the patterns of the Heavens, collecting and scrutinizing the constellations and their positions, and calculating the shape of the four seasons."

This passage shows that these concepts were connected intimately with astronomical observations, calendrics, and meteorology. We thus have a series of interrelated ideas beginning to form a system: Heaven and Earth dualism, Yin-Ying dualism, the concept of the *qi* vapors, and the seasons. The intent of these ideas was to explain the process of change and to interpret it in naturalistic terms. Yin and Yang were thought to affect the ripening of the grains, the mood of the people, and the effectiveness of the army. Scholars interested in such speculations dealt with the phenomena explained by the Yin-Yang theory.

The theory also occurs in the *Zuo zhuan*, in various contexts that are dated to events from the middle of the seventh century and to events contemporaneous with Fan Li and Confucius. In 645, a minister observed that "when the *qi* vital spirit of animals is in confusion, they become perverse and uncontrollable. Their Yin blood humour everywhere rises up, and their expanded veins swell and stand out" (*Zuo*, Xi 15). In this passage, we see the application of Yin-Yang theories to medical explanations based on the *qi* vital humour theory.

At this same time, it is recorded in the *Zuo zhuan* that five stones fell from the sky and that six fishhawks flew backward over the capital of Song. These were understood as omens from Heaven by the Duke of Song, and he asked about their meaning. A scholar offered the duke an interpretation, but privately observed: "His lordship asked the wrong question. This is a matter of the action of Yin and Yang. It is not something that produces good luck or misfortune. I did not presume to contradict the reasoning of his lordship" (*Zuo*, Xi 16). The text explains that the five stones were meteorites and that the force of the wind made the fishhawks appear to fly backward. Both explanations are an attempt to substitute a naturalistic interpretation of the world for the older idea that Heaven responded to the world of men with signs and sent down disasters. This older view is amply documented in *Odes* composed at the time of the collapse of the Western Zhou dynasty in 771, but even then some preferred naturalistic explanations.

The most comprehensive early treatment of Yin-Yang theory is in the speeches of Prince Chan of Zheng, who links astronomical and meteorological lore with medical theory, pointing out that the Yin and Yang are but two of the varieties of *qi* vital vapors, the others being wind and rain and light and darkness. The illness of the Duke of Jin is not caused by spirits:

These two spirits do not influence your lord's body. The spirits of the hills and streams are offered sacrifice for fortune in times of flood, drought, and pestilence. The spirits of the sun, moon, stars, and constellations are offered sacrifice for fortune on occasions when there is unseasonable snow, hoarfrost, wind, or rain. As far as the body of your lord is concerned, it must be a matter of his movements about the palace, his food and drink, or his griefs and pleasures. What could spirits of hills and streams or celestial objects have to do with it?

Prince Chan thus distinguishes ritual offerings, which are appropriate for certain occasions, from the causation of bodily illness, which is related to sexual indulgence, diet, and emotional stress:

I have heard that the gentleman observes four divisions of the day: in the morning he listens to matters of government, at noon he makes inquiries about these
and consults others, in the evening he puts his commands in good order, and at
night he rests his body. By this practice he keeps his *qi* humours within their
natural bounds so that they are not allowed to be shut up, stopped, constricted,
or congested, whereby they might cause the body to waste away. Should that
happen, his mind will lose its vigor and all his various measures will become
dark and confused. (*Zuo*, Zhao 1)

Prince Chan is also responsible for one of the earliest statements of the
theory of "two souls," which compose the person, one Yang soul from
the father and one Yin soul from the mother (*Zuo*, Zhao 7).

A physician from Qin summoned to treat the Duke of Jin offers a
parallel explanation. He, too, links illness with the failure to observe
natural bounds. He associates these natural bounds with those defined by
and observed in music, particularly in the tuning of instruments, and he
cautions against "loose sounds" (*Zuo*, Zhao 1). The problem of "loose
sounds" is well known from Confucius, who condemns the music of
Zheng and Wey for its looseness (*LY*, 15.11, 17.16). At about the same
time, a minister offers a naturalistic interpretation of a ritual calendar
preserved in the "Seventh Month" Ode (*Zuo*, Zhao 4; *Shi*, "Airs of
Bin," "Qi yue" 七月, Mao 154). Thus, Yin-Yang was becoming a general
theory that attempted a naturalistic explanation of change without the
older magical, ritual, and moralistic colorations. By Xunzi's time, the
theory also embraced symbolic correlations of the whole universe in
terms of other theories concerned with numerology and the Five Processes. Xunzi condemns this more general theory, which is to be associated with Zou Yan, particularly its adaptation by Ru scholars as seen in
the works of Fu Sheng ("Fei shier zi," 6.7).

THE QI VAPORS

No single English word can capture the full range of philosophical
meanings of the word *qi*. The *qi* is the essence, the substance, the breath,
the vital spirit or vapor, the humour, the energy of which the universe
and all things in it are composed. The oldest form of the written graph
appears to indicate steam and vapor. The modern graph depicts vapors
and aromas arising from cooking food. It designates the essence of things,
the very spirit that characterizes them, just as the aroma enables us immediately to identify foods. But the aroma and accompanying steam in
cooking are linked to the vapor of one's breathing, which makes us live,
the breath itself, and the air we breathe. All things are composed of *qi*,

either rarefied or condensed. It is part of all vital things. *Qi* thus indicates the fundamental character of things, what makes them what they are. To capture the essence of a thing is to capture not its external form, but its *qi*. If we are to capture the real thing, it must be the *qi* that is evoked in music and in art.

From the earliest times, the word appears to have been applied to meteorological phenomena. There was a lighter, more subtle *qi* and a heavier, coarser *qi*. From the primeval *qi* vapor, the lighter *qi* rose and by its accumulation formed the Heavens, the heavier *qi* sank and by its accumulation formed the Earth. The wind was the *qi* of the Heavens; rain the *qi* of the Earth. The movement of the winds was in response to the changing balance of the Yin and Yang as the seasons succeeded one another. The Yang *qi* was identified with fire and became the mind; the Yin *qi* was identified with water. Thunder was like water thrown into a furnace. The *qi* of the Heavens comes down, whereas that of Earth ascends.[12]

Life is the result of the collecting together of the *qi*. In one of his most important passages, Xunzi observes that fire and water possess *qi* but not life ("Wangzhi," 9.16). He thus distinguishes between the vital spirit that moving things like fire and water possess and the true life of plants, animals, and humans. The Yin and Yang were recognized as two types of "vital spirit" or "vapor." Others were Heaven and Earth, mentioned in the *Jiran*, the wind and rain, and light and dark.

Men were composed of Yin and Yang *qi* humours, which accounted for their moods and their individual temperaments. "To sustain the Yang at its height without reverting to the Yin puts one under great stress and the tension shows in one's face. It is something that ordinary people prefer not to defy, so they suppress what the other man is stirring up in them in order to calm their own hearts" (*Zhuangzi*, 4 "Renjianshi" 人間世, 2.6a; Graham, *Chuang-tzu*, p. 69). Xunzi speaks of those who have a "contentious *qi*," meaning mood, those who have evil and base *qi*, meaning sentiments, and those who have a rebellious *qi*, which is to be suppressed, in contrast to an obedient *qi*, which accords with nature. Xunzi describes a man who became so frightened that he lost his *qi* vital breath and died ("Jiebi," 21.8).

Men come into being from the union of the Yang and Yin vital spirits, which become their two souls. The Yang vapor is the seminal spirit that becomes the mind. The Yin vapor is the solid substance that becomes the bones and flesh. The process of coming into being is like that of water becoming ice and that of dying like that of ice melting. Each is only a change of form. The Yang becomes a spirit after death, whereas the Yin is buried in the earth.

So long as a man maintains the proper balance between these, he will live. Various medical and alchemical theories developed arcane strategies for maintaining the balance. The hope was to attain immortality. In Xunzi's day, pursuit of elixirs and medicines became an obsession among the nobility. From early times, it was thought that sexual excess depleted a man's Yang and hastened his death: "Women are associated with Yang things and with times of darkness. Loose excess in regard to them produces diseases of internal heat and deluded madness" (*Zuo*, Zhao 1). Zhuang Zhou points out that as the mind, which is the product of the Yang vapor, nears death, "nothing can make it revert to the Yang" (2 "Qiwulun," 1.12a). Xunzi discusses this doctrine in his book "On Self-Cultivation," which examines the theory of "controlling the *qi* vital breath."

LI: REASON, PRINCIPLE OF ORDER

The word *li* 理 originally meant the "pattern" or "order" inherent in a thing or given a thing. Its earliest attested meaning is "to mark out the divisions of fields." This is to be seen in the original phonetic part of the graph, which consists of elements meaning "field" and "earth." It refers as well to the distinctive markings in a piece of jade, to the grain in bamboo, to the lines that appear on the skin, and to the fibers of the muscle. As a verb, it meant to cut along the veins of a piece of jade or to lay out fields according to the requirements of land forms. Thus, wherever a distinctive pattern provided order in a thing, there was *li*. It was the principle of order that provided the pattern, regulated the thing, and made it recognizable as that thing and function as that thing functions. It is the reason and rationality common to the minds of all men. It delights the mind just as good food delights the palate (*Mengzi*, 6A.7). Xunzi stresses that the gentleman keeps to his reason in times of happiness and in times of sadness, so that he never loses hold on reality ("Bugou," 3.6; "Zhongni," 7.2).

The concept *qi* "vapor" serves something of the role that "matter" or "substance" plays in Western philosophy. The word that plays a role similar to that of *logos* or reason is *li*. The Dao or Way is formless and shapeless. It is the *li* that provides the pattern, the order ("Quanxue," 1.12; "Xiushen," 2.13). The *li* is the rational basis of all order. It is natural order, and it is reason. In his commentary on the *Daode jing*, Han Fei observes that the *li* is the pattern of the complete or whole thing.[13] It makes the square thing square and the round round, the short short and the long long, the coarse coarse and the fine fine, the hard hard and the soft soft (*HFZ*, 20 "Jie *Lao*" 解老 6.9a). When this order is observed, the jade can be cut, the bamboo woven into baskets, and the fields laid out to man's benefit.

One must use the *li* patterns of order that inhere in all the things of nature. The ancient sage Fuxi 伏羲 looked up at the Heavens to observe their configurations and scrutinized the patterns of earthly things in order to determine the proper category for each kind of thing. The mind enables us to discover this pattern and to understand its rationale. The sage makes use of it and so does not invent things out of his own heart, but understands by reason what cannot be apprehended, perceives what cannot be seen, and reckons what cannot be counted (*Mengzi*, 6A.7; *LSCQ*, 25/2 "Bielei" 別類, 25.3b—4a). The sage succeeds through using such reason. The sage "regulates and distinguishes according to the great natural principles of order all that is encompassed in space and time" ("Jiebi," 21.5e). But if one does not proceed in accordance with the natural and rational principles of order, then things cannot succeed (*DDLJ*, "Yibenming" 易本命; Wilhelm, p. 250). When we understand the *li* of Nature, then its processes are neither miraculous nor magical since everything is understandable, though profound and mysterious.

For philosophers such as the Mohist logicians, Xunzi, and Han Fei, *li* was preeminently "reason" as it applied to discourse and to the state. "Names derive from reality; reality derives from natural principles of order. Natural principles of order derive from the inner powers of things. The inner power of things derives from their harmoniousness. Their harmony derives from their congruity" (*Guanzi*, 55 "Jiushou" 九守, 18.4a).[14] The Mohists regarded the *li* as the basis of rational judgment by which we distinguish and classify things in discourse (*Mozi*, "Canons and Explanations," A75, B78 [Graham, *Later Mohist Logic*]). "Thus if the content of a discrimination does not coincide with rational principles of order, then it is false. 'Knowledge' that does not correspond to rational order is deceit.... [Because] *li* rational principles of order are the progenitor of any distinction of right and wrong" (*LSCQ*, 18/4 "Nanwei" 難謂, 18.8a).

Xunzi objected to the types of logical conundrums propounded by the sophists because they failed to conform to rational principles of order. The superiority of the gentleman over mere debaters consisted solely in the fact that the gentleman caused his "speech to be certain to accord with rational principles of order and undertakings to be certain to be properly attended to" ("Ruxiao," 8.3). The discriminations of sophists, though they appeared to have perfect logic, were fatally flawed because they understood only an aspect of the truth ("Fei shier zi," 6.1; "Jiebi," 21.1).

Xunzi held that the Dao, which provided the classical standards and natural order of things, must be discovered not through the study of the way of Heaven or through the way of Earth, but through the way of Man, because "as a general rule, it is through knowledge of the nature of man that it is possible to know the natural principles of order in things" ("Jiebi," 21.9). This means, in his view, that the "constant relationships" of human society and the natural categories of things should be considered an outgrowth of natural order. This is why men find a society based on such "constant relationships" reasonable and why such a society corresponds harmoniously with nature. "Heaven and Earth give birth to the gentleman, and the gentleman provides the organizing principle for Heaven and Earth. . . . The relationships between lord and minister, father and son, older and younger brothers, husband and wife, begin as they end and end as they begin. They share with Heaven and Earth the same natural principles of order. They endure in the same form through all eternity" ("Wangzhi," 9.15). For Xunzi, this meant that the sage could depend on his reason and the natural order he discovered within himself to understand everything else. "The classes of things do not become contradictory although a long time has elapsed because they have an identical principle of order" ("Fei xiang," 5.5).

Xunzi believed that the Dao provided the classical standards and the rational principles on which all social order rested ("Zhengming," 22.3e; "Fei xiang," 5.9). He asserts that the basic values of civilized society depend on following *li*, meaning natural and rational principles of order. These can be known and put into practice. This is what justifies the conviction that everyone could, if he had the will, become a sage like Yu the Great. "Every man has the capacity to know them and the full ability to put them into practice" ("Xing'e," 23.5a).

Petty men attach great importance to mere things because they minimize the significance of rational principles of order ("Zhengming," 22.6c). But when what the mind finds acceptable corresponds to natural order, then whether the desires be numerous or few, there will be no harm to social order ("Zhengming," 22.5a). The sage understands this; though the sage also follows his desires and fulfills his emotions, he regulates them in accord with the dictates of *li* reason. Confucius was a sage in whom this reached the completion of perfect harmony. Mencius (5B.1) describes it in musical terms: "To do this is to open the music with bells and conclude it with the jade tubes. To open with bells is to begin with *li* rational order. To conclude with jade is to end with *li* natural order. To begin in accord with rational principles of order is the concern of the wise, whereas to end in accord with natural principles of order is the concern of the sage."

When the fundamental divisions of society correspond to natural and rational order, there is harmony. People recognize the justness of their position, of their duties, and of their rewards. Things are as they ought to be is the general perception. The result of such order is that "the way of public-spiritedness will prevail everywhere, selfish private interests will be closed off, the public good will be made clear, and private affairs put to rest" ("Jundao" 君道, 12.7).

HE HARMONY

Chinese thought has always stressed the necessity of man to be harmonious with nature and emphasized *he* 和 harmony among men as the goal of society. Things do not exist in isolation. Each belongs to a specific logical and material class. When it has the qualities proper to its class, it is good. This class has its place in the scheme of things. Its position is determined by its relation to everything else encompassed in time and space and between Heaven and Earth. This is not the result of any plan or design or of any creator or external will. What is of Nature is spontaneous and effortless. Heaven does not command the seasons, nor does the sage ruler command his people. It is the Dao of Nature that no action is taken and yet each thing is perfected (*Liji*, "Aigongwen" 哀公文, 50.8a).

It is the nature of the world that every "this" creates a "that." Opposites generate each other and grow out of each other. This is the constant, unvarying manifestation of the Dao, whose natural movement is reversal. We have seen how this is true of the Yin and Yang principles, but it applies to every other pair of contrasting terms as well.

> Difficult and easy complete each other.
> Long and short demonstrate each other.
> High and low determine each other.
> Instrument and voice harmonize each other.
> Before and after follow each other.
>
> (*DDJ*, 2)

The meaning of a word becomes complete only when contrasted with its opposite. Xunzi observes that "trusting what is trustworthy is trust" but "doubting what is dubious is also trust" ("Fei shier zi," 6.9; see also Introduction to Book 6).

What Chinese philosophers sought was therefore the connectedness of all things. We have seen how the special talent of the sage was his ability to recognize the distinctive marks that express such connectedness. This enabled him to respond perfectly to every change. Responsiveness preserves the harmony between things. Perfect responsiveness was always compared to a reverberating echo or to the shadow of a moving object.

Again, things of the same kind attract and influence each other. When one cow lows, others respond. One dog causes others to bark. When one instrument is struck, the others resonate. There is nothing mysterious or magical about this; all things reject what is different and accept what is akin to them. Such sounding of their own accord and mutual reaction of things appears spontaneous because things of every class are affected by other things of that same class (*Yijing*, 1.15a).

Harmony is distinguished clearly from *tong* 同 "identity" as a logical concept and from solidarity as a social practice. "Harmony results in the production of things, but identity does not produce any issue. When one thing is used to balance something else, it is called 'harmony.' If one thing is added to something identical to itself, all that is new is rejected" (*Guoyu*, "Zhengyu" 鄭語, 16.4a). Yan Ying illustrated the fundamental difference by an analogy with soup. To make a good soup requires fire, water, vinegar, pickles, salt, plums, and fish. The fire boils the water, the ingredients are blended and their flavors equalized so that what is deficient is corrected and what is in excess is reduced. The success of the soup lies in blending, equalizing, and harmonizing the ingredients so that none loses its proper place. It is the same with music, where all the instruments and sounds must blend together if the form is to be united. "If you were to try to give water flavor with water, who would care to partake of the result? If lutes were to be confined to a single note, who would be able to listen to them? Such is the inadequacy of mere identity" (*Zuo*, Zhao 20). So it is with Nature and with society as well.

6

■ ■ ||||||||||||||||||||||||||||||||||||||||||||||||||||||||||||||||||||||||||||||||||||||||||||||||||||||||||||||||||||||||||||||||||||||||||||||||| ■ ■

Man and Society

HUMAN NATURE

For Ru philosophers the question of human nature was of great importance since they placed on the individual the whole success of society. Confucius himself was ambiguous in his teachings about man's nature. He objected when Ji Zicheng 棘子成 contended that a gentleman is nothing more than the stuff of which he is made. To Confucius the embellishments of culture were important: "shorn of its fur, the pelt of a tiger or leopard is no different from that of a dog or sheep" (*LY*, 12.8). He indicated that by nature all men were essentially alike. It is the process of education that causes them to become different (*LY*, 17.2, 15.39). He granted that some were so stupid that they could not be changed and others so wise that instruction was unnecessary (*LY*, 17.3). Since men differ but little in inborn nature, Confucius stressed that education should be open to all. He himself never failed to offer instruction to anyone who sought it eagerly (*LY*, 7.7). He recognized four categories of persons: those who are born wise, those who study to become wise, those who must toil away in study, and the common people who toil but do not study (*LY*, 16.9). Confucius admitted that he was not one of those who were born wise (*LY*, 7.20). He urged that the proper approach of the gentleman was to develop those qualities that are good and to suppress those that are bad. The words he used for this contrast mean as much "beautiful" and "ugly" as "good" and "bad" (*LY*, 12.16).

It seems clear that Confucius must have regarded man's inborn nature as a mixture of good qualities that education must develop and bad qualities that it must suppress. This is in any case certainly the view of his disciples. Wang Chong 王充 reports that the disciples Fu Zijian 宓子賤, Qidiao Kai 漆彫開, and Gongsun Nizi 公孫尼子 shared with Shi Shi 世碩[1] the view that human nature contains both good and evil elements: "If one emphasizes what is good in inborn nature, if one cultivates and regulates it, then its goodness will increase" (*Lunheng* 論衡, 3.12a). The same is true of the evil in man's nature. The explanation is to be found in the fact that "in everyone's inborn nature there are both Yin and Yang elements, and good and evil qualities depend on what is cultivated" (*Lunheng*, 3.12a). Wang Chong explains that the inborn nature with which we are initially endowed by Nature as our *ming* 命, "lot" or "fate," is determined by the particular mixture of fine and coarse *qi* vapor of which we are composed.[2]

Mencius held that man's nature was good, as proved by the fact that everyone has in him the "Four Beginnings": a sense of compassion for others, a sense of shame, a sense of modesty and courtesy, and a sense of right and wrong. Mencius cited the example of the spontaneous reaction of all people to a child about to fall into a well. Anyone that is human will try to rescue it. Mencius thus concluded that since the most important of the Ru virtues are prefigured in the Four Beginnings, man's inborn nature must be good (*Mengzi*, 2A.6). Xunzi explicitly rejects Mencius' analysis as flawed and devotes his book "Man's Nature Is Evil" to refuting Mencius' view. Realism forced Mencius to admit there was a "small part" in man's nature that the gentleman suppresses with his mind. Ordinary men remain ordinary because they do not use their minds to think and so find no answers (*Mengzi*, 6A.15). Xunzi argues that the "conscious effort" implied by such use of the mind shows that goodness is not a part of inborn nature, but is acquired. This, in Xunzi's view, allows man to overcome his nature, just as Mencius admits the great man overcomes the "small part" of his nature.

Whatever their arguments about man's inborn nature, all Ru philosophers agreed that to develop the good and suppress the bad, it was necessary to know the teachings of the sages, to observe the restrictions of ritual, to incorporate the harmony of music, to cultivate one's inner power, and to develop a sense of what is right. Because all of these had to be learned—no one was born knowing them—Xunzi concluded that man's nature is that of the petty man. Yet all men had the potential to become a sage, if they would accumulate good.

Just as Heaven provided the ruling dynasty with a *ming* or mandate to rule, so too Heaven (understood either as a deity or as Nature) endowed man at birth with a *ming*, which was his fate or destiny. We cannot be certain when this concept developed. The character for the word *ming* became distinguished from that for *ling* 令, "command, order," during the reign of King Mu 周穆王 (956–923).[3] The concept is certainly clearly developed by Confucius' time. One's *ming* determined how long one would live, whether one would have wealth or honor (*LY*, 12.5, 16.8), whether one would live in safety or danger. Old age or premature death, poverty or wealth, safety or danger, order or chaos—all are assuredly the preordained decree of Heaven that cannot be altered. Failure to get

office or success in office, reward or punishment, good fortune or bad—
all have a fixed limit. Man's knowledge and strength can do nothing to
influence them (*Mozi*, 39 "Fei Ru" 非儒, 9.16b).

Ming also determined whether there would be order or chaos in the
state of a ruler, whether his population would be large or small, and
whether it would be wealthy or poor (*Mozi*, 35 "Fei Ming," I 非命, 上,
9.1a). Mo Di found this doctrine widespread among the Ru scholars of
his day, and he argued forcefully against it. Believing that man can do
nothing, the Ru do not try to do what can be done. "If officials fail to
govern properly, there will be disorder. If agriculture is neglected,
poverty will result. Poverty and disorder destroy the foundation of
government. Yet the Ru accept such ideas, believing them to be the true
teachings of the Way" (*Mozi*, 39 "Fei Ru," 9.16b).

The Mohist criticism seems to have modified Ru views. In Xunzi, the
doctrine of fate is unimportant. He acknowledges that every living thing
has its *ming* fate or destiny and that we must be obedient to our destiny
("Wangzhi," 9.16; "Bugou," 3.9). But this destiny can be known and
those who know destiny do not resent Heaven ("Fei shier zi," 6.11;
"Rongru," 4.5). Xunzi even extends the doctrine of fate to encompass
"opportunities encountered unexpectedly" ("Zhengming," 22.1b).

A central theme of Xunzi's "Discourse on Nature" is that though
Nature has endowed man with a certain constitution, what happens to
him is the result of his own action. The state is the creation of man; it is
his contribution to the Triad between Heaven, Earth, and Man. Ritual
principles are to the state what destiny is to man. Just as man cannot
depart from his endowed nature and survive, so too the state cannot depart from ritual principles and survive ("Tianlun," 17.9; "Qiangguo,"
16.1).

THE STATE AS FAMILY

The ancient Chinese conceived the state on the model of the family.
The ruler occupied the position of a parent. He was to treat his subjects
with the solicitude of a parent, loving them, caring for them, nurturing
them, teaching them, leading them. His subjects were like children.
They were to admire him, emulate him, follow him, respect him, obey
him. Ru philosophers conceived the family and human relationships in
terms of unequal pairs: ruler and subject, husband and wife, father and
son, elder and younger brother. The superior position—ruler, husband,
father, elder brother—must deal gently with the lower position—subject,
wife, son, younger brother—who must obey the wishes of the superior
and follow his example. Thus, Confucius tells the Duke of Qi, whose

sons contested the succession and whose ministers usurped ducal pre-
rogatives, that the art of governing consisted in letting "lords be lords
and ministers be ministers" and in letting "fathers be fathers and sons be
sons" (LY, 12.11). One must begin with the individual who sets the example: the ruler. However he behaves, his subject will follow him, just
as children emulate their parents. His influence is great since he is like
the wind and his subjects are like the grasses that must bend as the wind
blows (LY, 12.19).

With the model of the family in mind, Ru philosophers assumed a
hierarchical class society that supported a rule of noble gentlemen who
performed all the functions of government for the masses whom they
ruled. The Ru did no more than assume what was the actuality of their
day. China was a feudal state ruled by an hereditary nobility that was
supported by the masses. At the top of the hierarchy was the Zhou king,
the Son of Heaven, who held a universal mandate recognized by Heaven
itself, which had indicated its approval. Under him were the feudal lords,
who ruled by right of a mandate from the Zhou king. The nobles themselves were arranged in a hierarchy, ranging from dukes and marquises at
the top to earls in the middle to the viscounts and barons at the bottom.
Though this hierarchy did not exist at the beginning of the dynasty, it
was clearly accepted in the political theory of later times. Under the
feudal lords were the great noble families, who held mandates either
from the Zhou king or the feudal lords to "assist" the rulers in governing
their states. These were the great ministerial families of the states, whose
wealth and influence often rivaled that of their lords. Younger sons of
feudal lords often founded ministerial families. Below them were the
aristocrats. They were the grand officers, who were below the ministers
but above the knights, who held minor ranks in the government bureau-
cracy and who were often very poor. Confucius himself originated from
the aristocracy, being a leader of the *shi* or "knights." At the bottom
were the commoners, the craftsmen, merchants, and farmers whose labor
supported society.

This conception of the state of affairs had long been rationalized by
the aristocrats themselves, who observed that "it was a rule of our former
kings that gentlemen should labor with their minds and that ordinary
men should toil with the strength of their bodies" (Zuo, Xiang 9; cf.
Guoyu, "Lu yu" 魯語, 5.9a). Mencius (3A.4) declared this to be a universal principle recognized throughout the world: gentlemen should rule,
and ordinary men should be ruled. Those who are ruled support those
who rule.

A ritual cycle supported the religious view that the authority of the
king and the feudal lords derived ultimately from Heaven itself. This was

the *li* 禮 ritual, which also encompasses the etiquette and courtesy with which gentlemen treated each other and the protocol governing formal behavior in court functions. Though Xunzi would greatly expand the significance of ritual to provide a rationale for the state, in earlier times it comprised the traditional standards by which the nobles justified their dealings with each other and with the people. Its basis was tradition, and it did not justify the rule of the king or the lords. Rule in ancient China was personal rule, and it was personal qualities that caused Heaven to give King Wen the Mandate to rule the world. Personal qualities gave a ruler authority, provided the prestige that influenced others, and gave his government moral power. The Chinese expressed this with a single term: *de* 德.

RULE BY DE VIRTUE

Of all Chinese philosophical concepts, the most ancient is *de*, "inner power," which recent research indicates is already present in Shang oracle bone inscriptions.[4] In these very early texts, many of the more complex, developed meanings of the term are in common use. This suggests that the origins of the concept must stretch far back into the primitive past of the Chinese people.

It is generally agreed that the word *de* inner power is cognate with another word *de* 得 meaning "to obtain, to get" (*LY*, 12.21). *De* refers to the benefits, material or spiritual, that one "gets" from another and that place one in debt to that person. Used in this meaning, the common convention is to translate *de* as "kindness," which must be repaid (*bao* 報). Such acts of kindness created goodwill, which attached those nearby to one and attracted those far away (*LY*, 13.16). The opposite of the goodwill created by *de* acts of kindness was *yuan* 怨, "illwill, resentment, enmity" (*LY*, 14.34). *De* kindness might be extended by the gods and spirits, by the lord or king, by a neighbor or stranger, but whenever it was extended, one felt a strong obligation to repay the consideration one enjoyed.

After the Marquis of Jin failed to repay the kindness of his brother-in-law, the Earl of Qin, who had sent food when Jin faced famine, he was captured in battle. His emissary told the Earl of Qin that the gentlemen of Jin would rather die than equivocate about repaying Qin's *de* act of kindness. The earl was admonished not to kill the marquis since to do so would take his previous "*de* kindness and turn it into a cause for enmity" (*Zuo*, Xi 15). When the Earl of Qin, for a third time, offered famine relief to Jin despite the deplorable conduct of its marquis, he noted that though he bore a grudge against the marquis, he pitied the people. Further, since he was intimidated by the prophecy that Jin should become great, he felt that he could not hope to conquer it, so that "for now let me plant more deeply my *de* inner power in order to await someone of real ability" (*Zuo*, Xi 15).

When the Zhou king made use of the barbarian Di 狄 army in a power struggle, he "*de* felt in debt to the Di for their kindness and was about to take the offer of a daughter as his queen when Fu Chen 富辰 warned against it: 'This is utterly impossible! Your servant has heard it said that "though those who recompense favors grow tired, the recipient of favors is never satisfied." The Di are assuredly avaricious and rapacious, and your majesty has opened a way for them.'" Fu Chen then observes that "a young woman's *de* is limitless and a wife's *yuan* enmity is undying." This is the single example that indicates that originally the notion of *de* power must have been connected with ideas of sexual potency and fertility (*Zuo*, Xi 24).

True Kingship and all true government were based on *de*. It was by and through *de* that a lord ruled. The sense of goodwill toward the ruler by those enjoying the *de* of his government was thought to be the ultimate foundation of legitimate rule. Such rule was said to be "gentle" since it did not involve any compulsion; rather it rested on the acceptance, or at least acquiescence, of the people. A True King would treat the disaffected with *li* courtesy and would cherish the remote with *de* kindness (*Zuo*, Xi 7, 24, Wen 7, Cheng 4). When a vassal failed to follow his lord, the lord should "deal gently with him, treating him with *de* kindness and continuing to offer him instruction, so that the vassal would submit voluntarily" (*Zuo*, Xi 7). True submission was obtained only by *de*, for which the ruler was cherished by his people. In its meaning as the foundation on which legitimate government rested, *de* thus describes the "moral force" or "inner power" of the born leader that attracts the masses to him with its "power" and "force." The Chinese discuss this personal quality in mystical terms analogous to those used in the West to describe charisma or leadership.

The opposite of moral force or inner power was physical force, compulsion, which relied on punishment. True Kings met with acceptance. People were anxious to be their subjects. In the Spring and Autumn period, feudal lords who gained paramountcy over their neighbors were cautioned against being harsh and demanding: "The ancients had the saying that . . . 'The deer driven to its death is not selective about its shelter.' When a small state serves a large state, if it is treated with *de* kindness, then it acts like humans act; when it is not treated with *de* kindness, it acts like the deer. The deer will run off straight over a precipice since in its urgent distress, how can it choose? A state driven by commands that know no limit will also know that it is doomed" (*Zuo*, Wen 17).

An ancient *Treatise on Armies* 軍志 contended that "those who possess *de* moral force cannot be opposed" (*Zuo*, Xi 28). When the Zhou conquest began, Mencius (1B.11, 7B.4) informs us, the people in distant regions wondered why the Zhou did not come to them first. Though the conquest was certainly quite bloody and a general revolt broke out shortly after the conquest, Mencius felt compelled to doubt the version of the events told in the ancient documents because a True King, such as Kings Wen and Wu certainly had been, should conquer without real opposition, as in his own day a very flawed King Xuan of Qi had conquered Yan: "When it is a state of 10,000 chariots [like Qi] attacking another of equal strength [like Yan] and your army is met by the people bringing baskets of rice and bottles of drink, what other reason can there be than that the people are fleeing from water and fire?" (*Mengzi*, 1B.10–11.)

Earlier when the Duke of Song laid siege to the capital of a small state for having the effrontery not to offer the submission he thought his due, a minister rebuked him with the example of King Wen, who, hearing that in Chong 崇 *de* moral force had fallen into anarchy, attacked it. Since there was no surrender, King Wen withdrew to put his teachings in better order; when he renewed the attack, Chong surrendered. The duke was told: "Now it would seem that my lord's *de* moral force must have in it some defect; otherwise, why should he have to attack others? Perhaps for the present he should examine himself for moral force, and when it is found to be without defect, he might then act" (*Zuo*, Xi 19).

Being the basis of all legitimate rule, the moral force of the ruling house had to be kept in "good repair" by constant cultivation lest it be allowed to deteriorate, which would permit the overthrow of the house. The "Announcement of Shao" 召誥 (*Documents*, 20), dating from the beginning of the Zhou dynasty, urges: "May the King treat with the utmost reverence the *de* moral force [which justified the Zhou Mandate from Heaven] and, by applying this moral force, pray for Heaven to grant its Mandate in perpetuity."

Kings and feudal lords were urged to "pile up inner power," to make it "bright," to make it "constant," to "ponder it unremittingly," to "keep in repair" the moral prestige they had inherited, to "cultivate" their own inner power, and to plant like a tree their own moral force that it might bear fruit in the future.[5] Such inner power was "excellent," "good," and "bright." It was "proper to its type" (*Zuo*, Huan 15, Cheng 2, Xi 24). Unless strict, reverent care were taken to preserve it, with time and neglect, the inherited moral force and prestige of a family would "decay," "wear away," and become "dark" (*Zuo*, Xi 24, Xuan 3). It was no longer "proper to its type," and it was "inconstant" (*Zuo*, Xi 24, Cheng 13).

With the collapse of the moral authority of the Zhou dynasty, thinkers attempted to find another basis of power. There was a natural tendency to employ physical force and coercion. In the Spring and Autumn period, this was a significant problem. Guan Zhong warned Duke Huan 桓公, the first of the lords-protector: "One calls the disaffected with *li* ritual courtesy and cherishes the remote with *de* kindness. When courteous and kind treatment are the unalterable rule, there is no one who is not cherished" (*Zuo*, Xi 7). Confronted with rulers who manifestly did not possess any inner power and who had inherited little moral power from their ancestors, statesmen-thinkers proposed three alternatives. One was to show anxious concern while treating those who offered submission gently. This was thought to have been the practice of King Wen, and it was represented as the practice of the Five Lords-Protector (*Zuo*, Xuan 11–12). A second theory rested on the practice of King Zhuang of Chu 楚莊王: "Where there is a lack of moral force that can be used to reach distant regions, no policy is better than treating one's people with generosity and compassion while using them well" (*Zuo*, Cheng 2). The third possibility, represented as "second only to moral force," was to show magnanimity in providing for the people, being hard and strong in defending them, appealing to the intelligent spirits to bind them, dealing gently with those who submit, and attacking those who are disloyal (*Zuo*, Cheng 9). In these theories are the germs of lines of thinking that would later develop into philosophies of government. When Xunzi concluded that the way of the Later Kings was beyond many of the rulers of his day, he turned to practices such as those followed by the Five Lords-Protector that rulers might at least save their countries.

The inner power of the individual and the moral force of a family or dynasty were made visible in court ceremonies and court dress. When a dynasty was established, these matters were settled by the founding kings as a way of informing the world of the dynasty's great moral force. Merely making a show of these signs of moral force would overawe one's opposition. They were the tokens of moral authority and as such had to be protected and kept unchanged. When the Marquis of Jin rescued the Zhou king, "the king feasted him with sweet spirits and mandated gifts of encouragement. The marquis requested that he be granted the privilege of a tomb tunnel. The king would not agree to his request, saying: 'It is a sumptuary token of distinction belonging to the king. As yet there is none to supersede our moral force and become a second king, a thing which you, My Uncle, moreover would hate'" (*Zuo*, Xi 25).

Later kings would be less scrupulous about protecting royal privileges. Confucius was particularly distressed that the Zhou kings and the dukes of Lu had allowed the usurpation of such tokens of authority by subordinates. When he was an envoy from the king to the Duke of Lu,

Duke Yue of Zhou 周公閱 was feasted with a banquet that included sweet flag root, white rice and black millet, and salt shaped in the form of a tiger. The array of dishes in such a feast was to "represent in images his inner power." The duke objected: "The presentation of the five flavors, the viands made from refined grains, and the salt formed in the shape of a tiger are used to exhibit meritorious accomplishments. How should I be worthy of them?" (*Zuo*, Xi 30.) By the time of Xunzi, such violations of sumptuary rules were the exception rather than the rule. He thus developed at length the proper hierarchy of tokens and signs of authority to represent a properly ordered society.

A lord of men "caused his inner power to be displayed in his actions" that he might thereby "influence his Hundred Officers with his illustrious presence." Appearing anxious that he "should in some way lose" the moral force inherited from his ancestors, a ruler should "seek to display an excellent *de* virtue for his sons and grandsons." The Duke of Lu was criticized for failing to cultivate his own inner power and to observe ritual practices that would protect the inherited moral force of his ancestor the Duke of Zhou. A ruler should observe a sense of thrift in his ritual observances. He should display his observance of prescribed measure in his personal costumes and court ornaments. He should keep to the enumeration proper to his rank in sumptuary regulations. The elements of design in decorations should observe good form. He should keep in the choice of colors of decorations to the indications given by natural objects. He should display in the bells ornamenting his chariots and carriage flags his "sound," which causes his reputation to be heard. His flags and standards should display the "shining luster" of his bright inner power. The goal in all this was to cause his officers to copy his example. The rationale for all this was:

> *De* virtue consists in his [the ruler's] thrift and observance of the prescribed measure. It lies in raising up and sending down with the enumerations proper to the rank. Good form in decorations and the indications given by natural objects are used to issue indications of it. All of this is done in order that he might thereby influence his Hundred Officers with his illustrious presence. When arrayed in this fashion, he presents himself to his Hundred Officers; they are overawed into proper caution so that they dare not alter the recorded regulations.
>
> (*Zuo*, Huan 2)

Ru scholars did not stress details of court ceremony and ritual because they loved historical detail but because they thought that the visible indications of an inner reality were important. If government was to be based on acquiescence and not on force, then tokens were an important instrument of social control and of recognition of worth and merit.

De has two other important meanings. We have seen that the Chinese conceived that the Dao has within it a Power and this power is *de*. In this usage, *de* is morally neutral. It might be "auspicious" or "greatly inauspicious."

To host a reputation as a concealer and to seek advantage from using a traitor is to act from a greatly inauspicious *de* inner power that must suffer the regular punishment without forgiveness. . . . It is thieving malefaction and concealment of traitors that produces inauspicious inner power. . . . If you protect him and profit from him, then you will be a principal in concealment. Were we to use his instructions and paradigm so blindly, our people would lack any proper paradigm of conduct and would all have in them inauspicious inner power.

(*Zuo*, Wen 18)

De conceived as "power" contrasts with mere physical strength. Talents such as those of Archer Yi 羿 that are based on physical efforts are less than the accomplishments of a Yu, which are based on moral power. This applies even to animals since "a thoroughbred like Ji is not praised for its physical strength but for its inner power" (*LY*, 14.5, 14.33). The morally neutral *de* becomes the Power associated with the *Dao*, the Way that accepted equally both what was "good" in the eyes of the Ru and Mohists and what they considered "bad." Critics of such moral notions cited this characteristic of the Way as proof that conventional views of morality were worthless.

But like the English word *virtue*, which can mean power, *de* also means virtue in the sense of moral excellence. Many passages list specific moral excellences that derive from *de* "virtue." In this usage, *de* virtue is contrasted with *jian* 姦 "wickedness." Fu Chen contrasts "four virtues" with "four wickednesses": "To employ the meritorious, to draw near those who are close to one, to treat with affection one's relatives, and to raise up for veneration those who are worthy—these are the greatest of virtues." These Fu considers characteristics of the Zhou family, in contrast to the "four wickednesses" that characterize the Di barbarians: "To side with the deaf, follow after the blind, agree with the stupid, and use the deceitful—these are the greatest of wickednesses" (*Zuo*, Xi 24).

BASIC ETHICAL VALUES

The root of all moral value was *de* inner power. Those who possessed it held an irresistible power that was constant and unwavering (*LY*, 13.22). It was the root and source of all excellence. It distinguished the sage and the gentleman from ordinary men. It does not occur in isolation but always "finds neighbors" (*LY*, 4.5). It comes from Heaven (*LY*,

7.23), but few understand it (*LY*, 15.4). Ordinary men neglect it because in man's nature, the love of virtue is not strong like the desire for sex (*LY*, 9.18, 15.15). The highest virtue is a "concealed" or "secret" virtue. This is to be seen in the Earl of Tai 泰伯, who renounced his claim to the world, and Yao 堯, who could copy Heaven. Their virtue, like the Dao, was so great that the people could find no name for it that they could use to praise them (*LY*, 8.1, 8.19). It was to be found in King Wen, who, though he possessed two-thirds of the world, continued to serve the Shang with perfect virtue (*LY*, 8.20). The concept of a "secret" or "concealed" virtue was based on the notion that to yield or to renounce the reward expected because of one's "kindness," "moral power," or "virtue" would result in still greater power and virtue. Xunzi repeatedly praises "yielding," "giving way," "giving up one's position" as high ethical actions because they demonstrate true inner power.

The term that meant morality in Chinese is *yi* 義. *Yi* expresses the "rightness" of a course of conduct that is proper, fitting, decent, suitable, appropriate in the circumstances in which it was done. Han Fei (20 "Jie Lao," 6.1b) provides an excellent summary of the relations encompassed within the meaning of *yi*: "*Yi* is the duty inherent in the official responsibilities of lord and minister, superior and inferior, in the formal relations between father and son, noble and humble, in receiving in welcome acquaintances and friends, and in the separate treatment of near and distant relatives and of those within and without the family." *Yi* thus designated the appropriateness, the fitness, and the suitability of the service the minister gave his lord and the son his father, the respect the humble gave the noble, the assistance friends gave each other, and the differences in treatment between near and far relatives.

What was inappropriate or unsuitable in some circumstances, even if it might have been proper in other circumstances, is not "right." Ladies could not leave the inner sanctum of the palace unless they had a chaperon. In 542 a noble lady was burned to death in the palace because there was no chaperon to escort her, but she was not praised for her scruples because it was not *yi* congruent with the circumstances (*Zuo*, Xiang 30). *Yi*, then, is the principle that expresses the congruity between action and situation, what is reasonable and right in the circumstances.

It becomes more than mere congruity since it reflects an inner sense for what is right (*Mengzi*, 6A.5). What is right is what "ought to be done." *Yi* expresses the "ought," our duty, whether moral or official. When things are done in accord with what "ought to be," they are *yi* just. Guan Zhong tells Duke Huan that virtue and justice are the indispensable conditions of true kingship and good government (*Guanzi*, 20 "Xiaokuang" 小匡, 8.15a). They are the root of all benefit (*Zuo*, Xi 28).

"A mind that does not pattern itself after the continuous thread provided by virtue and a sense of what is right acts stupidly" (*Zuo*, Xi 24). When we fulfill what ought to be done, we are *yi* "moral" and have obeyed what our sense of right has told us should be done because it is right. Acts that show a high sense of moral duty are called *yi* "righteous" and persons of incorruptible moral purity like Bo Yi 伯夷 and Shu Qi 叔齊 were called "righteous knights." In Xunzi, *yi* becomes the basic moral principles underlying all good, all order, all human relationships. He further argues that an *yi* "sense for what is right" is inborn and that it distinguishes us from the animals.

The virtue that distinguishes the gentleman is called *ren* 仁, the character for which is composed of elements meaning "man" and "two." It expressed the fundamental bond between men in society. It means "good" in the sense of "the good." It involves doing good for others out of an altruistic benevolence. It is the source of all humane feelings. It means to "love others." Han Fei (20 "Jie Lao," 6.1a) provides the best definition of the word: "*Ren* means the enjoyment that one feels in one's innermost heart in loving others. It is the feeling of joy at the good luck of others and the feeling of revulsion at their misfortune. It is an indispensable part of the heart with which we are born since it never seeks any recompense." "Humane feelings" are born of our empathy with and compassion for others. Thus, a man of humanity will "help others take their stand where he takes his and helps them go as far as he goes himself" (*LY*, 6.30). Confucius suggested that the single word "reciprocity" expressed the fundamental meaning of *ren*, humane feelings translated into action. He offered a golden rule to interpret it: "Do not do to others what you would not like yourself" (*LY*, 15.24). In all this, the virtue of humanity was shared by the Ru, the Mohists, the early Legalists, and others.

Ru scholars, beginning with Confucius, made two fundamental associations with *ren* humane principles that distinguished them from other schools. First, they regarded "submission to the precepts of ritual" as a necessary condition for true humanity (*LY*, 3.3, 12.1–2; *Zuo*, Zhao 12). Other schools, the Mohists and Legalists particularly, rejected this association if it meant the emphasis on funerals and musical performances that the Ru particularly stressed among ritual precepts. Second, Confucius and the Ru who followed him made a sharp distinction between the love one gave one's relatives and that bestowed on others. Favor to one's own kinsmen was an accepted practice of the day. The Duke of She 葉公 observed that in Chu sons were expected to report the crimes of their fathers. Confucius rejected this as uncivilized since in his view the special love of family required that sons protect their fathers (*LY*, 13.18).

The Ru regarded it as an essential fact of human nature that men give preference to their own relatives. Confucius contended that the special favor of gentlemen for their own relatives over others encouraged ordinary men to the humane feelings of benevolent love (*LY*, 8.2).

But the Mohists directed their strongest attacks against this view, advocating instead that love must be universal, that it could not be graded by recognizing "decreasing measures of love to more distant relatives" (*Zhongyong*, 30). Special preference given some over others was the root of evil in the world. Since the thief loves his own family but not others, he steals to benefit his family to the detriment of others. Ministers do the same on a larger scale. The warfare of the feudal lord is but thievery on a grand scale justified by love of one's own state at the expense of others (*Mozi*, 14 "Jianai," I 兼愛, 上, 4.1b–2a). It was an attack of great moral weight that the Ru were at pains to answer. The *Daode jing* (18, 38) regards as mere hypocrisy Ru concepts of *ren* humanity and the qualifications of *yi* morality that the Ru made to preserve the preference for kin.

Naturally the Ru had to make some answer. They did so by linking *ren* humanity with traditional doctrines of filial piety, the natural love and sense of obligation that children feel for their parents, and filial submission, the natural tendency of younger brothers to respect older brothers they admire and want to emulate (*LY*, 1.2; *Zhongyong*, 13). Since Mohists conceded that filial piety was both natural and desirable, Mencius (1A.7, 4A.27, 6B.3, 7A.15) argued that graded love was based on our inborn nature. The Mohist Yizi 夷子 is represented as admitting Mencius' point that love begins with love of parents (*Mengzi*, 3A.5). The Mohist *Canons* reflect a later stage of the argument, dating from just before Xunzi's time. *Ren* humane principle is defined as to love individually in contrast to collectively. The Mohists argue that humane feelings derive from a love that does not involve any thought of a benefit and that we should love a man "for the sake of the man he is." We should love others' parents as much as our own. Love of everyone and love of an individual are equal.[6]

Xunzi himself rarely discusses *ren* in an ethical sense. We may assume that in his view the issue had resolved itself in debates between Mencius and the Mohists. But as a principle of humanity, it was of great importance to his philosophy. He says that humanity consists in being loyal, trustworthy, straightforward, and diligent so that one does not cause harm or injury. "Loyalty and trustworthiness are to be considered as the raw substance of humanity, straightforwardness and diligence as its guiding norms, ritual and moral principles as its standard of good form. The Constant Relationships of human society and the natural categories of things are to be considered its principles of rational order" ("Chendao,"

13.7). For Xunzi, *ren* remained a philosophical problem in only (1) the actions of the gentleman and the ruler as a man of humane principles; and (2) *ren* the principle of humanity and *yi* justice as the foundation of society and government.

In addition to these three primary ethical values, most Chinese accepted other traditional terms. There were *xiao* 孝 filial piety and *ti* 弟 fraternal submission, which the Ru especially emphasized. There was *zhong* 忠 loyalty and honesty, which Xunzi usually mentions along with *xin* 信 trustworthiness and keeping one's word. The problem of true loyalty and trustworthiness in the face of adversity was raised in the case of the Lords of Pingyuan and Xinling, which Xunzi examined in his "On the Way of Ministers." To these should be added yielding precedence and polite refusals, which Xunzi especially emphasized. Because of the importance he gave ritual principles, Xunzi laid great stress on the need for respect and reverence. The character *gong* 恭, which depicts a man in a formal salute, means the respect paid one's elders and superiors. A higher level of respect is indicated by the term *jing* 敬, the strict and reverent care with which one should undertake sacrifices and the king's mandates. This word occurs often in bronze inscriptions. The opposite of *jing* was a lazy indifference that failed to nurture the spirits or fulfill the king's commands.

EVIL

Against these terms of ethical value, there was a rich vocabulary to describe evil and wickedness. Xunzi uses four terms to express evil: *liu* 流 wayward; *yin* 淫 wanton; *jian* 姦, wicked; and *e* 惡 evil. The term *liu* has as its root meaning "stream, outflow of a spring." By extension it designates what "flows" or "drifts"; applied to persons, it means "a drifter, vagrant"; in terms of a person's ideals, one who holds no fixed values, no principles, in short, one who is "wayward."

The term *yin* has as its root meaning "soak," by implication "over-soaked," thus "excessive, irregular." Another chain of meaning seems to have developed from the meaning, "soaking loose," thus "let loose, liberate"; combined with the implication of "excess," to be "abandoned," thus to abandon oneself to excess, to be "lewd" and "licentious," in short, "wanton."

The graph for *jian* consists of three women, and its root meaning appears to be "adultery," but more generally any kind of "open and selfish wickedness." Two examples of *jian* "treacherous, villainous" behavior are "a father being *jian* treacherous with his son" and a "son observing his father's command according to the exigencies of the moment." Anyone who offers such advice is himself a "villain" (*Zuo*, Xi 7). The idea of *jian* "evil" is antonymic to that of *de* virtue as "moral power, moral force." Anyone who "appropriates to himself what is actually the work of Heaven" is a *jian* "unworthy scoundrel" (*Zuo*, Xi 24). In terms of personal behavior, it means "debauched, licentious, lewd, obscene"; in public behavior, it means "wicked, villainous, treacherous, false, disloyal"; in characterizing acts and states of affairs, it means "dissolute, evil, lawless."

The term Xunzi uses to describe man's inborn nature is *e* "evil." Translating *e* as "evil" often overstates its meaning since the Chinese does not carry the sinister and baleful overtones of the English word. It is applied, for instance, to "bad relations" with another state, which should "not be prolonged," as opposed to "good relations, which should not be lost," because bad relations may get out of hand, like a fire burning on a plain (*Zuo*, Yin 6). An officer, fearing the duke's anger, murdered him, showing that "he had no regard for his lord in his heart and so proceeded in his evil movements" (*Zuo*, Huan 2). The character also means "ugly" as opposed to "beautiful." We have seen Confucius use it this way to refer to the qualities of men. It also means "dislike" as opposed to "like," "hate" as opposed to "love," "bad" as opposed to "good," and generally what men have a natural revulsion to in contrast to what they have a natural desire for. It is in this latter sense that Xunzi typically employs the term; he argues that the desires inherent in man's nature will, if unchecked, produce results that are ugly and bad that men will dislike and hate. He specifies that the "evil" is "what is wrong through partiality, what wickedly contravenes natural order, rebellion, and chaos" ("Xing'e," 23.3a). This clearly indicates that the inborn nature of man must be judged evil not because its inborn qualities are sinister or baleful, but because they lead to evil results. It is precisely because man's nature is evil that good is possible ("Xing'e," 23.2b).

For Xunzi, the problem of evil was linked to the problem of desire. The essential emotional nature of man is such that he feels love and hate, delight and anger, and joy and sorrow ("Zhengming," 22.1b; "Tianlun," 17.3). When hungry, he desires something to eat; when cold, warm clothing; and when weary, rest ("Xing'e," 23.1d). Men like what is beneficial and dislike what is harmful. They want honor and hate disgrace. They desire strength and hate weakness. They enjoy comfort and security, and they hate danger ("Rongru," 4.8; "Jundao," 12.8; "Ruxiao," 8.11). What men like and what they hate are common to all men, even those who seem quite exceptional ("Wangzhi," 9.3; "Rongru," 4.3). From the fact that desires are the same for all men, it follows that if society were not hierarchical, there could be no unity because men would be unwilling to serve each other since none would listen to the commands of another. The result would be contention and civil disorder, which would lead to universal poverty. Inequality is the norm of Nature. Kingship and the division of men into social classes are necessary conditions of order. "Just as there is Heaven and Earth, so too there exists the distinction between superior and inferior" ("Wangzhi," 9.3). The sage kings knew this and instituted their government of regulations, ritual principles, and moral duty.

THE PURPOSES OF SOCIETY

In the view of the ancient Chinese, "the great affairs of state consist in sacrifice and war" because "at sacrifice, there is the distribution of the sacrificial meat to the participants. In warfare, there is the distribution of what is offered at the altar of soil. These are the great ceremonies for the spirits" (*Zuo*, Cheng 13). Confucius conceived these "great affairs" as music and ritual pertaining to sacrifice and corrective expeditions and attacks to smite the wicked (*LY*, 16.2). Ritual practice also established the proper relation with the spirits. Among the Mohists, for whom a belief in the spirits was important, the function of ritual was religious. But the Ru, even in Confucius' time, were skeptical about the very existence of spirits. Xunzi denied their existence as effective agents. For him, then, ritual became a secular matter detached from the religious system that produced it. Men should perform the sacrifices not because the spirits existed or because they would "enjoy" them or because they would respond with good fortune, but because the sacrifices gave ornamented expression to the emotions that otherwise would have no proper outlet and would become socially dangerous. Early Ru concentrated on rituals connected with the details of musical performances, court receptions, and funerals. Such matters were less important to Xunzi, who conceived ritual principles to be the fundamental basis of society by defining the relationships between men.

Yan Ying, a minister of Qi and elder contemporary of Confucius, provided one of the finest early rationales of the purpose and function of ritual:

Ritual principles have long had the ability to govern the state since they are coeval with Heaven and Earth. That the lord issues commands and the minister discharges them, that the father is affectionately kind and the son dutiful, that the elder brother is loving and the younger brother reverent, that the husband is harmonious and the wife meek, and that the mother-in-law is affectionately kind and the daughter-in-law is docilely obedient are instances of ritual principles.

In this recital of the way ritual functioned in society, Yan Ying enumerates all the basic values of ancient Chinese society.

That the lord in issuing commands does not contravene what is right and the minister discharges them without duplicity, that the father is affectionately kind yet provides instruction and the son is dutiful yet capable of gentle admonition, that the older brother is loving and overtly friendly and the younger brother is reverent and submissive, that the husband is harmonious yet maintains moral principles and the wife is meek yet correct, and that the mother-in-law is affectionately kind and agreeable and the daughter-in-law is docilely obedient yet winning are instances of the excellence of ritual principles.   (*Zuo*, Zhao 26)

Beyond this, ritual was important, in Xunzi's view, because it gave men assurances that the purposes of society would be fulfilled with justice.

Many Ru were reluctant to discuss the other "great affair" of state, warfare, but even here the proper instruments are "inner power, just punishment, punctilious observance, right conduct, ritual propriety, and good faith. By inner power, one bestows generous kindness. By the just application of punishment, one corrects what is wrong. By punctilious observance, one serves the spirits. By right conduct, one raises up what is beneficial. By ritual propriety, one acts in natural accord with the seasons. With good faith, one tends the things in one's charge" (*Zuo*, Cheng 16). We have a definition of the seven "virtues possessed by true martial prowess" given by the king of Chu: "The true meaning of military prowess is to be seen in the suppression of cruelty, in the sheathing of weapons, in the safeguarding of the great Mandate, in the firm establishment of accomplishment, in giving repose to the people, in producing harmony among the multitude of states, and in producing abundance of resources" (*Zuo*, Xuan 12). Xunzi devoted a book to the principles of warfare. He continued the tradition represented in these words. A True King does not engage in aggression. Like King Wen in chastising the errant state of Chong, he displays his moral force, and his enemies are overawed. Without quitting the trenches, his troops triumph.

There was very little dispute between the Mohists and Ru as to the purposes of society. Mo Di argued that the state was to care for the people, to preside over the altars of soil and grain, and to bring order to the nation (9 "Shang xian," II 尚賢, 中, 2.5a). The tests of a good state derive from its purposes: it is rich, its population is numerous, and its application of punishments and the administration of its government are well ordered. Mo Di develops a well-argued strategy by which to achieve this result (8 "Shang xian," I 上, 2.1a). "In their exercise of government, the sage kings of antiquity distinguished men on the basis of their inner power and elevated those that were worthy. Those who had ability were raised up, given high office, with rank and honor, remunerated with a generous stipend, entrusted with important matters, and empowered to see orders carried out" (8 "Shang xian," I, 2.3a).

Mo Di argued that only virtue, worthiness, and ability counted; the sage kings were willing to take people who had labored in the ditches, sold in the marketplace, or cooked in the kitchen. The sages did not "show any special concern for their own kin," nor were they "partial to the eminent and wealthy," nor did they "favor the good-looking and attractive" (9 "Shang xian," II, 2.5a). Mo Di explains that the sages did so because they copied Heaven: "Heaven, too, makes no discrimination between rich and poor, eminent and humble, near and far, or close and distant relatives" (9 "Shang xian," II, 2.13a). The sage kings gave worthy and able men high rank and position so that the people would take strict, reverent care in obeying them. They gave them generous stipends so that the people would have confidence in them. They gave them the power to have their orders carried out so the people would stand in awe of them. For this reason, ranks were distinguished on the basis of the inner power of the individual. Responsibilities were determined by the office held. Rewards were given in relation to the labor involved. Stipends were decided by measuring the merit of their accomplishments (8 "Shang xian," I, 2.3a).

Xunzi develops his theories concerning the proper organization of society in several of his books. He observes that the nature of man being what it is, if society were not a hierarchy, no one would be willing to follow the orders of anyone else. The essential work of society could not be done. There could be no unity. "Two men of equal eminence cannot attend each other; two men of the same low status cannot command each other—such is the norm of Heaven" ("Wangzhi," 9.3). Since desires are limitless and material goods limited, were power and positions equally distributed, then the result would be that no man's desires would be satisfied. This would certainly lead to contention, which could only result in poverty. Society emerged because the Ancient Kings abhorred such disorder.

The Ancient Kings thus created the basic institutions of society on the basis of the family. Unequal positions were the base. Xunzi quotes with approval a passage from the Documents ("Lü xing" 呂刑, 19.30b): "There is equality only insofar as they are not equal." This was expressed by the division of society into social classes so that "there were gradation of wealth and eminence of station sufficient to bring everyone under supervision." The basic institutions of government were expressed in regulations and ordinances. Such institutions were themselves based on their idea of justice expressed in the precepts of ritual principles. The success of the enterprise rested on men of moral excellence. The imperatives of the sage kings consisted in this: "Select good and worthy men for office, promote those who are honest and reverent, reward filial piety and brotherly affection, gather under your protection orphans and widows, and offer assistance to those in poverty and need" ("Wangzhi," 9.4).

As his ideas developed, Xunzi gradually came to stress the need for law and punishments, for the administrative apparatus of government. Accordingly, his final position is closer to that of his student Han Fei than to the idealism of Mencius. Nonetheless, Xunzi still held that the supreme instrument of statecraft was the moral force of the ruler, who must rule with the acceptance of his subjects. He cannot impose his will on them through force of arms. "The lord is the boat; his subjects the water. It is the water that sustains the boat, and it is the water that capsizes the boat" ("Wangzhi," 9.4).

Xunzi recognizes four levels of moral excellence. There is the sage 聖人, who represents the pinnacle of human qualities. The great sages had founded human society, had bestowed on humanity all its treasures, and had developed the institutions that enable man to reach his noblest expressions. But the last sages had died almost a thousand years earlier. The Duke of Zhou is the last man Xunzi clearly regards as a sage. Confucius is not accorded that status in unequivocal terms. No ruler of his time aspired to be a sage. Rather, Xunzi discusses what would happen if a humane man 仁人 were to be ruler. Such a man need not be a sage, but his moral excellence must be high.

Xunzi does not include the humane man as one of his four categories. The sage is humane, but so is the gentleman and the worthy. It is a term that allows him to move from the category of the perfect excellence of the sage to that of the outstanding excellence of the worthy. The Chinese word *xian* 賢, conventionally translated "worthy," probably originally meant one who was morally steadfast, but it is applied generally to those who are wise, skillful, and morally worthy even in the *Odes*. The opposite is not someone who is "not worthy," but one who "does not resemble" 不肖—referring particularly to a son who does not resemble his father. It implies a lack of filial piety. Persons who are "unworthy" by "not resembling" are blameworthy, violent, stupid, and low.

Lower than the sage and the worthy in Xunzi's scheme is the *junzi* gentleman. The gentleman is the goal of all teaching and self-cultivation. He combines wide comprehension with high moral character. Xunzi devotes a substantial portion of his works to developing his ideas of the true character of the gentleman, how one becomes a gentleman, and why the rulers of his time should employ gentlemen. The common contrast in Xunzi, as in other philosophers, is between the gentleman, who has cultivated himself, and the *xiaoren* 小人, the small or petty man, who does not develop his talents.

Usually equivalent to the gentleman, but in Xunzi clearly representing a morally less developed person, is the *shi*, "knight" or "scholar." The first task of learning is to create a "scholar," but its final end to create a sage ("Quanxue," 1.8). For Xunzi, moral worth is tied to self-cultivation. Self-cultivation requires an understanding of ritual principles and cannot easily succeed without a teacher to lead one through the Classics. But, by repeating what his teacher has said, by grasping the meaning of the Classics, by incorporating the dictates of ritual in every facet of his conduct, any man can become morally excellent. "If he obtains a worthy teacher, then what he hears will be the way of Yao, Shun, Yu, and Tang. If he obtains good men as his friends, then what he sees will be conduct that is marked by loyalty, trust, respect, and politeness. Each day he will advance in true humanity and in morality without his being conscious of it because his environment has caused it" ("Xing'e," 23.9). For Xunzi, the environment created the man. It alone was critical. He taught that the accumulation of small acts and deeds through the course of our lives determines where we take our stand and what we accomplish. Learning and self-cultivation are the basis of everything else. Brought to completion, the gentleman is a whole man who can form a Triad with Heaven and Earth, as did the great sages. The gentleman becomes a different man: "The exigencies of time and place and considerations of personal profit cannot influence him, cliques and coteries cannot sway him, and the whole world cannot deter him" ("Quanxue," 1.14).

7

History and Authenticity of the Xunzi

The biography of Xunzi in the *Shiji* (74.14), repreated in the *Preface* of Liu Xiang, states that in Xunzi's last years in Lanling, he "arranged and ordered his writings, which consisted of several tens of thousands of characters." This is consistent with the present state of the work, which contains about 75,000 characters. We do not know the form of this text, but from numerous quotations in parallel texts, which rarely identify the *Xunzi* as their source, we can draw some conclusions. We may surmise that when parallel texts incorporate passages essentially identical with the present *Xunzi*, they are quoting from the text as it existed before Liu Xiang edited the text.[1] There are essentially three texts parallel to the *Xunzi*: the *Hanshi waizhuan*; the *Da Dai liji*; and the *Liji*. There are sound reasons, as we have seen, to believe that both the *Liji* and *Da Dai liji* in their present form date to a period after Liu Xiang's redaction. Nonetheless, it seems likely that ancestral forms of these texts existed in which the passages parallel to the *Xunzi* were derived from versions in circulation before Liu's work.

From such quotations it appears that Han compilers were familiar with a corpus comprising Books 1–3, 5–6, 8–10, 12–13, 15–17, 19–20, and 27–32. The absence of quotations from Books 4, 7, 11, 14, 18, 21–24, and the poetry collections 25–26 may indicate that versions of the text then in circulation lacked these books.

The *Hanshi waizhuan* contains passages from 19 of the *Xunzi's* 32 books, including considerable portions of some. Though we can demonstrate cross-collation between parallel texts and the *Xunzi* during the course of their transmission, such quotations suggest that Han Ying was familiar with a corpus essentially similar to the contents of the books as they now exist. The absence of quotations from Books 4, 7, and 14 may result from the facts that they are very short and contain only four quotations from the *Odes* or may arise from a perceived lack of relevance in explicating the *Odes*. We know from Han Ying's quotations from

"Contra Twelve Philosophers" that he excised those parts of Xunzi's works that offended contemporary notions.[2] Eight books in the *Da Dai* collection have passages in common with the *Xunzi*; most are short passages in the "Great Compendium," itself composed of short fragments.[3] Eight books in the *Liji* quote passages from the *Xunzi*, again mostly short passages from the "Great Compendium."[4] Nearly the whole, or the substance, of some of these books is derived from the *Xunzi*: the "Sannianwen" 三年問 of the *Liji* and "Sanben" 三本 of the *Da Dai* are contained in the "Discourse on Ritual Principles"; the "Yueji" 樂記 and "Xiangyinjiuyi" 鄉飲酒義 of the *Liji* are combined in the "Discourse on Music"; the "Pingyi" 聘義 of the *Liji* is in "On the Model for Conduct" 法行; the "Quanxue" 勸學 of the *Da Dai* corresponds to the first part of the "Exhortation to Learning" of the *Xunzi*; and the "Zengzi lishi" 曾子立事 of the *Da Dai* is divided between "On Self-Cultivation" and "The Great Compendium." Together these collections of ritual texts add books 19 and 20, the discourses on ritual and music, to those quoted in the *Hanshi waizhuan*. This is sufficient to indicate that the materials were in general circulation and evidently popular, except for the difficult and more philosophical Books 18 and 21–23.

LIU XIANG EDITION

The popularity of Xunzi's work is confirmed by the fact that when Liu started to prepare a standard edition of the works of Xunzi, he found in the Imperial Library some 322 manuscripts of Xunzi's writings. The Imperial Library had been an important institution since the time of Emperor Wu, when the Erudites were established and the Imperial University founded. Liu Xin, the son of Liu Xiang and himself an important scholar who prepared the catalogue of the Imperial Library, says that "Emperor Wu instructed Chancellor Gongsun Hong to provide ample facilities for presenting books to the throne. During the following century, books piled up into mounds as high as hills. Therefore, outside the palace there were the storehouses of the Minister for Public Works, the Grand Historian, and the Erudites, and within them were depositories in long galleries, spacious rooms, and private apartments."[5] In 26 B.C., an emissary was sent to collect books from all over the empire.[6] About this time Liu Xiang began his work on the imperial collections, where he labored for more than twenty years.[7]

When Liu collated and compared all these manuscripts, he found bundles of bamboo slips and silk scrolls of various origins that naturally contained many duplications. Of the 322 manuscripts of the *Xunzi*, he eliminated 290 as duplicates and established the standard text for 32 books, which were recorded on freshly prepared bamboo strips. From what we know, his procedure was to examine all independent manuscripts on bamboo and silk that were thought to have a common origin or authorship. From the embedded titles, such as "Renlun" 人論 in "The Teachings of the Ru" and "Xuguan" 序官 in "On the Regulations of a King," it is clear that at least some parts of the *Xunzi* circulated as independent essays before they were combined into the present books of the *Xunzi*. After examining all the manuscripts, he established a definitive text and prepared a table of contents. His work was then reported to the emperor in the form of a memorial of presentation that described the manuscripts and how they were collated; gave a biography of the author based, in the case of Xunzi and the other philosophers, on Sima Qian's *Shiji*, which contains a brief historical background; and concluded with a discussion of the authenticity, transmission, and value of the work. These reports were appended to the edited text and function as a preface to the works.[8] All modern editions of the *Xunzi* derive from the redaction of Liu Xiang.

Liu Xiang, who observed the Han custom of observing a taboo against using the emperors' personal names, entitled the work *Sunqingzi* 孫卿子.[9] He characterized his efforts as a "new book" and arranged Xunzi's books in the following order:

1. "Quanxue" 勸學, "Exhortation to Learning."
2. "Xiushen" 修身, "On Self-Cultivation."
3. "Bugou" 不苟, "Nothing Indecorous."
4. "Rongru" 榮辱, "Of Honor and Disgrace."
5. "Fei xiang" 非相, "Contra Physiognomy."
6. "Fei shier zi" 非十二子, "Contra Twelve Philosophers."
7. "Zhongni" 仲尼, "On Confucius."
8. "Chengxiang" 成相, "Working Songs."
9. "Ruxiao" 儒效, "The Teachings of the Ru."
10. "Wangzhi" 王制, "On the Regulations of a King."
11. "Fuguo" 富國, "Enriching the State."
12. "Wangba" 王霸, "Of Kings and Lords Protector."
13. "Jundao" 君道, "On the Way of a Lord."
14. "Chendao" 臣道, "On the Way of Ministers."
15. "Zhishi" 致士, "On Attracting Scholars"
16. "Yibing" 議兵, "Debate on the Principles of Warfare."
17. "Qiangguo" 彊國, "On Strengthening the State."
18. "Tianlun" 天論, "Discourse on Nature."
19. "Zhenglun" 正論, "Rectifying Theses."
20. "Yuelun" 樂論, "Discourse on Music."

21. "Jiebi" 解蔽, "Dispelling Blindness."
22. "Zhengming" 正名, "On the Correct Use of Names."
23. "Lilun" 禮論, "Discourse on Ritual Principles."
24. "Youzuo" 宥坐, "The Warning Vessel on the Right."
25. "Zidao" 子道, "On the Way of Sons."
26. "Xing'e" 性惡, "Man's Nature Is Evil."
27. "Faxing" 法行, "On the Model for Conduct."
28. "Aigong" 哀公, "Duke Ai."
29. "Dalue" 大略, "The Great Compendium."
30. "Yaowen" 堯問, "The Questions of Yao."
31. "Junzi" 君子, "On the Gentleman."
32. "Fu" 賦, "Rhyme-prose Poems."

The poems of Xunzi, which Liu included in his edition, also maintained an independent existence for several centuries thereafter.[10] In addition to the *Xunzi*, Liu also prepared the standard editions of the *Hanfeizi* 韓非子, the *Guanzi* 管子, the *Liezi* 列子, and the *Yanzi chunqiu* 晏子春秋. His contribution to the study of ancient Chinese thought is thus immense.

After being written on bamboo strips, the books of the *Xunzi* were then bound together with leather. Sometimes the name of the book was written on the back of the strip, though we do not know the actual practice in the Imperial Library. Each book consisted of a single "bundle" called a *pian* 篇. Xunzi's complete works were thus 32 bundles. We find them listed this way in the Imperial Catalogue, with an additional bundle for the *Preface* of Liu Xiang.[11] Later the *Xunzi* was copied onto scrolls of silk (*juan* 卷). Since silk scrolls of convenient size could hold more text than a bundle of bamboo pieces, shorter books were combined on the same scroll.

Each form of book had liabilities. The leather strips binding the bamboo strips tended to rot or be eaten by insects. Sometimes when restrung, they were not put back together in proper order. There is evidence of such damage in the *Xunzi* today. Silk scrolls did not get out of order, but the beginnings and ends became frayed, with resultant damage to the text. Such damage is also detectable in the *Xunzi*. Other errors creep into any text that is hand-copied repeatedly, as were all ancient texts. Such errors include miscopied characters, characters or lines left out, lines repeated, and lines put in the wrong order. Some such errors are obvious; others are hard to discover.

During the Han dynasty, many sections of the *Xunzi* were quoted in other works, some of which, as we have seen, were compiled before Liu Xiang prepared his edition of the text. They sometimes offer insight into the earlier version of the text and sometimes can be used to correct problems in the *Xunzi* itself. But since texts were often collated, the value of these as independent testimony is compromised. Liu Xiang himself extracted a number of passages from the *Xunzi* in the other works he compiled. From a somewhat later date, there are occasional quotations of the *Xunzi* in commentaries prepared for other texts. The later period of the Han Dynasty, called the Later Han or Eastern Han, saw the need to prepare commentaries to classical texts, which were becoming obscure because of changes in the language and the gradual decay of knowledge of ancient matters. All the officially recognized Classics had commentaries prepared for them. Zhao Qi 趙岐 (d. A.D. 201) prepared a particularly fine commentary that paraphrases the text of the *Mencius* and enables us to understand it with uncommon clarity and precision. Eastern Han commentaries, though of uneven quality, are of great value in helping us understand ancient texts, which had traditions of interpretation and scholarship that were then still alive. With the collapse of the Han dynasty, the traditions were broken. It is unfortunate that the *Xunzi* had no commentary written for it at this time, but the fact that there was none testifies to the declining influence Xunzi's works exercised on an age turning increasingly to magic and mysticism.

During the medieval period, the *Xunzi* was often quoted in the florilegia and encyclopedia that were the fashion of the time. The most important were four extensive compilations: *Beitang shuchao* 北堂書鈔, *Yiwen leiju* 藝文類聚, *Chuxue ji* 初學記, and the *Taiping yulan* 太平御覽. To these should be added the many citations of ancient literature contained in the extensive commentaries to the *Wenxuan* 文選. Today these citations often provide our only source of knowledge of the ideas of some ancient philosophers. Quotations provide independent testimony to the reading of the text and occasionally enable us to correct errors that have crept into the text. They also assure us of the essential integrity of the *Xunzi* since the current text omits only a few sentences attributed to Xunzi in all the numerous quotations of his works.

More important than the isolated quotations found in these encyclopedia and florilegia is the long extract from the *Xunzi* found in the thirty-eighth chapter of the *Qunshu zhiyao* 群書治要, a Tang anthology of political philosophy collected at imperial command under the leadership of Wei Zheng 魏徵 (A.D. 580–643).[12] It appears that this anthology was collected from works in the Imperial Library, of which Wei Zheng was director.[13] He was assited in his work by Yu Shinan 虞世南, the assistant director, Chu Liang 褚亮, and Xiao Deyan 蕭德言. The work was completed and presented to the throne on November 6, 631.[14] Though the work seems to have been lost in China by the twelfth century, it survived in Japan, where it enjoyed considerable prestige and was reprinted under

TABLE I
Extracted Passages from the Xunzi in the Qunshu zhiyao

Xunzi	Zhiyao	Xunzi	Zhiyao	Xunzi	Zhiyao
1.1	38.1a	10.2	38.6b	17.1	38.17b
2.1	38.1b	11.1	38.9a	17.5	38.18a
2.8	38.2a	11.12	38.12a	18.1	38.18b
3.9	38.2b	12.1	38.12b	29.1	38.19a
4.8	38.3b	12.5	38.13a	23.9	38.19b
6.10	38.3b	12.8	38.14a	31.6	38.20a
7.1	38.4a	12.9	38.14b	27.24	38.20a
8.2	38.4b	13.2	38.15a	27.51	38.20a
9.1	38.5b	14.4	38.16a	24.2	38.21a
9.4	38.6a	15.1	38.16b		

the aegis of Tokugawa Ieyasu.[15] The work was recovered in China, apparently from Japan, only in the late eighteenth or nineteenth century.[16]

The thirty-eighth chapter of the *Qunshu zhiyao* is an extended extract from the *Xunzi*. The beginning paragraph of the *Xunzi* from which each extracted passage was taken is listed in Table 1. These excerpts are usually whole paragraphs from the text, sometimes abridged and simplified in language. Parts of 21 books are included in the extract.[17] The order of the extracts corresponds to the order of the Liu Xiang edition. Comparison of the *Qunshu* readings with the *Xunzi* confirm the essential integrity of the text.

The revival of a centralized, universal empire under the Sui and Tang dynasties resulted in the restoration of such imperial institutions as a library. Once again, ancient texts were collected, but a comparison of the catalogues of these libraries with that of the Han dynasty shows that in the interval the writings of most ancient philosophers had been lost. The *Xunzi*, however, survived. We know that in the early medieval period the *Xunzi* was written on twelve silk scrolls. It is only in this form that we find the work during the medieval period.[18]

YANG LIANG'S COMMENTARY

Toward the end of the Tang dynasty, the learned Yang Liang 楊倞, who held a minor office and is otherwise unknown, wrote the first commentary for the *Xunzi*.[19] In his *Preface*, dated in December of A.D. 818, Yang gives his reasons for preparing a commentary:

Alone among the ancient texts, the *Xunzi* has never been provided with a commentary and explanation. Further, the work contains repetitions. Its bamboo slips have been damaged, some having rotted and others being lost. The received text contains inaccuracies from mistakes in copying. Even if a man of good intentions had the time and, in addition, were equal to the task, he would come to passages whose purpose was baffling and there would often be inclined to close the book.

Yang's commentary is a masterpiece of Tang scholarship. Exhaustive and lacking doctrinaire biases, its interpretations are almost always correct, and it never fails to offer profitable insights into the significance of Xunzi's point. An understanding of the *Xunzi* would be possible without

TABLE 2
Yang Liang's Arrangement of the Xunzi

SCROLL 1	SCROLL 11
1. "Quanxue," "Exhortation to Learning"	16. "Qiangguo," "On Strengthening the State"
2. "Xiushen," "On Self-Cultivation"	17. "Tianlun" "Discourse on Nature"
SCROLL 2	SCROLL 12
3. "Bugou," "Nothing Indecorous"	18. Zhenglun," "Rectifying Theses"
4. "Rongru," "Of Honor and Disgrace"	SCROLL 13
SCROLL 3	19. "Lilun," "Discourse on Ritual Principles"
5. "Fei xiang," "Contra Physiognomy"	
6. "Fei shier zi," "Contra Twelve Philosophers"	SCROLL 14
7. "Zhongni," "On Confucius"	20. "Yuelun," "Discourse on Music"
SCROLL 4	SCROLL 15
8. "Ruxiao," "The Teachings of the Ru"	21. "Jiebi," "Dispelling Blindness"
SCROLL 5	SCROLL 16
9. "Wangzhi," "On the Regulations of a King"	22. "Zhengming," "On the Correct Use of Names"
SCROLL 6	SCROLL 17
10. "Fuguo," "Enriching the State"	23. "Xing'e," "Man's Nature Is Evil"
	24. "Junzi," "On the Gentleman"
SCROLL 7	SCROLL 18
11. "Wangba," "Of Kings and Lords-Protector"	25. "Chengxiang," "Working Songs"
	26. "Fu," "Rhyme-Prose Poems"
SCROLL 8	SCROLL 19
12. "Jundao," "On the Way of a Lord"	27. "Dalue," "The Great Compendium"
SCROLL 9	SCROLL 20
13. "Chendao," "On the Way of Ministers"	28. "Youzuo," "The Warning Vessel on the Right"
14. "Zhishi," "On Attracting Scholars"	29. "Zidao," "On the Way of Sons"
SCROLL 10	30. "Faxing," "On the Model for Conduct"
15. "Yibing," "Debate on the Principles of Warfare"	31. "Aigong," "Duke Ai"
	32. "Yaowen," "The Questions of Yao"

Yang's commentary, but it is certainly made much easier thanks to his efforts.

Yang found Liu Xiang's arrangement of the text inappropriate when transferred from bamboo to silk: "The divisions of the text were troublesomely numerous, so I redivided the old twelve silk scrolls and 32 bundles into twenty scrolls. The sequence of the bundles has been changed as a result of grouping together bundles with similar topics into the same scroll." Yang rearranged only two of the first 23 books, putting the "Working Songs" with the "Rhyme-prose Poems" and the "Discourse on Ritual Principles" before the "Discourse on Music." But he had serious reservations about the authenticity of the books at the end of the Liu Xiang edition. He regarded "Man's Nature Is Evil" as genuine and hence placed it earlier in the text. He suggested that "The Great Compendium" was an assemblage by Xunzi's students from miscellaneous quotations that belong to no particular book but brought out important points. He thought that "On the Gentleman" had become mistitled in the course of transmission since its subject was the "Son of Heaven." Other works he regarded as the efforts not of Xunzi but of his students, who had culled material from various historical texts and scholarly traditions. These works comprised Books 28–32 in his arrangement (see Table 2). Yang Liang consciously followed the order of the *Analects* of Confucius by beginning with "learning" and ending with "Yao." Yang Liang also restored the original name, *Xunzi*, to the work, though he did not change occurrences of the name in the text itself from *sun* 孫 to *xun* 荀. The Yang Liang edition of *Xunzi* first appears in the "Bibliographic Treatise" of the *Xin Tangshu* in twenty scrolls. From Song times, this has been the standard format.

PRINTED EDITIONS

When printing became common in China during the Song dynasty (A.D. 960–1280), the *Xunzi* was issued in several different editions. Fortunately in addition to the edition with Yang Liang's commentary, unannotated copies of the *Xunzi* had survived; in the Song editions, there are sections and a whole chapter that lack Yang's commentary and must have been taken from such editions. The *Xunzi* went through perhaps twelve editions in various formats with different woodblocks being used. Of these, eight survived until they could be described by eighteenth- and nineteenth-century scholars and book collectors. Most of these are editions of only marginal value for establishing the proper readings of the text.[20]

Lü Xiaqing Edition

The earliest printed edition of which we have knowledge is that prepared by Wang Zishao 王子韶 and Lü Xiaqing 呂夏卿 and printed by the Guozi jian 國子監 (National Education Bureau) in response to an imperial edict. The report of the bureau is dated to the first year of the Xining 熙寧 reign period (A.D. 1068), the ninth month and eighth day. The edition is commonly called the Lü edition because Lü Xiaqing was the chief collator of the text. It is one of the most important of the editions and the first to correct problems of transmission in the text since Yang Liang's commentary. The basis of such corrections appears to have been collation with such parallel texts as the *Da Dai liji*. The Lü edition divided the text of each book into paragraphs covering single topics. Some of these paragraphs contain embedded titles. This may indicate that paragraphing was characteristic of the *Xunzi* text in the Liu Xiang redaction or in the Yang Liang redaction, or in both, though paragraph divisions were not made in the popular editions. But of the 29 extracts from the *Xunzi* in the *Qunshu zhiyao*, 23 do begin at the start of a paragraph. In 5 instances, the opening of the paragraph is omitted, probably because it was not considered relevant to the political theme of the anthology. One passage is not associated with a paragraph beginning.[21] Since the *Qunshu zhiyao* antedates the Yang commentary, it seems reasonable to assume that such divisions reflect the text of the redaction of Liu Xiang, if not perhaps the original bundles of Xunzi's works from which he assembled his *Xunzi*.

The edition contains the prefaces of Liu Xiang and Yang Liang, and tables of contents reflecting the order of the text in the arrangement of both Yang and Liu, in twenty scrolls with the 32 books. Each page contained eight columns with 16 characters, with interlinear annotation in double columns of 24 to 25 characters.[22] Qian Dian 錢佃 tells us that the original Lü edition was never issued and that he used as his basic text a Yuanfeng 元豐 reign period (A.D. 1078–85) printing that he found in the Provincial School Library of Lulang.[23] Much later in the Qing dynasty, even Lu Wenchao 盧文弨 (1717–96) had to use an imperfect copy (*chaoben* 抄本) for his collation.[24] Zhang Jinwu (1787–1829) 張金吾 in his *Airi jinglu cangshu zhi* 愛日精廬藏書志 (preface dated 1826) says that the existing exemplar of the Song woodblock edition had paper deterioration and damaged characters that had been traced over and pasted in and that the traced copies were more reliable.[25] Copies of the Lü edition, both the original printed edition and the traced copy, continued to exist until the middle of the nineteenth century.

The collector Huang Peilie 黃丕烈 (1763–1825), who had himself once owned a copy of the Lü edition, notes that he had had the opportunity to inspect the traced copy in the home of Zhou Xizan 周錫瓚 and the printed edition from which the copy had been made in the retreat of Gu Guangqi 顧廣圻 (1776–1835).[26] Qu Shaoji 瞿紹基 (1772–1836) and his son Qu Yong 瞿鏞 reassembled in their library the collections of Zhang Jinwu and Chen Kui 陳揆 (1780–1825) and a substantial part of that of Wang Shizhong 汪士鐘. They possessed two copies of the Lü edition, for which there is description.[27] Ye Linzong 葉林宗 had made a copy of the Song edition, called the Ye MS in the collection of Qian Zeng 錢曾, from a Song edition in the Ming dynastic library, the Wenyuan Ge 文淵閣.[28] Hui Dong 惠棟 added a collation to it. Gu Guangqi made use of its text to correct a total of 770 characters, and this copy had Gu's cinnabar notes at the head of each scroll. Within the chapters, there were notes of the Suzhou scholar Niu Shuyu 鈕樹玉.[29] In addition to the Ye-Hui MS, Qu also possessed another collated edition, the Baojing collation of Lu Wenchao with each chapter containing his reading notes in cinnabar.[30] Guan Tingfen 管庭芬 (1797–1880) mentions that it was still in existence, but there now seems to be no extant copy.[31]

Qian Dian Edition

In the twelfth century, Qian Dian reported, in a colophon dated the eighth year of the Chunzi 淳熙 reign period (1181), that he could find no well-preserved copy of the *Xunzi*. Qian assembled in his library four bookstore editions, which he called the Erzhe 二浙 and Xishu 西蜀 editions. These seem to have been fundamentally the same text since in his variorum, Qian Dian regularly groups them under the term *zhuben* 諸本. He prepared a collation from them, but could not establish what he regarded as the correct text. Later he obtained a copy of the Lü edition, which he used as his basic text. It appears that he followed the paragraph divisions of the Lü edition. But since this edition also had errors, he employed these other editions for collation and corrected a total of 154 characters. He found 126 lines that could not easily be resolved, and he discussed these in a separate chapter (*Kaoyi* 考異) that still survives.[32] Chen Zhensun 陳振孫 notes that Qian Dian listed a total of 296 discrepancies between the various texts. The format of the edition is unknown, except that each page contained ten columns with eighteen characters per column. Chen, whose library was said to have been the largest in existence in the mid-thirteenth century, had two editions of the *Xunzi*, one of them unidentifiable, the other the Qian Dian, which he regarded as the "most complete and perfect edition" available.[33]

The histories of both these editions show that virtually all the important Qing collations and editions are based on the same copies. Exemplars of both these editions were in the library of Huang Peilie, who described them as "a pair of jade *bi* discs." He observed that in addition to the original edition, there circulated a traced manuscript version of it. In his day, very few men had ever seen these works, and Huang was "happy that a collated edition had been made." He regarded both editions as treasures of the greatest value, to be handed down with great care and secrecy.[34] Huang sold them to Wang Shizhong, who in turn sold them to Qu Yong, whose descriptions provide us with much of what we know of them. In addition to having been used by Gu Guangqi and Lu Wenchao, Yang Shaohe 楊紹和 (1831–76) reports that Wang Niansun 王念孫 had examined these two editions and made textual notes based on them.[35] We are unfortunately unable to locate either of these editions today.

Taizhou Edition

In the thirteenth century, Wang Yinglin 王應麟 (1223–96) noted that the edition of Tang Yuzheng 唐與政 was the same as the Lü edition.[36] Generally known as the Taizhou 台州 edition, it is in fact simply a reprint of the Lü edition that Tang issued in 1181, a few months after Qian Dian issued his collated edition.[37] Mori Tachiyuki 森文之等 received a copy of Lu Wenchao's collation of the *Xunzi* in which Lu complains that his copy of the Lü edition was imperfect. He realized that if Lu Wenchao had had to use a defective copy, the virtually perfect copy of the Taizhou reprint that he had discovered in the Kanezawa Bunko 金澤文庫 must be extremely valuable since it was certainly the best exemplar in existence.[38] This edition contains the prefaces of Yang Liang and Liu Xiang with a postface by Tang Yuzheng, the table of contents of both Yang and Liu, with a format of eight columns per page containing uneven numbers of characters. Paragraphing is consistent with that in the Lü edition. Annotation is in double columns, also containing uneven numbers of characters. The original copy has since disappeared, but fortunately Yang Shoujing 楊守敬 had arranged its reprinting in the *Guyi congshu* 古逸叢書 (subsequently reprinted again in *Sibu congkan* 四部叢刊).[39] No other copy of this edition seems to be extant.

Zuantu Huzhu Edition

The bookstore editions that Qian Dian used in his collation are unknown, but another popular edition does survive. Bookstores issued sets of philosophers' writings in the then-popular *Zuantu huzhu* editions

纂圖互注本, which contained woodcuts illustrating the works, with annotations calling attention to parallel passages in other works, and to
repeated words and ideas. There were a set of four philosophers including *Xunzi*, Yang Xiong's 楊雄 *Fayan* 法言, *Daode jing*, and *Zhuangzi*; a set
of six philosophers, which added the *Wenzhongzi* 文仲子 and *Liezi*; and a
set of six philosophers printed in a reduced size, all issued in the Song
dynasty with reprints in both the Yuan and early Ming dynasties.[40] Pan
Zongzhou 潘宗周 says that the Jianyang 建陽 bookshop, which was responsible for the *Xunzi* and the philosophers, also published similar editions of the Classics, including the *Zhou Yi* 周易, *Mao Shi* 毛詩, and the
Chunqiu jingzhuan jijie 春秋經傳集解.[41] Today there are exemplars of these
editions in the East Asiatic Library of the University of California at
Berkeley, the National Palace Collection in Taibei, the Library of the
Academia Sinica in Taibei, the National Central Library in Taibei, the
Shanghai Library, and the Imperial Household Collection in Tokyo.
Some of these appear to be of Song date, others of Yuan date. Though
of lowly origin, this edition has preserved important text variants. Lu
Xinyuan 陸心源 (1834–94), a famous collector, identified 31 instances
where the reading of this edition was superior to that of the Lü edition.[42]

Shide Tang Edition

The basis of modern editions is the Ming dynasty Shide Tang edition
世德堂本, which Lu Wenchao used as the basic text for his collation. Each
page contains eight columns of seventeen characters with annotations in
double columns of seventeen characters. The edition was first printed in
1530, reprinted in 1533, issued in a small-character edition, reprinted by
Hu Dongtang 胡東塘 in 1583, and reprinted again in 1914 by the Yuwen
Company. It was issued as part of a set of six philosophers: the *Daode jing*
with the commentary of He Shanggong 河上公; the *Zhuangzi* with the
commentary of Guo Xiang 郭象; the *Liezi* with the commentary of Zhang
Zhan 張湛; the *Fayan* of Yang Xiong; the *Wenzhongzi*; and the *Xunzi*.
This edition was apparently readily available in the early Qing dynasty,
and copies used by famous scholars with their marginal notes survive.
Gu Guangqi discovered that the text was identical with the Yuan dynasty *Zuantu huzhu* edition except that it omitted the "repeated ideas"
annotations in all but two instances, which confirms the origin of the
text.[43] The East Asiatic Library at Berkeley has a copy collated by Gu
Chun 顧春 with manuscript notes supplied by Hui Dong and Liu Fu 劉復,
transcribed by Ling Yanchi 凌焱暹 from the copy in the collection of Gu
Guangqi, dated to August 1753. The Shanghai Library has a copy with
collation notes of Hui Shiqi 惠士奇 and Hui Dong transcribed by Ye Yi

葉奕, another with the collation notes of Niu Shuyu and Gu Guangqi, and a third with collation notes of Hui Dong transcribed by Shen Dacheng 沈大成.

QING DYNASTY SCHOLARSHIP

With the development of philological research in the eighteenth and nineteenth centuries, textual studies of ancient Chinese works advanced rapidly, leading to a greatly improved grasp of ancient writings. Scholars and bibliophiles exerted great effort to locate and preserve rare editions and works. They shared notes on differences they had observed and collaborated to produce collations of different editions. This led to the creation of accurate editions of the text based on all the surviving material. The *Xunzi* text used today is based on the collations of Lu Wenchao and Gu Guangqi, who provided extensive notes on variations among the editions, some of which have since disappeared.

Lu Wenchao's Collation

The *Xunzi* was one of many texts that Lu collated during the course of his career. He was among the first Qing scholars to devote his entire life to the establishment of reliable text readings for passages in ancient texts that centuries of miscopying and reprinting had rendered incomprehensible. Lu spent almost 45 years collating texts, continuously comparing texts, noting differences, and preparing correct versions. He used as his basic text for the *Xunzi* the Shide Tang edition, which he then compared to the Yuan printing of the *Zuantu huzhu* edition, a traced manuscript of the Song Lü edition in large characters, and several other editions he encountered in the collections of famous bibliophiles. Unfortunately, the traced copy of the Lü edition he saw was quite defective, and Lu occasionally adopted an erroneous reading on its authority. Wang Xianqian notes that "On Self-Cultivation" and "On the Regulations of a King," in particular, bear this out.[44]

Xie Yong 謝墉 (1719–95), the commissioner of education of Jiangsu province, arranged in 1786 for detailed comparisons and publication of a collation of the *Xunzi* prepared by Lu Wenchao. In his preface, Xie makes it plain that the critical collation was derived from Lu Wenchao and that his contribution was comparatively minor. To Lu's collation and his own contributions, he added annotations from Zhao Ximing 趙曦明, Duan Yucai 段玉裁, Wu Qian 吳騫, Zhu Huan 朱奂, and Wang Zhong 汪中. These annotations were placed after the Yang Liang commentary, following a circle to distinguish them. At the end of the text, he added a separate chapter containing a supplement discussing points of difficulty in the collation. Lu generally followed the paragraph divisions in the Lü edition, though he introduced additional paragraphs where parallel texts indicate that a division should be made. This edition has been reprinted more than ten times in China and three times in Japan and is the basis of the well-known *Sibu beiyao* 四部備要 edition. Its critical importance to the study of the *Xunzi* lies in the fact that both Wang Xianqian and Kubo Ai 久保愛 used it as the basis of their critical editions with collected commentaries.

Commentaries

In addition to preparing accurate editions of the texts of ancient works, Qing scholars devoted their efforts to textual studies of rare words, unusual constructions, idioms, and other problems that hindered real understanding of their meaning. Several of these commentaries are the basis of our modern understanding of the text.

The first modern Chinese commentary was prepared by Liu Taigong 劉台拱 (1751–1805), who identified problems in the text, which he attacked combining contemporary philological exegesis with traditional Song interpretative ideas. His work *Xunzi buzhu* 荀子補注 was published with two other works in 1806 by his son-in-law Ruan Changsheng 阮常生 and has been reprinted four times since.

A work of equal importance is the *Xunzi buzhu* 荀子補注 of Hao Yixing 郝懿行 (1757–1825), which annotates over 300 passages in the *Xunzi*. Hao's annotations are often extremely perceptive, no doubt because of his wide range of interests. His work was published in 1865 and reprinted three times thereafter.

More important than either of these is the work of Wang Niansun (1744–1832), who had a profound grasp of etymology and phonetics because of his work on the *Guangya* 廣雅 dictionary and an encyclopedic acquaintance with the major works of ancient philosophy. His *Dushu zazhi* 讀書雜誌, published 1812–31, contained detailed annotations and emendations of the *Shiji*, *Hanshu* 漢書, *Guanzi*, and *Mozi*, in addition to the *Xunzi*. Wang Niansun based his work on the Lu collation, correcting it with the Qian Dian edition, the Song dynasty *Xunzi zhujie* 荀子注解 of Gong Shixie 龔士卨, and a manuscript collation he obtained from Gu Guangqi. His annotations take into consideration the previous work of Hao Yixing, Liu Taigong, Wang Zhong, and Chen Huan 陳奐, with a few notes contributed by his son Wang Yinzhi 王引之. Wang also collected fragments no longer appearing in the text from early quotations. His work is indispensable.

Another work of importance is the *Zhuzi pingyi* 諸子平議 of Yu Yue 俞越 (1821–1907). Patterned in the tradition of textual criticism and philology established by Wang Niansun and continued by Wang Yinzhi, his work is filled with erudition and insight. Finally there are the annotations of Yu Chang 于鬯 (1850–1910), which are included in his collected works, *Xiangcao xujiao shu* 香草續校書 (1897).

Wang Xianqian

The extensive range of scholarly philological exegesis of texts made it imperative that these be combined with the established text of the *Xunzi*. This was done by Wang Xianqian at the end of the last century in his *Xunzi jijie* 荀子集解 ("Collected Explanations on the Xunzi"; 1891). This important work includes virtually all Chinese work on the text up to his time. Wang was able to correct Lu's text on many important points by reference to the recently recovered Taizhou edition.

JAPANESE SCHOLARSHIP

In Japan a related tradition of scholarship developed. The first important work is the *Doku Junshi* 讀荀子 of Ogyū Sorai 荻生徂徠 (1666–1728). Other important contributions were made by Katayama Kenzan 片山兼山 (1730–81), Tsukada Taihō 冢田大峰 (1745–1832), Momoi Hakuroku 桃井白鹿 (1722–1801), and Furuya Sekiyō 古屋昔陽 (1734–1806).[45] On the basis of the Lu collation and his own study of old editions, Kubo Ai (1759–1832) prepared an edition with a detailed commentary incorporating the substance of earlier Japanese scholarship that is indispensable to serious study of the *Xunzi*. Kubo made use of his acquaintance with old editions to introduce additional paragraph divisions where indicated by internal textual evidence and by quotations in parallel texts. His *Junshi zōchū* 荀子增注 ranks with Wang Niansun's annotations, and the two scholars often reach the same conclusions. Important additional notes were made by Igai Hikohiro 猪飼彦博 (1761–1845), Asakawa Kanae 朝川鼎 (1780–1848), Muraoka Reisai 村岡樂齊 (1845–1917), and Haoshi Banri 帆足萬里 (1778–1852).

CONTEMPORARY SCHOLARSHIP

During this century, serious study, independent of old prejudices against Xunzi, has proceeded with more than a dozen excellent studies of textual and interpretative problems. Among the most important are those of Zhong Tai 鍾泰, Liang Qixiong 梁啓雄, Liu Shipei 劉師培, Tao

Hongqing 陶鴻慶, Yu Xingwu 于省吾, Ruan Tingzhuo 阮廷卓, Gao Heng 高亨, Kanaya Osamu 金谷治, Zhang Heng 張亨, Fujii Sen'ei 藤井專英, and Yan Lingfeng 嚴靈峯.

A complete concordance, with a collation of the complete text, was published as part of the Harvard–Yenching Institute Sinological Index Series, *Xunzi yinde* 荀子引得 (1950). In Taiwan, Xiong Gongzhe 熊公哲 has produced a contemporary edition providing the complete text, brief annotations, and a full translation, *Xunzi jinzhu jinshi* 荀子今註今釋 (1975). In China, Xunzi's "materialism," in Marxist terminology, makes him an attractive thinker and has resulted in a new edition of his works, *Xunzi xinzhu* 荀子新注 (1979), prepared by Beijing University, the reprinting of several older works, and the publication of several studies. In 1977, Yan Lingfeng 嚴靈峯 issued a 49-volume reprint of editions and critical studies on the *Xunzi*. He included four editions of the *Xunzi* without the Yang Liang commentary, reprints of the Song dynasty Taizhou and *Zuantu* editions, the Ming dynasty Shide Tang edition, and numerous critical studies, for a total of 72 titles by Chinese authors and 11 by Japanese writers.

Western Scholarship

The study of Xunzi has been neglected in the West. There is in English a partial translation by H. H. Dubs, *The Works of Hsüntze* (1928), and his general study *Hsüntze: The Moulder of Ancient Confucianism* (1927). J.J.L. Duyvendak provided detailed corrections to Dubs's translation, a study on the life of Xunzi, and a translation of the book "On the Correct Use of Names." Burton Watson published an uncommonly readable translation of many of the most important books from the *Xunzi* (1963). Hermann Köster has produced a complete translation into German, *Hsün-tzu* (1967).

AUTHENTICITY OF THE TEXT

Among ancient texts, the *Xunzi* is very well preserved. There are remarkably few interpolations and passages requiring substantial emendation. That damage to the text is relatively minor is also indicated by the small number of passages quoted in the encyclopedia and florilegia that are not in the present text.[46] Nonetheless, as we have seen, Yang Liang noted that several books pose problems. He suggested that the "Great Compendium" was collected by Xunzi's disciples (Wang Xianqian, *Xunzi jijie*, 19.1a), rearranged the books to place at the end five books that he regarded as belonging to Xunzi's disciples rather than to Xunzi himself (*Xunzi jijie*, 20.1a), and thought that the title of "On the Gentleman" was perhaps a copyist's error (*Xunzi jijie*, 17.12a). Beyond these reservations, Yang Liang regarded the works as representing the authentic words and teachings of Xunzi. In the Song dynasty, Wang Yinglin, *Kunxue jiwen* (10.15b), noting that the *Hanshi waizhuan* quotes the criticism of only ten philosophers, suggested that "Contra Twelve Philosophers," which criticized Zisi and Mencius as well, must have been interpolated by Li Si and Han Fei.

Qing Criticism

Qing dynasty scholars found more passages that were problematic. Lu Wenchao suggested that there were a number of problems in "Contra Physiognomy" and "On the Way of Ministers," where parts of the text appear misplaced. Lu had suspicions as well about paragraph 9.18 of "The Regulations of a King," where the Yang commentary is missing (*Xunzi jijie*, 5.16a). Hao Yixing suggested that the rhymed paragraph 14.3 is an interpolation since it seems intrusive in the context (*Xunzi jijie*, 9.10b). Wang Xianqian noted that paragraph 9.17, which has an embedded title, "On the Precedence of Offices," must be an independent essay since it is explicitly quoted in the "Discourse on Music" (20.2) as though it were an independent work (*Xunzi jijie*, 5.13a). Nonetheless, it did not seem to Wang that paragraph headings as embedded titles indicated that such sections had originally been independent books. The consensus of Qing scholars was that though the *Xunzi* had passages that had been misplaced and confused in the course of transmission, it was in the main reliable.

Modern Criticism

Liang Qichao 梁啓超 (1873–1929) concurred that the *Xunzi* was generally reliable, suspecting only the seven books that Yang had identified. These he considered to be the work of Han dynasty literati. He believed that Xunzi had written the basic text himself, but that his disciples had probably recorded those sections where he is directly engaged in debate or persuasion. Liang further proposed that where the *Liji* and *Da Dai* parallel the *Xunzi*, they are quoting from it. Liang concluded that the *Xunzi* was substantially free, apart from the suspect books, from interpolation and lacunae.[47]

More radical were the views of Hu Shi 胡適, who recognized only four books as constituting the "core of his doctrines": "Discourse on Nature," "Dispelling Blindness," "On the Correct Use of Names," and "Man's Nature Is Evil." Hu thought the last two paragraphs of the "Discourse on Nature" were unconnected with the theme of the book and accordingly found them suspect. The two books of poetry and the last six books he rejected entirely. To Hu, the remaining twenty books lacked any fundamental connection with Xunzi's essential teachings, even if genuine. Hu noted that the last part of "Contra Physiognomy" and the last paragraph of "Discourse on Music" are unconnected with what precedes and that in the case of parallels in the *Liji*, *Da Dai*, and *Hanshi waizhuan*, we cannot establish which is the primary source. Though this is the most radical attack on the authenticity of the *Xunzi*, it lacks systematic evidence and rigorous argument.[48]

Zhang Xitang 張西堂, reviewing the work of Liang and Hu, concluded that (1) fourteen books could be accepted as genuine, though with an occasional interpolation, namely Books 1–3, 6, 9–11, and 17–23; (2) four books include authentic paragraphs from the hand of Xunzi but contain passages that are extremely dubious, Books 4, 5, 12, and 13; (3) three books are the work of his students in that they present debates and persuasions of the master, Books 8, 15 and 16; (4) three books are probably not by Xunzi, nor do they reflect his views, Books 7, 14, and 24; (5) the two books of poetry are not the work of Xunzi the philosopher; and (6) the last six books in Yang's ordering are the works of Han literati. Zhang concurred with Hu that "Discourse on Nature," "Dispelling Blindness," "On the Correct Use of Names," and "Man's Nature Is Evil" best reflected Xunzi's teachings. He noted that an important point of evidence is the absence of quotation from three of these in parallel texts such as the *Liji*, *Da Dai*, and *Hanshi waizhuan*. He argued that the "Discourse on Nature" presupposes social circumstances that developed only in the lifetime of Xunzi, that it represents an attack on the Daoist notions that only then developed, and that it presents a world more developed than that in *Mengzi* but less developed than that in *Hanfeizi*. Finally, he argues that the internal consistency of argumentation and style of composition in these four books testifies to their authenticity. The *Xunzi* is primary in cases of parallels with the *Da Dai* and *Hanshi waizhuan*, and there is an internal consistency between the four primary books and such books as "Exhortation to Learning." Zhang's approach was considerably more sophisticated than that of either Hu or Liang.[49]

The most sophisticated and systematic exploration of the problem of authenticity was made by Yang Yunru 楊筠如, who concluded that the *Xunzi* was a heterogeneous text that included additions by later figures. Yang developed four classes of evidence that indicate the heteronomy of the text: discrepancies of style in headings and in composition; contradictions in thought; confusion in the order of paragraphs within books; and circumstantial evidence provided by discrepancies. Yang noted that book names in ancient texts are typically of two kinds: those that derive from the opening sentence of the book and those that express the theme or most important idea of the book. Titles in the *Analects* and *Mengzi* are of the first type as are those of the "Outer Books" of the *Zhuangzi*, whereas those of the "Inner Books" of the *Zhuangzi* and of the *Mozi* and *Hanfeizi* are of the latter type. The co-occurrence of both types of titles is evidence against the genuineness of the text. In the *Xunzi*, some books such as "Discourse on Nature" and "Man's Nature Is Evil" follow the latter pattern, whereas others such as "Duke Ai," "The Questions of Yao," and "On Confucius" follow the former.

Among the contradictions of thought, Yang cited the clear condemnation of the doctrine of fate in paragraph 17.1, but allusions to the "fate of man" lying with Heaven in paragraph 17.9, which agrees with paragraph 2.12. A second contradiction concerns the doctrine of *wei* 偽 "acquired nature" as developed in paragraph 23.1a and the use of the word to mean "hypocrisy" in the rhymed passage in paragraph 20.3. To Yang, this indicated that the author of paragraphs 17.1 and 23.1a is not the author of paragraphs 20.3, 17.9, and 2.12. Because paragraphs 17.7–8 are quoted in the *Hanshi waizhuan*, Yang suspected them. Paragraph 17.10 is a poem unconnected with paragraph 17.9 and paragraphs 17.11–12. Thus, Yang concluded, paragraphs 17.1–6 are the geuine work of Xunzi, but paragraphs 17.7–12 are suspect for various reasons. Though "Man's Nature Is Evil" is generally recognized as genuine, Yang thought that paragraphs 23.7–9 are interpolations since he considered them contradictory to this doctrine. That the "Discourse on Music" is heterogeneous is shown by the parallel texts, which establish that the work was assembled from independent texts. Finallly, Yang argued that since the "Great Compendium" contains passages in common with the *Guliang* and the *Gongyang* commentaries, which he dates to the Han dynasty, the *Xunzi* contains materials written long after the death of Xunzi.[50]

Book Titles

We know from the history of the text that Liu Xiang and not Xunzi is responsible for the original order not only of the books but also of sections or paragraphs within the books. Nor it is clear that Xunzi is responsible for any of the titles. A number, such as "Exhortation to Learning" and "Enriching the State," are relatively common titles.[51] Since we know that Liu Xiang assembled 32 books from the 322 bundles that he found, we must assume that substantial overlap in their contents was the basis of his elimination of "duplicate" bundles. The frequency with which embedded titles appear within the books suggests that they were assembled from paragraphs that may once have had independent status and thus that it was Liu Xiang who gave the books their present titles. Thus, arguments against the authenticity of a book because of the character of its title must be regarded as invalid. We cannot infer merely from the lack of a strong connection between the book's title and the contents of its constituent paragraphs that the book is interpolated or a forgery. On such grounds, it is not possible to argue either that a paragraph is an interpolation or that it is not the genuine work of Xunzi.

Parallel Texts

The problem of parallel texts is more complex than indicated by the discussion of previous scholars. It is reasonable to assume that in preparing his redaction of the *Xunzi*, Liu Xiang did not borrow from the *Liji*, the *Da Dai*, or the *Hanshi waizhuan*. To understand the interrelations between these texts, we need to distinguish three possible text relations: parallel texts, composed after the *Xunzi* and quoting from it, with or without acknowledgment; parallel texts, composed about the time of the *Xunzi* sharing material in common with the *Xunzi*, testifying to the traditional nature of the material and to the joint quotation from an unacknowledged and now-lost source; and interpolations of materials from sources outside Xunzi's own writings and those traditions concerning him collected by his disciples. Distinguishing these three requires a detailed examination of all the texts for evidence of direct quotation, paraphrase, or simplification of difficult readings indicating which is the source and which the quotation.

This can best be done by examining the relationship between the *Xunzi* text and its parallels in terms of a single book, the "Exhortation to Learning," that is representative of the problems. This book can be divided into two parts. The first, comprising paragraphs 1.1–1.7, is composed of traditional materials arranged to buttress Xunzi's argument. This material is widely attested in other works dating from Xunzi's time and later; parallels to parts occur in the *Yanzi chunqiu, Shangjun shu* 商君書, *Lüshi chunqiu*, and in the works of Xunzi's disciple Han Fei. Sentences are quoted or paraphrased in the *Yantie lun* 鹽鐵論, *Liuzi* 劉子, *Shiji*, *Wenzi* 文子, and the *Kongzi jiayu* 孔子家語. Phrases identical with or similar to those of the *Xunzi* occur in the *Mengzi* and *Zhanguo ce* 戰國策. Such "quotations" are without acknowledgment and testify only to the traditional nature of the materials and the proverbial character of some of the language in the book. The second part, comprising paragraphs 1.8–1.14, is mostly the original composition of Xunzi and as such is much more rarely "quoted."

Later texts extract long passages and whole paragraphs from the *Xunzi*, sometimes nearly verbatim, other times only as loose paraphrases. The most important of these is the *Da Dai*, which extracts paragraphs 1.1–1.7 and uses materials from paragraph 1.12. The *Hanshi waizhuan* makes use of a single sentence, clearly proverbial, from 1.1. It makes more extended use of the material in paragraph 1.4, which the *Shuoyuan* 說苑 parallel includes in a persuasion of Tian Wen, the Lord of Mengchang and Duke of Xue. The substance of paragraph 1.9 is quoted, but with significant changes in the language. Paragraph 1.12 is quoted directly with minor variations. In his *Shuoyuan*, Liu Xiang selected passages from paragraphs 1.1, 1.3, 1.4, and 1.6, which he often merely paraphrases.

In the first part, virtually every character is attested in a number of other sources, but in the second there are rare quotations. Only paragraph 1.12, which the *Da Dai* parallel indicates may be misplaced, has a substantial number of parallels or quotations. (See Table 3 for a summary of these facts.)

A close examination of the sources suggests that in every case the *Da Dai*, *Liji*, and *Hanshi waizhuan* are secondary. This is indicated by their regular simplification of the language and the grammar of the *Xunzi*, by their avoidance of its rare characters and names, and by their omission of certain materials to accommodate Han views on controversial matters. The *Shuoyuan* explicitly acknowledges some excerpts from the *Xunzi*, but quotes other passages without credit. There is no dependable pattern of relations between the texts in these two cases; the *Shuoyuan* has occasionally either used an earlier form of the *Xunzi* text, employed another source for traditional materials, or has been edited or paraphrased. Of the various parallel texts, the *Kongzi jiayu* is dependably the closest in language to the *Xunzi*, a fact consistent with its being a late compilation that could have used the version of the *Xunzi* edited by Liu Xiang.

When passages are shared with such works as the *Lüshi chunqiu*, *Hanfeizi*, *Zhanguo ce*, as well as the *Shiji* and *Huainanzi* 淮南子, there is no reason to consider the possibility of direct quotation since we are probably dealing with traditional material ancestral to both the *Xunzi* and these texts. Generally, it is best to assume that such material, particularly when short passages are involved, was part of the rhetorical tradition used in discriminations and persuasions. A typical example of this phenomenon is to be seen in the use of nearly identical languages in passages in the *Xunzi* and *Mengzi* and in the *Hanshi waizhuan* (6.8a) debate between Shunyu Kun and Mencius. Paragraph 1.7 of the *Xunzi* begins: "In antiquity, when Hu Ba 瓠巴 played the zither, deep-water sturgeons came up to listen, and when Bo Ya 伯牙 played the lute, the six horses

TABLE 3
Parallels to "Exhortation to Learning"

Xunzi	Hanshi	Shuo-yuan	Jiayu	Da Dai	Other
1.1	5.13b	3.4b; 3.7a	—	7.6a	*Shiji*, 60.21 *Yanzi*, 5.347 *Huainanzi*, 19.9a
1.2	—	—	—	7.6a	*Hanfeizi*, 8.13a
1.3	—	3.4b; 16.3a	—	7.6a	*Hanfeizi*, 8.13a, 4.16b *Huainanzi*, 9.13a *Wenzi*, B.33a *Lüshi chunqiu*, 17.12b
1.4	8.17a	11.4b 16.4a 17.11a	4.4b	7.6b 5.2a	*Shiji*, 60.24, 60.28 *Lunheng*, 12.5b, 2.11a *Yanzi chunqiu*, 5.347 *Huainanzi*, 18.9a *Liuzi*, 5.44a
1.5	—	—	—	7.7a	*Huainanzi*, 17.13b, 13.6b *Hanfeizi*, 5.3b *Shangjun shu*, 3.14a *Zhanguo ce*, 4.10b
1.6	—	3.4b	—	7.7ab	*Yantie lun*, 39.269 *Mengzi*, 3B.10 *Huainanzi*, 17.12a, 17.13b, 16.1b *Wenzi;* * *Shizi* ʃ* ʃ*
1.7	6.8a	—	—	7.8a	*Lunheng*, 5.11a, 2.13b *Huainanzi*, 16.1b *Shiji*, 128.9 *Liuzi*, 1.9a
1.8	—	—	—	—	—
1.9	9.7a	—	—	—	—
1.10	—	—	—	—	—
1.11	—	—	—	—	—
1.12	4.9a	—	—	7.7b	*Lüshi chunqiu*, 21.9a, 24.7a *Huainanzi*, 11.13b, 16.8a *Shiji* 86.25, 90.33
1.13	—	—	—	—	—
1.14	—	—	—	—	—

*Cited in commentaries.

looked up from their feed bags." Shunyu Kun uses identical language to rebuke Mencius for lacking true goodness, concluding: "If even fishes and horses recognize what is good, how much more then should a lord of men recognize them!" Mencius rejoined that one cannot make the deaf hear or the blind see. Shunyu countered, using language identical with the second sentence of paragraph 1.7 of the *Xunzi*: "Truly there is no sound so faint that it is not to be heard, and no action so concealed that it is not visible." Shunyu concludes that Mencius is no sage; if he were, then his country would not have been destroyed.

The debate between Shunyu Kun and Mencius, which must have been taken from an earlier collection of such pieces and incorporated into the *Hanshi waizhuan*, shows how proverbial comments were used in Warring States rhetoric. Xunzi frequently employs such materials. In paragraph 1.7, he cites yet a third proverbial saying and then concludes with a sentence that must represent his own thought: "Good deeds—do they not accumulate! Surely it is not true that no one will ever hear of them!" This shows that language common to two texts does not indicate "forgery" or "interpolation" but rather indebtedness to a common tradition of rhetoric.

Early Paragraph Organization

Previous arguments about the authenticity of the text have failed to consider the full circumstances of the early development of the *Xunzi*. The *Xunzi* collects together in its paragraphs several different types of compositions:

1. Expositions of *Odes, Documents,* or traditions usually quoted at the conclusion (for example, 2.2 and 4.8).

2. Disquisitions on a specific topic such as 5.1 on physiognomy.

3. Glosses to proverbial and traditional sayings (10.6).

4. Definitions of traditional terms (2.3, 6.9, and 6.11).

5. Apparently independent essays marked by embedded titles (2.4, 3.13, 5.8, 6.10, and 6.13).

6. Rhetorical antitheses, usually involving the gentleman and ordinary man or the wise and stupid ruler (3.6, 4.4).

7. Refutations of theses of other schools (3.7, 5.5).

8. Short essays on basic topics, possibly fragments of persuasions (5.4).

9. Answers to questions, possibly fragments of debates or of answers to students (8.2).

These various types of compositions are suggestive of the wide range of materials transmitted and collected into the 322 bundles Liu Xiang found in the Imperial Library.

The issue of authenticity is independent of the type of composition:

1. Paragraphs in the *Xunzi* are sometimes written by him as original essays. Paragraphs 1.8, 1.10, 1.11, 1.13, 1.14 of the "Exhortation" belong to this category.

2. Other paragraphs are compilations of traditional materials that were part of the heritage he received from his teachers and that he may

have edited or interpreted. Paragraphs 1.1–1.7, 1.9, and 1.12 belong to this category, as do passages in mnemonic poetic forms.

3. Others are traditions concerning his teachings handed down by his disciples. The "Debate on the Principles of Warfare" belongs to this category.

The diversity of types of paragraphs contributes to an impression of heteronomy in the books, but this cannot be taken as evidence that the works are therefore vitiated by "forged" sections or by "interpolations."

Beyond the paragraph level, we may assume that Liu Xiang encountered longer essays within the bundles he found in the Imperial Library. Both the long extract in the *Da Dai* from the "Exhortation" and the long quotation from "Contra Twelve Philosophers" in the *Hanshi waizhuan* indicate that the arrangement of paragraphs in Liu Xiang's redaction was not arbitrary but based on earlier compilations. The fact that paragraph 1.12 is contained in the *Da Dai* extract along with 1.1–1.7 may indicate that the present text of the *Xunzi* is out of order, or it may indicate that Liu Xiang rearranged, on grounds not now known, the original or that the editor of the *Da Dai* exercised editorial judgment by adding the passage. We are in no position to draw a definite conclusion in this instance.

Our lack of knowledge of the principles that Liu Xiang used to collate the numerous bundles into the books he recognized makes it difficult to draw firm conclusions. But his use of the term "duplicate" (*fuchong* 復重) for the 290 bundles he discarded suggests that the fundamental framework of each book existed at the time of his redaction. Though there is evidence of disturbances in the order of some books (see Appendix B), they seem generally well preserved. Most previous statements that this or that book or this or that paragraph are "forgeries" or "interpolations" do not rest on sound argument. We may conclude that the works transmitted by Liu Xiang and Yang Liang are in general the authentic works of Xunzi. Except for interpolations identified in the notes, the text is exceptionally reliable and may be used with confidence.

BOOKS 1-6
■■

BOOK I

An Exhortation to Learning

INTRODUCTION

A love of learning characterized most Ru thinkers, but for Xunzi learning was a matter of crucial importance; only through learning, involving conscious effort, could the original nature of man be overcome. Learning does not ornament or refine a basically good nature, or direct a neutral nature toward social good; rather, it conquers evil tendencies inherent in man through the conscious exertion entailed in all learning. The "Exhortation to Learning" stresses that learning continues so long as one lives and that the gentleman must accordingly examine himself each day to make sure that he applies his learning to his conduct. Learning improves our original nature and transcends it, just as ice, though made from water, is colder than water. Learning is a tincture that permanently alters us, like dye. Once we have been shaped by education, we will never revert to our original "evil" nature, just as a straight board steamed into the shape of a wheel will not revert to its original shape. Learning is the standard, the plumbline that straightens out our irregularities, and the technique, the whetstone, that sharpens our natural abilities.

Learning transforms our horizons and sense of perspective. The process of education effects changes in us so that though as children we are born much the same, we grow up to be very different people. The gentleman is distinguished from ordinary men by his willingness to "borrow" the useful and good qualities of other things and other people. Since we are affected by our environment, the gentleman takes great care to see that his surroundings are proper. Beginnings are important. Thus, the gentleman is cautious about his inner power and watches his speech.

One of Xunzi's most important doctrines is that of *ji* 積 "accumulation." Differences in accomplishment are the result not of differences in inborn talent but of steadfastness and constancy of purpose and the accumulation resulting from continuous effort. Though the earthworm lacks the advantages of the crab's legs and claws, by its persistence it can accomplish its ends, whereas the crab, which moves in every direction at once, accomplishes nothing. Good deeds accumulate, and achievements that may have been undertaken in obscurity are certain to be noticed.

Philosophers often cited well-known paragons to illustrate the effect of following a philosophical principle or to show that even with lesser abilities one could accomplish as much, if one mastered his philosophy. Xunzi contrasts a worn-out old nag with the fabulous Qiji 騏驥, famed as one of the remarkable horses belonging to King Mu of the Zhou dynasty, which, when driven by the great charioteer Zaofu 造父 on the western journey of the king, were able to cover 1,000 *li* in a single day.[1]

Hu Ba and Bo Ya. Hu Ba was an ancient expert at playing the zither, though it was not known when he lived. The *Liezi* (*jishi*, 5.109) records that "when Hu Ba played the lute, birds would dance and fishes leap."[2]

Bo Ya was an ancient who became accomplished at playing the lute, but no one knew when he lived.[3] When he played his lute, the six horses would raise their heads from their feeding sacks to listen. Bo Ya studied the lute under Cheng Lian 成連, who carried him to the fabulous Isles of the Blest, where his musical talent was developed. Later he became friends with a woodcutter named Zhong Ziqi 鍾子期, who fully grasped the beauty of his playing. Tradition records that once when Bo Ya was strumming his lute while Zhong Ziqi was listening, his thoughts turned to a high mountain. Ziqi remarked: "How excellent indeed! Lofty and majestic like Mount Tai." A short time later, when his thoughts turned to rippling waters, Ziqi said: "How beautifully done! Rolling and swelling like the Yangtze." Another time when he was caught in a sudden downpour, Bo Ya improvised an air about the constant drizzle, and then he composed a variation on the sound of crashing mountains. Whatever he played, Ziqi grasped the drift of his thinking. "How well you listen! Wherever my thoughts wander, you imagine just what is on my mind!" When Ziqi died, Bo Ya was disconsolate, tore the strings off his lute, and smashed it because he felt that there was no one in the world worth playing for. To the end of his life he never played again.[4]

It was a general Chinese belief that all nature reverberates in sympathetic harmony with the accomplishments and moral self-cultivation of the gentleman, just as of old fishes and horses had responded to Hu Ba and Bo Ya. In mentioning these men, Xunzi makes use of an important theory derived from magnetic and acoustical phenomena. The ancient belief, as we have seen, was that a continuum linked even things separated by space, as when the lodestone draws iron particles to itself or when a note played on one instrument causes another to vibrate. So, too, there were invisible links between men and through music between men and animals. The effect of music on animals was akin to that of the moon on sea creatures. When the theories of philosophers like Zou Yan were combined with the general conviction that music was of cosmic importance, even extraordinary things seemed possible.

The Process of Learning. Though Xunzi held that the process of learning should never cease, he realized that the program of learning must have a beginning and an end. Its immediate end is to create a scholar, its final end is to produce a sage. In this book, Xunzi distinguishes three levels of accomplishment: the scholar, the gentleman, and the sage. The scholar puts into practice his learning, he admires the model transmitted by tradition, and he seeks to emulate the example of the past. The gentleman exerts himself out of his love of learning, he embodies a firm sense of purpose, and he realizes the meaning of his learning in his conduct. The sage fully comprehends the meaning of things and possesses an inexhaustible and incisive intelligence that illuminates everything with its brilliance. For Xunzi, learning begins with the traditional materials learned through recitation, proceeds through the *Documents*, the *Odes*, the *Music*, and the *Spring and Autumn Annals*, until it reaches its conclusion with the *Rituals*. The supreme importance that Xunzi placed on ritual matters distinguishes his philosophy. To Xunzi, "ritual" meant less the details of ceremonial behavior that had seemed important to such earlier Ru as Ziyou, Zizhang, and Zixia and more the fundamental principles underlying all human behavior.

The works he mentions had become, as we have seen, canonical in Xunzi's time. Xunzi adapted this common heritage as the core of his program of education. These works, to be recited until memorized along with the teacher's explication of difficult points, were the foundation of thinking. They supplied an indispensable wealth of human experience and wisdom that enlarged one's own views and cautioned against overemphasis on the merely ephemeral. They held before one the splendid example of antiquity wherein all great ideas had once been exemplified in individuals and in society. An orator and a thinker would always preface his argument with "I have heard," so that he might repeat what he had learned from his own master. The learning of the gentleman was characterized by reflection, and it influenced his every thought and action. Not an ornament worn for the sake of others, it refined his character and molded his actions. The gentleman thus responded with perfect congruity to the requirements of his surroundings, like an echo.

With this view of learning, Xunzi naturally held that one cannot learn on one's own. The *Rituals* and *Music* have no explanations, the relevance of the *Odes* and *Documents* is not obvious, and the import of the *Annals* is not easily grasped. Thus, a teacher is necessary, both to provide explanations and to act as a model. Devotion to a teacher and learning to repeat his explanations are the best way of becoming a gentleman. The second best is exaltation of ritual principles, which will provide a guide to correct behavior. But if a man neither had a teacher nor exalted ritual principles, Xunzi believed that all such a person could expect to do is master unrelated facts or mechanically repeat the *Odes* and *Documents* without understanding their import. Such a person will be but a shallow and vain Ru, however skilled he might become in disputation.

Xunzi's gentleman is to be guided by ritual in all things. He does not engage in conversation and debate with those who are uncouth. He is careful to keep his speech appropriate to the occasion, speaking only where it is proper, saying only what is required by the situation, carefully observing the demeanor and mood of those with whom he talks. The gentleman, being catholic and universal, unifies all things with his learning and makes them secure, so that he does not leave with one principle and return with another. He fully comprehends the requirements of his various social roles—subject, son, father, husband, friend—and is at home with the requirements of a sense of humanity and moral duty. He is so expert that his responses perfectly suit the circumstances because his learning is entire and not of a piece.

Villains. Xunzi stressed that becoming expert only in a few things and neglecting a broad base of learning has unfortunate consequences for the individual. But, for Xunzi, such narrowness can have disastrous consequences for society as well. When such people occupy high positions and when there is no one of moral worth and true education to oppose them, they plunder and despoil the people and undermine the foundations of government. Xunzi recalls the three great villains of Chinese history: Jie, Zhou Xin, and Robber Zhi 盜跖. Notorious for their utterly irredeemable depravity and wickedness, each was a contemporary of one of the great heroes and paragons of Chinese society. Jie destroyed the Xia dynasty and Zhou Xin ruined the Shang, to be succeeded, respectively, by the sage kings Tang and Wen.

Robber Zhi does not fit into any scheme of political history. Rather, he is the hero of a dissident school that called into question the legitimacy of all Ru and Mohist notions of government. He was famous for intimidating Confucius and besting him in argument, the "record" of which is now contained in the *Zhuangzi* (29 "Dao Zhi" 盜跖, 9.17b–21b). To the Ru, he was a clever and dangerous brigand and nothing more. He was said to have been the younger brother of Liuxia Hui 柳下惠, a minister of Lu admired by Confucius. Zhi organized a band of 9,000 brigands and rampaged through the empire, stealing, looting, terrorizing the population, and carrying off wives and daughers. He ignored every custom and law, even to neglecting his family and offering no sacrifices to his ancestors. Confucius suggested that Liuxia Hui should do something about his brother, but Hui replied that Zhi was hopeless. So Confucius with two of his disciples went to reform him despite Hui's warnings. Confucius attempted to persuade him to follow the Way, but Zhi contemptuously dismissed all that Confucius had said as "inane, inadequate, fraudulent, sinister, vain, and hypocritical," in short, "not worth discussing." Confucius was utterly astonished and fled, fumbling three times when he tried to grasp the chariot reins, his expression blank and his face ashen. On his return, Confucius described the visit as like "patting a tiger's head and plaiting its whiskers."

Because Xunzi's gentleman understands the need for completeness, he recites and enumerates his studies so that no point escapes his notice, he ponders the overall meaning and significance. He translates his learning into action so that his conduct embodies the traditions of the ancients, and he carefully and attentively eliminates what is harmful and nurtures what is good. Even his senses are transformed, so that the world he experiences is quite different from that of the petty man. Thus, he is not swayed by temporal matters, and he cannot be deterred from doing what is right. "He was born to follow it, and he will die following it."

TEXT

1.1

The gentleman says: "Learning must never be concluded."

Though blue dye comes from the indigo plant, it is bluer than indigo. Ice is made from water, but it is colder than water.

A piece of wood straight as a plumbline can, by steaming, be made pliable enough to bend into the shape of a wheel rim, so its curvature will conform to the compass. Yet, even though it is then allowed to dry out completely in the sun, it will not return to its former straightness because the process of steaming has effected this change in it.

So, too, wood that has been marked with the plumbline will be straight and metal that has been put to the whetstone will be sharp.

In broadening his learning, the gentleman each day examines himself so that his awareness will be discerning and his actions without excess.

1.2

Truly if you do not climb a high mountain, you will be unaware of the height of the sky. If you do not look down into a deep gorge, you will be unaware of the thickness of the earth.

If you have not heard the words inherited from the Ancient Kings,[5] you will be unaware of the greatness of learning and inquiry. The children of Hann 干[6] and Yue 越 and of the tribes of Yi 夷 and Mo 貉[7] are all born making the same sounds, but they grow up having different customs because the process of education has effected such changes in them. An Ode says:[8]

O you gentlemen,
Be not constantly at ease and at rest.
Be thoughtful and respectful in your official position.
Love those who are upright and correct.
And the spirits will heed you,
And will increase your bright blessings.[9]

There is no spirit so great as the transformation of the self with the Way, and there is no blessing so long lasting as being without misfortune.[10]

1.3

I once spent a whole day in thought, but it was not so valuable as a moment in study.[11] I once stood on my tiptoes to look out into the distance, but it was not so effective as climbing up to a high place for a broader vista.

Climbing to a height and waving your arm does not cause the arm's length to increase, but your wave can be seen farther away.

Shouting downwind does not increase the tenseness of the sound, but it is heard more distinctly.[12]

A man who borrows a horse and carriage does not improve his feet, but he can extend his travels 1,000 *li*.[13] A man who borrows a boat and paddles does not gain any new ability in water, but he can cut across rivers and seas.[14]

The gentleman by birth is not different from other men;[15] he is just good at "borrowing" the use of external things.[16]

1.4

In the southern regions, there is a bird called the "dunce dove" that builds its nest out of feathers woven together with hair and attaches the nest to the flowering tassels of reeds. The winds come, the tassels snap off, the eggs break, and the baby birds are killed.[17]

It is not that the nest was not well made; rather, it resulted from what it was attached to.

In the western regions, there is a tree called the "servant's cane" that has a trunk only four inches long and grows on the top of high mountains, yet it looks down into chasms a hundred fathoms deep.[18]

It is not that this tree's trunk is able to grow to such length; rather, it is the result of its situation.

Raspberry vines growing among hemp plants are not staked, yet they grow up straight. [White sand put into a black slime will mix with it and become entirely black.][19]

If the root of the orchid and the rhizome of the valerian[20] are soaked in the water used to wash rice,[21] the gentleman will not go near them, and the petty man will not wear them.

It is not that their substance is unpleasing; it is the result of what they were soaked in. Accordingly,

where the gentleman resides is sure to be a carefully chosen neighborhood,[22] and when he travels, it is certain to be in the company of scholars,

so that he can keep away from what is untoward and low and draw near what is fair and upright.

1.5

There must be some beginning for every type of phenomenon that occurs. The coming of honor or disgrace must be a reflection of one's inner power.

From rotting meat come maggots; decaying wood produces woodworms.[23]

An insolent disregard for one's own person creates therewith calamity and misfortune.[24]

The rigid cause themselves to be broken; the pliable cause themselves to be bound.[25]

Those whose character is mean and vicious will rouse others to animosity against them.

When firewood is spread out evenly, fire will seek out the driest sticks. When the ground has been leveled out evenly, water will seek the dampest places.

Grasses and trees grow together with their own type; birds and beasts live together in their own groups; each thing follows after its own kind.[26]

Accordingly,

when the target is set out on the archery range, bows and arrows will arrive. Where the trees in the forest flourish, axes and halberds will come. Where things have turned sour, gnats will collect.

Truly, words have the potential to summon disaster, and actions the potential to invite disgrace, so the gentleman is cautious about where he takes his position.[27]

1.6

If you accumulate enough earth to build up a high hill, rain and wind will flourish because of it. If you accumulate enough water to fill a chasm, dragons and scaly dragons will be born within it. If you accumulate enough good to make whole your inner power, a divine clarity of intelligence will be naturally acquired and a sagelike mind will be fully realized.[28] Accordingly,

if you do not accumulate paces and double paces, you will lack the means to reach 1,000 li, and if you do not accumulate small streams, you will have no way to fill a river or sea.

Even a famous thoroughbred like Qiji cannot cover ten paces in a single stride. But in ten yokings even a worn-out nag can. Its achievement consists in its not giving up.[29]

If you start carving but give up, you cannot cut even a rotting piece of wood in two. Yet if you carve away and never give up, even metal and stone can be engraved.

Though the earthworm has neither the advantage of claws and teeth nor the strength of muscles and bones, it can eat dust and dirt above ground and drink from the waters of the Yellow Springs below,[30]

because its mind is fixed on a constant end.[31]

The crab has eight legs and two claws; still if there is no hole made by an eel or snake, it will have no safe place to live,

because its mind moves in every direction at once.

For these reasons, if there is no dark obscurity in purpose,[32] there will be no reputation for brilliance; if there is no hidden secretiveness in the performance of duties, there will be no awe-inspiring majesty in achievements. If you attempt to travel both forks of a road, you will arrive nowhere, and if you attempt to serve two masters, you will please neither.

The eye cannot look at two objects and see either clearly; the ear cannot listen to two things and hear either distinctly.

The wingless dragon has no limbs, but it can fly; the flying squirrel has five talents, but it is reduced to extremity.[33]

An Ode says:[34]

> The ring dove is in the mulberry tree,
> Its young ones are seven.
> The good man, my lord,
> His bearing is constant,
> His bearing is constant,
> As though his mind were tied.

Thus, the gentleman is tied to constancy.[35]

1.7

In antiquity, when Hu Ba played the zither, deep-water sturgeons came up to listen, and when Bo Ya played the lute, the six horses looked up from their feed bags.[36]

Truly there is no sound so faint that it is not to be heard, and no action so concealed that it is not visible.

Where jade is buried in the hills, the plants have a special sheen, and where pearls grow in the deeps, the banks do not parch.[37]

Good deeds—do they not accumulate! Surely it is not true that no one will ever hear of them![38]

1.8

Learning—where should it begin and where should it end! I say: Its proper method is to start with the recitation of the Classics and conclude with the reading of the *Rituals*.[39] Its real purpose is first to create a scholar and in the end to create a sage.[40] If you genuinely accumulate and earnestly practice for a long time, then you will become an initiate.[41] Learning continues until death and only then does it stop.[42] Thus, though the methods employed to learn come to a conclusion, the purpose of learning must never, even for an instant, be put aside. Those who undertake learning become men; those who neglect it become as wild beasts. Truly the *Documents* contain the record of governmental affairs. The *Odes* set the correct standards to which pronunciations should adhere.[43] The *Rituals* contain the model for the primary social distinctions and the categories used by analogical extension for the guiding rules and ordering norms of behavior. Accordingly, when learning has been perfected in the rituals, it has come to its terminus. Surely this may be called the culmination of the Way and its Power! The reverence and refinement of the *Rituals*, the concord and harmony of the *Music*, the breadth of the *Odes* and *Documents*, the subtlety of the *Annals*—all the creations of Heaven and Earth are completed in them.

1.9

The learning of the gentleman enters through the ear, is stored in the mind,[44] spreads through the four limbs, and is visible in his activity and repose.[45]

In his softest word and slightest movement,[46] in one and all,[47] the gentleman can be taken as a model and pattern.[48]

The learning of the petty man enters the ear and comes out the mouth. Since the distance between the mouth and ear is no more than four inches,[49] how could it be sufficient to refine the seven-foot body of a man![50]

In antiquity men undertook learning for the sake of self-improvement; today people undertake learning for the sake of others.[51]

The learning of the gentleman is used to refine his character. The learning of the petty man is used like ceremonial offerings of birds and calves.[52] Accordingly, informing where no question has been posed is called "forwardness,"[53] and offering information on two points when only one has been raised is called "garrulity."[54] Both forwardness and garrulity are to be condemned! The gentleman is responsive like an echo.[55]

1.10

In learning, no method is of more advantage than to be near a man of learning.

The *Rituals* and *Music* present models but do not offer explanation;[56] the *Odes* and *Documents* present matters of antiquity but are not always apposite; the *Annals* are laconic, and their import is not quickly grasped.[57] It is just on these occasions that the man of learning repeats the explanations of the gentleman. Thus, he is honored for his comprehensive and catholic acquaintance with the affairs of the world.[58] Therefore it is said: "In learning, no method is of more advantage than to be near a man of learning."

1.11

Of the direct routes to learning, none is quicker than devotion to a man of learning. The next best route is exaltation of ritual principles.[59] If you can neither be devoted to a man of learning nor exalt ritual principles, how will you do more than learn unordered facts or merely mechanically follow the *Odes* and *Documents*? In this case you will never, even to the end of your days, escape being nothing more than an untutored Ru. If you would take the Ancient Kings as your source and the principle of humanity and justice as your foundation, then ritual principles will rectify the warp and woof, the straightaways and byways of your life. It is like lifting a fur collar by turning under your fingers to grasp it to raise it up. Those that fall into their proper place are too many to be counted.[60] Not being led by the examples of ritual principles while using the *Odes* and *Documents* as the basis of action is like "using a finger to plumb the depth of the Yellow River," or "a lance to pound the husks off millet," or "an awl to eat the evening meal from a pot." It is doomed to failure. Thus, one who exalts ritual principles, though he may never gain a clear understanding of them, will be a model scholar, whereas one who does not exalt them, though he undertakes investigations and makes discriminations, will remain only an undisciplined Ru.[61]

1.12

Do not answer a person whose questions are uncouth. Do not ask questions of a person who is uncouth. Do not listen to a person whose theories are uncouth. Do not engage in discriminations with a person who is in a quarrelsome mood.[62] Thus, a person must first have become what he is by following the Way, and only then should you receive him. If he did not become what he is by following the Way, then he should be avoided. Thus, after ritual principles[63] are respected in his actions, you can discuss with him the methods of the Way; after his speech is guided by ritual principles, then you can discuss the principles of the Way; and after his demeanor[64] is obedient to ritual principles, then you can discuss the attainment of the Way. Accordingly, having discussions with one whom one ought not is termed "forwardness";[65] not having discussions with those with whom one ought is termed "secretiveness";[66] and having discussions but not observing the demeanor and mood of those to whom one speaks is termed "blindness."[67] Thus, the gentleman is not forward, not secretive, and not blind, but is cautious and submissive in his person.[68] An Ode says:[69]

> They are not rude, not remiss,[70]
> They are rewarded by the Son of Heaven.

This expresses my point.

1.13

One who misses a single shot out of 100 does not deserve to be called an expert archer. One who travels a journey of 1,000 *li*, but does not take the last half-step does not deserve to be called an expert carriage driver. One who does not fully grasp the appropriate connection between modes of behavior and the various categories of things[71] and who does not see the oneness between the requirements of the principle of humanity and the moral obligations that inhere in it[72] does not deserve to be called expert in learning. The truly learned are those who make sure that their studies keep this unity. Those who leave with one principle and return with another are men of the streets and alleys. They are expert in a few things, but inexpert in many, like Jie, Zhou Xin, and Robber Zhi. Be complete and whole in it, and then you will be truly learned.

1.14

The gentleman, knowing well that learning that is incomplete and impure does not deserve to be called fine, recites and enumerates his studies that he will be familiar with them, ponders over them and searches into them that he will fully penetrate their meaning,[73] acts in his person that they will come to dwell within him,[74] and eliminates what is harmful within him that he will hold on to them and be nourished by them. Thereby he causes his eye to be unwilling to see what is contrary to it,[75] his ear unwilling to hear what is contrary to it, his mouth unwilling to speak anything contrary to it, and his mind unwilling to contemplate anything contrary to it. When he has reached the limit of such perfection, he finds delight in it. His eye then finds greater enjoyment in the five colors, his ear in the five sounds, his mouth in the five tastes, and his mind benefits from possessing all that is in the world.[76] Therefore, the exigencies of time and place and considerations of personal profit cannot influence him, cliques and coteries cannot sway him, and the whole world cannot deter him. He was born to follow it, and he will die following it: truly this can be called "being resolute from inner power." Keep resolute from inner power because only then can you be firm of purpose. Be firm of purpose because only then can you be responsive to all.[77] One who can be both firm of purpose and responsive to all is truly to be called the "perfected man."[78] Just as the value of Heaven is to be seen in its brilliance and that of Earth in its vast expanses, so the gentleman is to be valued for his completeness.[79]

■ ■ ‖‖ ■ ■

BOOK 2

On Self-Cultivation

INTRODUCTION

Self-cultivation is a general theme of Chinese philosophy. Virtually the whole spectrum of thinkers and schools agreed with the statement in the *Daxue* 大學, "The Great Learning" (6), that "from the Son of Heaven down to the common masses, one and all regard cultivation of the self as the foundation." If a man cultivated the Way in his own self, the Daoists taught (*DDJ*, 54), his inner power would become real. The Ru taught that if the gentleman cleaved to the cultivation of this self, he could bring order to the world (*Mengzi*, 7B.32). What was meant by self-cultivation varied with the philosopher, but all agreed that it was vital.

The gentleman is anxious to preserve what is good within himself and correct what is bad. Xunzi contrasts the *shan* 善 "good" that teachers and friends do with the *zei* 賊 "injury" done by malefactors. In his "Man's Nature Is Evil" (23.3a), Xunzi defined "good" as what "is correct, is in accord with natural principles, is productive of tranquillity, and is well ordered." The basic meaning of *zei* is "to do injury, violence; malefaction; predatory." Ru philosophers applied it to those who are merely "useless pests" (*LY*, 14.46), who are "enemies of virtue" (*LY*, 17.13; *Mengzi* 7B.37), or who have utter disregard for the injurious consequences of their actions (*LY*, 20.2). Confucius observed that even a good quality such as love of honesty, unless tempered by a love of learning, can become an obsession that results in *zei* "malefaction" (*LY*, 17.7). Suggestive of extreme injury, *zei* is applied to assailants and murderers, to thieves and robbers, and to those given to sedition and villainy. Those who lead others astray through failing to correct them wrong them just as surely as if they had assaulted them, robbed them, or behaved in a predatory fashion against them. Xunzi believed that we must correct others when they are wrong, just as we must encourage them when they are right.

Nurturing Life. Yangsheng 養生 "nurturing life" consists in conserving one's vital powers to prolong physical and sexual vitality and thus life itself. The theme was common in the third century. Quite naturally it attracted nearly universal interest since, as Xunzi remarks, everyone wants warm clothing, filling food, and a long life ("Rongru," 4.7). Though the theme of "nurturing life" was especially associated with the Daoists, its universality may be seen in such diverse works as *Mozi*, *Zhuangzi*, *Guanzi*, *Hanfeizi*, *Lüshi chunqiu*, and *Huainanzi*. Originally *yangsheng* had meant only to "care for the living" and is so used by Mencius (1A.3). But prayers for long life are common in Zhou bronze inscriptions as early as the eight century.[1] Gradually a technical vocabulary developed, and *yangsheng* came to mean specifically "nurturing life." Other terms expressed different aspects of the common desire: *changsheng* 長生 "long life," "longevity," ultimately "immortality," meaning physical and material immortality; *baoshen* 保身 "preservation of the person," meaning the visible individual; *nanlao* 難老 "to make difficult the advance of old age," implying the retardation of senility; *quelao* 卻老 "warding off old age"; and, of course, *wusi* 無死 and *busi* 不死 "deathlessness," exemplified as well in the common greeting and toast *wansui* 萬歲 "May you live for 10,000 years!"[2]

The conviction gradually emerged during Xunzi's lifetime that not only could life be prolonged but one could attain deathlessness through an elixir of life. Han Fei relates that a certain traveling philosopher visited the king of Yan, who entertained him in exchange for being taught the way to deathlessness. Unfortunately, before the ministers of the king could be fully taught the technique, the philosopher died. The king, furious, chastised his ministers for being dilatory, never thinking that he might have been duped by the philosopher (*HFZ*, 34 "Waichu shui" 外儲說, I/B, 11.4b–5a). The First Emperor, at the end of Xunzi's life or shortly after his death, made extensive searches for the elixir and sent expeditions to distant lands in hopes of finding it.

The theme of nurturing life is associated in Xunzi's mind with prolonging life and possibly with the elixir of immortality and the physical preservation of the body. In "Rectifying Theses" (18.7), to refute the Mohist notion that burials should be modest, he mentions the elaborate equipment of tombs, which motivated robbers to dig into them. His catalogue of the contents of such tombs mentions various objects that appear to be connected with the physical immortality of the deceased. Having been a student and later a member of the Jixia Academy, he was fully familiar with the speculations of the cosmologists and alchemists who flourished in late third-century China. The hope for physical immortality, if not fully realized around 275 when Xunzi was writing this book, was at least a real possibility and not the mere fantasy of frauds who shamelessly exploited the superstitions of gullible rulers. Recent excavations have made it abundantly clear that the ancient Chinese were in fact successful in preserving the body from physical decay. The tomb of the Marchioness of Dai 軑侯妻子, dating from the lifetime of some of Xunzi's students, has been excavated, and her body found in the state of preservation of a person who had died only a week or two before— without embalming, mummification, tanning, or freezing.[3] A search of the historical literature shows that on various occasions at least five other such bodies were uncovered before A.D. 650, but these reports were previously dismissed as mere fables.[4]

Controlling the Qi Vital Breath. "Controlling the vital breath" is the only technique that Xunzi specifically mentions to nurture life. The primary sense of *zhi* 治 "control" is "good order, well governed"; as a verb it means to "regulate, govern, control, manipulate, arrange" so as to put into "good order." As a medical term, it meant to "restore to good order," thus "to heal." This is the meaning of "controlling" the vital breath in order to preserve its good order and thus make life and good health possible. The term *qi* "vital breath," as we have seen, is a primary philosophical concept requiring different translations as the context varies. Xunzi held that it is part of all vital things since fire and water possess it, as do all living things ("Wangzhi," 9.16).

According to contemporary cosmology, refined *qi* rose to form the heavens, and the grosser *qi* sank to form the earth. In the creation of all things and in the processes of the earth, the masculine Yang principle and the feminine Yin principle had interacted with the *qi* to form all living things. Man, being in the middle of the cosmic scheme, was a mixture of both, his body of the earthly *qi* to which it returned at death and his heart and mind of the rarefied *qi*. The distinction between the *bo* 魄 animal soul and the *hun* 魂 spiritual soul expressed the division between the Yin and Yang in the human. Blood being neither solid nor ethereal, lay between them, partaking of both, and was thus the basis of man's temperament, his emotions, his qualities of mind and character. Thus, control of the vital breath offered access to every aspect of man's nature and life.

The "Neiye" 內業 of the *Guanzi* explains how this is accomplished. The "seminal essence," when present within the person, "gives life naturally."[5] It acts as the fountainhead when stored up within. "Being harmonious and tranquil, it acts as the wellspring for the vital breath. So long as the wellspring does not dry up, the four parts of the body will remain firm." You must "concentrate the vital breath until you become like a spirit and the myriad things are complete within you." This enables you to comprehend even those matters that are not easily understood even through divination or through the power of the spirits themselves. Your knowing comes "through the utmost development of the seminal essence and vital breath." When this has been done, you can "unify your intellect and concentrate your mind" so that "though it be distant," the Way "will seem close" (*Guanzi*, 49 "Neiye," 16.4a–5a).

"Controlling the vital breath" is sometimes interpreted in a more mundane fashion as "breath control." Breath control was indeed one of several techniques thought to nurture life. Others were various sexual regimens, breathing techniques, physical exercises, and dietary restrictions, many of which continue in popular form today. Although we may be certain that Xunzi would have had nothing to do with sexual regimens, given the general abhorrence with which the Ru viewed such matters, and reasonably confident that he did not endorse physical exercises and dietary restrictions, we cannot absolutely exclude breathing exercises. It may be that "unifying the intellect" and "concentrating the mind" rested on the technique of "sitting in forgetfulness," which entailed meditation, severing the mind's connections with the limbs and body, dismissing the distractions of the senses, detaching the mind from the bodily frame, and expelling "knowledge" from the mind.[6]

The "Keyi" 刻意 of the *Zhuangzi* mentions the special terms used to designate particular breathing techniques: "To pant, to puff, to hail, to sip, to cast out old breath and induct the new, bear hangings and bird stretchings, with no aim but long life—such is the wont of the Inducer, nurturer of the bodily frame, aspirant to Patriarch's high longevity."[7] Unfortunately we do not know what technique was involved with each of these special terms.[8] But the author of the "Keyi" regarded such techniques as linked with the mere nurture of the bodily frame and not with nurture of life. As such, they were unimportant since there were men who "lived to great old age, though they never practiced Induction."

Similarly, the *Daode jing* (10) recommends: "Be intent on regulating your animal soul and spiritual soul and hold fast to unity so that it can be kept from separating. Concentrate the vital breath so that it will become soft and you will become like a babe."[9] But to try merely "to prolong life is ominous, and to let the mind try to direct the vital breath is violence. Whatever has reached its full maturity begins its decline to old age. We call these practices contrary to the Way, and what is contrary to the Way soon dies" (*DDJ*, 55).

Since Xunzi specifically links "controlling the vital breath" to "cultivating your character and strengthening your self," it seems likely that he meant something akin to the doctrines described in the "Neiye" and *Daode jing* rather than the physical breath control condemned in the "Keyi" of the *Zhuangzi*. Xunzi cites the example of Patriarch Peng 彭祖 to show the reality of longevity when one utilizes the proper method. Patriarch Peng serves in Chinese literature the same function as Nestor in

Greek and Methusaleh in Biblical literature. Confucius mentions that Peng was "faithful to and loved the Ancients" (*LY*, 7.1). It was said that he obtained mastery of the Way and lived from the time of Ancestor Shun 舜 to the time of the Five Lords-Protector, more than a millennium.[10]

Nurturing the Mind. Closely linked with the concept of nurturing life was the doctrine of "nurturing the mind." Here, the *xin* 心 "mind, heart" means not the ordinary brain, but the ruler of the body, the seat of nobility that urges man toward good and curbs the disruptive tendencies of the desires. Mencius (7B.35) observed that "there is nothing better for nurturing the mind than to reduce the number of one's desires." One method of doing so involved making proper use of the blood humour, the aspirations of the will, and foresight. One must take steps to conserve the vital breath that permeates the whole body and is responsible for all mental activity. If the desires are not controlled, then the vital breath is consumed uselessly in worry and fretting.

Xunzi uses the technical term *mao* 耗 "bewilderment" for dissipation of the vital breath through disorganization and lack of clear aims. Such "bewilderment" is the opposite of "control" and "order." It arises from the absence of the "unity of purpose" that he stressed in "Exhortation to Learning." "Bewilderment" diminishes the capacity of the mind and senses, producing dullness of vision and hearing with the confusion that results. It is produced by the failure to observe the natural and rational limits on behavior embedded in ritual and moral principles.

"Bewilderment" is also a technical term involving control of the vital breath. The *Huainanzi* (1.17b) points out that it is by repose, mental as well as physical, that the vital breath is conserved and retained. Persons who are impetuous in action, undisciplined in thought, and vehement in their emotions each day waste their life energy and so grow old prematurely. Excess of sensations also creates confusion and disorder because the five colors bring confusion to the eye, the five flavors to the mouth, the emotions of liking and hating to the mind, and this confusion and disorder, through the lack of control involved, cause the dissipation and exhaustion of the life energy (*HNZ*, 7.3b). Hence, bewilderment is not only unfortunate in its social consequences, it is deadly to the individual afflicted with it.

Xunzi prescribes ritual principles as the cure for bewilderment. Ritual provides the controls necessary to produce order in three things: *xueqi* 血氣 "blood humour," *zhiyi* 志意 "aspirations and ambitions," and *zhilü* 知慮 "knowledge and foresight." As Xunzi explains in his "Discourse on Ritual Principles" (19.1), ritual enables one to achieve satisfaction while preserving order within oneself and in society at large.

The "blood humour" is responsible for one's physical prowess and for the temperament that is derived from it. It is detectable as the pulse, which may be strong and vigorous or weak and declining. Although the term *xueqi* sometimes means merely "blood and breath," in this context it is best to translate *qi* by the archaic medical term "humour," which also originally meant "vapor, moisture." It is thus quite close in meaning to *qi*, and it has the advantage of a physiological meaning analogous to the Chinese. Confucius pointed out that the gentleman was careful to pay proper attention to the blood humour in regulating his behavior: "In youth, before his blood humour has settled down, he guards against avarice" (*LY*, 16.7).

By *zhiyi*, "aspirations and ambitions," Xunzi means the mental processes involved in projecting organized actions into the future and in forming a concept of their effects. These processes of projecting memory in the formation of wishes and goals were higher-level mental operations. The blood humour gave rise to the temperament of the individual. Within this, there arose the *qi* "sentiments," which might be noble or base. Music could move and stir these sentiments in men's hearts ("Yuelun," 20.1). The *zhiyi*, "aspirations and ambitions," combined intention and thought with such sentiment. The word *zhi* 志 meant "intention, ambition, aspiration," but it equally meant "memory." So, too, *yi* 意 meant "thought, intellect," but equally "intention, wish." Thus, in the "Discourse on Ritual Principles" (19.11), Xunzi remarks that sacrifice originates in the emotions stirred by *zhiyi* "remembrance of and longing for" the dead. Such processes are not inherited, but are the product of acculturation. "The people of Wu and Yue speak languages that are not mutually intelligible and have *zhiyi* ambitions and aspirations that cannot be communicated to each other, but when they are in the same boat amid mountainous waves, they rescue one another as though they were one people" (*ZGC*, 10.17b).

The highest-level mental processes were called *zhilü*, "knowing and foreseeing." These involved perceiving and recognizing, analyzing and classifying, then deliberating and pondering in order to project and anticipate future events. In Ru thinking, the Classics provided the materials necessary for perceiving and recognizing and for analyzing and classifying. In Xunzi's thinking, they, above all the *Rituals*, contained the logical categories on which knowledge of things was based. Philosophers of other traditions often rejected these mental processes. Shen Dao was "not taught by knowledge and foresight, did not recognize a before and after, but simply stayed put where he was" (*Zhuangzi*, 33 "Tianxia," 10.17b). A sagacious ruler "does not depend on knowledge and foresight," teaches the *Shangjun shu* (1.9a), but "creates unity among his people, and they will thus not scheme after private gain." But Mencius (6B.16) inquires whether Yuezheng Ke 樂正克 had "knowledge and foresight enough" for an official position. As the *Huainanzi* (18.1b) notes, "knowledge and foresight are the doorways to fortune and misfortune; activity and repose are the pivot on which turn benefit and harm."

Philosophical Controversies. The last part of this book turns to the problems of philosophical argument that characterized the dialecticians of the day. Debates over the nature of language and the relation of language to reality had arisen out of Ru debates on man's nature and out of the Mohist desire to defend propositions such as "to kill a robber is not to kill a man" against the attack of opponents who disputed whether they loved all men universally, as they claimed, if they were willing to execute robbers, who were, after all, men. Mo Di himself had made a precise distinction between the words "attack" (*gong* 攻) and "punish" (*zhu* 誅) to condemn aggression and yet condone punitive expeditions such as those of the Sage Di Ancestor Yu against the Miao 苗.[11] From such Mohist argumentation, many important logical discoveries were made, and a distinct group of Mohists specialized in logical problems.

A similar movement arose out of legal discussion. With the publication of the first law codes, need for precise distinctions arose, and their absence was often exploited by clever men. The first to achieve fame for this was Deng Xi, a contemporary of Prince Chan of Zheng, who published the first law code. Later we find philosophers who specialized in argumentation for its own sake. The significance of these various disputes is suggested by the preface Lu Sheng (fl. A.D. 291) wrote to the Mohist *Canons* of logic, which he edited:

Named entities must possess shape. No procedure for examining the shape compares with that of differentiating "shape" from "color." Thus, there exists the disputation concerning "hard and white." Names must possess evident distinctions. No distinction is more evident than that between "existence" and "nonexistence." Thus, there exists the disputation concerning the "dimensionless." The "correct" possesses the "not correct"; the "admissible" possesses the "not admissible." This is called the "admissibility of both alternatives." There are differences even among the similar and similarities even among the different. This is referred to as disputing "identity and difference."[12]

Xunzi frequently mentions these disputes but always to condemn them because they cannot be concluded. In several books, he criticizes particular disputations that he regards as vain or foolish.

Hard and White. Yang Liang identifies the "hard and white" 堅白 dispute with the famous argument of Gongsun Long, a contemporary of Xunzi's. Yang cites a passage from the "Discourse on Hard and White":

Is it admissible to regard "hard," "white," and "stone" [of the term "hard white stone"] as three items? I say that it would be inadmissible to do so. We may say that when the eye beholds a stone, it perceives only the "white" of the stone, but is not aware that it is "hard." As far as it is concerned, the stone may be referred to as a "white stone." If the hand squeezes a stone, it is aware that it is "hard," but not that it is "white." As far as the hand is concerned, the stone may be called a "hard stone." This being the case, in the final analysis, it is inadmissible to conjoin "hard and white" into a single thing.

Yang notes that the commentator Sima Biao 司馬彪 (A.D. 240–305) says that "hard and white" refers to the two propositions "a hard stone is not a stone" and "a white horse is not a horse." Recent scholarship suggests that the "Discourse on Hard and White" in the extant *Gongsun Longzi* is a forgery and that the original dispute concerned separating concepts that in commonsense terms were thought to be inseparable, such as the "hardness" from the stone and the "whiteness" from the horse. The view of Sima Biao is, then, probably correct in regard to this passage of the *Xunzi*.[13]

Identity and Difference. "Identity and difference" 同異 is one of the famous paradoxes of the Logicians, principally associated with Hui Shi, but also discussed by Gongsun Long. Yang Liang says that in the *Xunzi* "identity and difference" refers to "treating different entities as though they were identical and identical entities as though they were different." He quotes an alternate opinion contending that the "identity and difference" paradox was the same as the "similarity on a large scale and similarity on a minor scale" discussed in the *Zhuangzi* (33 "Tianxia," 10.20b). Yang Liang explains:

"'Similarity on a large scale' differs from a similarity on a minor scale, which is what is meant by 'similarity and difference in regard to minor points.'" This passage means that they are the same in that they exist in the interval between heaven and earth, which is called their "similarity on a large scale." Things all possess aspects in which they are the same, which is called "similarity on the minor scale."

"The myriad things being collectively similar and collectively different is called 'similarity and difference on the large scale.'"[14] This refers to the myriad of things as a whole being called "things." No one of them will not be the same in regard to the whole. This constitutes "the myriad of things being collectively similar and collectively different." If they are separated and distinguished from one another, the senses and faculties of men will make of them "grass," "trees," "leaves," "flowers," and other entities. Nothing will not in regard to the whole be different, which constitutes "the myriad of things being collectively different." These all take part in "sameness" and in "difference," and accordingly this is called "similarity and difference on the large scale."

Dimension and Dimensionless. "Dimension and dimensionless" 厚無厚 refers to yet another of the paradoxes of Hui Shi. The term "dimension" means commonly "to have thickness," and "dimensionless" "to be without thickness." "What is without thickness cannot be piled up, yet its extension can cover 1,000 *li*" (*Zhuangzi*, 33 "Tianxia," 10.20b). The idea is that things without thickness, even when piled on top of each other, cannot accumulate any thickness, this being a characteristic only of things that do possess thickness. Yet, though without thickness, such a thing can, like a geometric plane, be extended to cover 1,000 *li*. Although it lacks one dimension, the other two can be extended indefinitely to cover the whole earth. Zhong Tai argues that this paradox is more properly associated with Deng Xi than with Hui Shi since it is the title of one of his works.[15]

In pursuit of paradoxes, these men wasted their energies in vain and idle efforts. True knowledge is not attained thereby. Xunzi did not see the pursuit of knowledge for its own sake as contributing to self-cultivation. Self-cultivation must rest on ritual, which provided the model, and on following one's teacher, who kept ritual principles rectified. Xunzi's view stresses that the outcome of self-cultivation is socialization as a scholar, a gentleman, or, at the highest, a sage. It is not the cultivation of the individual self that Westerners esteem.

TEXT

2.1

When a man sees good, being filled with delight, he is sure to preserve it within himself. When he sees what is not good, being filled with sorrowful apprehension, he is certain to search for it within himself.[16] When he finds what is good within himself, with a sense of firm resolve he is sure to cherish its being there. When he sees what is not good within himself, filled with loathing,[17] he must hate that it is there. As of old, those who consider me to be in the wrong and are correct in doing so are my teachers; those who consider me to be in the right and are correct are my friends; but those who flatter me and toady after me are my malefactors.[18] Thus, the gentleman esteems his teachers, is intimate with his friends, that he might thereby utterly despise his malefactors. He never tires of cherishing what is good. He accepts reproofs and is able to take guard from their warnings. So even if he had no desire at all for advancement, how could he help but succeed!

The petty man is just the opposite. Despite his utter disorderliness, he hates for men to consider him in the wrong; despite his utter unworthiness, he desires that men should consider him worthy. Though his heart is like that of tigers and wolves and his behavior like that of wild beasts,[19] he nonetheless also despises those who are his malefactors. Intimate with flatterers and sycophants, he is estranged from those who would reprove or admonish him. His cultivation of uprightness becomes ludicrous and his complete loyalty injurious.[20] So though he wants to avoid death and destruction, how could he help but come to them! An Ode says:[21]

> They league together, they slander;[22]
> I am filled with grief at this.
> When counsels are good,
> they all act against them.
> When counsels are bad,
> they all cleave to them.

This expresses my meaning.

2.2

If you employ the measure of excellence in every circumstance[23] to control the vital breath and nourish life, you will outlive[24] even Patriarch Peng, and if you use it to cultivate your character and strengthen your self, you will establish a reputation equal to that of Yao or Yu.[25] It is suitable to living in times of success and beneficial when dwelling in impoverished circumstances.[26] This measure is ritual principles and being trustworthy.

In general, when the use a man makes of his blood humour, his aspirations and ambitions, and his knowledge and foresight

follow the requirements of ritual principles, good order penetrates every aspect of his activity. But when this is not so, then his actions become unreasonable and disorderly, dilatory and negligent.[27] When one's food and drink, clothing and dress, dwelling and home, activity and repose follow the dictates of ritual, they are harmonious and measured.[28] But when they do not, they become offensive and excessive and so will produce illness. If one's manner and appearance, bearing and deportment, entrances and exits, and one's rapid steps[29] proceed according to ritual principles, they will be cultured. But when they do not, they will seem arrogant and obstinate,[30] depraved and perverted, utterly commonplace and savage.[31] Thus, a man without ritual will not live; an undertaking lacking ritual will not be completed; and a nation without ritual will not be tranquil.[32]

An Ode says:[33]

> Their rituals and ceremonies are exact,
> their laughter and talk directly to the point.

This expresses my meaning.

2.3

To lead others with what is good is called "education." To agree with others for the sake of what is good is called "concord." To lead others with what is not good is called "flattery." To agree with others in the interests of what is not good is called "toadying." To recognize as right what is right and as wrong what is wrong is called "wisdom." To regard as wrong what is right and as right what is wrong is called "stupidity." "Slander" is doing injury to an honorable man; "malefaction" is doing him harm.[34] "Straightforwardness" is calling right what is right and wrong what is wrong.[35] "Robbery" is stealing property; "deceit" is concealing conduct; and "boasting" is treating words lightly. One whose inclinations and aversions are unsettled is called "inconstant." One who protects personal profit at the expense of abandoning his moral duty is called "utterly malicious." One who has heard much is "broad"; one who has heard little is "shallow." One who has seen much is "cultivated"; one who has seen little is "provincial."[36] He who has difficulty obtaining advancement in office is "dilatory"; and he who easily forgets is "oblivious."[37] One who, though he does only a few things, obeys natural principles in organizing what he does is "well ordered"; one who, though he does many things, lacks any principle of organization in what he does is "bewildered."

2.4
The Art of Controlling the Vital Breath and Nourishing the Mind[38]

If the blood humour is too strong and robust, calm it with balance and harmony. If knowledge and foresight are too penetrating and deep, unify them with ease and sincerity.[39] If the impulse to daring and bravery is too fierce and violent, stay it with guidance and instruction.[40] If the quickness of the mind and the fluency of the tongue are too punctilious and sharp, moderate them in your activity and rest. What is so narrow and restricted that it has become mean and petty, broaden with liberality and magnanimity. What is base and low from greed for selfish gain,[41] lift up with a sense of high purpose. What is common and mediocre, worthless and undisciplined, overcome with the help of teachers and friends.[42] What is negligent and self-indulgent, frivolous and heedless, warn against with omens and portents.[43] What is simpleminded but sincere,[44] upright and diligent, consolidate with ritual and music. [What is...], make comprehensive with thought and inquiry.[45] In summary, of all the methods of controlling the vital breath and nourishing the mind, none is more direct than proceeding according to ritual principles, none more essential than obtaining a good teacher, and none more intelligent than unifying one's likes.[46] Truly this procedure may properly be called "the method of controlling the vital breath and nourishing the mind."

2.5

If a person cultivates his will and sense of purpose, he can take more pride in them than in riches and eminence. If he gives due weight to the Way and what is congruent with it, he will have slight regard for kings and dukes. Absorbed in the examination of his inner self, he will scorn mere external things. A tradition expresses this:

The gentleman works external things; the petty man works for external things.[47]

Do whatever causes the mind to be serene, though it gives the body toil, and whatever causes one's sense for what is right to develop, though it diminishes the concern for profit. Serving a disruptive lord and being successful is not as good as serving an impoverished lord and being obedient in such service.[48] Accordingly, just as a good farmer does not fail to plow because of flooding and drought, or a good merchant does not fail to go to the marketplace because of occasional losses on the sale of his goods, so, too, the scholar and gentleman do not neglect the Way because of poverty and want.

2.6

If your deportment is respectful and reverent, your heart loyal and faithful, if you use only those methods sanctioned by ritual principles and moral duty, and if your emotional disposition is one of love and humanity,[49] then though you travel throughout the empire, and though you find yourself reduced to living among the Four Yi 夷 tribes, everyone would consider you to be an honorable person.[50] If you strive to be the first to undertake toilsome and bitter tasks and can leave pleasant and rewarding tasks to others, if your are proper, diligent, sincere, and trustworthy, if you take responsibility and oversee it meticulously, then wherever you travel in the civilized world and though you find yourself reduced to living with the Four Tribes, everyone would be willing to entrust you with official duties. But if your deportment is insolent and obstinate, if your heart is sly and deceptive, if your methods accord with blackly impure principles,[51] if your emotional disposition is confused and vile,[52] then wherever you travel in the world, even to the farthest directions, everyone will regard you with contempt. If you are evasive and timorous, if you shun and avoid toilsome and bitter tasks, if you are cleverly persuasive and shrewdly eager,[53] adaptable and accommodating, in seeking out rewarding and pleasant tasks, if you are depraved and perverted, if you are not diligent and do not conscientiously perform your regular tasks and duties,[54] then though you travel throughout the world, even to the farthest directions, everyone will cast you out.

2.7

He does not walk with his hands folded respectfully before him because he fears that he may soil his sleeves in the mud.[55] Nor does he walk with his head bowed because he is worried that he may collide with something.[56] He is not the first to lower his eyes when he encounters a colleague out of fear and trepidation. The scholar behaves in this way because he desires only to cultivate his own person and incur no blame from the common folk of his neighborhood.

2.8

Qiji could cover 1,000 *li* in a single day, but if a worn-out nag takes the journey in ten stages, then it, too, can cover the distance.[57] Are you going to try to exhaust the inexhaustible and pursue the boundless? If you do, then though you break your bones and wear out your flesh in the attempt, in the end it will be impossible to reach your goal. But if you undertake a journey that has an end, then though it be 1,000 *li* or more, whether quickly or slowly, before others or after them, how could you be unable to reach the goal! Will you be one of those who unwittingly marches along the road attempting to exhaust the inexhaustible and pursue the boundless? Or will you rather undertake only what has an end? Such problems as "hard and white," "identity and difference," and "dimension and dimensionless" are not inherently unexaminable, but the gentleman nonetheless does not engage in debate concerning them because he places them beyond the boundary of his endeavors.[58] It is not that performing strange and extraordinary feats is not difficult,[59] nonetheless the gentleman does not perform them because he places them beyond the boundary of his endeavors. Hence it is said:

Learning is slow-going.[60] That stopping place awaits us. If we set out for it and proceed toward the goal, though some will move quickly and others slowly, though some will lead the way and others follow, how could we all not be able to reach the same goal!

Thus,

moving ahead step by step and not resting, a lame turtle can go 1,000 *li*.

Pile up earth basket by basket and do not quit, and in the end a high mound will be completed.[61]

If you dam up their sources and open up their sluices, even the Yangtze and Yellow River can be drained dry.

With one advancing and another retreating, one moving to the left and another to the right, the six horses would get nowhere.[62]

Surely the natural abilities of men do not differ so widely as a lame turtle and the six horses, yet the lame turtle reaches the goal and the six horses do not. There is no other reason for this than that the one acts and the other does not.

2.9[63]

Though the Way is near, if you do not travel along it, you will not reach the end.

Though the task is small, if it is not acted upon, it will not be completed.

One who spends many days in idleness will not excel others by much.[64]

2.10

He who acts from a love of the model is a scholar.[65] He who embodies it with a firm sense of purpose is a gentlemen.[66] He who has an understanding of it that is acute without limit is a sage.[67] If a man lacks the model, he acts with rash and aimless confusion. If he possesses the model, but has no recognition of what is congruent with it, he nervously looks about, anxiously wondering what to do.[68] Only after he has come to rely on the model and then gone on to penetrate deeply into its application through analogical extension to other categories and types of things does he act with gentle warmth and calm confidence.

2.11

It is through ritual that the individual is rectified. It is by means of a teacher that ritual is rectified. If there were no ritual, how could the individual be rectified? If there were no teachers, how could you know which ritual is correct?

When what ritual mandates, you make so in your conduct, then your emotions will find peace in ritual. When what your teacher says you say also, then your knowledge will be like that of your teacher. When your emotions find peace in ritual and your knowledge is like that of your teacher, then you will become a sage. Hence to oppose ritual is the same as lacking a model. To oppose your teacher is the same as being without a teacher. Not to hold correct your teacher and the model, but to prefer instead to rely on your own notions is to employ a blind man to differentiate colors or a deaf person to distinguish sounds—you have nothing with which to reject confusion and error.[69] Therefore one who is in the process of learning is one who learns of ritual principles and of the model.[70] The teacher is one who makes his own person an erect gnomon indicating the proper standard of deportment and who values what is at peace with him. An Ode says:[71]

> Not from knowledge, not from wisdom,
> were you obedient to the Di Ancestor's rules.

This expresses my meaning.[72]

2.12

If you are straightforward and diligent, obedient and respectful of your elders, you are properly called a "good youth." If you add to these a love of learning combined with modesty and earnestness, then[73] you may properly be considered a gentleman. But if you are evasive, timorous, and shirk your duties, if you lack any sense of modesty or shame and have an inordinate fondness for food and drink as well, you are properly called a "despicable youth." If you add to these profligacy, cruelty, disobedience, treachery, malice, and disrespectfulness to elders, then you are properly called an "ill-omened youth." Although you may suffer dismemberment or death as punishment, it is entirely proper that it should be so.

Mature adults will flock to one who treats the elderly as they should be treated.[74] Successful men will congregate around one who does not place hardships on those already having difficulties.[75] If one conducts himself in obscurity and is kind when no recognition will result, then the worthy and unworthy alike will unite about him. A person who possess these three qualities, though he be sent a greatly inauspicious omen,[76] would Heaven have wrought his ruin?[77]

2.13

The gentleman treats summarily the pursuit of profit but is alert to keeping out of harm's way. He is apprehensive about avoiding disgrace but is courageous in conducting himself in accordance with the Way and the requirements of reason.

2.14

In times of hardship and poverty, the gentleman broadens his sense of purpose. In times of prosperity and honor, he comports himself with respectfulness. When tranquil and at ease, his blood humour is not enfeebled. In times of fatigue and exhaustion, his appearance is not slovenly.[78] He does not commit the excess of snatching things back out of anger or that of giving things away out of joy. The gentleman can broaden his sense of purpose even in times of hardship and poverty because he exalts the principle of humanity.[79] He is able to comport himself with respectfulness toward others even when he is wealthy and honored because he deprecates the power and influence that accompany them.[80] His blood humour is not enfeebled when he is tranquil and at ease because he is restrained by natural order.[81] His appearance is not slovenly in times of fatigue and exhaustion because he is fond of good form.[82] He does not commit the excess of snatching things back out of anger or that of giving things away out of joy because the model triumphs over merely private interest. One of the *Documents* says:

> Nothing have which predilections create,
> Follow the way of the King.
> Nothing have which aversions cause,
> Follow the King's road.[83]

This says that the gentleman's ability consists in his use of a sense of common good to triumph over merely personal desires.

BOOK 3

■ ■ |||||||||||||||||||||||||||||||||||||||||||||||||||||||||||||||||||||||||||||||||||||||||||||||||||||||||||||||||||||||||||||||||||||||||||||||| ■ ■

Nothing Indecorous

INTRODUCTION

We cannot with a single English word indicate Xunzi's theme in this book. The meaning of *gou* 苟 is "indecorous," and it applies to whatever is "unsuitable," thus to "unbecoming" behavior, "indecorous" conduct, "unseemly" actions. In the course of an interview with an envoy from Lu, Confucius' home state, an important minister in the royal court allowed that he was not fond of learning. When this was reported to a minister of Lu, he observed:

The kingdom of Zhou is going to face disorders. There must be many who engage in such talk because otherwise it would not have reached into the ranks of their great men. Great men, being troubled at deficiencies in learning, have become deluded, till they say: "It is quite permissible to lack learning because a lack of learning does not produce any harm." But if a lack of learning should not cause any harm, it can only result from a *gou* fluke circumstance.

(*Zuo*, Zhao 18)

In terms of difficult feats, *gou* implies that they are lacking in good judgment; in terms of argumentation, that a sound basis is missing; in terms of reputation, that it is undeserved and questionable. The *Shangjun shu* (4.14a) observes that what is meant by morality is "when ministers are loyal, sons filial, when there are proper ceremonies observed between juniors and seniors, proper distinctions between men and women, when a hungry man eats and a dying man lives, not *gou* improperly, but only in accordance with a sense of what is right." So, too, Mencius (6A.10) notes that though he loves life, "there is my sense of morality, which I value more"; if one must be given up, "I will let life go and choose morality," because "I will not seek to possess life by any *gou* improper means." When Confucius was unable to get the ruler of Lu to follow his advice, he left on the pretext of a minor slight at a sacrifice because he "preferred to be slightly at fault in this leaving rather than to appear to leave without some apparent cause *gou*" (*Mengzi*, 6B.6). What is *gou* indecorous is in conflict with one's moral duty, what occurs as a fluke or without cause.

Arthur Waley delineates the whole range of meanings of *gou*:

The Chinese have a special word for things done "after a fashion" . . . but not according to the proper ritual. What is done in this way may seem for the moment to "work," . . . but the gentleman's code, like that of the old-fashioned artisan, compels him to "make a good job" of whatever he undertakes. A temporary success secured by irregular means gives him no satisfaction; it is stolen, not honestly come by. *Gou* . . . is used when things are done "somehow or other," in a "hit or miss" offhand fashion, when everything is "left to chance." . . . It applies wherever a result is achieved by mere accident and not as a result of inner power (*de*).[1]

In this book, Xunzi characterizes foolhardy acts, sophistry, and notoriety as *gou* indecorous because they are "contrary to the mean of behavior prescribed by ritual and moral principles." In doing so, he is in accord with a long tradition amply attested in the *Analects, Zuo zhuan, Shangjun shu,* and the *Mencius.*

This book is the first of three books that date to the later periods of Xunzi's life and are related in concept and outlook. From his return to the restored Jixia Academy, Xunzi found himself faced with attacks on Ru doctrines from every direction. This in itself was nothing new. What was new, and to Xunzi very distressing, was that these attacks now seemed convincing to some Ru, who incorporated the ideas into their teachings. Xunzi regarded some of these as pernicious and wrongheaded ideas and felt obliged to attack them directly.

One of these was the concept of martyrdom to a high ideal. The vivid spectacle of men committing suicide on behalf of some principle captured the popular imagination. Men, as Nietzsche put it, demand a picturesque effect of the truth and expect a lover of knowledge to make a strong impression on the senses. Xunzi opposed such sentiments. More insidious still, and equally widespread, was the effect of dialecticians, who often created their reputations by the ingenuity of their arguments. They would sometimes maintain, just for effect, positions that flatly contradicted common sense. They delighted in arguing with such extraordinary skill that they silenced their unconvinced opponents. For some this was merely a means of showing off their rhetorical skills. A few were known to be able and willing to advocate any position on any question. These men Xunzi condemned.

The Suicide of Shentu Di. Xunzi cites the notorious example of Shentu Di as an illustration of indecorous conduct. Regretting that the Way was not followed, says Yang Liang, Shentu Di became exasperated and, carrying a stone on his back, drowned himself. The *Hanshi waizhuan* (1.12a) says that Cui Jia 崔嘉, hearing of his intention, tried to stop him, but to no avail. Shentu Di was one of a number of semilegendary paragons who committed suicide rather than continue to live in an immoral and decaying world where merit and personal virtue went unrecognized. He is mentioned along with several other figures in the *Zhuangzi* (6 "Da-zongshi," 3.3a), some of whom lived at the end of the Shang dynasty. Commentators therefore tended to date him to that period as well.[2] Liu Taigong observed that in his reply to Cui Jia, Shentu Di mentions that the state of Wu executed Wu Zixu and that Chen killed Xie Ye 泄冶, both of whom lived during the middle Zhou period.[3] The literary motif of committing suicide seems to have become popular during the late fourth century, the foremost example being Qu Yuan, who, clasping a stone to his breast, threw himself in the Milo River and drowned (*SJ*, 84.18). A number of other figures also committed suicide at the end of the Zhou dynasty. Kubo Ai suggests that Shentu was a title, meaning in the early Han period "minister of instruction." Several people with the name Shentu, perhaps deriving from an official title, were active during the late Zhou and early Han periods.

Xunzi, as Yang Liang observed, believed that "when the occasion requires that he stop, the gentleman stops; when it requires that he act, he acts; but it certainly never requires that he cause himself to wither away in starvation or to drown in the deep." Yang Xiong, troubled by the popularity of the suicide of Qu Yuan, asked in his "Essay Against Qu Yuan": "Why must the gentleman, whether he meets with the great change [the death of a sovereign or parent] or encounters dragons [good men], ever drown himself?"[4] With this sentiment, Xunzi concurred.

The Dialecticians and Their Paradoxes. Xunzi found the philosophers of his day bewitched by abstruse conundrums that baffled their intellect and distracted them from the serious pursuit of knowledge and from the self-cultivation that alone could make them gentlemen. Some of these men were interested only in rhetorical effect, silencing the tongues of others without winning their hearts. They were intent on rendering the intellect of others powerless, as Nietzsche complained of the dialectic of Socrates, on making them furious and helpless at the same time, and on making their opponents seem like idiots.

Xunzi would allow that some of these arcane philosophical arguments had serious import and examined abstract and difficult problems of logic. From these men Xunzi himself learned much. But too often their arguments were difficult to distinguish from the frivolous though clever distinctions that the dialecticians made to support their sophistries. Xunzi cites six such sophistries, which he associates with Hui Shi and Deng Xi.

"Mountains and abysses are level" 山淵平 is a paradox also identified with Hui Shi in the *Zhuangzi*, where it is linked with the second paradox mentioned by Xunzi, "Heaven and Earth are comparable" 天地比. It is generally thought that the purpose of these paradoxes is to indicate spatial relativity. Yang Liang says that "comparable" means that Heaven and Earth are "equal" in level. He cites the explanation of Lu Deming 陸德明: "If you take the level of the earth and compare it with that of the heavens, then earth is lower than the heavens, but were you to compare them from the heights of the Empyrean, then both the heavens and earth would appear low: If the heavens and earth were both low, then mountains would be on a level with marshes." Lu is, of course, commenting on the alternate reading of the paradoxes in the *Zhuangzi*, but Yang is correct in regarding the paradoxes as fully equivalent.

Yang also cites another explanation identified by Lu Wenchao as that of Zhang Zhan (fl. A.D. 370):

The heavens lack substantial form. Above the earth is the Void, the totality of which is the heavens. This constitutes the everlasting relationship of Heaven and Earth. It is the mutual accord of them wherein they are comparable. Without the height of the heavens, the earth below would be destroyed. Viewed from a high mountain, the heavens still appear high; viewed from a deep abyss, they also appear low. Thus, it is said that "Heaven and Earth are comparable." Earth went away from Heaven, but whether nearby or faraway, they resemble each other. This is the meaning of "mountains and marshes are level."

A third explanation is offered by Sun Yirang 孫詒讓, who takes "comparable" to mean "close" in space: "Heaven and Earth, being opposed to each other, originally separated from one another and became far apart, yet they may be said to be close to each other, just as mountains and marshes though originally not level may be called level. All of these statements were paradoxes propounded by the Logicians on the theme of 'joining the same and different.'"[5] It is evident that these two paradoxes are also related to the statement made by the God of the Northern Sea to the River Spirit in the *Zhuangzi*: "Heaven and Earth are as small as a grain of the smallest rice, and the tip of a hair is as vast as a mountain mass."[6]

Lu Deming is certainly correct in observing that from the heights of the Empyrean the height of the sky wherein weather occurs and the height of the ground are comparable and that from such heights mountains and abysses appear level. Contemporary scholars do not agree on the significance of such relativism. Hu Shi argued that Hui Shi intended to prove the monism of the universe.[7] Indeed, Hui taught that we must "love all things universally because Heaven and Earth are one body" (*Zhuangzi*, 33 "Tianxia," 10.20b). On the other hand, Zhang Binglin (in

Guogu lunheng, pp. 192–94) considered that the paradoxes attempted to demonstrate that all measurement and all spatial distinctions, such as high and low, were unreal and illusory.

"Qi and Qin are adjacent" 齊秦襲 is paradoxical because Qi was the easternmost country and Qin the westernmost, sharing no common border and separated from each other by the rest of the Chinese world. Yang Liang explains that we could accept this assertion were we to consider it from the viewpoint of the vastness of Heaven and Earth, which enclose them. From this perspective, they would appear to be undivided and without differences so that they could be joined together as though a single country. This interpretation links the paradox with the two preceding ones as arguing the relativity of space.

The word translated "adjacent" is understood by Yang in the sense "adjoin" and by Kubo Ai as "neighboring." Kubo Ai suggests that Qi and Qin are like a garment and its lining, which are separated by space but are "close together." Joseph Needham, however, translates "coterminous." Needham (2 : 197) offers the novel suggestion that "the abolition of the intervening states might bring the western state Qin and the eastern state Qi into juxtaposition." I suspect that the meaning of the paradox has something to do with the concept of the limits of space and is thus related to another of Hui Shi's paradoxes: "I know the center of the world—it is north of Yan and south of Yue" (referring to the northernmost and southernmost of the Chinese states [*Zhuangzi*, 33 "Tianxia," 10.20b]).

The paradox "Mountains issue out of mouths" 山出口 is an emendation of the text of the *Xunzi*. Virtually all commentators and editors from Yang Liang to the present agree that the six characters in the present text are excrescent and make no sense in this context. The present reading of the text, "it enters through the ear and comes out through the mouth," parallels language found in paragraph 1.9 above. Needham (2: 196), interpreting the text as it stands, suggests this may involve some epistemological consideration akin to the role of the mind in such paradoxes as "Fire is not hot" and "The eye does not see" (*Zhuangzi*, 33 "Tianxia," 10.21b–22a). It is, however, hard to see what mental operations might be involved in this "paradox," especially since Xunzi, who here is condemning it, used it as a mere commonsense phrase earlier. For this reason, it seems better to adopt the common emendation to "mountains issue from mouths."

Sima Biao interprets this paradox to refer to the fact that when you shout at a mountain, the whole mountain range responds in echo. Following this interpretation, the paradox is sometimes taken to be "mountains possess mouths" 山有口. Here, however, Needham (2 : 197; 3b : 610) offers a striking alternative. "I suggest, instead of the usual explanation about echoes, that it may refer to volcanoes. Mountains may indeed issue from mouths in the earth. The ancient Chinese were living on the edge of the circum-Pacific earthquake and volcanic belt; active volcanoes may possibly have been known to them." It is probable that volcanoes, possibly those in Japan, were known in Xunzi's day. They may have formed part of the geographical knowledge for which Zou Yan was famed.[8]

A. C. Graham (*Later Mohist Logic*, pp. 311–12) links this paradox with disputes about the nature of space. Commenting on three corrupt and defective passages in the Mohist *Canons*, he observes that "it would seem that there must have been sophists who built paradoxes on the assumption that a body can be regarded as filling intervals between the points on its surface. One of the sophisms . . . is a probable example, "Mountains come out of holes." One could think of the surface of the mountain as a hole in the sky, so that it descends out of the hole instead of rising out of the earth." This interpretation takes *kou* 口 "mouth" as "opening, hole."

"Old women have whiskers" 姁有須 is based on the emendation of Yu Yue. So emended, the paradox must refer either to the well-attested fact that older women, as a consequence of physiological changes after menopause, sometimes develop moustaches or to a more general, theoretical change based on sex reversals known among animals and sexual anormalies in man (cf. *Mozi*, 19 "Fei gong" 非攻, III 下, 5.16b). As it stands, the text reads "barbs have hairs," which Yang Liang attempts to equate with "frogs have tails" in the *Zhuangzi*. The *Zhuangzi* paradox involves notions of potentiality and actuality, but it is unclear what "potentiality," akin to the relation of tadpole to frog, barb could have to hairs.[9] It seems likely that the present reading is itself an editorial emendation to make the paradox present an issue of potentiality versus actuality like the paradox that follows.

"Eggs have feathers" 卵有毛 deals with the potential existence of the feathers of the baby chick already being in the egg. Everything that is characteristic of the chicken, which comes from the egg, must also be in the egg.

Hui Shi. In condemning the paradoxes and sophistries of men like Hui Shi and Deng Xi, Xunzi agrees with other schools of thinking. Zhuang Zhou condemned them, the Mohists condemned them, Zou Yan condemned them, and other Ru condemned them. Their objections lay more in the practical effect of such sophistries than in opposition to their logical argument. Since the sophistries of Hui Shi, however serious their original intent, seemed like the sophistical trickery of Deng Xi, Xunzi always links their names together in condemnation ("Fei shier zi," 6.6;

"Ruxiao," 8.3). Men like Hui Shi do not teach, nor do they reform; they are intent only on confounding the minds of men. The *Zhuangzi* (33 "Tianxia," 10.23a) expresses a similar view:

Seen from the point of view of the way of Heaven and Earth, the abilities of Hui Shi were like the laboring of one mosquito or of a single gadfly. Of what use was he to anything? To be sure, he was content with his monism, which was praiseworthy, but I say that had he increased his esteem of the Way, he would have gotten nearer. But Hui could find no tranquillity in this. So he dissipated himself on the myriad things, never being satisfied, and in the end he acquired only a reputation for being the most accomplished dialectician. Alas, Hui Shi for all his talents spent himself in a profusion of efforts that came to naught. His pursuit of the myriad things, from which he would never turn back, was like trying to stop an echo by shouting it down or a form trying to outrace its own shadow. How sad!

Deng Xi. Less is known of Deng Xi than of Hui Shi. He was a grand officer of the state of Zheng in the sixth century. A book that shelters under his name may contain some of his views, but it is generally admitted to be a much later work, possibly even a reconstruction of the fifth century A.D. Men were convinced that Deng Xi "made it his business to raise objections" so that with his lawyerly skills he could "turn the wrong into the right and the right into the wrong" (*LSCQ*, 18/4 "Nanwei" 難謂, 18.8a). Liu Xiang says that "Deng Xi was fond of the doctrine of 'performance and title,' upheld the theory that both of two alternatives were admissible, and devised propositions concerning the inexhaustible" (Liu Xiang, *Bielu*, apud the Yang commentary).

Since "discriminations that do not agree with the natural principles of things are dissimulation and knowledge that does not agree with the natural order of things is deception," the ancient kings regarded such practices as worthy of punishment (*LSCQ*, 18/4 "Liwei," 18.8a). Thus, the legend developed that Prince Chan of Zheng, whose laws Deng Xi distorted, was forced to have him beheaded (Liu Xiang, *Bielu*, apud the Yang commentary). Deng Xi was in fact executed by Si Chuan 駟歂, who had become prime minister in 501, 21 years after the death of Prince Chan. Deng Xi developed a code of penal laws, which was inscribed on bamboo tablets and which Si Chuan nonetheless used after executing him. Later scholars condemned Si Chuan for "casting away the man whose way he employed" (*Zuo*, Ding 9). In condemning Deng Xi and Hui Shi, Xunzi followed the general attitude of his time, but that he was also aware of the significance of their arguments is shown in "Dispelling Blindness" and "On the Correct Use of Names," where he refutes some of their positions.

Xunzi's Concept of the Gentleman. Against the indecorous conduct caused by the doctrines he criticizes, Xunzi argues that the gentleman venerates the inner power in others, celebrates excellence, and corrects and criticizes the faults of others, but never to excess. The gentleman is able to bend or straighten as the occasion demands and knows to keep things in their proper place and perspective; thus, with every step, he doubly moves forward, whereas the petty man twice regresses. The gentleman understands that order can come only from order and so never uses what is contrary to ritual and moral principles. Thus, the gentleman purifies his inner self. His self-purification attracts those whose nature is similar to his own. The gentleman will not subject his own full and clear understanding to the delusions of others. Yang Liang explains that this "full understanding" is one that, in the words of the *Changes* (9.3a), "exhausts the principle of the natural order in the world and contains within all human nature."

Xunzi's Use of Cheng "Truthfulness." Xunzi adapts the concepts of other schools and philosophies to his own doctrines in this book. One of these is *cheng* 誠, an elusive concept central to the *Zhongyong*, "Doctrine of the Mean," which is generally attributed to Confucius' grandson Zisi. Xunzi's language closely parallels that of the *Zhongyong*, which may indicate a debt to the school of Zisi. Few Chinese concepts are more difficult to make precise than *cheng*. In common usage, it means "sincere," what is "true" and "real," and as a verb to "verify" or "examine." It approximates the ideas of "genuine" and "authentic." The *Zhongyong* claims that *cheng* is the way of Heaven. In order to be *cheng*, one must understand what is good. One who has *cheng* effortlessly does what is right and apprehends things without thinking. When understanding results from *cheng*, it results from our inborn nature, but when *cheng* results from understanding, it is because of education. *Cheng* is necessary to fulfill our inborn nature; it is required for self-completion; without it we cannot complete others. It is *cheng* that can *hua* 化 transform us. *Cheng* makes us choose what is good and hold fast to it. Without *cheng* there is nothing. Absolute *cheng* is ceaseless. "Only he who possesses the most perfect *cheng* in the whole world can create the fabric of the great classical pattern for the world, establish the great fundamental of it, and know the transmutations and nurturing operations of Heaven and Earth. . . . Only one as extremely quick in apprehension, as perspicacious in sagelike awareness, as far reaching in the Power of Heaven as he could come to know him" (*Zhongyong*, 32, 16, 20–26).[10] It is apparent that *cheng* transcends "sincerity" to mean what is real, the recognition of the real and the true, truthfulness about things and about oneself, and a genuineness and authenticity that permit no falsity, no pretense, no illusion, no deception. Xunzi argues that being truthful, real, actual, authentic, free from hypocrisy, the mind will be untroubled by thoughts of deceit and will constantly be tranquil. As what has accumulated within a person is manifested in his external appearance, the gentleman's truthfulness will be apparent to all. The *Daxue* (6.2) observes that "what is truly within a man will be made palpable in his external characteristics."

An individual in realizing what he authentically is and being content with his authentic nature can become obedient to his destiny by according with his nature. "Destiny" refers, in Chinese thought, both to the allotted fate decreed by Heaven and to the nature that Heaven has endowed one with and that one must authentically realize. The sage perfects his destiny so that "when he is seen, the people all revere him; when he speaks, they all believe what he says; and when he acts, they are all pleased with what he does" (*Zhongyong*, 31). Such is the *Tiande*, the Power of Heaven.

Tiande, the Power of Heaven. Tiande 天德 is an old but comparatively rare term. It is used in the *Mozi* (27 "Tianzhi" 天志, II 中, 7.10b) to show that the government of the sage kings of the Three Dynasties was beneficial to Heaven above, to the spirits in the middle, and to mankind below. "Being beneficial to these three realms, there were none who did not benefit—this is called the Power of Heaven." The meaning here is the *de* "power" intrinsic in Heaven/Nature, a concept parallel to that of the power inherent in the Way in the *Daode jing*. In the *Zhuangzi* (15 "Keyi," 6.2ab), *tiande* is associated with the character of the sage: "His spirit is calm, his soul unwearied, empty and pure, he is then in agreement with the Power of Heaven." The "empty," "calm," and "pure" mind of the sage allows him to conform to, and join with, the Power inherent in Nature, a concept developed by Xunzi in "Dispelling Blindness," where he argues that since the characteristics of the mind mirror those of the Way, the mind can know the Way, though it is silent.

The Silence of Heaven. In the *Analects* (17.19), Confucius remarks that "Heaven does not speak." The *Daode jing* (23) says that "to speak sparingly is in accord with Nature."[11] Xunzi applies this principle of silence or of "few words" to the gentleman. Here, too, an important Daoist parallel is to be found:

Heaven and Earth have the greatest beauty, but they do not speak of them; the four seasons have clear laws (*fa* 法), but they do not discuss them; the myriad things have intrinsic principles of order (*li* 理) that complete them, but they do not explain them. The sage seeks the source of the beauty of Heaven and Earth and penetrates into the intrinsic principles of all things. For these reasons, the Perfect Man acts with assertion, and the Great Sage does not create. This is called observing Heaven and Earth. (*Zhuangzi*, 22 "Zhibeiyou," 7.23ab)[12]

Nature does not speak, but men can discover its truths. So, too, the gentleman, though he does not speak, is understood.

Xunzi adapts these ideas to his philosophy through four pairs of related terms. He first pairs the principle of humanity (*ren* 仁) with the sense of congruity (*yi* 義). This connection, of course, was not specific to his philosophy but was part of the common inheritance of all schools. The ancient Chinese believed that the basic humanity in all of us expressed itself in the love of individuals (*ren*). Similarly the sense of rightness, congruity, and justice (*yi*) expressed itself in the moral principles that govern our actions. How humanity was expressed might be subject to argument, whether in universal love or love for family or self, and what moral principles should be were contested among the various schools. For Xunzi, it was a sense for what was right that put things in their proper station and gave due measure to manifestations of humanity.

The pairing of humanity and morality is developed in terms of three contrasts, between the appearance or form (*xing* 形) of a thing and the principles of its natural order (*li* 理), between its "spirit" (*shen* 神) and its "brightness" (*ming* 明), and between its transmutation (*hua* 化) and its metamorphosis (*bian* 變). Each of these requires explication.

Chinese has three words that can be translated as "change," *yi* 易, *hua* 化, and *bian* 變. Though one cannot rigidly distinguish between them, especially in common usage, differences in the graphs themselves give insight into the conception fundamental to each word.

Yi as a graph was originally a drawing of a lizard, the idea of change perhaps deriving from the color change of a chameleon or the rapid movements of the lizard as it catches insects. Besides color changes and changes of position, the word means to exchange one thing for another, as when the king of Qi exchanged a sheep for an ox in a sacrifice (*Mengzi*, 1A.7). As change, its meaning encompasses mostly superficial changes like those of color, position, owner, and name.

Hua suggests sudden and complete change, especially of substance, as the transmutation of base metals into gold. It is used for smelting ores into metals, for ice melting into water, for the digestion of food, and to change and reform oneself. In modern usage, it is employed for chemical vocabulary. The idea behind *hua* is usually well translated by "transmutation" or "transformation."

Bian involves changes of weather, of circumstances, of views, the metamorphosis of insects, and gradual alterations of the personality. It is especially associated with changes of form rather than substance and changes involving rearrangement. An important usage is to "alter the laws" (*bian fa* 變法; *SJ*, 68.5), associated with the program of Shang Yang.

One cannot, however, insist on any radical distinction between these words. They could be, and often were, used in all these meanings, but the meanings tended to be specialized, though overlapping. We can see the difference in four passages: (1) "The sage alters (*bian*) with the times, but is not transformed (*hua*); he accords with things, but is not moved" (*Guanzi*, 49 "Neiye," 16.2b). Here the contrast is between the adjustments made necessary by the times in which the sage lives in contrast to any radical transformation of one's self or of one's principles. Thus, altering to adjust to changing circumstances or to new states of things is appropriate to the sage, but transformation and movement are not. (2) "A sage teaches without reforming (*yi*) the people, and the wise man acts without altering (*bian*) the laws" (*Shang jun shu*, 1.2a). Here the contrast is between *yi* "reforming the people," meaning to modify their natures, and *bian* "altering the laws," meaning a wholesale rearrangement or revolution in the laws. (3) "What makes possible transmutation (*hua*) of things into unity is called "spirit" (*shen*); what makes possible transformation (*bian*) of affairs into unity is called wisdom. To transmute (*hua*) and not alter (*yi*) one's vital breath and to transform (*bian*) and not alter (*yi*) one's wisdom—only the gentleman who holds fast to unity can do this!" (*Guanzi*, 49 "Neiye," 16.3a.) Here it is clear that *hua* refers to substantial modification of things without altering their "vital breath" and *bian* to modification of affairs without altering the conclusions, "wisdom," that are to be drawn from them; the contrast between the nature of "concrete things" and that of "events" and "affairs" is parallel to the contrast between *hua* and *bian*. Both are conceived to be more radical changes than the alteration (*yi*) of the vital breath or of wisdom. (4) "*Hua* 'transformation' is the distinguishing characteristic of *yi* general change."[13] To illustrate this point, the Mohists cite the example of a water-frog transmuting into a quail, an imaginary though commonly cited example of change that characterizes the radical, obvious change imposed by *hua*. In the Mohist *Canons*, where terminology is especially rigorous, *hua* entails "change *into*," *bian* "change *to*," and *yi* "change *for*."[14]

The concepts of "transmutation" and "transformation" are linked in the *Xunzi* with *shen* 神, understood by Yang Liang as "spirit-like,"[15] and *ming* 明 "bright." In this choice of wording, Xunzi makes use of ritual language that addresses, particularly in the worship at the altars of soil and grain and in ancestor worship, matters of the spirits. In such contexts, "spirit-like" referred to the magical efficacy of spirits, which made things happen by word or will and without evident causal mechanism.

Ming referred not to "bright," as light is bright, but to the sacred quality of vessels and implements used in ceremonies, where they become numinous, spirit-fraught, and thus effective. The meaning of both is thus parallel, "efficacious (like a spirit)" and "effective (like a ritual implement)" and the contrast between them is analogous to that between *hua* "transformation" and *bian* "metamorphosis." But Xunzi discounted the magical qualities of ritual and disbelieved entirely in the spirit realm. He rejected any notion of a sentient Heaven that might respond to prayers or curses. He endorsed ritual only as an embellishment to life that gave form and expression to our emotions. In the *Xunzi*, *shen* refers to "intelligence" (as in paragraph 2.4 above) or, as here, to things that are rendered "intelligible." *Ming* refers to what is "clear" or has become clear to our understanding. There is nothing magical and nothing mystical.

The third pair of contrasts is between *xing* 形 and *li* 理. *Xing* means "form, appearance" and "to appear, be manifested"; to be given visible form. *Li*, which usually means rational order or the "principle of natural order" in a thing, means here, since it is parallel to *xing*, to give a thing its distinguishing natural marks.

By persisting, things becomes easy for the gentleman because they become part of his very nature. Xunzi expresses this with two concepts, *shen* 慎 and *du* 獨. By *shen* he means "to make genuine," "to be real," "to be as one authentically is." The meaning of *du* is primarily "what is singular to oneself," thus one's innermost feelings and thoughts. Here the meaning is extended to what characterizes oneself alone, what is unique and individual. Combined, they express the singular characteristics of the individual made real, actual, genuine, in short fully, utterly, and authentically to be what one *is*.

The Daoist Sage and Xunzi's Gentleman. During the third century, thinkers of the Daoist persuasion developed technical vocabulary to describe the sage. Their thought is preserved in the *Daode jing* and *Zhuangzi*, as well as in the eclectic Han dynasty *Huainanzi*. Xunzi systematically adapts this technical language used by Daoists to describe the sage to his concept of the gentleman:

Thus the sage ponders the turning and twisting of affairs and simply accommodates himself to them as they bend or unbend, lying back and looking up without possessing any constancy of outward forms of deportment. On some occasions he bends; on others he is rigidly straight. He can be humble, weak, and flexible like rushes and reeds, but this is not the result of any fear of making a decision. He can be unyieldingly strong and fiercely resolute, his sense of purpose sternly pure and noble like a white cloud, but this is not the result of haughtiness. He responds and changes with the requirements of the occasion.

(HNZ, 13.12a)

Rejecting the Daoist notion that the sage has no "constancy of outward forms of deportment," Xunzi asserts that the gentleman must act in accord with ritual principles, humanity, and justice. This is necessary because the gentleman is a social being. His life and his thoughts are tied up with activity within society. He is unprepared to become a recluse, to abandon society, or to retreat into himself. These require that the gentleman be different from the Daoist sage, despite the qualities that they share.

The gentleman holds fast to the Way, realizing that the nature of all men is in a single man, that the beginning of Heaven and Earth are present today, and that the model of all True Kings is to be found in the actions of the Later Kings. But in stressing that the large can be seen in the small, the distant in the near, and the old in the new, Xunzi is again following a precept of Daoist thinking about the knowledge of the sage and adapting it to Ru purposes. The model of the Later Kings is one of the distinctive doctrines of Xunzi. Whereas most philosophers advocated the model of kings who lived at the dawn of history, as Mencius with Yao and Shun, or Mo Di with Yu, or Zhuang Zhou with Huang Di, Xunzi would have the gentleman scrutinize the actions of the kings of more recent history, about whom much was known. With Confucius, Xunzi advocated following the model of the Zhou dynasty. Confucius explains that he did so because the state of Qiy 杞, founded to maintain sacrifices to the ancestors of the Xia dynasty, supplied no adequate evidence for its rituals 禮 and the state of Song 宋, founded to maintain sacrifices to the ancestors of the Shang dynasty, supplied inadequate evidence of its rituals. "The cause is the insufficiency of literary records and of learned men" (*LY*, 3.9). Confucius thus determines that "Zhou has the advantage of surveying these two dynasties. What a wealth of culture this was! I follow Zhou" (*LY*, 3.14).

Stolen Reputations. Xunzi used the doctrine of the model of the later kings to combat the abnormal and detestable state of the world of his day, which was often rationalized by appeal to the doctrines of primordial worthies about whom next to nothing was known. When the rich and eminent were arrogant while the poor and humble starved, it could only be because the world sanctioned "stolen reputations." A world wherein indecorous conduct is celebrated at the expense of what is proper will praise such men as Tian Zhong 田仲 and Shi Qiu 史鰌.

Tian Zhong. Xunzi singles out these men to illustrate the general malady affecting his time. Also known as Chen 陳 Zhong (see paragraph 6.3 below), Tian Zhong was a scion of the ruling family of Qi. The Tian family had seized the throne of Qi some generations earlier, and Tian

Zhong was a relative, though distant, of the reigning king. Since the Tian family were originally refugees from the old state of Chen 陳, they were often referred to as Chen. Zhong worked in his own garden and wove sandals, and his wife made hemp and silk threads that they bartered to get food and clothing. Mencius relates that because Zhong considered his elder brother's income of 10,000 bushels to be ill-gotten, he refused to partake of it or even live in his brother's home. Instead he left and went to live in the wilderness of Wuling, where he supported himself in a bare existence, occasionally verging on starvation (*Mengzi*, 3B.10). The eccentric behavior of Tian Zhong seems based on the doctrines of Xu Xing 許行 and the Agronomists, who taught that a man should live a simple life based only on his own labors.

The upper classes were outraged at his conduct. The queen of Zhao asked of an emissary from Qi if Tian Zhong were still alive, remarking: "He is a man who does not serve his king, has neglected his familial obligations, and does not seek suitable social ties with the feudal lords. He sets for the people an example of utter uselessness. Why has he not been executed?" (*ZGC*, 4.64b.)

The king of Chu, in contrast, hearing that Tian Zhong was a worthy man, dispatched a messenger with 100 catties of gold to offer him the office of premier of Chu. Reminded by his wife that he was content there as a gardener surrounded by his books and lute and that by accepting the offer he was likely to come to harm, Tian declined the offer (Liu Xiang, *Lienu zhuan* 列女傳, 1.13ab). He developed a reputation for incorruptible moral purity, would not attend the court of the corrupt lords of his day, and would not eat food grown by others, and so supported himself by his own labors.[16] Mencius (3B.10) considered him "among the finest gentlemen of the state of Qi," but rejected his style of life as fit only for an "earthworm."

Shi Qiu. Shi Qiu was a grand officer of Wey during the Spring and Autumn period. He held office as court historian during the reign of Duke Ling 衛靈公 (r. 534–493). Confucius, who was his contemporary, knew of his reputation and praised him for the advice he gave the duke (*LY*, 15.6) and noted that "he possessed three aspects of the way of a gentleman: even when not holding office, he was respectful of the ruler; when not sacrificing, he was reverent toward the spirits; and though personally upright, he was able to accommodate himself to others" (*SY*, 17.10b). The reason for Xunzi's criticism is thus not evident from anything that is recorded elsewhere in the Ru tradition of Shi Qiu. Some have thought it possible that there was another, later Shi Qiu whose behavior was like that of Tian Zhong, but no record of such a person exists.

Though we do not know what specifically in Shi Qiu's conduct Xunzi found objectionable, his opinion was not unique. In the *Zhuangzi* (8 "Bianmu" 骈拇, 4.2a), we find Shi criticized for "tearing out the inner power given him and stifling his inborn nature to seize fame and reputation" by leading the world "to an unattainable ideal."[17] He and Zengzi, the disciple of Confucius, are said to have applied their efforts to excelling in matters of humanity and morality to such an extreme degree that "they cannot be called expert" (8 "Bianmu," 4.5a). Indeed, to preserve "inner power" and make it reach the high state of mysterious leveling, one must "put a stop to the ways of Zeng and Shi, gag the mouths of Yang and Mo, and wipe out and reject [the Ru doctrines of] 'humanity' and 'morality'" (*Zhuangzi*, 10 "Quqie" 胠箧, 4.12b).

The *Zhuangzi* (12 "Tiandi," 5.11a; 11 "Zaiyou" 在宥, 4.17b–18a) also notes that though Robber Zhi is quite different from Master Zeng and Shi Qiu in matters of conduct and morality, yet what they did amounted to the same thing because all of them "lost their inborn nature." Xunzi apparently agreed; in "Contra Twelve Philosophers," he expressly criticizes Tian Zhong and Shi Qiu for "repressing their emotions and inborn nature." The reputations of Tian Zhong for incorruptible purity and of Shi Qiu for uprightness were both undeserved because they obtained them not through cultivating the principle of humanity but through eccentric practices and pernicious doctrines.

TEXT

3.1

In matters of conduct the gentleman does not esteem indecorous, though difficult, feats; in his explanations he does not prize improper investigations; in matters of reputation he does not value unsuitable traditions. Rather, only what is fitting to the occasion does he esteem.[18]

To be sure "carrying[19] a stone on one's back and drowning oneself in the Yellow River" is a difficult feat, but Shentu Di was capable of it. Nonetheless, the gentleman does not esteem his feat because it is contrary to the mean of behavior prescribed by ritual principles and by a sense of what is right.[20]

> Mountains and abysses are level.
> Heaven and Earth are comparable.
> Qi and Qin are adjacent.[21]
> [Mountains issue out of mouths.][22]
> Old women have whiskers.[23]
> Eggs have feathers.

All these are theories that are difficult to uphold, yet Hui Shi and Deng Xi were capable of doing so. Nonetheless, the gentleman does not prize their feats of sophistry because they are contrary to the mean of behavior prescribed by ritual and moral principles. The name and reputation of Robber Zhi are on everyone's lips,[24] and his fame shines everywhere like the sun and moon, being unfailingly transmitted to posterity just as are those of Yu and Shun. Nonetheless, the gentleman does not value his reputation because it is contrary to the mean of behavior prescribed by ritual and moral principles. Thus, it is said:

> In matters of conduct the gentleman does not esteem indecorous, though difficult, feats; in his explanations he does not prize improper investigations; and in matters of reputation he does not value unsuitable traditions. Rather, only what is fitting to the occasion does he esteem.

An Ode says:[25]

> Things are in quantities
> only in their proper season.[26]

This expresses my meaning.

3.2

The gentleman is easy to come to know, but difficult to be familiar with.[27] He is easily made apprehensive but is difficult to intimidate. He dreads suffering but will not avoid what is required by his moral duty, even at the risk of death. He desires what is beneficial but will not do what is wrong. In his personal relations he is considerate but not partial.[28] His discussions are in the form of discriminations but are not disordered formulations.[29] How magnificently he possesses all that differentiates him from the vulgar world about him!

3.3

Whether the gentleman is capable or not, he is loved all the same; conversely the petty man is loathed all the same. If the gentleman has ability, he is magnanimous, generous, tolerant, and straightforward, through which he opens the way to instruct others. If he is incapable, he is respectful, reverent, moderate, and modest,[30] through which, being awe-inspired, he undertakes to serve others.

If the petty man is capable, he is rude and arrogant, perverted and depraved, so that he is filled with an overweening pride around others. If he has no ability, he is envious, jealous, resentful, and given to backbiting, so that he subverts and undermines others. Accordingly, it is said:

> If the gentleman is capable, others will consider it an honor to learn from him, and if he lacks ability, they will be pleased to inform him about things. If the petty man has ability, others will consider it contemptible to learn from him, and if he is capable, they will be ashamed to inform him about things.

This constitutes the distinction between the gentleman and the petty man.

3.4

The gentleman is magnanimous, but not to the point of being remiss. He is scrupulous, but not to the point of inflicting suffering. He engages in argumentation, but not to the point of causing a quarrel. He is critical, but not to the point of provoking others.[31] When he upholds an upright position, he is not merely interested in victory.[32] When hard and strong, he is not haughty. When flexible and tractable, he does not merely drift with the demands of the occasion. He is respectful, reverent, attentive, and cautious, but still remains inwardly at ease. Truly this may be called the "perfection of good form." An Ode says:[33]

> Mildly gentle and respectful men,
> only they are the foundation for inner power.

This expresses my meaning.

3.5

In venerating the inner power in others or in celebrating their excellence, the gentleman does not engage in flattery or toady after others. In correcting and criticizing others in blunt terms and in pointing out their faults,[34] he does not engage in backbiting or slander. To speak of the glory and beauty of his self, to compare it with that of Yu or Shun, and to place it in a triadic relation with Heaven and Earth is not to engage in idle boasting and bragging. That he bends and unbends[35] as the occasion demands and that he is flexible and tractable like rushes and reeds is not because of fear and cowardice. That he is unyieldingly strong and fiercely resolute and that there is nothing in him that has not been made straight[36] are not because of pride or haughtiness. His use of his sense of what is morally right[37] to change in response to every situation[38] is because of knowledge that is precisely fitting for every occasion, whether curved or straight. An Ode says:[39]

> As he moves to the left, moves to the left,
> the gentleman moves with perfect fittingness.[40]
> As he moves to the right, to the right,
> the gentleman possesses what is needed.

This says that the gentleman is able to employ his sense of what is morally right to bend or straighten, changing and responding to every occasion.

3.6

The gentleman and the petty man are opposites. When the gentleman is bold of heart, he [reveres][41] Heaven and follows its Way. When faint of heart, he is awe-inspired by his sense of moral duty and regulates his conduct to accord with it. When knowledgeable, he understands the interconnections between phenomena and can assign them to their proper logical category. When ignorant, he is honest and diligent and can follow the model. If he is followed by others, with respect he restrains himself: when they refuse to follow his lead, with reverence he regulates himself.[42] When he is happy, he is concordant with others and well ordered in his person.[43] When saddened, he maintains inner quietude and preserves his distinctive qualities.[44] If he meets with success, he maintains good form and makes it illustrious. If he encounters hardship, he is frugal and proceeds with care.

The petty man does not behave in this way. When he is bold of heart, he is indolent and haughty. When faint of heart, he drifts into lechery and is subversive. When knowledgeable, he is predatory and clandestine.[45] When ignorant, he is poisonously malicious and given to rebelliousness. If he is followed by others, being pleased with himself, he becomes imperious.[46] If they refuse to follow his lead, he is resentful and engages in underhanded schemes.[47] When he is happy, he is frivolous and flighty.[48] When saddened, he is crushed and despondent.[49] When he meets with success, he is filled with pride and is unfair. When he encounters hardship, he becomes negligent and unambitious.[50] A tradition says:[51]

The gentleman doubly advances; the petty man doubly regresses.

This expresses my meaning.

3.7

The gentleman creates order with what is itself well ordered and not with what is itself chaotic.

What is the meaning of this? I say that "well ordered" refers to ritual and moral principles and that "chaotic" refers to what is contrary to them. Accordingly, a gentleman creates order in terms of ritual and moral principles; he does not create order with what is contrary to them.

This being the case, were a country to fall into chaos, would he then not attempt to restore order? I say that "restoring order to a country that has fallen into chaos" does not mean that one will depend on what is itself chaotic to restore the country to a state of order. Rather, it entails leaving what is chaotic behind and reaching over it to what is well ordered. Similarly, "to make cultivated a vile person"[52] does not mean that one will depend on his vileness for his cultivation, but that one will leave behind what is vile and transform him through the process of cultivation. Accordingly, it is a case of "leaving behind what is chaotic" and not of "making well ordered what is chaotic," and of "leaving behind what is vile" and not of "cultivating the vile." The meaning of "order" is illustrated in the maxim:

> The gentleman acts in the interests of order and not in the interests of chaos, in the interests of cultivation and not in the interests of vileness.

3.8

When the gentleman purifies his character,[53] those of a kindred spirit join with him. When he refines his speech, those who are of his kind respond. Just as when one horse neighs, other horses respond to it [and when one cow lows, other cows respond to it].[54] This is not because of any knowledge on their part, it is because such is their inner constitution. Accordingly, that

> one who has just washed his body will shake out his robes and that one who has just washed his hair will dust off his cap[55]

is because of the essential nature of humans. Who among them could bear to subject his own full understanding to the delusions of others![56]

3.9a[57]

> For the gentleman to nurture his mind, nothing is more excellent than truthfulness.

If a man has attained perfection of truthfulness,[58] he will have no other concern than to uphold the principle of humanity and to behave with justice. If with truthfulness of mind he upholds the principle of humanity, it will be given form.

> Having been given form, it becomes intelligible. Having become intelligible, it can produce transmutation. If with truthfulness of mind he behaves with justice, it will accord with natural order. Ac-

cording with natural order, it will become clear. Having become clear, it can produce transformation.

To cause transmutation and transformation to flourish in succession is called the "Power of Nature."

3.9b

> Though the sky does not speak, men can infer that it is high; though the earth does not speak, men can infer that it is thick; though the four seasons do not speak, the Hundred Clans[59] anticipate their proper sequence.

This is because having attained perfect truthfulness, they possess a constant regularity. Similarly, when the gentleman has attained to perfect inner power, though he remains silent, he is understood; though he has never bestowed any favor, he is considered affectionate; and though he does not display anger, he possesses an awe-inspiring dignity. Because he preserves the authenticity of his individual uniqueness, he is obedient to his destiny.[60] Though a man is adept at acting in accord with the Way,

> if he lacks truthfulness, he will not be individual. Not being individual, his character will not be given form.

His character not having form, though he creates it in his mind, displays his intentions on his face, and expresses his will in words, the common people will nonetheless never follow him, and insofar as they must, it will be with suspicion.

3.9c

> Heaven and Earth are indeed great, but were they to lack truthfulness, they could not transmute the myriad things. Sages to be sure are wise, but were they to lack truthfulness, they could not transmute the people. Fathers and sons naturally possess affection for each other, but were they to be untruthful, they would drift apart.

The ruler being superior in position is honored, but were he to be untruthful, he would be considered base. It is to just such truthfulness that the gentleman cleaves, and just this truthfulness forms the foundation of his government, so that wherever he may dwell, those who are of his own kind will come to him.

> If he persists in it, he will obtain it; but if he gives up, it will be lost. By persisting in it and obtaining it, it will become easy for him. Having become easy for him, his conduct will become individual. Being individual and not giving up, he will be fulfilled.

Brought to fulfillment, his talents completely realized, continually pro-
gressing, and never reverting to his beginnings, he has indeed undergone
transmutation.

3.10

The gentleman, though he occupies an eminent position, is respectful
in his disposition because he realizes that the mind is small but the Way is
great. Having heard and seen directly what is near him, he grasps what is
far away. How is this possible? It is because of his holding on to the
method.[61] Accordingly, the essential nature of 1,000 or 10,000 men is in
that of a single man. The beginnings of Heaven and Earth are still present today. And the way of all True Kings is in that of the Later Kings.[62]
The gentleman carefully scrutinizes the way of the Later Kings before
arranging in their proper grades the various kings of earlier times, as
though he were deliberating in court robes with arms folded in formal
stance.[63] He derives guidelines from ritual and moral principles, makes
sharp the division between right and wrong, binds together the essentials
of the world, and makes well ordered the multitude within the seas, as
though in the service of a single man.

Hence by holding on to what is very small, he can undertake tasks
that are extremely large, just as with a short ruler only five inches long
one can measure the whole square of the world. Thus, the gentleman
need not leave his own house, yet the essential nature of all that is within
the seas is established and accumulated there.[64] This is because of his
holding on to the method in this fashion.

3.11

There are successful scholars, public-spirited scholars, upright scholars,
cautious scholars, and those who are merely petty men. Only one who
can honor his lord and love the people, who can respond to things
whenever they come and manage situations as they turn up,[65] is properly
called a "successful scholar."

Only one who does not form cliques with his inferiors to deceive his
superiors, who does not conform to the opinions of his superiors out of
envy of those in lower positions,[66] who settles disputes with fairness and
does not bring harm to others by acting out of considerations of private
ends, is properly called a "public-spirited scholar."

Only one who does not harbor resentments[67] against his lord when
superiors do not recognize his good personal qualities and who does not
accept rewards when superiors are unaware of his shortcomings, who
neither shows off his good qualities nor glosses over his faults but uses

the true circumstances[68] to recommend himself, is properly termed an "upright scholar."

Only one who is certain to be honest in ordinary speech and prudent in ordinary behavior, who is awe-inspired by the model and goes along with popular customs, and does not presume to consider what is unique to himself as correct, is properly termed a "cautious scholar."[69]

Only one who is inconstantly honest in his speech and inconstantly correct in his conduct, who is partial to whatever involves profit to himself to the exclusion of all else, is properly considered a "petty man."[70]

3.12

Public-spiritedness produces clear understanding; partisanship produces dark obscurity. Straightforwardness and diligence produce success; deceitfulness and falsity produce obstructions. Sincerity and honesty produce perspicacity; boastfulness and bragging produce self-delusion. These are the "Six Productions" about which the gentleman is prudent. It is just these that separate sage emperor Yu from the tyrant Jie.

3.13
Weighing the Relative Merits of Choosing
or Refusing Desires and Aversions[71]

When a man sees something desirable, he must reflect on the fact that with time it could come to involve what is detestable. When he sees something that is beneficial, he should reflect that sooner or later it, too, could come to involve harm. Only after weighing the total of the one against that of the other and maturely calculating should he determine the relative merits of choosing or refusing his desires and aversions. In this fashion, he will regularly avoid failure and being ensnared by what he has chosen. In general, the calamities that beset mankind are the result of prejudices and the damage they cause. If, when a man sees something desirable, he does not reflect that it may come to be detestable and, something beneficial, that it could come to be harmful, then it is inevitable that his movements will ensnare him and his actions will bring disgrace. Just this constitutes the calamity of prejudice and the damages that result from it.

3.14

[What other men desire, I desire also;] what other men detest, I detest also.[72] To treat the rich and eminent as a group with arrogance or to be intent on demeaning oneself before the poor and humble—to act thusly is contrary to the essential nature of the humane man.[73] Rather, it is characteristic of wretched men who would deceptively steal a reputation for humaneness in this benighted world.[74] No threat is as great as this! Hence it is said:

To steal a reputation is not like stealing mere property.

Men like Tian Zhong and Shi Qiu are not like ordinary robbers.

BOOK 4

Of Honor and Disgrace

INTRODUCTION

How to gain honor and avoid disgrace was the most practical advice philosophy could offer. Honor brought riches, but disgrace brought certain poverty and perhaps death as well. Since reputations were quickly made in the chaotic world of the Warring States China, and even more quickly lost, the relation between achievement and reputation became a frequent theme in literature. Words and actions were obvious factors, but philosophers differed as to which words and what actions would bring success and avoid failure. The *Changes* ("Xici," 7.17b) says: "Words and actions are the guiding force of the gentleman. The manifestation of this guiding force is the lord and master of honor and disgrace. Words and actions are what the gentleman uses to move Heaven and Earth."

Lord Shang, who reformed the state of Qin with his New Laws and built the foundation of its later conquest of the Chinese world, held that anyone "who is hesitant in the execution of his duties will be without reputation."[1] The famous general Yue Yi, a contemporary of Xunzi's, wrote a letter to King Hui of Yan, who had foolishly dismissed him and was trying to reemploy him: "I have heard that the worthy and sage-like among the lords would never lay waste to the achievements they had established and thus were written about in the annals of their country, and that prescient scholars would never ruin the reputation they had perfected and thus were extolled by later generations" (*SJ*, 80.10).

Being such an important theme, the problem of honor and disgrace was discussed in such diverse books as the *Zhanguo ce*, *Hanfeizi*, *Guanzi*, *Liezi*, *Lüshi chunqiu*, and in the works of Shen Dao. These philosophers differed with Xunzi, but none so dramatically as the "Xiaoyaoyou" 逍遙遊 (1.4b) of the *Zhuangzi*, which cites approvingly Song Xing, who "settled the distinction between internal and external qualities and explained the true nature of honor and disgrace." Song Xing argued that "he whose achievements have been perfected will be brought to ruin; he whose reputation is perfect will be brought down."[2] This is the Song Xing who outraged Xunzi with his notion that "to suffer insult is no disgrace."[3] Xunzi believed that the desire for honor and the hatred of disgrace belonged to man's inborn nature. Song's theory overlooked that fundamental and unalterable fact. Xunzi stated in "Exhortation to Learning" (1.5) that "the coming of honor and disgrace must be a reflection of one's inner power," and here he develops the theme more extensively.

The Technique of Proper Discrimination. Argument, debate, and intellectual controversy within the courts of ancient China took place in a formal setting in which opponents attacked each other's positions before the king, lord, or patron. A sample of what such debates were like can be seen in Xunzi's "Debate on the Principles of Warfare," which records his debate with the Lord of Linwu before the king of Zhao. Intellectual disputes within the Jixia Academy and in the entourages of the great patrons of learning like the Lord of Chunshen were more technical in nature and were commonly called *bian* 辯, generally translated "discrimination." *Bian* refers to a logical inquiry that resolves a disputed point. The *shuo* 説 was the "explanation" that resulted. The system was well developed in Xunzi's day, having been perfected by over a century of argumentation. Opponents of this system contended that "discriminations are unable to explain" (*HNZ*, 2.12a). The Mohist logicians argued that a proper discrimination occurred when the disputants contended "over claims that are the converse of each other" as when one party contends that "*X* is an ox" while the other contends that "*X* is not an ox." There is a *sheng* 勝, "victory in a discrimination," when one side *dang* 當 "fits with the facts." Since both of two converse propositions cannot fit the facts, "of necessity one of them does not fit."[4]

A proper discrimination thus resulted in the victory of one position over the other. This "victory" indicated that one position had been shown to be valid or the other invalid. "If what is advocated [by debaters] is not similar, then it is different. When it is a case of similar, the one may contend that it is a 'puppy' while the other says that it is a 'dog.' When it is a case of different, the one may say that it is an 'ox' while the other says that it is a 'horse.' If in neither is there a victory for one position over the other, there is no discrimination."[5]

What Xunzi objects to in this book is that "discriminations," especially as employed by those who imitated Hui Shi and Deng Xi, did not result in explanations because those who pursued them were interested not in understanding but in debate. The technical term *zheng* 爭, translated "debate," has as well the common meaning "quarrel," which is what such debates seemed to others. Similarly the practitioners of discriminations were concerned not with knowledge but solely with victory in debate. Xunzi did not condemn logical inquiry as such, only the idle exploitation of logical distinctions for startling effects and for confounding common sense. He in fact frequently used the techniques of logical argumentation developed by the Mohist logicians and exploited by the followers of Hui Shi.

Bellicosity. Xunzi particularly criticizes the bellicose, who allow a moment of danger to destroy everything of value: their lives, those of their family, and their service to their lord. He contrasts them with a nursing sow that attacks a tiger to save her offspring. Their error lies in their considering themselves alone correct and others entirely wrong. Others may be attracted by their "bravery" and "boldness," but in the end such behavior results in great stupidity, harm, and danger. It is not something born of delusion or disease, nor is it atavism to an animal nature; it is an extreme condition of normal likes and dislikes. Song Xing, who argued that men would not display such a willingness to fight if they could be taught that it was no disgrace to suffer insult, failed to grasp this essential point ("Zhenglun," 18.8).

Xunzi is here criticizing the knights of his day who made great displays of their bravery and boldness. It seems evident that a branch of the Ru retained the "knight" image of the *shi*, rather than the "scholar" image cultivated by most Ru. Mozi condemns this tendency in a conversation with a follower of the disciple Zixia (*Mozi*, 46 "Geng Zhu" 耕柱, 11.19a). He suggests that a number of men closely associated with Confucius proved prone to rebellion (39 "Fei Ru," 9.30ab). Han Fei specifically mentions that Song Xing's ideas opposed the doctrines of the Qidiao 漆雕 school of Ru (50 "Xianxue" 顯學, 19.9b). Xunzi considered a bellicose spirit the foundation of harm and held that the gentleman should be "without bellicosity and rancor" ("Chendao," 13.8). Rather than depend on a "fighting spirit," the gentleman relies on the superior strength of *de* inner power ("Wangzhi," 9.7).

Society and Natural Inequality. In the view of Ru philosophers, the nature of society is hierarchical and inheres in the natural inequality of things, but Heaven, which produced the "teeming masses," also provided an appropriate station of life that is the due lot of each. Those highest in ability, wisdom, intelligence, and inner power, by general assent, become rulers, as did Yao and Shun of old. Those of lesser talents become feudal lords, grand officers, and officials. Each serves an appropriate role in the structure of human society. The responsibilities, income, and prestige of each is commensurate with the position he occupies. Since antiquity each office had been handed down from father to son who conscientiously carried out their duty. Office consisted of defined functions that were taught and of practical activities that would be learned independently of understanding their original purpose or their relation to other activities. Thus, we can know the model of government, even though the Three Dynasties have all perished.

When society takes proper account of the natural inequality of things, each group performs the functions appropriate to its lot. This is expressed in the *renlun* 人倫, or "constant relationships" between people. Mencius (3A.4) provides the classic expression of these: "Shun... appointed Xie 禼 minister of education in order that the *renlun* constant relationships be taught: that between father and son there be affection; between lord and subject, justice; between husband and wife, due separation of functions; between old and young, proper precedence; and between friends, good faith." It was thought that these constant relationships, which all men share, inhered in nature, just like the fruits of the various trees and vines. A sage knew of them and would not go against them.[6] Xunzi expands the concept to encompass the grades of men, from lesser to greater, who compose society and form its government: the common mass of humanity, who must perform the basic work of society; the lesser Ru scholars, who should be ministers and officials of the government; and the greater Ru scholars, who should be rulers.[7]

When this is fully realized, one attains "perfect peace," a concept that occurs twice in the *Xunzi*. The term *ping* 平 basically means "level," by extension, "even, equal," and thus "calm, pacific, tranquil." It also refers to the "even," normal, regular course of life in contrast to the upheavals associated with a death in the family and the mourning period that follows. The sage king, without lifting his hand, "levels" his opposition and so creates peace. Xunzi explains that in the government of the sage, the "people find joy and security in encouraging each other in the ruler's undertakings" and "imitate the frame of his mind," so that as even "rival states submit," the whole world is "unified without waiting for a decree" ("Jundao," 12.1).

Human Nature. Nature does not distinguish between the gentleman and the petty man. Both have similar natural talents, awareness, and capabilities. Their desires and their aversions are the same. "It is the nature of the people, when they are hungry to strive for food; when they are tired to strive for rest; when they suffer hardship to seek enjoyment; when they are in a state of humiliation to strive for honor. Such is the essential nature of the people" (*Shangjun shu*, 2.5b). What distinguishes the gentleman from the petty man is the choices he makes. Though all men, whether a Yu or a Jie, have, according to the philosopher Gaozi 告子, "an inborn appetite for food and sex" (*Mengzi*, 6A.4), and though their eyes, ears, mouths, noses, and skins react to the same things in the same way, a Yu becomes different from a Jie through self-cultivation.

Xunzi observes that if a man has no teacher, then, since his inborn nature is that of a petty man, he will think only in terms of benefit to himself and will assume that the customs of his land and his age are proper. His mind will be just like his mouth or stomach, seeking only what is immediately gratifying. What transforms him is a teacher who acquaints him with the model, with the way of the sage kings, and with the guiding principles of humanity and justice. A petty man, though his natural disposition is to desire the best of foods, can learn to husband his resources in order to perpetuate his wealth. But he does not know how much more valuable is the pattern of life that derives from the classics of the *Odes*, *Documents*, *Rituals*, and *Music*. What is needed is a teacher to help one master them. Then one must reflect on them so that he can attain inner peace and come to love them.

TEXT

4.1

Pride and excess bring disaster for man.[8] Respectfulness and moderation ward off the five weapons,[9] for although the lance and spear are piercing, they are not so sharp as respectfulness and moderation. Hence words of praise for another are warmer than clothing of linen and silk. The wound caused by words is deeper than that of spears and halberds. Thus, that one can find no place to walk through the breadth of the earth[10] is not because the earth is not tranquil but because the danger to every step of the traveler lies generally with words. When the roadway is broad, people yield the way; when the roadway is narrow, they are crowded together. Although they have no desire to be heedful, it is as if circumstances forced them to move thusly.[11]

4.2

For all their cheerfulness,[12] they perish because of their anger. For all their careful investigations, they are destroyed by their viciousness. For all their breadth of knowledge, they are reduced to poverty because of their penchant for slander.[13] For all their appearance of personal probity,[14] they sink further into corruption because they revile others.[15] For all the fine foods they eat, they become ever more emaciated because they associate indiscriminately.[16] For all their discriminations, they do not provide convincing explanations because they are interested only in debate. Though they have an upright position, they are not recognized because they are interested only in "victory." Though they are scrupulous, they are not valued because they are injurious to others. Though they are bold, they do not inspire dread in others because they are greedy. Though they are trustworthy, they are not respected because they are fond of acting on their own.[17] The petty man is intent on behaving in these ways, but the gentleman will not do so.

4.3

The bellicose are neglectful of their own person, of their kin, and of their lord. Though to act in the flush of a blind rage puts life and limb in jeopardy, still they do it. This is to be neglectful of their own person.[18] Though to place the position of their household in such danger that their kin are unable to avoid the death penalty, still they do it. This is to be neglectful of their kin.[19] Even when it involves what their lord dislikes and when it is against the most extreme prohibitions of the laws and punishments, still they do it. This is to be neglectful of their lord. Below[20] neglectful of their own person, within neglectful of their kin, and above neglectful of their lord—such behavior is neither condoned[21] by the laws and punishments nor supported by the sage kings.

A nursing sow will charge a tiger, and a bitch with pups will not wander far away.

They are not neglectful of their kin. It is only man who below is neglectful of his own person, within neglectful of his kin, and above neglectful of his lord. If only mankind were not so unlike the bitch and sow![22]

Every such bellicose person is sure to consider himself right and others wrong. Considering that he alone is truly right and others are truly wrong, he becomes the "gentleman" and others become "petty men." By these means both the "gentleman" and the "petty man" are wronged and harmed because below he was neglectful of his own self, within neglectful of his kin, and above neglectful of his lord. How utterly extreme indeed is his fault!

This kind of man is what is called "using a Hufu 狐父 lance to behead an ox."[23] Were one to consider this wisdom, no stupidity could be greater; were one to consider it beneficial, no harm could be greater;

were one to consider it honorable, no disgrace could be greater; and were one to consider it security, no danger could be greater. Why do men become bellicose? Were I to wish to associate their bellicosity with delusion, madness, disease, or illness, it would be impermissible because the sage king also punishes them. Were I to wish to connect it with something animal or bestial in such a man, it would not be permissible because they have the form and substance of a normal man and their likes and dislikes are in large measure the same as those of a normal man. Why then do men become bellicose? I am ashamed lest I, too, might share this fault.[24]

4.4

There is the bravery of the dog and boar and that of the peddler and robber. There is the courage of the petty man and that of the scholar and gentleman. Quarreling over food and drink, having neither scruples nor shame, not knowing right from wrong, not trying to avoid[25] death or injury, not fearful of greater strength or of greater numbers, greedily aware only of food and drink[26]—such is the bravery of the dog and boar. Dealing in transactions of profit, quarreling over goods and valuables, having no concern for polite refusals or for yielding precedence, being audacious and daring,[27] given to temerity and effrontery, greedily aware only of profit—such is the bravery of peddlers and robbers. Scorning death when filled with passionate intensity, [...][28]—such is the courage of the petty man. Staying with what is just, not swayed by the exigencies of the moment, not given to looking after his own benefit, elevating the interests of the whole state and assisting in realizing them, not acting to change his point of view, weighing the threat of death but[29] upholding his moral duty and not backing away from it— such is the courage of the scholar and gentleman.[30]

4.5

The mullet dart about near the surface of the water, but when they are netted and lying on the sand, though they may long for water, they will never reach it again.[31] Similarly when a man is caught in the midst of calamity, though he may wish he had been cautious, his wishing will be in vain. Those who know themselves do not resent others; those who know fate do not resent Heaven. Those who resent others are bound to fail; those who resent Heaven do not learn from experience.[32] Erring oneself but attributing it to others—is this not far wide of the mark indeed!

4.6[33]

The Great Distinction Between Honor and Disgrace and the Invariable Conditions of Security and Benefit and of Danger and Harm

Those who put first what is just and later matters of benefit are honorable; those who put first what is beneficial and later what is just are shameful. Those who are honorable always gain success; those who are shameful invariably fail.[34] The successful always administer others; failures are always administered by others. Such is the great distinction between honor and disgrace.

Those who are natural[35] and honest invariably obtain security and benefit; those who are profligate and cruel invariably obtain danger and harm. Those who have gained security and benefits are always happy and relaxed. Those who feel endangered and threatened with harm are always melancholy and insecure. Those who are happy and relaxed always live to a great age; those who are melancholy and insecure always are cut down while youths.[36] Such are the invariable conditions, respectively, of security and benefit and of danger and harm.

4.7

As "heaven produced the teeming masses,"[37] so there exists a means through which they obtain their station in life.[38] The man who becomes Son of Heaven and obtains the whole world is the person who has most developed his will and aspirations, is most substantial in behavior springing from moral power, and has the most lucid wisdom and insight. The feudal lords who are given the various nations are those persons who govern and issue commands according to the model, who initiate projects in accord with the proper season, who hold hearings and make decisions impartially, and who are able to obey the mandates of the Son of Heaven and protect the Hundred Clans.[39] Those who become the grand officers and knights and are given cities and fields are those persons who are cultivated in their ambitions and conduct, well ordered in overseeing their official functions, and able to obey their superiors and preserve the official duties.[40] The reason that the model of the Three Dynasties still exists even though they have perished is that officers and bureaucrats[41] have meticulously observed the rules and laws,[42] the weights and measures,[43] criminal sanctions and penalties, and maps[44] and registers.[45] This has been accomplished even when they no longer understood the meaning because they conscientiously safeguarded the calculations[46] and out of prudence never presumed either to increase or diminish them. Rather, they handed them from father to son in order to aid the king or duke.[47] This is the reason they are given emoluments and ranks. The commoners obtain warm clothing, filling food, and a long life. They see many days[48] through avoiding the death penalty by being filial, by respecting their elders, by being attentive, diligent, restrained, controlled,[49] and quick in exerting themselves, and by earnestly executing[50] their tasks and duties and not daring to be indolent or haughty. Traitors get into danger, fall into disgrace, and face execution because they cloak pernicious doctrines in beautiful language, present treacherous statements in elegantly composed form, perform strange feats, spread false rumors,[51] are given to boasting, break in and rob, act in profligate, cruel, proud, and haughty fashion,[52] and turn from one side to another during chaotic times in an attempt to save their lives. They are imperiled because their reflections are not deep, their choices are not carefully made, and their decisions regarding what should be chosen and what refused are defective or haphazard.

4.8

In natural talent, inborn nature, awareness, and capability, the gentleman and the petty man are one. In cherishing honor and detesting disgrace, in loving benefit and hating harm, the gentleman and the petty man are the same. Rather, it appears that the Way they employ to make their choices produces the difference. The petty man is eager to make boasts, yet desires that others should believe in him. He enthusiastically engages in deception, yet wants others to have affection for him. He conducts himself like an animal, yet wants others to think well of him. When he reflects on something, it is understood only with difficulty. When he acts in regard to something, it is difficult for him to make it secure. When he tries to sustain something, he has difficulty establishing it. In the end,[53] he is certain to fail to obtain what he loves and sure to encounter what he hates.

Accordingly, the gentleman is trustworthy and so desires that other men should trust him as well. He is loyal and so wants other men to have affection for him. He cultivates rectitude and makes orderly his management of situations,[54] and so desires that others should think well of him. When he reflects on something, it is easily understood. When he acts, it is easy for him to make it secure. When he tries to sustain something, it is easily established. In the end, he is certain to obtain what he loves and sure not to encounter what he hates. For these reasons, when he is unsuccessful in seeking office, he will not live in obscurity; when he is successful, he will become greatly illustrious; and when he dies, his reputation will be still more extensively declared.

The petty man, craning his neck and standing on tiptoes, wishfully remarks: "In awareness, thought, ability, and inborn nature, I certainly possess the characteristics of a Worthy." He does not realize that if there are no differences between him and other men, then it must be that the gentleman concentrates on devising plans[55] that are suitable to the occasion, whereas the petty man concentrates on transgressing what is appropriate. Thus, a thorough investigation of the awareness and capacity of the petty man is sufficient to make one aware that he possesses more than he appears to and that he could do what the gentleman does do. Consider the fact that though the native of Yue is content with Yue and the native of Chu with Chu, the gentleman is content only with Xia.[56] This is not because of any difference in awareness, capacity, talent, or inborn nature, but, rather, the differences are because of the moderating influence of what they concentrate on in laying plans and of the habits instilled by their customs.[57]

Conduct marked by humanity, justice, and inner power is normally the method of assuring safety, but there is no necessity that it will never involve peril. Conduct marked by baseness and recklessness,[58] and breaking in and robbing others are normally methods involving peril, but there is no necessity that they will never produce security. Therefore it is said:[59]

The gentleman is led by the normal, but the petty man is led by the exceptional.[60]

4.9

All men possess one and the same nature: when hungry, they desire food; when cold, they desire to be warm; when exhausted from toil, they desire rest; and they all desire benefit and hate harm. Such is the nature that men are born possessing. They do not have to await development before they become so. It is the same in the case of a Yu and in that of a Jie. The eye distinguishes white from black, the beautiful from the ugly. The ear distinguishes sounds and tones as to their shrillness or sonority.[61] The mouth distinguishes the sour and salty, the sweet and bitter. The nose distinguishes perfumes and fragrances, rancid and fetid odors. The bones, flesh, and skin-lines[62] distinguish hot and cold, pain and itching. These, too, are part of the nature that man is born possessing,[63] that he does not have to develop, and that is true of both Yu and Jie.

Whether a man can become a Yao or Yu or be a Jie or Robber Zhi, whether he becomes a workman or artisan, a farmer or merchant, lies entirely with the accumulated effect of circumstances,[64] with what they concentrate on in laying their plans, and on the influence of habits and customs.[65] If one becomes a Yao or Yu, one normally enjoys tranquillity and honor; if one is a Jie or Robber Zhi, one normally falls into peril and disgrace. If one becomes a Yao or Yu, one constantly finds enjoyment and ease; if one becomes a workman, artisan, farmer, or merchant, one must constantly toil and trouble oneself. Though this is so, many[66] men are like the latter, but only a few men are like the former. Why should this be so? I say that it is because they remain uncultivated; even Yao and Yu were not born wholly what they became, but rose up by transforming their old selves, brought them to perfection through cultivation and conscious exertion, and only after first putting forth the utmost effort did they become complete.[67]

4.10

The inborn nature of man is certainly that of the petty man.[68] If he is without a teacher and lacks the model, he will see things solely in terms of benefit to himself. As the nature of man is assuredly that of the petty man, if the age in which he lives is chaotic, he will acquire its chaotic customs. For this reason, he will use the small to redouble what is small and use the chaotic to begat more chaos.[69] If the gentleman does not use the power inherent in his circumstances to control them, then he will have no means to develop their inherent possibilities. Now the mouth and stomach of a man can only lead to smacking and chewing away, feasting and gorging himself to satisfaction.[70] How can they be aware of ritual principles and his moral duty? Or know when to offer polite refusals or to yield precedence? Or know shame more keenly or sharpen what he accumulates?[71] If a man lacks a teacher and the model, then his mind will be just like his mouth and stomach.

Now if a man were caused to live without ever having tasted the meat of pastured and grain-fed animals[72] or rice and millet, but knew only beans, coarse greens, dregs and husks, then he would be satisfied with such food. Were there suddenly to arrive a platter filled with the finest and most delicate of meats, he would look at them with astonishment and exclaim: "What strange things!" But since when savored, they are not unpleasing to the nose;[73] when tasted, they are sweet to the mouth; and when eaten, they are satisfying to the body, everyone who tries them will reject their old foods and choose these new ones instead.

Consider the way of the Ancient Kings and the guiding principles of humanity and justice. Are they not the means by which we live together in societies, by which we protect and nurture each other, by which we hedge in our faults[74] and refine each other, and by which together we become tranquil and secure? Consider then the way of Jie and Robber Zhi. Does it not contrast with that of the Ancient Kings just as the meat of pastured and grain-fed animals contrasts with dregs and husks![75] Though this is so, many[76] men still become like them and few like the Ancient Kings. Why is this? I say: They are uncultivated rustics. A lack of cultivation is a misfortune common to the whole world; it is the greatest calamity for man and does him the greatest harm. Anciently it was said:

The humane man delights in proclaiming and manifesting it to others.[77]

If it is proclaimed and manifested, smoothed and polished,[78] imitated and repeated,[79] then the myopic will suddenly become comprehensive, the uncultivated suddenly refined,[80] and the stupid suddenly wise. If this could not be done, though a Tang or Wu held supreme power, what advantage would result, and though a Jie or Zhou Xin held supreme power, what damage could they cause? But when Tang and Wu lived, the world followed them and order prevailed, and when Jie and Zhou Xin lived, the world followed them and was chaotic. How could this be if such were contrary to the essential nature of man because certainly it is as possible for a man to be like the one as like the other?

4.11

It is the essential nature of man that for food he desires the meat of pastured and grain-fed animals, that he desires clothing decorated with patterns and brocades, that to travel he wants a horse and carriage, and even that he wants wealth in the form of surplus money and hoards of provisions so that even in lean periods stretching over years, he will not know insufficiency.[81] Such is the essential nature of man.

Now in real life, though a man knows how to raise chickens, dogs, pigs, and swine as well as oxen and sheep, when he eats he dares not have wine and meat. Though he has surplus knife- and spade-shaped coins and stores in cellars and storehouses, he does not presume to dress in silk. Though the miser has treasures deposited in boxes and trunks,[82] he dares not travel by horse and carriage. Why is this? Not that men do not desire to do this, but[83] because, considering the long view of things and thinking of the consequences of their actions, they are apprehensive that they may lack means adequate to perpetuate their wealth. In this way, they, too, moderate what they expend and control[84] what they desire, harvesting, gathering, hoarding, and storing up goods in order to perpetuate their wealth. In itself is not this "considering the long view of things and thinking of the consequences" something quite excellent indeed! Now, the sort of person who lives in a haphazard manner and is only superficially aware of things does not grasp even this. So he consumes his provisions in an utterly extravagant manner,[85] not considering the consequences, and suddenly he finds himself forced into difficult straits and impoverished. This is why he will freeze, starve, be reduced to holding a begging gourd and sack, and will wind up as a skeleton lying in a drainage ditch.[86]

How much more important, then, are the way of the Ancient Kings, the guiding principles of humanity and justice, and the pattern of life[87] given in the *Odes*, *Documents*, *Rituals*, and *Music*; they certainly contain the most important thoughts in the world. They will cause anyone born to the world to consider the long view of things and think of the consequences, thereby protecting a myriad of generations. Their influence is eternal, their accumulated wisdom to be reanimated is substantial, and their achievements and accomplishments stretch far and wide.[88] None but those who have thoroughly cultivated themselves through conscious exertion so as to become gentlemen can be wise. There is the ancient saying:

> You cannot draw water from a deep well with a short rope. One whose knowledge is not intimately detailed cannot have words with the perfected sage.[89]

The patterns of life given in the *Odes*, *Documents*, *Rituals*, and *Music* are certainly opposed to what the common lot of men know about. Thus, it is said:

> Concentrate your mind on them, and you can master them twice over. Possess them, and you can follow them forever. Broaden them, and you can be successful in office. Reflect on them, and you can attain inner peace. Repeat, imitate, and investigate them, and you will love them all the more.

If you use them to bring order to your essential nature, you will benefit. If you employ them to make a name for yourself, you will gain honor. If you use them in the company of others, you will become concordant with them. If you employ them when you are alone, you will be satisfied. What could bring greater joy to your intellect than this!

4.12

To be as honored as the Son of Heaven and to be as wealthy by possessing the whole world—this natural human desire is shared by all men alike. But if all men gave free rein[90] to their desires, the result would be impossible to endure, and the material goods of the whole world would be inadequate to satisfy them. Accordingly, the Ancient Kings acted to control them with regulations, ritual, and moral principles, in order thereby to divide society into classes, creating therewith differences in status between the noble and base, disparities between the privileges of age and youth, and the division of the wise from the stupid, the able from the incapable. All of this caused men to perform the duties of their station in life and each to receive his due; only after this had been done was the amount and substance of the emolument paid by grain[91] made to fit their respective stations. This indeed is the Way to make the whole populace live together in harmony and unity.

Accordingly, when a humane man occupies the highest position, farmers labor with all their energy to exhaust the potential of their fields, merchants scrutinize with keen eyes to get the utmost from their goods, the various artisans use their skills to the fullest in making utensils and wares, and the officials, from the knights and grand officers up to the feudal lords, all execute fully the functions of their offices with humanity, generosity, wisdom, and ability. This may be called "perfect peace." So though one may have as his emolument the whole world, he need not consider it excessive, and though one be only a gatekeeper, receptionist, guard, or nightwatchman,[92] he need never think his salary too meager. Anciently it was said:[93]

Unequal yet equivalent, bent yet obedient, not the same yet uniform.[94]

This refers to the constant relationships of mankind. An Ode says:[95]

He received the large and small *gong* 共 jade regalia,[96]
and thus was thought truly great by the states below him.[97]

This expresses my meaning.[98]

BOOK 5

■ ■ |||||||||||||||||||||||||||||||||||||||||||||||||||||||||||||||||||||||||||||||||||||||||||||||||||||||||||||||||||||||||||||||||||||||||||||||||||||||||||||||||||||| ■ ■

Contra Physiognomy

INTRODUCTION

The Chinese version of physiognomy included not only determining a person's character from his physical appearance but also foretelling his future. It was but one of many pseudo-scientific beliefs that purported to be "techniques of destiny." Prognostication by scapulimancy and milfoil lots and by the trigrams of the *Changes* were ancient in Xunzi's day and were widely respected. But these concerned affairs of state and matters of war, harvests, and weather, not matters of individual destiny. Individuals, apart from kings and certain other royal persons, were not proper subjects.[1] The same is largely true of astrology, which flourished in Xunzi's day, as is amply documented in the *Lüshi chunqiu*.[2] Bound, as these matters were, with known facts of astronomy and equally explained by the same intellectual constructs, it was difficult to challenge the astrological element without simultaneously condemning the astronomical truths embedded in the same system.[3] Another system that was developing as Xunzi wrote this book was geomancy, defined by Herbert Chatley as: "the art of adapting the residences of the living and the dead so as to cooperate and harmonize with the local currents of the cosmic breath [*qi* 氣]."[4] Its theoretical origins can be seen in the *Guanzi* in passages dating from perhaps the fourth century, but it does not appear to have been well developed until the first century A.D., when Wang Chong criticized it.[5]

Physiognomy. The origins of physiognomy are unknown. In the seventh century, Bole 伯樂, a retainer of Duke Mu of Qin (r. 659–621), became famous for his ability to judge horses by physiognomizing their features (*HNZ*, 12.9a). Han Fei (50 "Xianxue," 19.11a) remarks that "if one only looks at the teeth and surveys the general shape of the horse, then even Bole could not be sure of the quality of the horse." Bole judged the quality of a horse by physiognomizing it on the basis of its shape, appearance, tendons, and bones (*HNZ*, 12.9a). So expert was he that a merchant once increased the price of his horse tenfold merely by having Bole look it over once and look back at it as he left (*ZGC*, 9.8b). Xunzi, like most of his contemporaries, regarded Bole as a paragon who could not be deceived when it came to horses, just as the gentleman could not be deceived concerning men.[6] "Prince Ao of Lu 魯公孫敖 had his sons physiognomized by Shufu 叔服, historiographer of the royal court, who concluded: Your son Gu 穀 will feed you. Your son Nan 難 will bury you. The lower part of Gu's face is large, so he is sure to have posterity in the state of Lu" (*Zuo*, Wen 1).

Physiognomy here offered the possibility of knowing one's future and the future of one's children. Kings could determine which ministers would prove helpful and which dangerous. Xunzi singled out physiognomy for special condemnation because it involved individuals rather than matters of state. He was perhaps also sensitive to the criticisms that Mozi and his followers had made of the fatalism adopted by some early Ru.

Xunzi mentions that in the past Gubu Ziqing 姑布子卿 had physiognomized Confucius during the latter's visit to the state of Wey.[7] Gubu recognized immediately that Confucius was a sage. Regarding Confucius as he walked 50 paces to meet him and then following Confucius for 50 paces, Gubu asked who this remarkable man was. Told that he was Confucius from Lu, he allowed that he had heard of him (*HSWZ*, 9.9a). Asked how Confucius impressed him, he responded: "He has the forehead of a Yao, the eyes of a Shun, the neck of a Yu, and the beak-like nose of a Gaoyao 皋陶. Viewed from the front, he is so perfect that he resembled those who possess territory. From the rear, he has high shoulders and a weak back; only in this regard does he not equal those four sages."[8] Gubu added that Confucius was like a "dog in the house of a family in mourning,"[9] that he was not hated because of his sunken face, and that it was because of his beak of a nose, which was like a bulrush, that no ruler had availed himself of Confucius' talents.[10] When this was reported to Confucius, he responded that the bodily form and facial appearance are of little importance.[11] In this he agreed with Xunzi.

The doctrine that the destiny of a person could be read in his physical form reached a high point during Xunzi's lifetime. A traveling physiognomist, Tang Ju, correctly foretold that Li Dui would become dictator of Zhao (*SJ*, 43.67–68; *HFZ*, 21 "Yu *Lao*" 喻老, 7.1b) and that Cai Ze would live for 43 more years and would become prime minister of Qin (*SJ*, 79.34–35). The marvelous accuracy of these two predictions stunned the intellectual world and gave credence to the doctrine. Testimony to the remarkable interest created in physiognomy is the list of 24 books on the subject to be found in the catalogue to the Han Imperial Library. For these reasons, Xunzi felt compelled to refute its claims and to demonstrate that there was nothing of substance in physiognomy. Any prediction that came true was the result of mere chance. The methods of physiognomy could not produce consistent results.

More important still, physiognomy distracted men with its emphasis on the mere external form of a man. What was vastly more important in Xunzi's view was his mind. Of still greater importance were the methods because they lead the man to great accomplishment. These are what should be examined. Xunzi believed that in the age of the sage kings of antiquity, doctrines such as physiognomy could not have existed since men would then have never paid attention to such foolishness. By paying attention to height, size, or weight, we cheat ourselves and cause others to scorn us.

Those who are concerned with mere external superficialities forget the examples of Jie and Zhou Xin, who, though attractive and handsome, lost their kingdoms and came to be regarded as the greatest of villains. Their failures were the result not of their looks but of the baseness of the things they discussed. The untutored masses who place high regard on fashionable attire are as naive as infatuated young girls. That such men end in disaster arises not from their looks but from the uselessness and incompleteness of what they value.

History as the Refutation of Physiognomy. To confute the claims of the physiognomists, Xunzi cites many examples from history intended to show that since human characteristics are randomly distributed among men, good and bad, it is impossible to judge a man or predict his fate from his looks. Most of Xunzi's examples were stock figures drawn from the rhetorical traditions of his times—men like Confucius and the Duke of Zhou compared with Jie and Zhou Xin. Others were figures then well known, but now so obscure that the full force of Xunzi's point is lost. Three others are of interest because all were associated with the history of Chu, where Xunzi was teaching at Lanling when he wrote his book: King Yan of Xu 徐偃王; Sunshu Ao 孫叔敖; and the Duke of She 葉公.

King Yan of Xu. Of these, King Yan is the most obscure, partly because of the conflicting testimony of the various sources and commentaries. According to Han Fei, King Yan of Xu ruled a territory of 500 square *li* located east of the Han river. His government was so humane and just that 36 states ceded territory and paid him court visits.[12] King Wen of Chu 楚文王 (r. 689-671), fearing that King Yan would cause him harm, raised his armies, attacked, and destroyed him. According to the

Shiji (5.6–8), however, when King Mu of Zhou (r. 956–923) was inspecting his lands in the far west, it became necessary for him to return by forced marches to meet the revolt of King Yan of Xu. Because of the urgency of the threat, his charioteer, Zaofu, drove the magnificent steeds of the king's chariot a distance of 1,000 *li* per day, for which accomplishment he was awarded a fief. As long ago as Qiao Zhou 譙周 (fl. A.D. 200–270), in his *Gushi kao* 古史考, it was noted that these two stories are incompatible, that even the historical tables of the *Shiji* list King Wen of Chu ruling 318 years after King Mu and that the *Shiji* story is obviously mythological.[13] We may be sure that Xunzi refers to the same King Yan as his student Han Fei.

Sunshu Ao. In common with other philosophers of the late Warring States period, Xunzi thought of Sunshu Ao as a model minister. But little is known of his career. He is only briefly mentioned in the *Zuo zhuan*, which provides the most detailed record of the period. He was premier of Chu under King Zhuang and established his reputation by diverting the waters of the Qisi into the wilderness of Yunlou, thereby causing the king to think him worthy of being premier.[14] During the twelve years he held office, the king of Chu became lord-protector. It is related in the *Zhuangzi* (21 "Tian Zifang" 田子方, 7.21a) that he was thrice appointed to office and thrice removed during his career. He predeceased the king (*HNZ*, 18.2a). His conversation in the *Zhuangzi* (24 "Xu Wugui" 徐無鬼, 8.16b) with Confucius may be dismissed as legend.

The Duke of She. Prince Gao 子高, the Duke of She, also known as Shen Zhuliang 沈諸梁, was most famous for suppressing the revolt of the Duke of Bo 白公. His career spanned the years 523 to 475. The duke was an important figure of his time, and when engaged in the pacification of Cai, he had a famous interview with Confucius and his disciples, probably about 493. Confucius had reason to think that the duke was one of the feudal lords of the day who would be sympathetic to his views.[15]

The revolt of the Duke of Bo was one of the most famous events of the late Spring and Autumn period. The main figures were the high nobility of Chu. Prince Xi 子西, Gongsun Shen 公孫申, the premier, was a son by a senior concubine of King Ping 楚平王. Prince Qi 子期, the minister of war, was also a son of King Ping. The Duke of Bo was the son of the crown prince of Chu and the grandson of King Ping. Having been forced into exile with his father by slanderers in the royal court, he sought revenge on his royal relatives. He plotted to raise 500 men to attack the king, premier, and minister of war, but this could not be accomplished. He next approached a strong man with his scheme but was rebuffed. Finally, an incursion by a raiding party from Wu provided the pretext to raise forces. Having defeated the raiders, he then asked that he be permitted to offer the spoils to the court. Once there, he raised an insurrection, killed both the premier and the minister of war, and took King Hui prisoner. He was advised to burn the treasury and murder the king, but refused: "To murder the king would be inauspicious. And if I burn the treasury, I would have no stores. With what should I then maintain myself?" At this time, the Duke of She was still in Cai, where he was advised to advance on the capital, but he demurred. Later when he heard that the Duke of Bo had put Guan Xiu 管修, a descendant of Guan Zhong, to death, he knew that the time was ripe and proceeded to advance toward the capital.

In the interim, the Duke of Bo tried to force Prince Lu 楚王子閭 to become king, but he refused, and the duke had him removed. Therewith the duke put him to death and went for the king, who was kept in the treasury. But a retainer had surreptitiously dug through the wall and carried the king on his back to the palace of the queen dowager. At this juncture, the Duke of She arrived, attacked the Duke of Bo, defeated him, and crushed his rebellion. The Duke of Bo committed suicide, and his retainers were boiled. Having brought peace to Chu, the Duke of She became both premier and minister of war while order was being completely restored. He then resigned the office of premier, which he turned over to Prince Xi's son, and the office of minister of war, which he turned over to Prince Qi's son. He retired to She, where he spent his old age. By his actions, the Duke of She saved his country and preserved its royal house. In the code of his day, he exemplified at its finest the loyal behavior of a minister (*Zuo*, Zhao 19–20, Ding 5, Ai 4, 16–17). As such he was celebrated by philosophers.

Whereas Sunshu Ao and the Duke of She should be regarded as historical persons whose career and accomplishments were real and well known, other "ministers" from the hoary past must be regarded as paragons whose accomplishments are legend, even though they may have been real persons and not fictions. In this book, we encounter a group of four such paragons, the good ministers who assist the good first king in founding the dynasty and securing the Mandate of Heaven to rule: Gaoyao; Hongyao 閎夭; Fuyue 傅說; and Yi Yin (see Vol. 2 for a discussion of their putative role in the development of ancient Chinese society).

The Scheme of Ancient History. By the late Warring States period, antiquity had been divided into four main periods: the eras of the Three Huang August Ones 三皇, the Five Di Ancestors 五帝, the Three Dynasties 三代, and the Five Lords-Protector 五霸.[16] The age of the Three August Ones stretched back to the very beginnings of human society. Xunzi mentions in "Rectifying Theses" (18.6) Taihao 太昊 (= Fuxi 伏羲) and Suiren 燧人, two figures who existed in this primordial time. Contemporary works such as the encyclopedic *Lüshi chunqiu* mention the age of the Three August Ones, and its omission in the *Xunzi* is chance. The Three Dynasties are mentioned in "Of Honor and Disgrace" ("Rongru," 4.7) and the Five Lords-Protector are the major theme of "On Confucius." "Of Kings and Lords-Protector" contrasts the lords-protector unfavorably with the True Kings of antiquity.

In Xunzi's day the Ru found themselves subjected to two lines of attack on historical grounds. Radical primitivists and utopians harked back to the age of the August Ones to criticize the government of later times, arguing for a continuous devolution of society from the Golden Age. Ru scholars, who argued for the restoration of the government of the sages, found these attacks disconcerting. Revolutionary philosophies, which contended that a total transformation of the structure of government was necessary, argued that since the present is different from the past, we must depart from the methods of the sage kings of antiquity.

Xunzi noted that stupid men and fools can be deceived about almost anything, but the sage cannot. To teach that we must neglect the past because it differs from the present, as did his students Han Fei and Li Si, is foolish. By keeping each thing to its proper class, however different the time, however long the elapsed interval, conclusions will be valid because things of the same class share an identical principle of order. This is what the gentleman pursues. Thus, though the details of the past are lost because of the extreme antiquity involved, we can understand what is important because we have a standard of measurement. Against the primitivists and others who advocated a return to the model of extreme antiquity, Xunzi argues (in 5.4 below) that we should follow the Later Kings, who founded the Zhou dynasty.

Persuasions and Discriminations. Xunzi argues in this book that observing the forms and rules of persuasions 說 and discriminations 辯 is not enough. One's conclusions must correspond with the truths that we have inherited from the past and that are embedded in ritual and moral principles. The gentleman must engage in discriminations not only because he must compete with others in court, but because he loves the good they develop and the refinements of form they bring to his life. Without discussion of ritual, morality, the lessons of antiquity, and the model of the sages, life would be inescapably base, common, and vulgar.

The view Xunzi held was common in aristocratic ancient China. According to the *Zuo zhuan* (Xi 24), "words are the embellishment of the person." Confucius discussed (*Zuo*, Xiang 25) the skill of Prince Chan, prime minister of Zheng, in argument and literary compositions: "There is an ancient saying: 'Words are to give adequate expression to one's thoughts and compositions are to provide adequate form to one's words.' If there were no words, how could anyone know your thoughts and intentions; and if there were no form to compositions, one's words, though given expression, would not penetrate far." With such consummate skill, Prince Chan was able to save his country through the power of his oratory. Almost alone among ancient Chinese thinkers, Xunzi appreciated and celebrated the aesthetic quality of life. It was no idle adornment, no mere distraction, as the Mohists thought; it inhered in all self-cultivation and all self-improvement. Without such beauty, life is concerned with bare actualities and becomes, as the *Changes* say, "a tied sack."

Philosophers of Xunzi's day had considerable difficulty in persuading rulers to follow the dictates of ritual, observe the requirements of justice and humanity, and emulate the model of the sage kings. Han Fei devoted four books to an exposition of the problems. He observed (3 "Nanyan" 難言, 1.7b–8a): "If one discusses contemporary affairs in language that is not disrespectful and offensive, he appears to be interested only in preserving his own life and in toadying after his superiors; if he discusses distant customs and matters that seem weird or fantastic to ordinary experience, he appears to be given to exaggerated and extravagant statements."

The difficulties faced by the philosopher are clearly illustrated by the case of the Lord of Shang, who, when he discussed the way of kings that he had been taught, got nowhere with the Duke of Qin, but when he discussed how to become powerful and rich, the duke made him prime minister. The gentleman, Xunzi taught, overcame these problems not by pandering to the whims of rulers, but by acting as the standard of measurement and by adhering to the universal method.

Man and Animals. In this book, probably because of the confused order of the paragraphs between Books 3–5 (see Appendix B), Xunzi returns to the problem of man's inborn nature. What distinguishes man from the animals is not his external characteristics, but his ability to draw distinctions and to make discriminations. This ability enables him to give good and proper form to his behavior through ritual principles, which he alone can conceive. Apes generally resemble men, and parrots can talk, but neither can draw boundaries between things. The *Liji* ("Quli" 曲禮, 1.6b–7a) amplifies this point:

The parrot can talk, but it is not distinct from other flying birds; the orangutan can speak, but it too is not apart from other animals. Now when men today are lacking ritual principles, though they too can speak, do they not also have merely the mind of an animal? Only wild animals lack ritual principles. Hence parents and offspring indiscriminately share females of the species. For this reason, the sages created ritual principles to instruct man and cause him to know that it is only through rites that they are different from the beasts.

Men to be men must draw boundaries, separate social classes, and follow ritual principles. In Xunzi's mind, this meant to adopt the usages of the Zhou dynasty because it was the most-recent and best-known exemplar and the heir to a great tradition.

TEXT

5.1

In antiquity, physiognomy[17] did not exist, and the learned did not discuss it. In the past there was Gubu Ziqing,[18] and in the present generation there is Tang Ju of Liang,[19] who physiognomized the form and features of other men in order to learn whether their fortune would be good or bad, auspicious or inauspicious. Because they could do this, the unlearned men of our age praise them. But in antiquity, such men did not exist, and the learned did not discuss them.

Hence, to physiognomize the external form is not as important as evaluating[20] the mind, and evaluating the mind is not as important as selecting the proper methodology.[21] The external form cannot overcome the mind, and the mind cannot overcome the methodology. When methodology is correct and the mind is in accord with it, then though a man's external form is physiognomized as evil, since his mind and methods are good, nothing will hinder his becoming a gentleman. So, too, although a man's external form may be physiognomized as good, if his mind and methods are evil, nothing will prevent his being a petty man. Being a gentleman is properly called "good fortune," and being a petty man is properly called "bad fortune." Thus, being tall or short, small or large, having a good or bad physiognomy, is not to be fortunate or unfortunate. In antiquity, such men did not exist, and the learned did not discuss them.

Were not Ancestor Yao tall and Ancestor Shun short, King Wen tall and the Duke of Zhou short, and Confucius tall and Zigong 子弓[22] short?

Formerly Duke Ling of Wey (r. 534–493) had a minister named Gongsun Lü 公孫呂,[23] whose body was seven feet tall, his face three feet long
with his forehead[24] three inches across, with his nostrils, eyes, and ears
all pushed together;[25] nonetheless, his reputation agitated the whole
world.[26] In Chu, Sunshu Ao, a native of the small hamlet Qisi,[27] was
bald with splotches of short hair, had a left leg that was too long, and was
short enough to go under the upturning poles of a state carriage; nonetheless, he made Chu lord-protector over all the states.[28] Prince Gao, the
Duke of She, was so frail, small, short, and skinny that when he walked,
it looked as if he could not support even his clothes, but during the revolt of the Duke of Bo in which both Premier Prince Xi and Minister of
War Prince Qi were put to death, the Duke of She entered the capital
and occupied it, executed the Duke of Bo, and pacified the whole of
Chu as easily as turning his hand over, so that his humanity, justice,
meritorious accomplishment, and fame have won the praise of posterity.[29] Accordingly, scholars[30] should not estimate the height, measure the
size,[31] or reckon the weight, but should fix their attention on the mind
and on nothing else.[32] What reason could there be to consider whether
he is short or tall, large or small, or the physiognomy of his external
form good or bad.

Moreover, in appearance King Yan of Xu's eyes were so protruded
that he could see his forehead.[33] Confucius' face looked like it was
covered with an exorcist's mask,[34] the Duke of Zhou's body was like a
broken stump.[35] Gaoyao's complexion was like that of a shaved melon.
Hongyao's face had no visible skin. Fuyue looked like he had a fin
emerging from his back.[36] Yi Yin had neither beard nor eyebrows.
Yu was lame, and Tang was paralyzed.[37] Yao and Shun had irregular
pupils.[38] Should we who follow them consider critically their will and
intellect and compare them in terms of the character of their culture and
learning? Or should we take note only of differences in size to discriminate between good and bad and so cheat and bring scorn upon
ourselves?

5.2

In antiquity, Jie and Zhou Xin were tall, well built, attractive, and
handsome, heroes of the whole world, whose musculature was so
powerful and whose strength was so great that they could hold their
own against a hundred men.[39] Nonetheless, both lost their lives, and
their kingdoms perished. They are now regarded as the greatest of crimi-
nals. Whenever we of later generations speak about evil, we must always
examine their cases.[40] Their calamitous end resulted not from their ap-

pearance but from the fact that what they had heard and seen was not the whole and from the baseness of what they discussed and deliberated, and from nothing else.

It is the custom of the anarchic masses[41] of the present day that the "smart" youth of every village are all beautifully elegant and seductively fascinating. They wear striking clothing with effeminate decorations and exhibit the physical desires and bearing of a young girl. Married women once all hoped to get such a man for their husband. Unmarried girls all hope to have one of them as their knight and would even be willing to abandon their father's house so they could elope with him and take the wife's position at his side. Nonetheless, the average lord would be ashamed to have them as ministers, the average father to have them as sons, and the average man to have them as friends. And no doubt one day they will suddenly be bound and fettered before a magistrate and taken to the large marketplace for execution. When this happens, they will cry out to Heaven, weeping and wailing, bitterly aggrieved at their present circumstances and regretting too late their past. Their calamity as well resulted not from their manner, but from the fact that their experience was not whole and what they talked about was worthless. In such cases, what should we who follow afterwards depend on![42]

5.3

Man has three sure signs of misfortune: to be young and yet unwilling to serve one's elders; to be of humble origins and yet be unwilling to serve the noble; and to be lacking in worth yet be unwilling to serve the worthy. Such are the three sure signs of misfortune.

Man has three patterns of behavior that certainly will reduce him to dire need.

To occupy a superior position and yet be unable to love those inferior to him or to occupy an inferior position and to be fond of condemning his superiors—this is the first way to bring certainty of dire need;

To be agreeable to a person's face,[43] yet when he turns his back, to insult him—this is the second way to bring certainty of dire need; and

To be so superficial and shallow in knowledge and behavior that one makes no distinction between crookedness and uprightness[44] and thus is unable to encourage humane men and to bring glory to wise scholars[45]—this is the third way to bring certainty of dire need.

If the man who practices these modes[46] of behavior occupies a high position, he is certain to be imperiled. If he occupies a low position, he is certain to be destroyed. An Ode says:[47]

The snow falls so thickly, so thickly,
but when it is cloudless and hot, it melts.[48]
None of them is willing to fall down,
but their mode of living is empty and arrogant.[49]

This expresses my meaning.

5.4

What is it that makes a man human? I say that it lies in his ability to draw boundaries. To desire food when hungry, to desire warmth when cold, to desire rest when tired, and to be fond of what is beneficial and to hate what is harmful—these characteristics man is born possessing, and he does not have to wait to develop them.[50] They are identical in the case of a Yu and in that of a Jie. But even so, what makes a man really human lies not primarily in his being a featherless biped,[51] but rather in his ability to draw boundaries. For example, the Shengsheng 猩猩 ape[52] resembles a man in form[53] and is also a featherless biped,[54] but the gentleman will nonetheless sip a broth and eat minced meat made from him.[55] Hence, what makes a man human lies not in his being a featherless biped but in his ability to draw boundaries.[56] Even though wild animals have parents and offspring, there is no natural affection between them as between father and son, and though there are male and female of the species, there is no proper separation of sexes. Hence, the proper way of Man lies in nothing other than his ability to draw boundaries.

Of such boundaries, none is more important than that between social classes. Of the instruments for distinguishing social classes, none is more important than ritual principles.[57] Of the sources of ritual principles, none is more important than the sage kings. But one asks: There are a hundred sage kings, which one ought I to use as my model?[58] There is an old saying:

Inscriptions with the passing of time perish,
Rhythms that are too prolonged break apart.[59]

Officers entrusted with preserving the model and methods in the end become lax in keeping them.[60] Hence I say: If you want to observe the footprints of the sage kings, you must look where they are most clearly preserved—that is, with the Later Kings.[61] These Later Kings were lords over the whole world. To put them aside and to discuss instead extreme antiquity is like giving up your own lord and serving another. Hence I say: If you want to observe a millennium, you must look at today.[62] If you would know ten thousand or a million, you must scrutinize one or two. If you would know the ages of antiquity, you must closely examine the way of Zhou. If you would know the way of Zhou, you must carefully observe the ideal of the gentleman prized by its men.⁶³ There is an ancient saying:

> Use the near to know the remote,
> Use the one to know the myriad,
> Use the insignificant to know the glorious.

This expresses my meaning.

5.5

Fools say:

The circumstances of the past and the present are quite different, and the Way by which to bring order to the anarchy of today must be different.⁶⁴

The mass of humanity are beguiled by this argument. The petty masses are so stupid that they lack any counterargument and so uncultivated that they have no counterstandard for measure. If they can be deceived about what they have seen with their own eye, how much more easily can they be deceived about what has been handed down over a thousand generations. Fools mislead and deceive them about what transpires within their own courtyards, how much more easily can they be misled about events that occurred a thousand years in the past.

But why can the sage not be deceived as well?⁶⁵ I say that it is because the sage uses himself as the standard for measurement. Hence, the sage uses men to measure men, circumstances to gauge circumstances,⁶⁶ each class of thing to measure that class, the persuasion to measure the achievement, and the Way to observe the totality, so that for him the ancient and modern are one and the same.⁶⁷ Things of the same class do not become contradictory even though a long time has elapsed because they share an identical principle of order. Hence, because the sage uses himself as a standard of measurement, when he encounters what is perverse and deviant, he is not led astray, and when he observes the diversity of objects of the external world, he is not confused.

That before the Five Di Ancestors there are no traditions concerning individuals is not because of the absence of sages during that time, but because of the extreme antiquity of the period. That for the period of the Five Di Ancestors there are no traditions concerning affairs of government is not because of the lack of good government, but again because of the extreme antiquity of the period. For Yu and Tang there are traditions concerning their government, but they cannot be ascertained with the detail of those for the Zhou dynasty. This again is not because of any absence of good government but because of the great antiquity of the period. What has been transmitted over a long span of time can be discussed only in broad outlines; what is recent can be discussed in greater detail. When only the broad outlines exist, major events are recorded; when the details survive, minor events are mentioned. The stupid, hearing of their broad outlines, do not know the details and, hearing of minute details, do not know the major events. This is because

> Inscriptions with the passing of time perish,
> Rhythms that are too prolonged break apart.

5.6

Every doctrine that is neither consistent with Ancient Kings[68] nor in accord with the requirements of ritual and moral principles is properly described as a "treacherous doctrine." Although they may be the product of a discrimination, the gentleman will not heed it. Though one models himself after the example of the Ancient Kings, is in accord in his actions with the requirements of ritual and moral principles, and is a partisan[69] of learning, but nonetheless is not fond of advocating the truth and does not take enjoyment in it, he certainly is no true scholar. Hence the gentleman's relation to advocating the truth is such that his innermost mind loves it, his actions find peace in it, and his joy is in approving it.[70] Thus,

> the gentleman must engage in discriminations. Every man without exception is fond of discussing what he finds to be good, but this is especially so with the gentleman.[71]

Accordingly, to make the gift of true doctrines to another is more valuable than gold, gems, pearls, and jade.[72] To show them to another is more beautiful than the embroidered emblems on the ceremonial court robes of the king.[73] To cause him to hear them is more enjoyable than the music of bells and drums and of zithers and lutes. For this reason, the gentleman never grows weary of advocating his doctrines. The uncultivated rustic is opposed to such things because he loves only the bare actuality and cares nothing for refinements of form; thus, his whole life is inescapably low, base, common, and vulgar.[74] Hence the *Changes* say:

> A tied sack: nothing to blame, nothing to praise.[75]

This describes the corrupt Ru.

5.7

All the difficulties of persuasions lie in this: that the highest must be juxtaposed with the lowest, that the most orderly must be connected with the most chaotic, and that this may never be done by the most direct route. If one adduces distant examples, they are annoyed at the exaggerations; if one cites[76] recent examples, they are annoyed at their commonplaceness. A true expert in this pursuit is sure to avoid both difficulties by adducing only distant examples that are not exaggerated and by citing recent examples that are not commonplace. He modifies and changes them with the occasion, adapting and adjusting them to the age, sometimes indulgent, sometimes urgent, sometimes expansive, other times restrictive. Channel them like canal ditches, force them like the press-frame,[77] accommodating them to the circumstances so that your audience will get hold of the idea under discussion, yet will not be given offense or be insulted.

Hence, the gentleman measures himself with the exactness of the plumbline, but when he comes into contact with others, he uses the less demanding bow-frame.[78] Because he measures himself with the plumbline, he deserves to be considered the model and paradigm of the whole world. Because when he comes into contact with others he uses the bow-frame, he is capable of magnanimity and tolerance. In consequence he can help to bring[79] the great undertakings of the world to fruition. Hence, the gentleman, though worthy, is able to tolerate the unfit. Though wise, he is able to suffer the stupid. Though profound, he is able to endure the superficial. Though pure, he can tolerate the adulterated. This may be described as the "universal method." An Ode says:[80]

> That the region of Xu was joined to the realm[81]
> was the accomplishment of the Son of Heaven.

This expresses my meaning.

5.8[82]
The Proper Methodology for Debate and Persuasion

Introduce the topic with dignity and earnestness, dwell on it with modesty and sincerity, hold to it with firmness and strength, illustrate its meaning with parables and praiseworthy examples,[83] elucidate its significance by making distinctions and drawing boundaries,[84] and present it with exuberance and ardor.[85] If you make it something precious and rare, valuable and magical, your persuasion will always and invariably be well received, and even if you do not please them, none will fail to esteem you. This may indeed be described as "being able to bring esteem to what one prizes." A tradition says:

> It is only the gentleman who is capable of bringing esteem to what he prizes.

This expresses my meaning.[86]

5.9

The gentleman must engage in discriminations. Every man without exception is fond of discussing what he finds to be good, but this is especially so with the gentleman.[87]

For this reason, whereas the petty man engages in discriminations to discuss threats of danger, the gentleman engages in them to discuss the principle of humanity. If a line of discussion does not coincide with the requirements of the principle of humanity, its words are worse than remaining silent and the discrimination not as good as stuttering. If the tenor of one's words coincides with the principle of humanity, the person who enjoys advocating true doctrines is superior to the man who does not. Hence, advocating the principle of humanity is of primary importance. Arising among the ruling classes, advocacy is used to guide the lower classes. Government regulations and ordinances are examples.[88] Arising from the lower classes, it is expressed in a loyalty to the ruling classes. Remonstrances and reproofs are examples.[89] Accordingly,

the gentleman never grows weary of the principle of humanity,
for he loves it in his innermost mind, his actions find peace in it,
and his joy is in discussing it.[90]

Thus it is said:

The gentleman must engage in discriminations.

Discrimination of secondary matters is not as important as making visible the first manifestations. Making visible the first manifestations is not as important as tracing social distinctions to their origins.[91] Through discrimination of secondary matters, one gains precision; through making visible the first manifestations, one gains understanding; and through tracing social distinctions to their origins, one discovers their principle of order. The division between the sage and the scholar and gentleman is provided for.

5.10

There are the discriminations of the petty man, those of the gentleman, and those of the sage. The discriminations of the sage involve no prior consideration and no planning beforehand, yet whatever he expresses is appropriate, perfected in form, and exactly proper to its type. In raising up issues or in setting them aside, in removing them or shifting them, he responds inexhaustibly to every change. The discriminations of the scholar and gentleman consider problems in advance and plan for them early, so that when they speak even on the spur of the moment, their advice deserves a hearing. They are well composed yet convey realities and are wide in learning yet committed to what is upright.[92]

If one listens to their discussion, though they appear to offer propositions and discriminations, they lack any guiding principle that connects everything together. If you employ them, they are so given to deception that they are devoid of accomplishment. On the one hand, they are incapable of gaining the acquiescence of an enlightened king and, on the other hand, inadequate to get agreement and common accord from the Hundred Clans. Further, through a clever and glib tongue,[93] whether with garrulity or with but a simple yes, they give the appearance of being in full accord,[94] but they ought to be regarded like braggarts, arrogant attendants,[95] and others of their ilk. Such persons may be described as the most dominant of villainous men. Should a sage king arise, his first task would be to execute them and only then deal with thieves and robbers. Because although one can succeed in getting robbers and thieves to transform themselves, one cannot get these men to change.

BOOK 6

▪▪ ▏▏▏ ▪▪

Contra Twelve Philosophers

INTRODUCTION

Xunzi's "Contra Twelve Philosophers" criticizes those philosophers whose doctrines and influence he regarded as dangerous to society. In doing so, he provides a rare survey of currents of contemporary thought. Together with the "World of Thought" of the *Zhuangzi* and the "Eminence in Learning" in the *Hanfeizi*, this book offers important insight into the intellectual life of late Warring States China. One might understand the title to be harsher than "contra," if one takes this book to be in the Mohist polemical tradition. As such it would be a successor to Mo Di's "Condemnation of the Ru" and should be considered Xunzi's "Condemnation of Twelve Philosophers." [1]

None of Xunzi's books has done more damage to his reputation. In other books, we have seen his censure of "worthless" and "base" Ru philosophers, but in none was criticism so directly aimed at particular heroes of the conventional, officially sanctioned Confucianism of the imperial period. Yang Liang, who shared the pieties of Tang Confucianism, felt embarrassed that Xunzi had attacked Mencius, whose canonization had then just begun, and Zisi, who was, after all, a grandson of Confucius. He and many others after him offered the lame suggestion that the offending passage had been inserted into the text by some opponent of Ru doctrines, possibly either Han Fei or Li Si, to use Xunzi to discredit the Ru. But this suggestion is absurd (see Appendix B). Other disciples of Xunzi, who may well have had a hand in the compilation of his works, were more conventional than their master insofar as we may judge from the sparse indications.

Xunzi attacks the twelve philosophers and the six philosophical positions their theories represent because they confuse the world with false notions of right and wrong and of what produces order and what anarchy. The Chinese terms for "right" and "wrong" (*shi*/*fei* 是/非) embrace not only the moral distinction but also the epistemological distinction between "what is the case" and "what is not the case." Here Xunzi undoubtedly means the epistemological as well as the moral distinction since he advocates in his "On the Correct Use of Names" the rectification of names. Like Nietzsche, Xunzi had no use for false but beautiful notions that lead to error and anarchy.

Wei Mou and Tuo Xiao. The innate nature of man embraces a love of profit and the natural desire for sex, food, clothing, and other bodily comforts, as well as the emotions. The inevitable result of following one's innate nature, as Tuo Xiao 它囂 and Wei Mou 魏牟 propose, can lead only to the conflict, disorder, and anarchy that the Ancient Kings abhorred. Xunzi thus considered that since man's nature was evil, the views of these two must necessarily lead to social chaos. Nothing whatever is known of Tuo Xiao except what is said here. Even his name does not occur elsewhere in the literature. This surprising fact, and the substitution of Fan Sui for his name in the *Hanshi waizhuan* parallel, has caused some scholars to surmise that the reading is an error for some other name, these characters having been mistaken for others similar in appearance. Guo Moruo suggests that he is Huan Yuan, a member of the Jixia Academy whose works are now lost. Unfortunately, we know very little of Huan Yuan other than that the *Hanshu* "Bibliographic Treatise" classifies him as a Daoist. We are thus unable to say that Huan's views match those described in this book.[2] Wei Mou, as we have seen, was influential in the court of the Lord of Pingyuan, where Xunzi undoubtedly first encountered his views.

Chen Zhong and Shi Qiu. The position opposite to that of Tuo Xiao and Wei Mou, that of repressing the desires by denying them, is equally in error. Such a way is cultivated only by those who pretend to superiority by having transcended the desires that all men manifestly have. Such men as Chen Zhong, called by his alternate name Tian Zhong in "Nothing Indecorous," and Shi Qiu want to do injury to the natural distinctions of wealth and honor on which society is founded.

Mo Di and Song Xing. To ignore gradations of rank and to abolish the social distance proper between ruler and subject out of concern for principles of mere utility or frugality undermine society in Xunzi's view. In advocating these principles, Song Xing seems to Xunzi the successor of Mo Di.

Shen Dao and Tian Pian. Elevating the principle of law without providing for the classical norm and masking a fondness for innovation behind the appearance of "following along" with the customs of the past destroy the state and undermine social distinctions. Shen Dao was concerned with the need for law, to be understood as the abstract principles of positive law rather than the enactment of specific rules with punishments, and thought it the proper basis of society. But Xunzi faulted his views because they failed to recognize the fundamental importance of the customary usages contained in ritual principles. It was not enough to have a "public" law that superseded private interests; the rationale for society and its institutions had to be based on common consent expressed through the voluntary submission of the people to the prince. The sage consolidated the submission of the people through ritual and observance of practices sanctioned by tradition. Like all thinkers of the Ru persuasion, Xunzi disliked innovation or change for its own sake. We have seen that Confucius had remarked that he was a "transmitter and not a creator" (*LY*, 7.1) and the *Mozi* confirms that the Ru claimed that a "gentleman is a follower and not a creator" (39 "Fei Ru," 9.21a). Shen Dao, like most philosophers, observed the practice of citing ancient authority to support his theories because in the milieu of the day to characterize one's thoughts as "innovative" or "modern" was to condemn them utterly. To Xunzi this was a ruse because there was no recurrent theme or main topic to which Shen Dao and Tian Pian returned as he himself returned to the principles of humanity and justice or to ritual principles and the ideal of the gentleman.

Hui Shi and Deng Xi. Shocking propositions, useless conclusions, and meager results are all that those who pursue abstruse matters of logic have to offer. Xunzi accepted and used improvements in exactness of formulation, in precision of definition, and in elegance of argument that Deng Xi and Hui Shi made through their analysis of discriminations, but he thought that their doctrines and conclusions lacked any guiding rules and ordering norms for the government and were thus worthless to kings and commoners alike.

Zisi and Mencius. Zisi was Kong Ji 孔伋, the grandson of Confucius (*SJ*, 74.3), and, through his disciples, the teacher of Mencius (*Mengzi*, 2B.2, 5B.6–7, 6B.6). He is known to have been active during the reign of Duke Mu of Lu 魯穆公 (r. 415–383) and is traditionally credited with the *Zhongyong*, "Doctrine of the Mean."[3] Though the present text by that name may include sections by Zisi, it clearly was not compiled or at least finally edited until the beginning of the Qin dynasty. We are thus uncertain of the specific ideas of Zisi. Mencius' works, in contrast, are the best preserved of any philosopher of the period. The evidence of Mencius' works dates him to the last two decades of the fourth century, and his conception of man's inborn nature is refuted by Xunzi in "Man's Nature Is Evil."

Xunzi contends that other philosophers did follow the model of the Ancient Kings, but in a fragmentary way. But since knowledge of the model had decayed with the passage of time, Xunzi advocated following the model of the Later Kings, particularly the founding kings of the Zhou dynasty, which was still well known. Philosophers of Xunzi's own time who adhered to the model of the Ancient Kings had begun to contaminate the true doctrines of Confucius with the Five Processes 五行 theory by passing them off as transmitted by Zisi and Mencius. They debased the true heritage of the sage to give a cloak of respectability to pernicious doctrines.

This contention of Xunzi's has caused much of the opprobrium from which Xunzi has suffered since the canonization of Mencius in the Song period. It has also puzzled scholars since nothing in the surviving works and fragments of Mencius and, insofar as can be known, those of Zisi indicates even the slightest connection with the Five Processes theory.[4] Yang Liang, knowing that Mencius did not discuss the Five Processes, identified the term with the Five Constants of correct behavior: humanity, ritual, morality, wisdom, and honesty. Though these words are often used by Confucius and Mencius, there is no reason to think that Xunzi would criticize Mencius for them since he endorses them all himself.[5] The problem must therefore lie elsewhere.

The central point at issue is the meaning of two sentences: Does Xunzi say that Zisi and Mencius transmitted these doctrines; and does he blame them for the corruption of traditional Ru values? Most scholars have answered yes to both questions and have been faced with the problem of accounting for Xunzi's statement, which so patently contradicts historical fact, at least insofar as the evidence indicates. Arthur Waley first offered another view: this paragraph is "not (as has been supposed) an attack on [Zisi and] Mencius but on the 'Cosmologists,'" who advocated the Five Processes theory.[6] This interpretation causes the dilemma simply to disappear by squaring the passage with the facts. What Xunzi is here criticizing is not the original doctrines of Zisi and Mencius, though elsewhere he criticizes some of these, but their corruption through admixture with the Five Processes theory.

The Adaptation of Wu Xing Theory. The Five Processes theory was of major importance in Xunzi's day and assumed even greater significance in the Han dynasty, when it penetrated the official Confucianism of the Imperial University. The origins of the theory perhaps date to the fifth century, and possibly earlier, depending on how one dates the composition of the "Hongfan" 洪范, one of the *Documents*,[7] which possibly testifies to an early incorporation of primitive Five Processes ideas into the traditions of the Ru philosophers. But its systematization into a comprehensive philosophy appears to have occurred only after 300 in the works of Zou Yan. By 250 its ideas were known to all schools of Chinese philosophy, as witnessed by references to the theory in such varied works as the *Guanzi, Mozi, Lüshi chunqiu, Zhuangzi*, and *Xunzi*. The amalgamation of Ru concepts with Five Processes ideas is associated with the transmission of the *Documents*. Proscribed during the Qin dynasty, the *Documents* were transmitted to the Han period solely through Fu Sheng (250–175). The commentary he prepared for the *Documents*, his *Shangshu dazhuan*, testifies to the fusion of the ideas of the Ru with those of the Five Processes theory that Xunzi condemns. Though now surviving only in fragments, Fu Sheng's line of argument is preserved in the "Treatise on the Five Processes" in Ban Gu's *Hanshu* (written about A.D. 90).

Xunzi may have had cause to be alarmed that even his own students, among them probably Zhang Cang, had been seduced by such notions. Zhang was clearly interested in the Five Processes theory. When he "rectified" the calendar and pitchpipes for the newly established Han dynasty, he took as the starting point the fact that it was in the tenth month that Gaozu, who founded the dynasty, reached Baoshang. Thus, he advocated continuing the old Qin practice of using the tenth month as the beginning of the new year. Drawing inferences from the cycle of mutations of the Five Powers, he concluded that the Power by which Han ruled should be water and that black should be its heraldic color, as it had been for Qin before it (*SJ*, 96.10). Sima Qian reports that Zhang loved every kind of book, examined everything that came his way, and understood them all. He excelled in everything connected with calendrics and pitchpipes (*SJ*, 96.11). Liu Xin includes a book by Zhang among the treatises concerned with the Yin-Yang school (*HSBZ*, 30.39b).

By 150, the Five Processes theory was an integral part of the mainstream of Confucian thinking, as witnessed by the *Chunqiu fanlu* 春秋繁露 of Dong Zhongshu. With the establishment of the Imperial University and the naming of Erudites for the Five Classics (in 136), the synthesis became the dominant philosophy.[8] Xunzi's condemnation should thus be taken as the earliest protest against a tendency that would later become triumphant by giving a "cloak of respectability," as he put it, to such ideas by attributing them to Confucius and claiming that they had been transmitted by Zisi and Mencius.

Five Processes Theory. The term *wu xing* 五行 has commonly been translated "Five Elements" since its five terms were fire, water, earth, wood, and metal, which, in a general way, resembled Greek notions usually translated "elements." But *xing* 行 never meant a constituent of matter. Translating it "element" inevitably leads to this misunderstanding. In common language, the character *xing* means "walk, move" and, by extension, when understood in a causal sense, "put into effect." It also means "row or column" as the "column of troops" of a moving army. It is out of these ordinary meanings of the character that the technical term *wu xing* developed. The *xing* were not the "agent," "force," or "mechanism" of change, but they could be the *phases* of change as when H_2O changes from ice to water to steam, or the *stages* of change associated with transformations of the hexagrams in the *Changes*, or the *activities* appropriate to the various seasons, or the *processes* of change symbolized by each of the *xing*. Each meaning is appropriate in certain contexts, but none is adequate to all. I have adopted the translation "processes" because it best illustrates the kinds of meaning that Xunzi seems to have had in mind in criticizing the theory.[9]

The description of each of the five "processes" is found in the "Hongfan" (5; Karlgren, "Book of Documents," p. 29), where the *wu xing* are among the invariable principles of Nature:[10] "The first of them are called the Five Processes. They are called: first, water; second, fire; third, wood; fourth, metal; and fifth, earth. 'Water' designates what soaks and descends. 'Fire' designates what blazes and ascends. 'Wood' designates what can be made curved or straight. 'Metal' designates what can follow its nature or be made to change.[11] 'Earth' designates what permits sowing and reaping." Here we are confronted with a passage using common words in a technical sense. Consequently we are undertranslating or loosely and ambiguously translating a passage that once had a precise sense now lost or unclear. This is suggested by the statements that follow in the "Hongfan."

It is said that "soaking" and "descending" produce saltiness, which seems to imply the chemical process of dissolving and precipitation that produces salts. What the text means by "blazing" and "ascending" producing "bitterness" is difficult to construe, though, as Needham (2:244) notes, it "may imply the use of heat in preparing decoctions of medicinal plants, which would be the bitterest substances likely to be known." "Wood" can be "made straight or curved," as Xunzi noted in his "Exhortation to Learning" (1.1). This suggests "workability" since it has no unalterable shape; with decomposition it becomes "sour." The meaning of "metal" being able to "follow its nature or made to change" apparently involves the "moldability" of metals, which, when heated, are reduced to liquids. The steaming of wood and the sharpening of metal were recurrent metaphors for the permanent improvements that education effected on inborn nature ("Xing'e," 23.1b). But in the Five Processes theory, smelting is associated with "acridity" as "wood" is with "sour." "Earth," which stands for the fundamental activity of society, sowing and reaping, is associated with "sweet," which is common throughout the world, as in "sweet" water, "sweet" soil, "sweet" milk, meaning "good, productive."

Interesting though the five processes are in suggesting the emergence of Chinese ideas about science and scientific theory, it was the social and political implications that interested the kings of the Warring States period. The "theory" they desired to understand contended that there was a periodical dominance of each of the five "processes" in turn during the cycles of history. Each dynasty had been characterized by dominance of one of the "processes." Each was in turn succeeded by a different dynasty characterized by dominance of a different process.[12] Two basic questions, in the view of the day, needed to be answered: How do the processes succeed one another; and what is the state or phase of the present age and what is its dominant process?

To the first question, several answers were current in Xunzi's day: the processes evolve from one into the other;[13] they produce one another;[14] they conquer one another.[15] This last is the theory for which Zou Yan was famous. It is usually thought that this is the version that Xunzi condemns in this book. The Mohists as well condemned this version, arguing that "the Five Processes do not constantly conquer. That fire melts metal is because there is much fire; that the metal uses the charcoal fuel is because there is much metal."[16]

To the second question there were also several answers, but it was the theory systematized by Zou Yan that dominated the age. It had direct and immediate political consequences since it taught that each epoch of history was ruled by a particular process that determined its character. Each ruling house had come to power through the natural succession of these processes, which in turn made its decline inevitable. Since it was obvious that the Zhou dynasty was in decline, the burning issue of political speculation was who would succeed. Knowing the process that would rule the next epoch and understanding how to use it would give a man such immense powers that he could gain the empire. Zou Yan said:

When any Di ancestor or king is about to arise, Heaven is certain first to exhibit auspicious omens to the people. In the time of Huang Di, Heaven first had large earthworms and large ants appear. He said: "The Earth essence (qi 氣) is conquering. For this reason our heraldry should honor yellow and our affairs should be modeled after Earth." ... In the time of King Wen, Heaven first exhibited Fire. Red birds holding documents written in cinnabar script flocked to the altars of Zhou. He said: "The Fire essence is conquering. For this reason, our heraldry should honor red, and our affairs should be modeled after Fire."

Following Fire, Water is sure to come. Heaven will first exhibit signs when the Water essence is about to conquer. Then the heraldry should honor black, and affairs should be modeled after Water. And that dispensation in turn will come to an end at its appointed time, though we know not when, and all will return once more to Earth. (LSCQ, 13/2 "Yingtong" 應同, 13.4a)

Associated with the wu xing Five Processes were the wu de "Five Powers," that is, the "power" (de 德) intrinsic to, and inherent in, each of the processes. Each of the Five Powers was followed, according to Zou Yan (as quoted in *Wenxuan* 59.9b), by the power it could not conquer.

Who would succeed and when they would succeed, all were anxious to learn. Zou Yan taught that it would be by the process Water and that there would be omens indicating its impending conquest. But how these could be anticipated and identified was uncertain and required "expert" judgments. Nonetheless, despite arguments over details, most apparently believed the theory was true. So when Qin conquered the empire and the First Emperor was proclaimed, "black" became the heraldic color, and the affairs of government were modeled after water. With the founding of the Han dynasty, it was thought that the power Water still prevailed, and so the color black was adopted,[17] in part, as we have seen, because of the influence of Xunzi's disciple Zhang Cang,[18] which may explain further the strength of Xunzi's denunciation of the admixture of *wu xing* ideas with Ru traditions.

The Condemnation of Aberrant Ru Schools. In this book, Xunzi singles out three specific groups of Ru for condemnation: those who claimed the disciples Zizhang, Zixia, and Ziyou as the founders of their school. We have seen that these disciples and their students are responsible for the *Analects* of Confucius and that Mencius apparently regarded them as a party or group. Writing about the same time as this book, Han Fei (50 "Xianxue," 19.9a) mentions only Zizhang among the founders of separate branches or schools of Ru. Xunzi, however, distinguishes between them, though all are condemned as "base Ru."

Zizhang is the style name of Zhuansun Shi 顓孫師, a native of Chen, who is said to have been 49 years younger than Confucius (*SJ*, 67.30–32). In the *Analects*, he frequently asks Confucius questions about humaneness and other topics[19] and is credited with several sayings of his own (*LY*, 19.1–3). He is described by the master as "going too far" and being "self-important," characteristics perhaps exaggerated in the behavior of his disciples in Xunzi's day (*LY*, 11.16, 19.16). Zizhang is ridiculed by a fictional eccentric called Mr. "Full of Ill-gotten Gains" in the *Zhuangzi* (29 "Dao Zhi," 9.22a). In the *Analects* (2.18), it is admitted that he studied in order to get an official emolument.

Zixia is the style name of Bu Shang 卜商, whose origins are unclear, though he is said to have been 44 years younger than Confucius (*SJ*, 67.28–30). He is especially important in the spread of Ru doctrines because late in life he became the adviser to Marquis Wen of Wei, who, alone among the feudal lords of that time, was fond of learning (*SJ*, 121.4). He is known to have been especially interested in ritual and is credited with the transmission of the *Odes*, which he had received from Confucius. He discusses rituals with Confucius and asks about the true meaning of the *Odes* (*LY*, 12.5, 3.8). He offers interpretations of the Master's words, has numerous sayings of his own (*LY*, 1.7, 19.4–13), and is specifically credited with "disciples and scholars" (19.3 19.12). Mo Di had a conversation with one of his disciples (46 "Geng Zhu" 耕柱, 11.19a). It is apparent that he was very important in the formation of the *Analects* tradition and that he founded a school, though not one of the eight mentioned by Han Fei (50 "Xianxue," 19.9a). Zixia is described as "not going far enough," in contrast to Zizhang (*LY*, 11.16), and praised together with Ziyou for his culture and learning (*LY*, 11.3). Confucius once admonished him to be a gentleman Ru and not a common, petty Ru (*LY*, 6.13), which may have been the basis of Xunzi's criticism of his followers, who exaggerated his faults and shortcomings.

Ziyou, whose name was Yan Yan 言偃, is not well known (*SJ*, 121.4), but he held office as commandant of Wu during the lifetime of Confucius (*LY*, 6.14, 17.4), is credited with several sayings in the *Analects* (4.26, 19.14–15), and identified the Way with music performances and the rites, which perhaps led his disciples to excess (*LY*, 17.4). He severely criticized the disciples of Zixia, saying that they were fit only for "sprinkling and sweeping floors" and other "minor matters" (*LY*, 19.12).

Other than what Xunzi says in this paragraph, we have no direct knowledge of the distinctive features of each of these schools. The syncretism of the Han period indiscriminately combined materials from diverse schools. In the process, differences between the followers of the various disciples have largely been obliterated. Today, it is all but impossible to identify with a particular individual or school such differences as are still apparent in the individual books of large compendiums of various ritual texts such as the *Liji* and *Da Dai liji*.

The True Ru Heritage. Alone among the disciples who founded schools, Xunzi thought Zigong transmitted the true doctrines of the Master.[20] Even such great men in better ages than the present, Xunzi concluded, did not always wield power. But if they do, as did Shun and Yu, the whole world benefits. When they do not, as Confucius and Zigong did not, they leave behind a perfected sense of what is morally right. This later generations must honor because it is what all who aspire to be a humane man in an evil age, such as that in which Xunzi lived, should do. Following these precepts, such a man will be able to silence the theories of the twelve philosophers, and he can make manifest the heritage of the sages. But if he fails to do this, then dissolute undertakings, outlooks, and theories will develop. However difficult such theories are to grasp or master, they can lead to nothing.

Philosophy and Language. In this book, we encounter an excellent example of the kind of sentence that accounts for the notion that Chinese "is vague and general" and that its utterances are accordingly always "ambiguous." The laconic character of Chinese propositions is indeed illustrated by Xunzi's remark *xin xin xin ye* 信信信也, "trust trust trust indeed." The absence of inflection of the word stem makes the three occurrences of the word apparently the same, the meaning being determined by syntax alone. Because Chinese has few traces of inflection, abstract ideas sometimes seem strange and peculiar, masked as they are behind common, ordinary forms. Specialized and technical usages—forms distinguished in English by inflection or by borrowing from a learned language like Greek or Latin—are often overlooked in ancient Chinese because they have been forgotten over the centuries that separate Xunzi's language from contemporary Chinese, where only the common meaning or an altered meaning remains known. Recent research has uncovered many such terms, particularly important technical terms applied to technical and scientific pursuits or the specialized language of mathematics, logic, and philosophy.

The meaning of the sentence is quite clear: "trusting what is trustworthy constitutes true trust." But, as Yang Liang notes, this is to be understood with its complement "doubting what should be doubted" (or "doubting what is dubious") also "constitutes true trust." This complementarity illustrates the Chinese tendency, especially evident in the concept of Yin and Yang, to analyze reality into contrasting, opposite terms, the union of which constitutes reality. Thus, the concept of "trust" understood fully must encompass not only "trusting the trustworthy" but also "doubting the dubious." Confucius made the same point with regard to knowledge: "When you know something, to recognize that you know it, and when you do not know something, to recognize that you do not know it—this is knowledge" (*LY*, 2.17).[21] Xunzi applies this way of thinking not only to "trust" but also to humaneness.

The Gentleman. The whole world willingly submits to a man who has the heart of a sage because it senses that his inner power, his intelligence, his wisdom, and his high position will benefit everyone and that he would not harm them, or trick them, or behave arrogantly toward them. The gentleman asks when he does not know, studies what he has not mastered, and yields to superior talent even where he has ability. Whatever his strength, courage, or resolution, the gentleman will never cause injury to others. Thus, he loves all, respects all, and will contend with none. He is complete like Heaven and Earth, so that all but the recalcitrant submit to him.

Students of Xunzi's day wanted to gain high office and the wealth that went with it, as did Li Si. They thus intended to be "scholar-officials." But Xunzi believed that the ancient ideal had been corrupted into mere greed and avarice by those who used high office as the occasion for arrogant and insulting displays. Similarly, the noble ideal of "scholar-recluse" had been debased by ignorant fools who pretended to esoteric knowledge, by desire-ridden creatures who feigned desirelessness, and by false and impure hypocrites who spoke loftily of integrity and prudence. In antiquity, Xunzi believed, scholar-recluses were worthy men who lived away from court in remote rural places. Most would not hold office because they thought it would compromise their principles to do so. Stories of venerable recluses were current even in Confucius' time.[22] Such men were thought to pursue Inner Quiet (*jing* 靜), which was induced by stilling the mind and blocking out sensory distractions, until a state of empty, blank, pure consciousness was reached.

> When the mind is quiet and the life-breath regular,
> the Way can be made to stay.
> . . . .
> When the mind is cultivated and the intellect made quiet,
> the Way can be obtained.
>
> (*Guanzi*, 49 "Neiye," 16.2a)[23]

But by Xunzi's time, one could find only frauds who pretended to be "scholar-recluses" to justify their eccentric and unrestrained conduct.

Xunzi concludes this book with the admonition that the gentleman should not be ashamed that he does not hold office and is unable to cause others to believe that he is honorable and trustworthy because shame comes not from what others think of him but from what he really is. The gentleman is distinguished by never being remiss in the performance of his duty and in being responsive to every transformation. In this he is utterly unlike the base Ru who follow the disciples Zizhang, Zixia, and Ziyou.

TEXT

6.1

Some men of the present generation[24] cloak pernicious persuasions in beautiful language and present elegantly composed but treacherous doctrines[25] and so create disorder and anarchy in the world. Such men are personally insidious and ostentatious, conceited and vulgar,[26] yet they spread through the whole world their confused ignorance of wherein lies the distinction between right and wrong and between order and anarchy.

6.2

Some men indulge their inborn nature and emotions,[27] are content with unrestrained passion and an overbearing manner,[28] and behave like animals. They are unfit for employment to put usages in conformity with good form[29] or bring success to government. Nonetheless, some of what they advocate has a rational basis, and their statements have perfect logic, enough indeed to deceive and mislead the ignorant masses.[30] Such men are Tuo Xiao[31] and Wei Mou.

6.3

Some men repress their emotions and innate nature. Theirs is an excessively narrow path and a harsh and intricate way,[32] and they foolishly consider that the differences that separate them from other men constitute their superiority over others. But they are adequate neither to the task of bringing concord to the great mass of the people nor to that of clarifying the fundamental distinctions in society. Nonetheless, some of what they advocate has a rational basis, and their statements have perfect logic, enough indeed to deceive and mislead the ignorant masses. Such men are Chen Zhong and Shi Qiu.[33]

6.4

Some men do not know how to unify the world or how to establish the "evaluations and designations" for the nation,[34] but, rather, elevate the principles of merit and utility, place great stress on frugality and economy, and ignore[35] gradations of rank and status. They are unwilling to admit that there are differences that must be explained and that there must be social distance between the lord and his subjects. Nonetheless, some of what they advocate has a rational basis, and their statements have perfect logic, enough indeed to deceive and mislead the ignorant masses. Such men are Mo Di and Song Xing.

6.5

Some men honor the principle of law but are themselves without law. They deprecate the principle of "following along with the usages of the past" and are fond of innovation.[36] They obtain a hearing from the ruling class and a following among the unsophisticated.[37] On every occasion their doctrines are perfected in form, well composed, and fully documented, but if one turns around[38] and closely examines what they say, it turns out to be masterfully grandiose but to lack any basic theme or main topic to which it returns. It is impossible for them to provide a classical norm for the state or to fix social distinctions. Nonetheless, some of what they advocate has a rational basis, and their statements have perfect logic, enough indeed to deceive and mislead the ignorant masses. Such men are Shen Dao and Tian Pian.

6.6

Some men do not model their doctrines after the Early Kings and do not affirm ritual or moral principles, but are fond of treating abstruse theories and playing with shocking propositions.[39] Although formulated with extreme exactness, their propositions concern matters of no urgency,[40] and their theories, though defended by discriminations, are quite useless.[41] Though they treat many topics, their results are meager, and they cannot be considered to have provided any guiding rules or ordering norms for government.[42] Nonetheless, some of what they advocate has a rational basis, and their statements have perfect logic, enough indeed to deceive and mislead the ignorant masses. Such men are Hui Shi and Deng Xi.

6.7[43]

Some men follow the model of the Ancient Kings in a fragmentary way, but they do not understand its guiding principles. Still[44] their abilities are manifold, their memory great,[45] and their experience and knowledge both varied and broad. They have initiated a theory for which they claim great antiquity, calling it the Five Processes theory. Peculiar and unreasonable in the extreme, it lacks proper logical categories.[46] Mysterious and enigmatic, it lacks a satisfactory theoretical basis. Esoteric and laconic in its statements, it lacks adequate explanations.[47] To give their propositions a cloak of respectability and to win respect and veneration for them, they claim:

> These doctrines represent the genuine words of the gentleman of former times. Zisi provided the tune for them, and Mencius harmonized it.[48]

The stupid, indecisive, deluded Ru of today enthusiastically welcome these notions, unaware that they are false.[49] They pass on what they have received, believing that, on account of these theories, Confucius and Zigong[50] would be highly esteemed by later generations. It is in just this that they offend against Zisi and Mencius.[51]

6.8

If a man[52] combined specific methods with general strategies, made what he said equal what he did, united guiding principles with the proper categories for each thing, and assembled the most talented heroes of the world, informing them of the greatness of antiquity[53] and teaching them perfect obedience, then by merely facing toward the south wall of his room and sitting upon his mat,[54] the full array of forms and outward signs of the sage king would gather about him, and because of him the customs of a tranquil age would develop abundantly.[55] The practitioners of the six theories could not gain entry to his court, and men like these twelve philosophers could not associate with him. Though he lacked so much as a pinpoint of land, kings and dukes could not rival his fame. Should he once occupy the position of grand officer, a single ruler could not keep him to himself, and a single state could not contain him.[56] The greatness of his reputation would exceed that of the feudal lords, each of whom would long to employ him as their minister.[57] Even such a sage does not always gain a position of power. Such were Confucius and Zigong.

If a man unifies the whole empire, controls[58] the myriad things, rears and nourishes the common people,[59] benefits the whole world universally—so that wherever his influence reaches or knowledge of him penetrates,[60] none will but follow and submit to him—and if the practitioners of the six theories instantly become silent and men like these twelve philosophers are converted, then a sage has attained power. Such were Shun and Yu.

With what task should the humane man of today occupy himself? On the one hand, he should model himself after the regulations of Shun and Yu; and on the other hand, he should model himself after the moral principles manifested by Confucius and Zigong, thereby making it his task to silence the theories of the twelve philosophers. When this has been done, then harm to the world is eliminated, the undertakings of the humane man are completed, and the footprints of the sage kings are made visible.[61]

6.9

Trusting the trustworthy is trust; suspecting the suspect is also trust. Esteeming the worthy is humaneness; deprecating the unworthy is humaneness as well. Speaking when it is appropriate to do so is knowledge; remaining silent when appropriate is also knowledge. Hence knowing when to remain silent is as important as knowing when to speak. Therefore, a sage, though he speaks often, always observes the logical categories appropriate to what he discusses. A gentleman, though he speaks but seldom, always accords with the model.[62] The petty man speaks frequently but in a manner that does not adhere to the model, his thoughts drowning in the verbiage of his idle chatter[63] even when he engages in the disciplined discourse of formal discriminations.

Hence labor, though toilsome, that is not a suitable occupation for the people[64] is termed a "dissolute undertaking." Knowledge that does not fit with the standards of the Ancient Kings, though hard won, is said to be that of a "dissolute mind." Discriminations and theories, illustrations and examples, though clever and sufficient, convenient and profitable, that do not follow the requirements of ritual and moral principles are termed "dissolute theories." The sage kings forbade these three dissolute things.

Those who most threaten public order are men who are wise but engage in daring exploits, who are malefactors with diabolic cleverness, who are skillful yet given to falseness and deception,[65] who discuss the useless but with formal discriminations, and who deal with matters of no urgency yet use precise investigations.[66] The great prohibitions of antiquity were against peculiar conduct engaged in with obstinate persistence, glossing over wrongs with fondness, playing with dissoluteness out of considerations of benefit,[67] and subversion of rational order yet engaging in advocacy and using discriminations.[68] The whole world scorns those who have knowledge but lack the model, those who are brave but reckless, those who, though capable of precise discriminations, hold on to perverse principles, those who have an excess of goods but are niggardly in their use,[69] those who are fond of debauchery and entice others to it, those who despite adequate material gain still go astray, and those who "carrying a stone on their back" throw themselves away.[70]

6.10
The Heart of One to Whom the Whole World Would Willingly Submit[71]

Exalted, highly esteemed, and honored—he does not use these to be arrogant toward others. Astutely intelligent and possessing sage-like wisdom—he does not use these to place others in difficulty. Quickwitted, fluent, agile, and universal in his intellectual grasp—he does not employ[72] these to gain precedence over others. Strong, resolute, brave, and daring—he does not use these to cause injury to others. When he does not know, he asks others; when he lacks an ability he studies; and even when he possesses an ability, he always yields to others. Only thusly does a man develop inner power.

When such a man unexpectedly encounters his lord, he devotes himself to observing the protocol appropriate to a minister and subject.[73] When he meets a fellow villager, he makes it his object to employ all the courtesy due age and accomplishment. When he encounters an older person, he devotes himself to observing the demeanor of a son or younger brother. When he meets a friend, he devotes himself to showing the appropriate courtesies and rules, polite refusals, and yielding precedence. When he encounters someone of lower station or younger than himself, he devotes himself to the manner appropriate to guidance, instruction, magnanimity, and tolerance. There are none he does not love, none he does not respect, and none with whom he would contend. He is as complete as Heaven and Earth, which embrace the myriad things.[74] One who is like this esteems the worthy and is kind to those who are not worthy. Those who do not willingly submit to such a person can only be called eccentric or weird, a rogue or a rascal. Though they should be his own son or his younger brother, it is altogether fitting that he should permit the punishment to reach them. An Ode says:[75]

> Is not the Supreme Di Ancestor[76] always timely!
> Yin does not use the old ways,
> but though it lacks old and perfected men,
> still it has the corpus of punishments,
> yet none will listen to them.
> For this the Great Mandate is tumbling down.[77]

This expresses my meaning.

6.11

The ancients called "scholar-official"[78] those who exerted themselves with a generous earnestness, made the masses concordant, and took pleasure in riches and honors.[79] Such men took delight in dividing and sharing. They kept their distance from offenses and transgressions. They were devoted to their duties and to reasoned order and were ashamed to keep wealth for themselves alone.[80]

Those who today are called "scholar-officials" are base and reckless, given to villainy and anarchy, to self-indulgence and excesses of passion, and to sheer greed. They are offensive and insulting,[81] and they lack any sense of ritual principle or moral duty, except when motivated by the desire for positions of power and influence.

The ancients called "scholar-recluses" those who possessed the highest inner power, who were able to obtain Inner Quiet, and who cultivated uprightness, knew destiny, and manifested in their person what was right and true.

Those who today are called "scholar-recluses" lack ability but are said to have ability,[82] and lack knowledge but are said to have it. They are insatiably profit-minded but feign desirelessness. They are false and secretly foul in conduct but forceful and lofty in speaking about integrity and prudence. They take the extraordinary as the ordinary, behaving eccentrically and without restraint, out of conceit and self-indulgence.[83]

6.12

There are both some things a scholar and gentleman can do and others they cannot do.[84] The gentleman can do what is honorable, but he cannot cause others to be certain to show him honor. He can act in a trustworthy fashion, but he cannot cause others to be sure to trust him. He can act so that he is employable, but he cannot cause others to be certain to use him. Hence, the gentleman is ashamed not to cultivate himself, but he is not ashamed to appear to have flaws. He would be ashamed not to be trustworthy, but he is not ashamed that he does not appear trustable. He would be ashamed to be lacking in ability, but he is not ashamed that he remains unused. For these reasons, he is not seduced by praise and is not made apprehensive by criticism. Rather, he follows the Way in his conduct, truly intent on rectifying himself, and is not swayed or turned away from it by mere external things. One who is like this may be described as a "true gentleman." An Ode says:[85]

> Mildly gentle and reverent men
> alone possess the foundation for inner power.

This expresses my meaning.

6.13
The Demeanor of the Scholar and Gentleman[86]

When he plays the role of a father or elder brother, his cap should protrude straight out and his robes be full, his demeanor should be relaxed and his manner should be dignified, grave, inspiring, correct but comfortable to be around,[87] noble and imposing, broad-minded, enlightened, and calmly at ease.[88] When he plays the role of son or younger brother, his cap should protrude and his robes be full, his demeanor should be attentive, and his manner should be temperate,[89] confident, helpful, honest, constantly striving,[90] respectful, exemplary, and unassuming.[91]

Let me now discuss the conceited manner of your students. Their caps are bent low over their foreheads.[92] Their cap strings are loose and slack.[93] Their manner is insolent and rude. They seem smug and pretentious as they amble about,[94] but their eyes dart nervously around.[95]

They may seem complacent, comfortable, and settled, but their gaze is confused and frightened.[96] With that excited and flurried air,[97] they betray an inner impurity and foulness[98] through their wide-eyed stares.[99] In the midst of official banquets or musical and dance performances, they sit blankly, unaware and unconscious, as though asleep or befuddled.[100] In the execution of ritual ceremonies, they are overeager and anxious, unrestrained and wanton.[101] In those trying and bitter functions of official life, they become dispirited and passive, evasive, timorous, and irresolute,[102] lacking integrity and a sense of shame, but rather acting cruelly, disgracefully, and insultingly. Such is the conceited manner of your students.

Their caps bent and twisted,[103] their robes billowing and flowing,[104] they move to and fro as though they were a Yu or a Shun—such are the base Ru of Zizhang's school.

Wearing their caps in perfectly correct form, maintaining their expression in perfect equanimity, they sit there all day long as though they were about to gag on a bit,[105] but say nothing—such are the base Ru of the school of Zixia.

Evasive and timorous, disliking work, lacking integrity, shameless, interested only in food and drink, they insist that "a gentleman naturally would not engage in manual labor"—such are the base Ru of the school of Ziyou.

The gentleman I have described is not like these. When he is at leisure, he is not remiss in his duties. When he is working, he is never indolent. To the ancestral origins and ultimate roots of things, he is responsive to every transformation, modifying as necessary to obtain for each thing its proper place. For only in this way can he ultimately become a sage.

APPENDIXES
∎∎

APPENDIX A

The Correct Form of Xunzi's Family Name

In citations of Xunzi's works before the Yang Liang edition, his name is sometimes given as Xun 荀 Qing and other times as Sun 孫 Qing. The usual explanation provided in Tang works was that Liu Xiang and other Han writers changed his name from Xun to Sun in order to observe the taboo against use of the personal names of the Han emperors—so Yan Shigu 顏師古 ("Bibliographic Treatise," *HSBZ*, 30.29a), Kong Yingda 孔穎達 (*Zuo zhuan zhushu*, Shisanjing ed., 41.29a), Sima Chen 司馬貞 (*SJ*, 74.12), and Li Xian 李賢 (*Hou Hanshu jijie*, 52.1a). In June of 64 B.C., Han Emperor Xuan (r. 76–48), whose original personal name had been Bingyi 病已 (meaning "his illness is over," an apotropaic name), issued an edict that his name was to be changed to *xun* 詢 (*Hanshu*, 8.21a). Though the taboo explanation seems to have been universally accepted by Tang commentators and scholars, the facts are not easily reconciled with the theory.

The *Shiji* regularly refers to Xunzi as Xun Qing. The *Yantie lun* (2.11a), written shortly after 81 B.C., also refers to him as Xun Qing. In contrast, in the *Hanfeizi* (16.4a), the *Zhanguo ce* (5.38b), the *Hanshi waizhuan* (4.13b), and Liu Xiang's *Preface*, in the text itself, in the *Hanshu* "Bibliographic Treatise," in the *Lunheng* (13.11b), and in Ying Shao 應劭 *Fengsu tongyi* (7.2a), he is referred to as Sun Qing, Sun Qingzi, or Sunzi. In Yan Zhitui's *Yanshi jiaxun*, he is called both Xun Qing (*huizhu*, 38b) and Sun Qing (58a, 104b).

Yan Shigu and the others are undoubtedly correct that Liu Xiang is responsible for the form *Sun*. Liu Xiang edited the texts of the *Xunzi*, *Zhanguo ce*, and probably the *Hanfeizi* as well. (For the problems connected with the *Hanfeizi* preface, see Li Duqing.) The passages excerpted by Liu Xiang for his *Shuoyuan* (2.10a, 5.9ab, 11.1ab) and *Xinxu* (*jiaozhu*, 22b–23b, 49ab) always read "Sun Qing." Ying Shao based his discussion of Xunzi on Liu Xiang's *Preface*, and Ban Gu 班固 depended on Liu Xiang not only for the "Bibliographic Treatise" but also probably for quotations from the *Xunzi* and for references to him (36.1a, 38.31a, and perhaps 88.2b). It is unclear whether Ban Gu himself observed the taboo against *xun*. In all references to Xunzi, the form is *sun*, even in 88.2b (same as *SJ*, 121.4). On the other hand, the character *xun* is used in the name Xun Zhi (*HSBZ*, 95.16b–18a).

The *Hanshi waizhuan* would seem to be an independent source for the form *sun*. The *Shiji* uses the form *xun* and since the *Yantie lun* quotes from the section on Zou Yan in the "Biography" (2.11a, 4.5b–7a), we may presume that its references are based on *Shiji* usage. (The first passage reads "Sun Qing," one occurrence; the latter "Xun Qing," two occurrences. Wang Liqi, *Yantie lun jiaozhu*, 131, *n*7, says that the Hua 華 movable-type edition has *Sun* in one of the two latter occurrences. Since characters were sometimes "corrected" by editors, it is impossible to be certain of the original reading. But the occurrence of the name Xun Xi at 4.6a shows that the taboo was not observed. Since the passages concerning Xunzi are based on the *Shiji*, I think it reasonable to conclude that the original reading was *xun* 荀.)

We thus have three apparently independent sources for Xunzi's name: the *Shiji*, which uses only *xun* 荀; the *Preface* and edition of Liu Xiang, which use only *sun* 孫; and the *Hanshi waizhuan*, nominally earlier than either of these, which uses *sun*.

In notes placed at the beginning of each of the "Basic Annals" of the *Hanshu*, Yan Shigu quotes Xun Yue 荀悅 (148–206 A.D.), who gives the standard taboo substitution character. For Emperor Xuan, he says that the tabooed *xun* was to be written *mou* 謀 (8.1a). H. H. Dubs believed that Xun Yue was quoting directly from the taboo tablets that were set up in public places so that persons might be apprised of the regulations and proper substitutions (*History of the Former Han Dynasty*, 2:267). In changing the name back to *xun*, Yang Liang apparently accepted the taboo explanation. After the Tang period, this explanation was generally accepted as adequate (see, for example, Wang Guanguo, *Xuelin*, 3.68).

In the Qing period, however, alternate explanations were advanced. Gu Yanwu (1613–82), *Rizhilu jishi*, 27.32a, argued that in Han times the tabooed name was not avoided altogether; rather, the sound of it was altered. Thus *xun* became *sun*, just as *meng* 孟 was changed to *mang* 芒 and Situ 司徒 became Shentu 申徒. Xie Yong (1719–95), in the preface to his edition of the *Xunzi* (2b–3a), examined the problem in more detail, pointing out that the personal name of the emperor was not *xun* and that throughout the Han period writers did not continue to avoid the personal names; thus, the names of numerous Later Han figures were written with the character *xun*. Further, though Liu Xiang's son Liu Xin edited the *Zuo zhuan*, the form of such names of numerous persons of the Xun family were not altered. In addition, Xie points to Ren Ao 任敖 and Gongsun Ao 公孫敖 as examples showing that the tabooed personal name Ao 驁 of Emperor Yuan 元帝 did not lead Han men to alter their names in order to avoid the taboo. Xie suggests instead that the graphic variation is to be understood as a result of the similarity of the pronunciation of the two characters; in support of this he cites certain well-known examples (examined first by Wang Fu, *Qianfu lun*, 9.21a). Takigawa Kametarō (*SJ*, 74.14) accepted Xie's argument.

Yan Kejun proposed a variation, suggesting that the interchangeability of *sun* and *xun* reflects a dialectical homophony of the two characters, much like the homophony that exists today in such southern Chinese areas as Hunan (*Quan shanggu sandai wen*, 9.9a). H. H. Dubs advanced the same argument (*History of the Former Han Dynasty*, 2:268–69). Ruan Tingzhuo, in a recent review of the evidence, concurs that this offers the best explanation of the phenomenon ("Xunzi tongkao").

Hu Yuanyi offered a third explanation based on the suggestion of Lin Bao 林寶, a contemporary of Yang Liang, in his *Yuanhe xingzuan* 元和姓纂. Lin Bao has no biography, but the preface to his work is dated to the seventh year of the Yuanhe reign period, A.D. 812 (*Siku quanshu zongmu*, 135.11a–13a). Lin and Hu proposed that Xunzi was descended from the marquises of Xun 郇. This house, which was enfeoffed at the beginning of the Zhou dynasty, was descended from one of the seventeen sons of King Wen. In the common practice of the time, later descendants took their name from the name of the state. (*Yuanhe xingzuan* s.v. *xun* 郇, quoted in Yu Jiaxi, *Siku tiyao bianzheng*, p. 514; and Hu quoted in Wang Xianqian, *Xunzi jijie*, "Kaoyi," 31a–39b. Ruan Tingzhuo, "Xunzi shulu," p. 415. Hu's work was never published.) In accord with custom, such descendants were also known as *gongsun* 公孫, in this case shortened to *sun* 孫. In support, Hu adduces the statement of Wang Fu, *Qianfu lun*, 9.2b, that the surnames Wangsun and Gongsun were posthumously awarded officials in the various states and that the surname Sun developed from Wangsun, according to some, or from Gongsun, according to others. When genealogical rules fell into disuse at the end of the Warring States period, confusion of names resulted. Double surnames are common, as in the case of the alternation between Chen and Tian for relatives of the ruling family in Qi. This alone, according to Hu, can account for all the facts. In his "Prolegomena" to the *Xunzi jijie* ("Kaoyi," 38a–39b), Wang Xianqian accepts this view. Liu Baonan (*Lunyu zhengyi*, 11.1a), Liu Shipei (*Liu Xiang*, 4.16ab), and Wang Shumin ("Shiji," p. 80) support this view.

The interpretation that the alternation of the two characters, *xun* and *sun*, is based on their homophony or on their being loan characters is not adequately founded on solid phonetic grounds, and it offers no adequate explanation of the distribution found in the texts. In a study of the "latitude of phonetical variation permissible" in an "authorized" loan character (that is, one found in a *xiesheng* series), Karlgren ("Loan Characters," pp. 10–17) concluded that the final of *xun* (case 33) could be not associated with the final of *sun* (case 45), though the final of *sun* was associated commonly with six other finals and rarely with three additional ones. The two characters do not belong to the same homonym category of the *Zhongyuan yinyun* 中原音韻, being respectively numbers 589 and 607 in the numbering of Hattori Shirō and Tōdō Akiyasu (pp. 109, 111). The qualification that it was dialectical does not help inasmuch as both Sima Qian and Liu Xiang could be expected to use the pronunciation of the capital; no dialectical difference can be supposed. Most striking is that in the case of the large numbers of people with the Xun surname in the *Zuo zhuan*, no such alternation is found; nor is it found among Xunzi's posterity (Zhang Senjie, p. 2452).

There is no doubt, as Liu Shipei points out, that a large number of names in pre-Han texts are written with more than one graph, but in the vast majority of cases the variation is merely orthographic with no difference in pronunciation implied. There are such cases as *fou* 浮 alternating with *bao* 包 in the name of Xunzi's disciple Fouqiu Bo/Baoqiu Bo, but these can be satisfactorily explained in accord with Karlgren's rules. (Cf. Wang Niansun, *Dushu zazhi*, 12.14a apud *Huainanzi*.) Variations in the *Lunyu* and other texts cited by Liu and others often involve problems of alternate text traditions rather than differences of orthography of the same text reading. It would therefore seem that, as Karlgren remarks, "too much should not be concluded from Han variants" ("Loan Characters," case 1433).

Hu Yuanyi's theory that the surname *Xun* 荀 developed from the ancient state of Xun 郇 is not easily confirmed since evidence concerning this ancient state is very limited. The oldest reference is *Shi*, Mao 153, one of the Guofeng (dated to seventh-sixth centuries by Dobson, "Origin and Development," pp. 246–49) associated with the reign of Duke Gong of Cao 曹共公 (652–18) in the "Little Preface," after the state of Xun 郇 had ceased to be important. (Dobson, "Linguistic Evidence," pp. 332–34, holds there is no good reason for entirely rejecting the dates of the "Little Preface," which seem, on the whole, to accord with the dates suggested by modern linguistic evidence.) The Marquis of Xun 荀 is mentioned in *Zuo zhuan*, Huan 9, where one version of the text reads *xun* 郇 and the Mao commentary to *Shi* 153 says that the two are the same. The fact that the Mao commentary derives from Xunzi gives weight to this equation. Textual variation in the fragments of the *Zhushu jinian* 竹書紀年 show the same variation. As quoted in the notes of Li Daoyuan 麗道元 to the *Shuijing* 水經 (in Wang Guowei, *Guben Zhushu jinian jijiao*, in *Zhushu jinian bazhong*, 1.17a) and in the notes of Ying Shao to the *Hanshu* "Treatise on Geography" (*Hanshu*, 28A.12a), a passage concerning Yuan Yan 原黶 becoming Xun Shu 荀叔 reads *xun* 荀, but as quoted in the Li Shan 李善 commentary to the *Wenxuan* (9.20b) reads *xun* 郇. The same variation can be found in the name Xun 荀 Ren (*Hou Hanshu jijie* 39.3b–4a, where Wang Xianqian notes that some editions have *xun* 荀 for *xun* 郇), and Xun 郇 Ren (53.1b, where Hui Dong observed that the *Dongguan ji* 東觀記 writes *xun* 荀 while the *Yuanhong ji* 袁宏記 writes *xun* 郇). Such variation in orthography often indicates that the signific of the character was omitted in the earliest manuscript tradition, to be added variously by later scholars and editors.

The quotation from the *Zhushu jinian*, regardless of the textual variants, shows that the Xun family of the Spring and Autumn period had the surname Yuan before being awarded with the fief of Xun. From the *Zuo zhuan*, we can determine that branches of the Xun family adopted alternate surnames: Zhonghang 中行 in the case of the descendants of Xun Linfu 荀林父; Zhi 知 in the case of the descendants of Xun Shou 荀首; and Fu 輔 in the case of the descendants of Zhi Guo 知果 (*Guoyu*, 15.7a; Sun Yue, p. 170.) In addition to the Xun surname, descendants of Yuan Chen 元軫 took the Xian 先 surname (*Guoyu*, 10.5a; Sun Yue, p. 171). Shuxiang 叔向, a grand officer of Jin, remarks (in 539) that the Yuan clan, along with seven others, had been reduced to the level of menials, that the government was run by the heads of the great families, and that of the eleven families descended from the ducal house of Jin, only his own family survived

(*Zuo*, Zhao 3). Shuxiang makes two interesting observations: that the old family, or main branch, of the Yuan clan no longer held high position; and that the old families descended from the ducal house had died off. It seems probable that the house of the original earl of Xun 荀, descending from a son of King Wen, had been completely destroyed by the early years of the seventh century and that therefore the Spring and Autumn name Xun 荀 is related to the descendants of Yuan Yan/Xun Shu. This removed any basis for associating *gongsun*, "duke's grandson/descendant," with the Xun family in that period since they never ruled an independent state. Second, though the surname Gongsun is fairly common among the Central States, the surname Sun, as it appears in the *Zuo zhuan*, is restricted to the states of Zheng, Chu, and Wey, and it is only in this last state that Sun as a family name, properly speaking, occurs—in the case of Sun Linfu and his posterity, who descended from Duke Wu of Wey.

Not only do the theories of Gu, Xie, and Hu have difficulties in themselves, but their critique of the taboo theory is itself open to challenge. Although centuries of editing have removed many of the taboos and restored the original characters, enough evidence remains to show that taboos were certainly observed in the Han period. Chen Yuan, p. 545, notes that the surname Shi 奭 was changed to avoid the tabooed personal name of Emperor Yuan (49–33) and the surname Zhuang 莊 changed to avoid that of Emperor An 安帝 (A.D. 107–25). The *Hanshu* avoids, even in quotations, the personal name of Emperor Gaozu 高祖 and that of his consort, the Empress Lü 呂后, and the *Shiji* avoids the personal names of Emperors Hui 惠帝 and Jing 景帝 (Chen Yuan, pp. 624–25). In the examples cited by Chen, Sima Qian and Ban Gu employ the substitution character given by Xun Yue as standard and approved. One would thus expect that if they were to observe the taboo, Xunzi's name would have become Mou Qing rather than Sun Qing. In personal names, the approved substitution has the important drawback that in Han orthography *mou* 謀 was interchangeable with *mou* 某 "so and so."

To avoid his father's personal name, Sima Qian changed the character *tan* 談 in the names of Zhao Tan 趙談, Li Tan 李談, and Zhang Mengtan 張孟談 to *tong* 同 (Qian Daxin, 5.12b; Chen Yuan, p. 555), but in the "Chronological Tables" he substituted *tan* 譚 in the names Lü Tan 呂譚 and Liu Tan 劉譚 (*Shiji zhiyi*, 21.27b). This shows that more than one character was sometimes used. Characters chosen as taboo substitutes commonly had a close phonetic or semantic relation to the original character, though not the precise phonetic relation customary in loan equations and substitutions. Given this situation, it would not seem exceptional that Liu Xiang substituted *sun* 孫 for the authorized *mou* 謀 to approximate the sound and avoid the unfortunate consequences of *mou* 某.

A second difficulty with the taboo theory is the uncertainty whether the taboo extended to *xun* 荀 since the emperor's name was *xun* 詢. Zhang Weixiang (1.6a) believes that it did. The early history of the characters *xun* 荀 and *xun* 郇 is uncertain since neither character appears in the *Erya* Lexicon and *xun* 郇 does not occur in the *Shuowen*. The available evidence testifies to considerable uncertainty and variation in orthography between *xun* 荀, 郇, 詢 and extending to *xun*

恂,洵,栒,拘,捑,樰,旬,巡, and 茊 as well. (See Gui Fu, 7.5ab: Yan Shigu apud *HSBZ*, 38A.35a, 35B.10a; *Shiji* 18.76, with the variants in other editions; *Shiji zhiyi*, 11.48; *Shuowen tongxun dingsheng*, 16.25a, 16.36b, 16.16b; Karlgren, LC 1437, with Lu Deming gloss to the character apud *Shi*, Mao 262. This indicates a lack of uniformity and regularization of forms in the characters in the series *xun* 旬, 郇, 詢, 恂, 洵, 栒, 旬, even as late as Tang times.) All this indicates that the taboo extended to other characters sharing the same phonetic.

One fact stands in the way of acceptance of this explanation: the character *xun* 荀 occurs in the *Xunzi* itself and in the *Zhanguo ce*, which was also edited by Liu Xiang. The character xun 荀 occurs once in Xunzi's name in the seven-character phrase introducing his persuasion of Tian Wen ("Qiangguo," 16.4), but this phrase is lacking in some editions (see the collection notes and discussion of Gu Guangqi regarding this passage, *Xunzi jijie* 11.4a). The character *xun* 郇 occurs in a quotation from *Shi*, Mao 254 (*Xunzi jijie*, 19.9b), which probably reflects an editorial correction by a later editor. The case of the *Zhanguo ce* is probably similar since given the numerous hands through which the work has passed, the presence of a character tabooed in Han times can mean little except that it was probably corrected by a later copyist or editor. Certainly it is inadequate evidence that the taboo was not observed.

Fortunately we possess positive evidence that at least in the *Xunzi* Liu Xiang did observe Han taboos. Weizi Qi 啟 is mentioned twice in the *Xunzi*, once as Weizi Qi (*Xunzi jijie*, 15.2b) and once as Weizi Kai 開 (*Xunzi jijie*, 10.10ab). At this latter reference, Yang Liang calls attention to the form, noting that it resulted from Liu Xiang's observation of the taboo on the personal name of Emperor Jing. (Xun Yue gives the taboo substitution at *Hanshu* 5.1a. The taboo is observed in the name Qidiao Qi/Kai in the *Shiji*. An interesting case is the occurrence of the name Weizi Qi apud *Lüshi chunqiu*, 11.9a [SBCK ed.], which has been corrected in other editions; for example, SBBY, 11.8a; see Gu Yanwu, 4.33ab.) We possess corroborative evidence that the correct name was *xun* 荀. When the *Qilue* was prepared, the taboo was observed not only in the *Xunzi*, which Liu Xiang had edited, but also in the collection of *fu*, which he had not and where the original name should have been preserved if no taboo were in effect. Significantly the *fu* collection, which survived into Tang times, is always quoted as *xun* both in commentaries and in encyclopedias, whereas the *Xunzi*, whose title was changed to observe the taboo, is always cited as *Sun Qingzi* (confirmed in the *Beitang shuchao*, *Yiwen leiju*, *Chuxue ji*, and *Taiping yulan*, and in the commentary of Li Shan to the *Wenxuan*). Similarly in the "Bibliographic Treatises" to the *Suishu* and both Tang histories, the *Xunzi* is listed as *Sun Qingzi* (*Suishu jingjizhi*, p. 71; *Tangshu jingji yiwen hezhi*, p. 169), whereas the *fu* collection is listed as *Xun Kuang ji* (*Suishu*, p. 112; *Tangshu hezhi*, p. 290). This clearly indicated that the correct form of the name is *xun* 荀 and not *sun* 孫. Final confirmation is provided by the statement that Xun Shu was the eleventh-generation descendant of Xunzi (*Hou Hanshu jijie*, 73.2b). Since this statement was written by Fan Ye (A.D. 398–445) long before the taboo theory was proposed, it cannot have been influenced by that explanation. In a work included in the *Wenxuan*

(50.12b), Fan Ye uses the form "Xun Qing" in a direct quotation of fourteen characters from the *Xunzi* text (*Xunzi jijie*, 1.17b). This confirms that he regarded the correct form as Xun, which doubtlessly, in view of his association with the Xun family, reflects the family tradition. We may thus conclude that the correct form of the name was Xun and that the taboo theory offers the only reasonable explanation of the historical alternation between Xun and Sun.

APPENDIX B

■ ■ IIIIIIIIIIIIIIIIIIIIIIIIIIIIIIIIIIIIIIIIIIIIIIIIIIIIIIIIIIIIIIIIIIIIIIIIIIIIIIIIIIIIIIIIIIIIIIIIIIIIIIIIIIIIIIIIIIIIIIIIIIIIIIIIIIIIIIIIIIIIIIIIIIIIIII ■ ■

Composition of Each Book

BOOK I: "EXHORTATION TO LEARNING"

In terms of the "Exhortation," there are no internal grounds for rejecting any part as not genuine, though quite clearly the first part is not an *original* composition in *original* language by Xunzi. It would, however, be entirely wrong to apply such modern notions of authorship to ancient texts such as the *Xunzi*. What we have appears to be an essay composed of the two parts we have distinguished (see Chapter 7). The book was probably not originally a single work, as is indicated by the *Da Dai* extract. We cannot be sure how the materials were combined to form this book, but they also continued to circulate independently in earlier forms.

The traditional materials adapted by Xunzi to his argument, paragraphs 1.1–1.7, 1.9, and 1.12, contain some of his own work and thinking. This can be illustrated in paragraph 1.1. The first sentence—The gentleman says: "Learning must never be concluded"—introduces the theme of the book. There then follow several sentences of traditional material illustrating the effect of learning that were also exploited by other thinkers for similar purposes. The paragraph concludes: "In broadening his learning, the gentleman each day examines himself so that his awareness will be discerning and his actions without excess." The first and last sentences occur only in the extracts in the *Da Dai* and *Qunshu zhiyao*, but the other sentences, which are traditional in character, are widely attested elsewhere. A similar pattern can be observed in the other paragraphs of the first part. This suggests that the first part (possibly also including paragraph 1.12, if one follows the *Da Dai* extract), was an essay that collected traditional material for explication in terms of the arguments of Xunzi's own philosophy. The relation between the first and second parts of the book cannot be precisely determined. It may be that the book as it stands was composed by Xunzi and that we are accordingly entitled to draw inferences from the order of the whole. This is in part justified by the close connection each paragraph has with the theme of the gentleman and his learning.

In dating the book, we must look to the core of material most closely associated with Xunzi, paragraphs 1.8, 1.10–11, and 1.13–14. The theme in these is the relation of learning to a curriculum of study in which the primary importance of ritual is indicated and in which the necessity of a teacher is argued. The traditional outlook of the material and the relative lack of sophistication in the language and conceptual framework bespeak an early date, consonant with his stay in Chu.

BOOK 2: "ON SELF-CULTIVATION"

In contrast, this book makes little use of traditional figures or stock figures and stories. The result is few parallels with other texts and infrequent excerpts in the parallel texts or quotations in Tang encyclopedia and florilegia. The *Hanshi waizhuan* quotes paragraphs 2.2 and 2.4 (see Table B1). Paragraph 2.4, both in the *Xunzi* and in the parallel text, begins with an embedded title indicating its once-independent status. In the *Hanshi waizhuan*, paragraph 2.9 is incorporated into a larger essay, unfortunately very corrupt, perhaps indicating a fuller context now lost in the *Xunzi*. This quotation is the basis of identifying these sentences as a separate paragraph, unconnected with what precedes it. The *Hanshi waizhuan* presents an alternate version of paragraph 2.11 in similar language but with a quite different context and form. Paragraph 2.13 is short and appears to be a fragment of a more extended comment or an isolated apothegm on the gentleman. In total, the book seems to have been assembled from independent paragraphs collected together because of their common theme. It cannot be determined whether this was done by Xunzi, his disciples, or by Liu Xiang.

In terms of dating, the core should be taken as paragraphs 2.2–4 and 2.8, which refer to doctrines associated with other schools. Paragraphs 2.3 and 2.10 allude to the concept of "bewilderment," which is to be linked with nurturing the vital breath. Paragraphs 2.1, 2.5–7, and 2.14 are concerned with the gentleman. Paragraph 2.11 is an essay on the importance of a teacher, connected with the theme of the "Exhortation." The book attempts to connect such non-Ru ideas as "nurturing the vital breath" with the traditional ideal of the gentleman, which requires that the gentleman not engage in inexhaustible disputes that are

TABLE B1
Parallels to Books 2, 3, 5, and 6

Xunzi	Hanshi waizhuan	Da Dai liji	Xunzi	Hanshi waizhuan	Dai Dai liji
2.2	1.3b	—	6.1	4.11a	—
2.4	2.18a	—	6.2	4.11a	—
2.9	4.16a	—	6.3	4.11a	—
2.11	5.7b	—	6.4	4.11a	—
3.1	3.21a	—	6.5	4.11a	—
3.2	2.10b	—	6.6	4.11a	—
3.5	2.11a	—	6.7	—	—
3.6	4.12b	—	6.8	4.11a	—
3.8	1.6a	—	6.9	—	—
5.5	3.17b	—	6.10	6.3b	10.13b
5.8	5.12b	11.1a			

beyond his limit. Aside from the apparently fragmentary paragraphs 2.9 and 2.13, the book is well preserved, and it has reasonable unity of theme. Xunzi's adaptation of such non-Ru notions as "nurturing the vital breath" suggests that the book was written in response to the intellectual milieu he found at the court of Chu.

BOOK 3: "NOTHING INDECOROUS"

The contents of Book 3, "Nothing Indecorous," are more uniform than those of the two previous books. The book introduces in paragraph 3.1, which provides the title, a theme quite ancient in Chinese society and of wider appeal than many other Ru concepts. The illustration that Xunzi uses, Shentu Di, was one of a stock of characters who, having failed to reform the world, committed suicide in some dramatic way. Shentu, and others like him, caught the attention and imagination of many writers, and accordingly there are allusions to him in the Zhuangzi, Huainanzi, Shuoyuan, Hanshi waizhuan, and Heguanzi 鶡冠子. Paragraph 3.2 contains rhymed material that was possibly a traditional mnemonic glossed by Xunzi with his philosophy. Later this paragraph became the basis of a gloss in the Mao commentary to the Odes. Paragraph 3.6 incorporates a theme from the Changes and quotes a "tradition" not otherwise known. One suspects that a substantial part of this paragraph is a paraphrase of, or allusion to, traditional material from sources now lost, but then commonly known. Paragraph 3.7 is a reply to various arguments attacking positions Xunzi held. These attacks are within the traditions of the dialecticians and were intended to show the absurdity or impossibility of creating order out of chaos or of reforming a vile character into a cultivated person. Traditional material in paragraph 3.8 can be identified as such because of its recurrence in other sources.

The latter part of this book, beginning with paragraph 3.9, discusses the idea of cheng 誠, "truthfulness," "sincerity," in contexts and language that closely parallel the Zhongyong and Daxue 大學, books traditionally associated with Confucius' grandson Zisi. Paragraph 3.10 uses language reminiscent of Daode jing, 47; paragraph 3.4 uses the technical language "lopping" in common with Daode jing, 58; and paragraph 3.9 discusses the concept of the "silence of Heaven and Earth," which is related both to Daode jing, 23, and to the "Zhibeiyou" of the Zhuangzi. Paragraph 3.10 makes reference to the doctrine of the Later Kings, which characterizes Xunzi's later thought. All this argues for a late date, probably the period when Xunzi was magistrate of Lanling.

BOOK 4: "OF HONOR AND DISGRACE"

This book appears to have suffered damage in the course of its transmission. The theme of honor and disgrace begins only with paragraph 4.6; paragraphs 4.1 to 4.5 do not address the topic. Since the opening paragraphs of each book usually discuss the topic designated by the title, many scholars believe that the first five paragraphs have been wrongly placed at the beginning. Since the topics of paragraphs 4.1 to 4.5 resemble those discussed in Book 3, it is thought they were once part of it. Further damage to the text is evident in paragraph 4.4, where parallelism suggests that there is now a long lacuna where once there was a description of the qualities of the petty man.

Individual paragraphs are closely related to those of other books. Paragraph 4.2 is akin to 2.3. The theme of 4.5 recurs in 17.1 and 30.5, where it is restated as part of a speech attributed to Zengzi, the disciple of Confucius, which indicates that the material is of a traditional nature. The topic of paragraph 4.7 derives from the *Odes*, Mao 260, and is part of the common heritage of Confucian scholars, as is indicated by its quotation in the *Mencius* as well. Paragraph 4.12 introduces a theme that is more extensively developed in paragraph 9.3. Paragraph 4.9 opens Xunzi's investigation of the problem of human nature. This appears to be a preliminary statement that was later developed in "Man's Nature Is Evil." The consensus of Chinese philosophers that human nature embraced certain fundamental desires and aversions is the starting point of his argument. Paragraph 4.7 mentions that the Zhou dynasty had perished, as had the Shang and Xia before it. The extinction of Zhou occurred in 256, when Qin conquered it, annexed its lands, and deposed the last Zhou ruler. Though this suggests that this passage was written after that date, the work as a whole should probably be dated to Xunzi's stay at the Jixia Academy as its most eminent elder scholar. The Zhou would then still have existed, but its imminent demise was obvious to all and its actual authority had ceased more than a century before Xunzi's time.

There are no texts parallel to any paragraph of Book 4.

BOOK 5: "CONTRA PHYSIOGNOMY"

Book 5 is unusual in that it is an attack on an issue so contemporary that there is no other discussion of it in the literature. The result is that the facts and events mentioned in this book are otherwise unknown. The *Xunzi* is the locus classicus for innumerable quotations of physiognomical lore recorded in Tang encyclopedia and florilegia. We have seen that one of the figures mentioned in this book, Tang Ju, dates the book to after 255. Other unusual features include paragraph 5.3, which incorporates an anomalous quotation from the *Odes* not agreeing with any of the extant traditions, even though three schools trace their roots to Xunzi. Paragraph 5.6 includes a quotation from the *Changes*, which is rarely quoted in the *Xunzi*. This may also be indicative of the late date of the work since an interest in the *Changes* seems to mark Xunzi's old age. Most parallels and direct quotations concern the various anomalies in the appearances of the sages of the past. There are two extracts in the *Hanshi waizhuan*, corresponding to paragraphs 5.5 and 5.8 (Table B1). The latter passage is attributed to Confucius, but in the *Shuoyuan*, the source is correctly identified as Xunzi.

LU RECONSTRUCTION OF BOOKS 3−5

Book 5 seems, like Book 4, to have suffered damage in the course of its transmission. Lu Wenchao observed that the discussion of the topic of physiognomy ends with paragraph 5.2 and that the remaining paragraphs deal with topics related in theme to those of Book 4. This suggested to Lu that the present text has been reordered since Liu Xiang's redaction of the text.

A possible reconstruction of the order of the text based on Lu's surmise would be:

1. The present Book 3 is a fragment of the original text.

2. The present Book 4 is composed of a fragment from Book 3, probably the end of the book, which precedes the original text of Book 4.

3. The present Book 5 is composed of the original text of Book 5 plus a fragment from Book 4 added at the end. This would make the text of Book 5 very short, and possibly some portions of the original text were lost during the course of transmission.

Lu's theory is attractive for its account of the anomalous organization of the text. It is in part corroborated by quotations from Tang encyclopedias suggesting that the present text is damaged and by the unusual number of variants between the Song and Yuan editions. Unfortunately, we do not know the division of the books between scrolls in the twelve-scroll editions. However, in Yang Liang's edition, Books 3 and 4 occupy Scroll 2, while Books 5–7 occupy Scroll 3. The type of damage presupposed in the reconstruction is difficult to account for in terms of scrolls, but easily understood in terms of damage to bamboo bundles. After Liu Xiang's redaction, but in a copy still written on bamboo rather than silk, the bundles for Books 3–5 were broken and then erroneously recombined when copied onto a silk scroll.

The editor would have been confronted with the following fragments:

1. A bundle of slips comprising the title slip and paragraphs 3.1–3.14;

2. A bundle of slips comprising material originally following paragraph 3.14, which he interpreted as the first part of Book 4 and incorporated in the ancestral form of the present text as paragraphs 4.1–4.5;

3. The title slip from Book 4 detached from the remainder of the book;

4. A bundle of slips comprising material originally the first part of Book 4, but which the editor made the second part of Book 4, comprising paragraphs 4.6–4.12 in the present text;

5. A bundle of slips containing material originally the last part of Book 4, but which the editor interpreted as the missing last section of Book 5;

6. An intact bundle comprising Book 5, which then consisted only of paragraphs 5.1–5.2, which the editor interpreted as a fragment of a larger work.

A RECONSTRUCTION OF BOOKS 3–5

Lu's thesis is an interesting attempt to reconstruct the original state of the text, but it is, I believe, inadequate. There is internal evidence that supports part of his thesis. Lu notes that in earlier editions, there is no paragraph indicated between 4.5, the end of the fragment taken from Book 3, and 4.6, the original beginning of Book 4. This suggests that the first bamboo slip with the title of

Book 4 became detached from the remainder of the book and that paragraphs 4.5 and 4.6 were combined during the reconstruction of the book as indicated in the hypothesis. But the fact that not all the paragraphs of Book 5 relate to the theme of the title cannot in itself be taken as adequate evidence that the later part of the book is an erroneous editorial reconstruction. I propose the following reconstruction, which, I believe, better explains the evidence:

1. Paragraphs 3.1–3.10 are the core of Book 3;
2. Paragraphs 3.11–3.12 are a separate fragment;
3. Paragraphs 3.13–3.14 are another fragment dealing with the problem of desire;
4. Paragraphs 4.1–4.5 are a fragment;
5. Paragraphs 4.6–4.12 are the core of Book 4;
6. Paragraphs 5.1–5.2 are the title portion of Book 5;
7. Paragraphs 5.3–5.6 are a fragment;
8. Paragraphs 5.7–5.10 are a fragment.

These fragments were originally combined in the following fashion:

1. Paragraphs 3.1–3.10 and paragraphs 5.7–5.10 agree in discussing the gentleman and should be regarded as the original corpus of Book 3.
2. Paragraphs 4.6–4.12 comprise the original core of Book 4, a principal topic of which is human nature. The discussion of desire in paragraphs 3.13–3.14 should be regarded as their continuation.
3. Paragraphs 5.1–5.2 are the title paragraphs of Book 5, with paragraphs 5.3–5.6 being their continuation. The language and themes of paragraphs 3.11–3.12 and 4.1–4.5 that are not consonant with either Books 3 or 4 should be considered the conclusion to Book 5.

This reconstruction produces books of relatively coherent content that can be regarded as wholes of essentially uniform dates of composition. Books 3 and 5 would still be dated to the period when Xunzi was magistrate of Lanling, with Book 4 still dated to the period of the Jixia Academy.

BOOK 6: "CONTRA TWELVE PHILOSOPHERS"

Since this book criticizes twelve philosophers, several scarcely known outside these pages, it is an unlikely source of "quotable" material. It is, therefore, surprising that paragraphs 6.1–6.6 and 6.8 are excerpted and paraphrased in the *Hanshi waizhuan*, with the criticism of Zisi and Mencius in paragraph 6.7 of the original omitted to conform to Han orthodoxies (Table B1). As we have seen, scholars since Wang Yinglin have used this fact to argue that the criticism of Zisi and Mencius is an interpolation. In this view, the book should be entitled "Contra Ten Philosophers." This view must be rejected since we have proof from Yang Xiong (*Fayan*, 12.1b), a contemporary of Liu Xiang, that Xunzi did "criticize" the views of numerous schools, including those of Zisi and Mencius. Paragraph 6.10 is quoted in the *Hanshi waizhuan* (6.3b), where it is introduced as a reply to a question or a riposte to some unstated point. The *Shuoyuan* (10.13b) provides an alternate version that has some language in common with the *Xunzi* and seems to be a free adaptation of the material. Paragraphs 6.8–6.12 provide corrections to the views of the various censured schools. The final paragraph (6.13) appears to have been originally an independent essay that harshly criticized the followers of Zizhang, Zixia, and Ziyou. The views expressed here are consistent with those to be found in paragraph 5.6.

We have seen that the intellectual milieu presupposed in the book developed in the court of the Lord of Pingyuan about the time Xunzi was in Zhao and debated the principles of warfare with the Lord of Linwu. The book must therefore postdate the siege of Handan (256). The language of the criticism of Zisi and Mencius also suggests a late date. The developments to which Xunzi objected belong to the generation before Fu Sheng, who transmitted the *Documents* to the Han dynasty. This would suggest composition about 240 or perhaps a decade later.

APPENDIX C

Concordances

Para-graph no.	Harvard-Yenching line no.	Wang Xianqian juan/ pg./line	Para-graph no.	Harvard-Yenching line no.	Wang Xianqian juan/ pg./line	Para-graph no.	Harvard-Yenching line no.	Wang Xianqian juan/ pg./line
1. Quanxue			**3. Bugou**			**5. Fei xiang**		
1.1	1	1.1a/5	3.1	1	2.1a/5	5.1	1	3.1a/7
1.2	3	1.2a/1	3.2	6	2.2b/7	5.2	13	3.3a/7
1.3	6	1.3a/1	3.3	7	2.3a/5	5.3	19	3.4a/6
1.4	9	1.3a/8	3.4	10	2.3a/10	5.4	23	3.5a/8
1.5	13	1.4b/5	3.5	12	2.3b/9	5.5	32	3.7a/9
1.6	17	1.5a/6	3.6	16	2.4b/7	5.6	40	3.8b/3
1.7	24	1.7a/2	3.7	20	2.6a/1	5.7	45	3.9b/1
1.8	26	1.7b/2	3.8	24	2.6a/9	5.8	50	3.10b/3
1.9	30	1.8b/1	3.9	26	2.6b/10	5.9	54	3.11a/1
1.10	30	1.9b/1	3.10	35	2.8b/3	5.10	59	3.11b/6
1.11	35	1.9b/4	3.11	39	2.9a/8	**6. Fei shier zi**		
1.12	39	1.11b/4	3.12	44	2.10a/10	6.1	1	3.12b/7
1.13	43	1.12a/8	3.13	45	2.10b/2	6.2	2	3.13b/2
1.14	46	1.12b/2	3.14	48	2.10b/9	6.3	3	3.14a/4
2. Xiushen			**4. Rongru**			6.4	4	3.14a/7
2.1	1	1.13b/9	4.1	1	2.11b/1	6.5	6	3.14b/6
2.2	6	1.14b/3	4.2	3	2.12a/8	6.6	8	3.15a/5
2.3	11	1.15b/9	4.3	6	2.12b/11	6.7	10	3.15a/10
2.4	14	1.16b/7	4.4	16	2.13b/10	6.8	14	3.16b/1
2.5	19	1.17b/10	4.5	20	2.14a/11	6.9	21	3.17b/6
2.6	22	1.18b/2	4.6	22	2.15a/8	6.10	27	3.19a/3
2.7	26	1.19b/6	4.7	25	2.15b/6	6.11	33	3.19b/4
2.8	27	1.20a/7	4.8	32	2.17a/2	6.12	38	3.20b/4
2.9	34	1.21b/3	4.9	42	2.18b/3	6.13	42	3.21a/4
2.10	35	1.21b/8	4.10	49	2.19a/8			
2.11	37	1.22a/6	4.11	60	2.21a/9			
2.12	41	1.22b/3	4.12	72	2.23a/9			
2.13	43	1.23a/9						
2.14	46	1.24a/1						

REFERENCE MATTER

■■

Glossary

FEN

Fen 分 has as its primary meaning "to divide" or "to differentiate" things. Division was conceived by Ru thinkers to be the way of Nature. Inequality of relationships was implicit in the very nature of man and of society—differences in age, sex, and position required differences in function, in behavior, and even in dress. In the *Xunzi*, *fen* regularly has the technical sense of the divisions or distinctions that characterize the hierarchal society the Ru thinkers advocated. Like the term *dike*, "division," in Greek philosophy, *fen* also meant the share belonging to one, the pattern of life customary to the "division" of society to which one belonged.

FIVE COLORS, FIVE TASTES, FIVE NOTES

In common with people all over the world, the Chinese grouped things by numbers and saw some mystical or occult significance in groups that shared the same number, here the number five. The five tastes 五味 are universal: sweet, acrid, sour, bitter, and salty. The colors 五色 are less so: blue-green (glaucous), yellow-brown (the color of earth in North China), red, white, and black. The five notes 五音 are those of the pentatonic scale that characterizes Chinese music to Westerners. In the *Xunzi*, there is no occult significance, and nothing more is meant than the association of the sense with its objects of apprehension.

GANG

Like many important terms in Chinese thinking, *gang* 網 is derived from the technical terminology of textiles. Originally it meant the cord that formed the selvage of a net. As the main cord of the net to which all the other cords were attached, it kept the net in order and controlled the entire net. The *Document* "Bangeng" 盤庚 (Karlgren, "Book of Documents," p. 8) notes that "when the net is arranged on its *gang* main cord, it is kept in order and does not become tangled." By extension, *gang* came to mean whatever "held together" or "gave shape" to a thing, thus "to rule, regulate, put in order." Xunzi uses it to refer to the guiding rules that give shape to society and keep it in order.

JI

Ji 紀, too, came originally from the textile term meaning "to separate and disentangle silk threads." It meant as well the main thread binding a skein of silk, and by extension the "continuous or leading thread." Its meaning then developed in two directions: "regulate, rule; norm; series"; and "continue; sequel; record." The word thus includes both the idea of norms and of relating things in serial order through time, and hence in the *Xunzi*, the ordering norms of society expressed in the institutions that bind it together.

LEI

Lei 類 "general categories" means in the *Xunzi* the extended applications by analogy of the models contained in the *Rituals* to categories not expressly covered by the models themselves. In Mohist logic, the term *lei* refers to "classifying" words such as "horse" in contrast to private names and general names like "thing." It designated the characteristics that all things of the same class have in common. It is one type of "agreement," the others being "identity," "part to whole," and "coexistence." The opposite are types of "difference" such as "duality," "not part to whole," "separation," and "generic otherness." The *lei* "fixed category" consists of changing individuals. Graham (*Later Mohist Logic*, A86–87, 336) observes that *lei* differs from "class" in that "*X* and *Y* are inside a class but not inside a *lei*"; rather, they are "the same in kind [*lei tong* 類同] or not of a kind [*bu lei* 不類]."

SHEN

The most common and ancient meaning of *shen* 神 is spirits who dwell in the mountains and streams. In the *Guanzi*, 39 "Shuidi" 水地 (14.1b), the power of water to nurture plants and animals and to be stored up in all things is described as *shen*, "mysterious and magical." In the *Xunzi*, *shen* generally means the "mysterious" or "magical" when applied to things that happen without apparent cause and "godlike" or "divine" when applied to abilities that transcend those of ordinary people.

SHENMING

Though among the more obscure terms in ancient Chinese philosophy, *shenming* 神明 is widely used in ancient Chinese texts. Maspero ("Le mot *ming*") observes that originally the term meant "the 'spirits' and, as a verb, 'to give the qualities of the spirits,' 'to deify.'" (The *Guanzi* frequently uses the term in the meaning "spirits" or "sacred and divine"—e.g., 13.2a, 14.10b, 16.3a, 18.3a. Two uses occur in *Guanzi* 55, "Jiushou" 九守, which Haloun, "Legalist Fragments," p. 85, has shown to be fragments of a widely preserved series of rhymed stanzas from an early legalist "Glass on Government," the archetype of which dates from the fourth century.) Yan Shigu says that in the passage "Some say that the Northeast is the dwelling place of the *shenming* and that the Western region is their burial place" (*SJ*, 28.42), the *shenming* are the gods in general. In 104, Emperor Wu of the Han dynasty built a Shenming Terrace following a great conflagration (*HS* 6.31b; 25B.4ab). Music Master Kuang 師曠 observed that a good ruler will be "loved like a parent, looked up to like the sun and moon, revered like the *shenming*, and stood in awe of like great claps of thunder" (*Zuo*, Xiang 14). In these cases the term clearly means "divine beings," and this meaning is attested even in the philosophical literature of the Warring States period.

The earliest datable philosophical usage is to be found in the *Mozi* (48 "Gongmeng" 公孟, 12.12a): "The ancient sages all considered spirits and ghosts to be *shenming* and able to cause fortune or misfortune, . . . [but] from Jie and Zhou Xin onward, everyone has considered the spirits and ghosts not to be *shenming* and unable to cause fortune or misfortune." Here it is clear that *shenming* designates not the "spirits generally" but some characteristic of the spirits that enables them to be the effective agent of fortune and misfortune. In numerous compounds the word *ming* refers to a kind of passive "sacred" quality that is attached to anything used in sacrifices, or associated with them, whether consecrated or not. In this respect, its meaning approaches *ling* 靈 "spiritfraught, efficacious." This meaning is appropriate in the *Mozi* passage. Elsewhere Mo Di (48 "Gongmeng," 12.17b) is said to have considered that the spirits and ghosts were "sacred and aware [*mingzhi* 明知] and able to cause fortune and misfortune." Finally, he complains that the Ru: "consider that Heaven is insensible [*bu ming* 不明] and that ghosts are not divine [*shen* 神]" (48 "Gongmeng," 12.15a).

The term *shenming* also occurs frequently in the *Zhuangzi* (e.g., 19 "Dasheng" 達生, 7.23b), where it usually means "spirits" or "sacred and spiritual." The way is described as *shenming* that has reached the highest purity. The ancients are "mates to the *shenming*, nurses to the 10,000 things, harmonizers of the world, whose bounty extends to all mankind" (33 "Tianxia," 10.13b). In contrast, mere scholars who possess only "one corner" attempt "to judge the beauties of Heaven and Earth, . . . [but seldom are able] to determine the [true] appearance of the *shenming*" (33 "Tianxia," 10.14b). The ancients whose views had been received by Lao Dan are described as "serenely solitary, dwelling in the company of the *shenming*" (33 "Tianxia," 10.18b).

There are, however, a number of passages that require a different interpretation. The "Qiwulun" of the *Zhuangzi* (2/1.16b) reads: "They wear out their *shenming* trying to unite things and are unaware that they are always the same. Such is called 'three in the morning.'" Here commentators agree that *shenming* must mean something like "brain," "mind," or "intelligence." The *Huainanzi* (19.8b) mentions several persons who "all possessed the way of *shenming* and the effects of sagely wisdom." Thus, *shenming* is similar to sagely wisdom and might be translated as "spirit-like intelligence," a translation that would also be appropriate in the "Qiwulun" passage as well. Two other passages in the *Huainanzi* seem to require this meaning rather than "spirits" or "sacred and divine":

> What is called the Way is round in body and square in pattern. . . . This is called *shenming*. What is round is of Heaven; what is square is of Earth.
> (*HNZ*, 15.3a)

> Heaven established the sun and moon, arranged the stars and planets. . . . It produced all living things. No one sees it nourishing them and yet things mature. It kills all living things. No one sees it destroying them, and yet they perish. This is referred to as *shenming*. The sage reflects on this, and thus he gives rise to good fortune. (*HNZ* 20.1a)

In the *Lunheng* (24.5b), there is yet another passage that has this same meaning: "Some say that man carries within his bosom the vital breath of Heaven and Earth. Their vital breath is within his body. It is the *shenming*."

Though the passages from the *Huainanzi* and *Lunheng* are considerably later than the *Xunzi*, they reflect earlier usages. The late Warring States meaning of the term *shenming* was (1) it is efficacious, being able to relate to the Way and to produce fortune or misfortune; (2) it is within the person and possessed by him; and (3) it is a faculty or state involving mental functions. This last is clearly shown by the "Neiye" (*Guanzi*, 49/16.3a), which says that "the highest degree of *shenming* is to know clearly the myriad things."

Prince Chan of Zheng in explaining how it is possible for a man to become a ghost after death sheds additional light on the mental functions that *shenming* entailed: "The animal soul (*po*) is what is present at conception. With the manifestation of the Yang principle, it is termed the spiritual soul (*hun*). By making use of matter, the seminal essence multiplies, and thereby the spiritual and animal souls grow in strength so that there is vitality and quickness. Thus, they attain *shenming*" (*Zuo*, Zhao 7).

The *shenming* is present from the beginning of life itself. In the theories of the day, the *po* animal soul was a manifestation of the Yin principle complementing the *hun* spiritual soul, which was a manifestation of the Yang principle (Gao You apud *HNZ*, 16.1a). The *qi* 氣, "vital breath," of Heaven created the *hun*, whereas that of Earth created the *po*, the *hun* being ethereal, the *po* material (*HNZ*, 9.1b). The connection of the *po* and *hun* with the mind is explicitly stated in the *Zuo zhuan* (Zhao 24): "I have heard that when there is joy where there should be grief and grief where there should be joy, it is a sign that one has lost his mind. The vitality and quickness of the mind are called the *hun* spiritual soul and *po* animal soul. Should they depart from the mind, how could it long maintain its abilities?"

Here the quickness and vitality of the mind come from the *po* animal and *hun* spiritual souls, whereas Prince Chan said this vitality and quickness were what enabled the *po* and *hun* to attain *shenming* intelligence. The idea of *shenming* intelligence seems to have been connected more with perspicacity and balance of judgment than with mere intellection or ratiocination. It seems a characteristic not of cogitation or analysis but of awareness and consciousness in evaluating circumstances and in making an appropriate response rather than in thinking reflectively or in logically analyzing problems. It is not learned, but inborn. It suggests a "divine" or "magical" clarity and sharpness of awareness, unmediated by conscious effort or thought, which enables those who possess it to discern subtle and minute distinctions that others miss. In this way, the myriad things are known, the Way is understood, and one can command and respond to things without transgression. The concept of *shenming* certainly was behind the notion, common to Chinese philosophers of the Warring States period, that some men, notably sages, needed no teaching and as such possessed a wisdom superior to any that could be learned since it was infallible, or nearly so.

Notes

Complete authors' names, titles, publication data, and characters are given in the Bibliography, pp. 308–22.

In the notes to the translations, I have not given the location of parallel passages, which are listed in Tables 3 and B1. I mention only the authority but do not cite pages since these vary between editions.

Commentaries regularly examine the materials in the order of the *Xunzi* text with a quotation of the passage to be examined.

Citations out of numerical order (e.g., *SJ*, 44.3, 5.82) indicate that the material in the narrative occurs in this order in the text indicated, or that there is a double entry of the material, or that the first reference is judged primary or more important.

Translations in both the text and the notes are my own, though I have consulted the standard translations of most works. I cite a particular translator when his rendering provides a difference in meaning that would affect the argument or when it makes additional points that cannot be made by a single version of the Chinese original in English.

In matters of the pronunciation of characters, I have generally followed Karlgren, *Grammata Serica Recensa*.

CHAPTER I

1. *SJ*, 74.12–14. To this should be added information included in the biographies of Li Si 李斯 and the Lord of Chunshen 春申君, *SJ*, 78.15 and 87.1–2, 14.

2. Wang Xianqian, 20.24a–28a. Cf. Liu Shipei, *Liu Xiang*, 4.16ab.

3. The detailed argumentation for this and other dates in this chapter is given in my article "Chronology." In brief, the date of Xunzi's birth is inferred from his arrival in Qi when he was fifteen (according to Liu Xiang's *Preface* to the *Xunzi*) and his interview with the Tian Wen, the Duke of Xue, between 286 and 284. If we assume that he was in his mid-twenties when the interview occurred, this provides a date of about 310 for his birth.

4. The *SJ* and Liu Xiang's *Preface* read "fiftieth," but the *FSTY*, 7.2a, which is based on the *Preface*, reads "fifteenth." Since Xunzi was said to have been a "flowering talent" at the time, this is the preferred reading. The whole issue is examined in Knoblock, pp. 33–34.

5. Xunzi offers the persuasion after the destruction and absorption of Song by Qi in 286. The persuasion is found in *Xunzi*, "Qiangguo" 強國, 16.4, but

since this passage occurs only in the Lü 呂 edition, some scholars suspect that it is an interpolation made by the Lü editors on the basis of the Yang Liang commentary.

6. *SJ*, 75.15. We gain some insight into the complex events from a persuasion datable to about 271 in which Fan Sui 范睢, who had been in Qi shortly after the restoration of King Xiang 襄王, says that the states united against Qi, leading to the failure of its victorious campaign against Chu, and that the humiliation this occasioned caused the ministers to agitate for a scapegoat, who was Tian Wen. *SJ*, 79.17.

7. *HFZ*, 14 "Jianjieshi chen" 姦劫弒臣, 4.18a, quoting from the letter Xunzi wrote the Lord of Chunshen; 36 "Nan" 難, I 上, 15.8a; 35 "Waichu shui" 外儲說, II/B 右/二, 14.2b, 14.8b.

8. "Qiangguo," 16.5. So says Yang Liang on the basis of a now-lost quotation of this passage from the *Xinxu* of Liu Xiang.

9. *SJ*, 73.3. This is the event to which Xunzi alludes when he refers to "moving the ancestral temples." It is uncertain which ancestral temples were moved when King Qingxiang was forced to abandon his capital, but they were probably those of the founder and the two immediate predecessors of the reigning king.

10. Chen was an independent state until Chu annexed it in 479. Nearby Cai was annexed in 477. These two states now became the center of Chu.

11. Mozi's interview with King Hui of Chu is recorded in *Mozi*, 40 "Guiyi" 貴義, 12.1b, and in *LSCQ*, 21/5 "Ailei" 愛類, Xu 1018. Mozi also saw the king of Yue, whose kingdom had been incorporated into Chu by the time of Xunzi's visit. *Mozi*, 49 "Luwen" 魯文, 13.7ab; *LSCQ*, 19/2 "Gaoyi" 高義, Xu 883.

12. According to the story, Meng Sheng and 183 of his followers died at Yangcheng, which testifies to a substantial Mohist community in Chu. *LSCQ*, 19/3 "Shangde" 上德, Xu 894–96.

13. *Zhuangzi*, 33 "Tianxia" 天下, 10.15b mentions Ku Huo 苦獲, Ji Chi 已齒, and the Master of Dengling 鄧陵子 as "Mohists of the South" who disputed such problems as "hard and white," "same and different," and "odd and even." *HFZ*, 50 "Xianxue" 顯學, 19.9a, Chen 1080, says that one of the three schools into which the Mohists had divided in Han Fei's time was called the Dengling school. Composition of the Mohist *Canons* cannot be confidently associated with any school or name.

14. *SJ*, 46.43 says that King Xiang was in Ju five years. It then discusses Tian Dan's liberation of Qi from the Yan invaders and the return of King Xiang to Linzi, implying that these took place after the five-year period when the king was in Ju. This is confirmed by *SJ*, 15.97, which dates the death of Yan General Qi Jie, and thus the beginning of the liberation, to the fifth year of King Xiang, 279.

15. *Yantie lun*, 2.10b–11a, says that Shen Dao disappeared and that Tian Pian took refuge in Xue. *HNZ*, 18.12a, adds that Tian Pian and his disciples were received by the Lord of Mengchang, Tian Wan, but dates the events to the reign of King Wei of Qi 齊威王. This is, of course, an error; the Lord of Meng-

chang was a contemporary of King Min. Neither is mentioned in a datable context to any later time.

16. Qian Mu, nos. 448–49, examines the many problems connected with Huan Yuan's identification and chronology. In *LSCQ*, 16/8 "Zhengming" 正名, Xu 737–38, Yin Wen persuades King Min of Qi. Gao You 高誘 says that he preceded Gongsun Long 公孫龍, who cites him. In *Zhuangzi*, 33 "Tianxia," 10.16ab, he is associated with Song Xing. The *Yinwenzi*, which purports to be Yin Wen's work, cites Peng Meng 彭蒙, Tian Pian, Song Xing, and the *Laozi*, which suggests that he postdates them all (Wu Feibai, pp. 483, 493, 494). In a passage dating to the reign of King Xiang's successor, the queen of Zhao asks whether Chen Zhong is still alive (*ZGC*, 4.64b). Since he is mentioned by Mencius (*Mengzi*, 3B.10) during the reign of King Xuan 齊宣王, he must have lived to an advanced age.

17. Tradition associates Zou Yan with King Hui of Wei 魏惠王, King Xuan of Qi, and King Zhao of Yan, which makes him a contemporary of Mencius, but it is clear that he must be a contemporary of Gongsun Long and thus younger than Xunzi. On these problems, see Qian Mu, nos. 438–43.

CHAPTER 2

1. Liu Xiang, *Preface*, confirmed by "Ruxiao" 儒效 8.2 and "Qiangguo," 16.6.

2. Though substantial parts of the *Zhuangzi* are to be dated to after Xunzi, Shang Yang is not mentioned in it.

3. Three books of the *HFZ* treat Shang Yang prominently: "Heshi" 和氏, "Jianjieshi chen" 姦劫弒臣, and "Dingfa" 定法.

4. This is a technical term, *xingming* 刑名, associated with the Shen Buhai, the philosopher prime minister of Han, who died in 337 (*SJ*, 45.7–8) and was thus a contemporary of Shang Yang. Since it is not clear that Sima Qian is correct in associating the term with Shang Yang, some understand the term to mean simply "criminal law" here. See Creel, *Shen Pu-hai*, pp. 119–24.

5. This is quoted as a proverbial saying in the *Shangjun shu*, 1.1b.

6. In the *Shangjun shu* (1.1b) version, this is represented as being part of the "laws" of Guo Yan 郭偃, whose reform of the laws of Jin was said to have made possible the hegemony of Duke Wen of Jin 晉文公.

7. *SJ*, 68.5–6; *Shangjun shu*, 1.1b. On the relation of these texts and certain other parallels and the general problem of the reliability of these texts, see Duyvendak, *Book of Lord Shang*, pp. 33–40.

8. Compare the language used to describe Confucius' government in Lu; *LSCQ*, 16/5 "Yuecheng" 樂成, 16.10ab.

9. Duyvendak, *Book of Lord Shang*, pp. 41–65, provides detailed analysis of the nature of Shang Yang's reforms.

10. That this greatly increased the prestige of Qin is indicated by the Zhou king's sending Duke Xiao meat from the royal sacrifice (*SJ*, 68.11).

11. *SJ*, 79.2 Fan Sui's visit to Qi occurred shortly before 271 when Xunzi was an eminent member of the Jixia Academy.

12. Dated to the eighth year that Chunshen was prime minister of Chu. This

was the year that the last remnant of the Zhou dynasty was eliminated and Lu, the old home state of Confucius, was annihilated.

13. Conveniently summarized in English by Duyvendak, "Chronology," 91.

14. *ZGC*, 5.38b; *HZF*, 14 "Jianjieshi chen," 4.18a; *HSWZ*, 4.13b.

15. This episode appears in the *Zuo zhuan*, which Xunzi is said to have received from Yu Qing. The form of citation indicates that "Spring and Autumn Annals" refers not to a particular work but generally to historical records in chronicle form. The events mentioned in the quotation are fully described in *Zuo*, Zhao 1, Xiang 25; and *SJ*, 32.42–44, 40.23–24.

16. Du Guoxiang, "Zong Xunzi de Chengxiang pian kan tade fashu sixiang" 從荀子的成相篇看他的法術思想, in *Wenji*, pp. 184–90.

17. Bodde, *China's First Unifier*, p. 80, examines the chronological problems associated with this phase of Li Si's career.

CHAPTER 3

1. Of Chen Xiao, nothing is known except his discussion with Xunzi after the debate with the Lord of Linwu on the principles of warfare. "Yibing" 議兵, 15.2.

2. *SJ*, 63.28; *HFZ*, 2 "Cun Han" 存韓, 1.4b–7b; Qian Mu, nos. 477–80; Bodde, *China's First Unifier*, pp. 55–77.

3. Most of these measures are mentioned by Li Si as his accomplishments; *SJ*, 87.14, 87.41–42.

4. *Yantie lun*, 4.5b.

5. Liu Xiang, *Preface*, in *Xunzi jijie*, 20.27a; *SJ*, 121.14–15; *HSBZ*, 36.1b, 88.23ab.

6. *SJ*, 96.1–13; *HSBZ*, 19B.8a–9a.

7. Liu Xiang, *Bielu*, apud *Chunqiu Zuo zhuan zhengyi*, 1.1b.

8. These are studied in detail by Chen Huan, who cites numerous examples. See his *Maoshi zhuan shu*.

9. *SJ*, 121.14–15.

10. *SJ*, 121.16. Among them are Kong Anguo 孔安國, grand administrator of Linhui, editor of the Old Script text of the *Documents*; Lu Ci 魯賜 of Tang, grand administrator of Tonghai (in which Lanling was located); Zhou Ba 周霸, clerk of the capital at Jiaoxi; Xia Kuan 夏寬, clerk of the capital at Chengyang; Xu Yan 徐偃, commandant of the capital at Jiaoxi; Quemen Qingji 闕門慶忌 of Zou, clerk of the capital at Jiaotong; and Master Miao 繆生 of Lanling.

11. Zhao Qi 趙岐, "Preface to the Mencius," *Mengzi zhengyi*, 1.9a.

12. Dubs, *History of the Former Han Dynasty*, 2:23.

13. Ibid., 2:32.

14. *HSBZ*, 6.3b; cf. 88.6a, 88.11a, 88.15b, 88.20b, and 88.21b, for the listing of the Erudites according to specialty.

15. Kong Zixian 孔子威 became an Erudite under Emperor Wen, his grandsons Kong Anguo and Kong Yannian 孔延年 were Erudites under Emperor Wu. The latter's son Kong Ba 孔霸 became an Erudite under Emperor Zhao, was made a marquis of the Imperial Domain, and was offered the position of lieute-

nant chancellor. His son Kong Guang 孔光 became an Erudite under Emperor Cheng. He was promoted to master of writing, was made a full marquis, and was given a splendid funeral by the government.

16. The classic study of the problems involved in the Old and New Script texts is Pelliot. More recent reviews include Chen Mengjia, *Shangshu tonglun,* pp. 114–35, and Qu Wanli, pp. 12–14.

17. Waley, *Book of Songs,* p. 11; Dobson, "Linguistic Evidence."

18. See Hightower, "The *Han-shih wai-chuan* and the *San chia shih,*" p. 249 with table 3 of appendix 3, pp. 293–300.

19. I am inclined to agree with the conclusions of Broman, esp. pp. 73–74.

20. See William Hung's "Prolegomena" to the *Li Chi yin-te,* pp. i–xl; and Tsuda Sokichi.

21. Sima Chen 司馬貞 theorizes (*SJ,* 130.65) that the interpolator took the "Document on the Rites" directly from the "Discourse" of the *Xunzi,* but the quotation may have come either from the *Xunzi* after its redaction by Liu Xiang or from the *Liji* after its form was stabilized by a group of Eastern Han scholars under the leadership of Cao Bao 曹褒. The materials that later formed the *DDLJ* and *Liji* were already in circulation in Sima Qian's time since he mentions the titles of five works that are part of the materials from which they were compiled: "Zhongyong" 中庸, "Wangzhi" 王制, "Xiaxiaozheng" 夏小正, "Wudide" 五帝德, "Dixixing" 帝繫姓. See Jin Dejian.

22. *Zuo,* Xiang 25, records that when the grand historiographer recorded that Cui Shu assassinated his lord, he was executed. His two younger brothers made the same entry and were also executed. When the third brother again made the same entry, he was left alone.

23. Malmquist, "Studies," p. 22.

24. Liu Xiang, *Bielu,* apud *Chunqiu Zuozhuan zhengyi,* 1.1b.

25. Zheng Liangshu, pp. 342–63, examines the evidence.

26. Karlgren, "Early History," p. 19.

CHAPTER 4

1. *HSBZ,* "Bibliographic Treatise," 30.33a, 38a, 40a, 41b–42a, 42b, 44a, and 51a.

2. Cf. *Mozi,* 46 "Geng Zhu" 耕柱, 11.22b, where Gongmeng 公孟, a Ru scholar of Mo Di's day, says that "a gentleman does not create things but does no more than transmit."

3. Creel, *Confucius and the Chinese Way,* pp. 173–76.

4. *HFZ,* 50 "Xianxue," 19.8b–9a. On the identity of these schools, see the annotations in Chen Qiyou, *Hanfeizi jishi,* pp. 1080–83.

5. Cui Shu, pp. 24–35. Cf. Waley, *Analects,* pp. 21–26; and Creel, Chang, and Rudolph. 2:9–20.

6. He has a biography in *SJ,* 67.8–9, on which this paragraph is based. On the alternate theories on Zigong's identity, see *n*22 to the translation of Book 5 below.

7. *HSBZ,* 24A.7a, contains a fragment applying his methods to the economic problems of the peasants.

8. Cf. Duyvendak, *Book of Lord Shang*, pp. 71–72.

9. So Liu Xiang, *Bielu*, apud the *Jijie* and *Soyin* commentaries to *SJ*, 46.31. The *Soyin* quotes the geographical treatise *Qi diji*, saying that "in the vicinity of the watercourse to the side of the West Gate in the wall of the capital of Qi, there was a debating chamber, ruins of which still survive." An alternate opinion is attributed to Yu Xi: "Qi has a Mt. Ji, below which was established a rest house for the reception of traveling scholars." There is no necessary incompatibility between these explanations since the gate itself might well have been named after the mountain. Qian Mu, no. 75, notes that since Qi also had a Deer Gate and the state of Lu had both a Deer Gate facing east and a Ji gate facing south, this may indicate that the names of city gates were consistent among states, probably because of some general sacrificial scheme. This suggests that the name of the academy may have come neither from the name of the mountain nor from the nearby watercourse, but from the name of the gate itself.

10. *Zhonglun*, "Wang guo" 亡國, 2.27a. How this *guan* 官 "academy" was organized is unknown, but the ancestral form of the organization in Xunzi's day appeared in the fact that it was a department of government in which distinguished scholars held official rank as grand officers.

11. Liu Xiang, *Xinxu*, "Zashi" 雜事, 2.5b (Shijie ed.). The *Xinxu* reads "King Xuan," an obvious error. *SJ*, 74.5 and 46.20–30, confirm that Zou Ji was prime minister in the time of King Wei.

12. Cf. *Mengzi*, 4A.22, taking *ze* 責 as "responsibility for" (cf. 2B.5) rather than as "criticize."

13. See V. A. Rubin.

14. Sun Yirang dates him 468–376, Qian Mu 479–381, and Fang Shouchu 490–403.

15. *SJ*, 74.17, knows virtually nothing of Mo Di, not even when he lived. Sun Yirang, *Mozi jiangu*, "Postface," 1.2a, examines the theories on his origins.

16. *LSCQ*, 2/4 "Dangran" 當染, 2.9b, says that Mo Di studied in Lu under the descendants of Shi Jue 史角, who had been sent from Zhou by King Xuan 周桓王 (r. 827–782) to Duke Hui of Lu 魯惠公. *HNZ*, "Yaolue" 要略, 21.6b, says that Mo Di studied under Ru scholars, but rejected their advocacy of the way of Zhou and followed instead the way of Xia. *Mozi*, 46 "Geng Zhu," 11.14a, contains a dialogue between Mo Di and Master Wuma 巫馬, who is identified either as the Disciple Wuma Qi 期 or his son; 11.19a contains a question put to Mo Di by a pupil of the disciple Zixia; 11.22b and *Mozi*, 48 "Gongmeng" 公孟, 12.8a, contain dialogues between Gong Mengzi and Mo Di. This Gongmeng is identified by Hui Dong 惠棟, in the commentary to this passage, with Gongming Yi 公明儀 or Gongming Gao 高 in *Mengzi* (3A.1 and 5A.1, respectively) and identified by Zheng Xuan and Zhao Qi as disciples of Zengzi.

17. Fang Shouchu, pp. 15–17, concludes that he was probably a wheelwright. Feng Youlan, pp. 141–42, concludes that he was a craftsman who rose to the rank of a *shi* "knight" and supported the interests of those engaged in handicrafts.

18. *LSCQ*, 21/5 "Ailei," 21.7b, 19/2 "Gaoyi," 19.4a; *Mozi*, 47 "Guiyi," 12.2a. The king pled old age and had Mo Di see Mu He 穆賀, who refers to his base origins. Mo Di is said to have been "black," i.e., darkened by the sun,

which is indicative of one who engages in manual labor, 12.7a. *Mengzi*, 3A.5; *Xunzi*, "Wangba" 王霸, 11.5b.

19. *Zhuangzi*, 33 "Tianxia," 10.16b. There are four books in the *Guanzi* collection that deal with the mind: 16/49 "Neiye" 內業; 13/38 "Baixin" 白心; 13/37; "Xinshu B" and 13/36 "Xinshu A" 心術, 上, 下. Of these, the "Neiye" and "Baixin" seem earliest, dating in content to the time of Mencius and Song Xing. The "Xinshu B" seems to be a commentary on the "Neiye," which it quotes. The "Xinshu A" consists of a "canon" composed of definitions and apothegms as well as a commentary in which they are explained in detail. Scholars are not agreed on the relation of these works. Guo Moruo, *Qingtong shidai*, pp. 210–32, and Liu Jie et al., pp. 238–58, argue that these works are the product of Song Xing and his associates. This is rejected by Machida Saburō. Rickett, *Kuan-tzu*, pp. 152–58, reviews the problems and rejects Song's authorship as "unlikely" in the cases of the "Neiye," Xinshu A," and "Xinshu B." I am inclined to suggest that all four belong to the school of Yin Wen and Song Xing. The "Neiye" seems to be the earliest of the texts. It may represent the state of thought at the beginning of Song Xing's career. This would date it to about 320 and possibly earlier. The "Baixin," dated I surmise to the beginning of the third century B.C., most probably represents the mature views of Song Xing. The "canon" of "Xinshu A" also dates to this time, with the "commentary" dating about half a century later, as does "Xinshu B." In this scheme, the "Neiye" represents the views of Jixia scholars antecedent to Song, the "Baixin" his mature views, the canon of "Xinshu A" traditional teachings to which he subscribed, and the "commentary" of "Xinshu A" and the discussion of the "Neiye" in "Xinshu B" the adaptations of his teachings to the climate of opinion about 250.

20. Despite his evident fame, the life of Hui Shi is scarcely known. He served King Hui of Wei from about 341 to his death in 320. He figures frequently in the diplomatic intrigues of his day. Cf. ZGC, 5.14b, 5.23a, 6.14a, 7.9b, 7.10b, 7.11a, 7.17a, 7.26b; LSCQ, 18/6 "Buqu" 不屈, 18.11b–14a.

21. LSCQ, 12/5 "Buqin" 不侵, 12.8ab. It should be noted that Hui Shi does not use the term *jianai* 兼愛 "ungraded love," which is the traditional Mohist concept, but rather *fan* 凡 "universal," which perhaps includes all things and not just humans.

22. See Guo Moruo, *Shi pipan shu*, p. 234.

23. What survives of Shen Dao's corpus has been assembled by Paul Thompson.

24. *Kongcongzi*, 12 "Gongsun Longzi" 公孫龍子, 4.1a–2b; *Gongsun Longzi*, 1 "Jifu" 跡府, 1.1b–2b.

25. Liu Xiang, *Bielu*, p. 13.

26. Graham, "Composition of the Gongsuen Long tzyy."

27. *Jinshu*, 94.6ab, which quotes from the preface of his work in his biography.

28. LSCQ, 18/1 "Shenying" 審應, 18.2ab, 18/7 "Yingyan" 應言, 18.14b–15a.

29. Yang Bojun, *Liezi jishi*, 4.86–89. The *Zhuangzi*, 17 "Qiushui" 秋水, 6.13a–14b, has Gongsun Long confounded by the doctrines of Zhuang Zhou and

seeking an explanation from Wei Mou, who chastises him for his foolishness. Gongsun Long was so astonished that "his mouth fell open and would not stay closed," "his tongue stuck to the roof of his mouth," and "he fled." This story is surely apocryphal.

30. Because of the faulty chronology in the *SJ*, Zou Yan is linked with Mencius and Shunyu Kun (44.21) and with King Hui, who had died long before.

31. Some Han dynasty titles are included in the totals, but the number of pre-Qin titles is extraordinary.

CHAPTER 5

1. The concept is probably attested in *Shu*, "Gan shi" 甘誓, 3 (confirmed as early by citation in *Mozi*, 31 "Ming gui" 明鬼, 8.13b–14b, as the "Yu shi" 禹誓); in *Yijing*, "Shuo gua" 說卦; and in *Zuo*, Cheng 15.

2. On the theory that the Dao provides no Mandate, see the discussion in Needham, 2:561.

3. Ibid., 2:37; Waley, *Way and Its Power*, p. 205; Lau, *Lao Tzu*, p. 112.

4. Graham, *Chuang-tzu*, p. 86; Needham, 2:38.

5. Graham, *Chuang-tzu*, p. 132; Needham, 2:38–39; cf. *DDJ*, 51.

6. Lau, *Lao Tzu*, p. 72; Waley, *Way and Its Power*, p. 162; Needham, 2:64.

7. The first line quoted is the first line of paragraph 20 in the present text. It is generally agreed that this line had been misplaced. With Lau, I believe that it should be placed at the head of paragraph 19. Lau, *Lao Tzu*, p. 76; Waley, *Way and Its Power*, pp. 166–68.

8. Forke, p. 170.

9. Thus, Li Jingchi; cf. Guo Moruo, *Qingtong shidai*, 81–84. These views are conveniently summarized in Needham, 2:307. The recent discovery of a copy of the *Yijing* with the Great Appendix among the Mawangdui texts may require a reevaluation of this whole issue.

10. Zhang Yachu and Liu Yu.

11. Quoted from the *Jiran*, "Fuguo" 富國, in *Wu Yue chunqiu*, 9.246. The rare term *guxu* is associated with lucky and unlucky in divination in later times and is connected with the relation of the denary and duodenary cyclical signs.

12. *Jiran*, apud Ma Guohan, 69.19b; *TPYL*, 10.9a.

13. *HFZ*, 20 "Jie Lao" 解老, 6.8ab. Cf. *Mozi*, "Names and Objects," no. 10 (Graham, *Later Mohist Logic*).

14. See Haloun, "Legalist Fragments," p. 118, for a detailed study and emended text that is the basis of this translation.

CHAPTER 6

1. That Shi Shi was a disciple of Confucius is stated by Ban Gu apud *HSBZ*, 30.13b.

2. Qian Mu, no. 497, believes that since the arguments summarized in the *Lunheng* as being those of Shi Shi and the other disciples use the term "evil"

rather than "not good," they must postdate Xunzi, who, he believes, originated this nomenclature.

3. Kane, p. 25, *n*5.

4. See Nivison; and Rao Zongyi.

5. *LY*, 12.10, 13.22; *Zuo*, Xi 7, Cheng 2, Wen 2, Zhuang 8.

6. *Mozi*, "Explaining the Canons," 2.7; "Canons and Explanations," A45, B76 (Graham, *Later Mohist Logic*).

CHAPTER 7

1. There is a possibility, particularly with short passages of a proverbial character, that both the *Xunzi* and the parallel text are quoting a third, unidentifiable source. I suspect that some of the quotations from the "Dalue" are derived from such sources. There are, for example, in the "Dalue" passages in common with the *Zuo zhuan* (Xiang 21), *Gongyang* (Yin 1, Zhuang 24, Wen 12, Huan 3), and *Guliang* (Yin 1, 3, 8, Zhuang 24) that certainly do not originate in the *Xunzi*.

2. Han Ying omits Xunzi's discussion of Zisi and Mencius, which he understood as condemning their views.

3. These are "Quanxue" 勸學, "Zengzi lishi" 曾子立事, "Lisanben" 禮三本, "Yudaide" 虞戴德, "Yibenming" 易本命, "Zengzi zhiyan" 曾子制言, "Zengzi benxiao" 曾子本孝, and "Aigong wen wuyi" 哀公問五義.

4. These are "Jingjie" 經解, "Yueji" 樂記, "Sangdaji" 喪大記, "Jiyi" 祭義, "Shaoyi" 少義, "Liyun" 禮運, "Wangzhi" 王制, and "Pingyi" 聘義.

5. *Qilue*, apud Ru Shun citation at *HSBZ*, 30.1b.

6. References to the acquisition of books can be found in the memorials concerning the *Liezi*, *SY*, and *Shenzi*, apud Pei Yin, *SJ jijie*, 63.5b; and concerning the *Zhouxun* 周訓, apud Yan Shigu, *HSBZ*, 30.21a.

7. *HSBZ* 10.6a, 30.1b, and 36.21a; *FSTY*, apud *TPYL*, 606.2a.

8. These various reports were collected together in the *Bielu*, which maintained an independent existence into the Tang Dynasty. The *Bielu* was frequently used by commentators, and what we know of it now is assembled from their citations.

9. Thus, Yan Shigu 顏師古, apud the entry in the *HS*, "Bibliographic Treatise" [*HSBZ*, 30.29a], Kong Yingda 孔穎達, apud *Zuo zhuan zhushu*, 41.29a; Sima Chen 司馬貞 apud *SJ*, 74.12; and Li Xian 李賢, apud *Hou Hanshu jijie*, 52.1a. On the details of this issue, see Appendix A.

10. The difficult problem of the independent existence of a military treatise, probably the "Yibing," mentioned in the *HSBZ*, "Bibliographic Treatise," 30.60a, is deferred to the introduction to that book.

11. *HSBZ*, 30.29a. This explanation of Shen Qinhan 沈欽韓 is generally accepted.

12. Before the preface and each chapter of the present text stands the credit: "Written by His Majesty's servant, the Director of the Department of the Library, the Viscount of Julu, Wei Zheng, and others, at imperial command."

13. A total of 67 works were excerpted, all of which are listed in the *Suishu* "Bibliography" and all but one in the "Bibliography" of the *Jiu Tangshu*. Wei

Zheng became director of the library in 628 and created a staff to edit and re-copy the holdings of the Library (*Jiu Tangshu*, 71.4a).

14. *Tang huiyao*, 36.651. Confirmed in the biography of Xiao Deyan, *Xin Tangshu*, 198.17ab.

15. The work is listed in the bibliography of the *Xin Tangshu*, but not in the *Chongwen zongmu* 崇文總目 and is known only as a fragment of ten chapters in the *Zhongxing shumu* 中興書目 of A.D. 1178 (cited in *Yuhai* 54.29a). The early history of the *Qunshu zhiyao* in Japan is summarized in the introduction to the 1940 typeset edition published by the Imperial Household Library. On the Tokugawa reprinting under the leadership of Hayashi Dōshun, Chief Erudite to Ieyasu, see *Dōshun nenpu*, apud Kimiya Yasuhiko.

16. It was not available to the editors of the *Siku*, but was used by Yan Kejun in his textual criticism, was copied by Ruan Yuan into his *Wanwei biecang* 苑委別藏 (never published), and was reprinted in the *Lianyunyi congshu* 連筠簃叢書 (1847) and in the *Yueya tang congshu* 粵雅堂叢書 (1857).

17. Most of the books that are unrepresented can be accounted for in terms of the limited scope of the *Qunshu zhiyao*. This applies to Books 5, 19–22, and 25–26. Other factors such as preferences must account for the failure to include material from Books 16, 28–30, and 32.

18. The "Bibliographic Treatise" of the *Suishu* and that of the *Jiu Tangshu*, which is based on it, record this edition. The *Xin Tangshu* includes the edition of Yang Liang as well.

19. Chao Gongwu, 10.7b–8a. Yang Liang apparently wrote the commentary when he was relatively young since his career continued for many years thereafter. See Zhao Yue and Lao Ge, 25.10a–11b. Though the commentary is generally well preserved, there is evidence of additions and modifications of the commentary at the hands of later scholars and editors. See Kimura Eiichi, pp. 281–82.

20. These editions are described by Ruan Tingzhuo, "Xunzi shulu," pp. 405–12. Several of them no longer exist and are known only from the brief notes of collectors and colophons of scholars.

21. The beginnings of paragraphs 12.8, 12.9, 13.2, 18.1, and 31.6 are omitted in the extract because of the inappropriateness of the openings to the topic of the book. The passage taken from 23.9 begins in the middle and is not easily explained.

22. Wang Wenjin, p. 223, describing the edition that Gu Guangqi had used for his collation with the Shide Tang edition.

23. Colophon of Qian Dian, apud his "Kaoyi" 考異; quoted in Qu Yong, 13.2b–3b.

24. Wang Xianqian, "Lilue" 例略, 2a.

25. Apud Mo Baiji, p. 1038.

26. Huang Peilie cited by Guan Tingfan in his annotation to the *Xunzi* in Qian Zeng, 3A.2a; and in Huang Peilie, 2.1a–2a.

27. Qu Yong assembled the bibliographic notes to the collection in 1860 in *Tieqin tongjian lou cangshu mulu*.

28. *Jingdian shiwen*, Postface, 1b.36.

29. Niu Shuyu (1760–1827) was an associate of Gu Guangqi and a follower of Hui Dong. Qu Yong, 13.2a.

30. Ibid., 13.2ab.

31. Guan, apud Qian Zeng, 3A.2a.

32. Qu Yong (13.2b–3b) quotes the entire colophon of Qian Dian. He possessed no copy of the edition but had a manuscript copy of the *Kaoyi*.

33. Chen Zhensun, 9.1b–2a. The original edition was lost and the work recollected and edited by the compilers of the *Siku quanshu* 四庫全書 from the *Yongle dadian* 永樂大典.

34. Huang Peilie, 2.2b.

35. Yang Shaohe, 3.1ab.

36. Wang Yinglin, 10.849.

37. Tang's Postface is dated to the eleventh month, five months later than Qian's. Tang reprinted not only the *Xunzi* but also the *Mengzi*, Yang Xiong's *Fayan*, and the *Wenzhongzi*; Yang Shaohe, 3.1ab.

38. Mori Tachiyuki, pp. 156–58.

39. Yang Shoujing, 7.18a–19a, describes the circumstances of the discovery and reprinting of the Taizhou edition.

40. Lu Xinyuan, *Yigutang xuba*, 9.2a–3b, provides detailed descriptions of these editions. Lu observed that this edition was known to Wang Yinglin, who called it the Fujian edition. Additional details are offered in Mo Baiji, pp. 1038–40. There is a general tendency to represent every edition as a Song edition.

41. Pan Zongzhou, Zi, 1ab.

42. Lu Xinyuan, *Yigutang xuba*, 9.2a–3b.

43. Ding Bing, 15.2b; Miao Quansun, p. 35.

44. Wang Xianqian, "Lilue," 2a.

45. The contribution of Japanese scholars and their relation to Chinese works are examined at length by Fujikawa Masukazu.

46. Wang Niansun included in his *Dushu zazhi* a list of passages not included in the present text. This was expanded by Ruan Tingzhuo, "*Xunzi* tongkao."

47. Liang Qichao, "Xun Qing yu *Xunzi*," pp. 110–14; idem, *Yaoji jieti*, p. 84.

48. Hu Shi, p. 306.

49. Zhang Xitang, "*Xunzi* 'Quanxue' pian."

50. Yang Yunru, "Guanyu *Xunzi*."

51. On the titles of the books, see the introduction to each book.

BOOK I

1. *SJ*, 5.6. The *Mu tianzi zhuan* (1.4a) lists the eight thoroughbreds owned by the king. All eight names, in a different orthography and order, are mentioned in the *Soyin* commentary to *SJ*, 5.6, and in the *Liezi jishi*, 3.59–60. *HFZ*, apud *YWLJ*, 93.1613. It was thought that only one such horse existed in any age.

2. The Han commentator Gao You 高誘 says (apud *HNZ*, 16.16a) that Hu Ba

was a native of Chu (other sources say Qi) whose playing so pleased the fish that they stuck their heads out of the water to listen to him.

3. Gao You thought him to be a native of Chu, but only because many adepts came from that strange country. Liu Xiang adds that his lute was named "Ringing Bell," such was the purity and fullness of its sound.

4. Recorded with various details in Liu Xiang, "Qiu Tan" 九歎, *Chuci,* 16.22b; *LSCQ,* 14/2 "Muwei" 木味, 14.4ab; *HSWZ,* 9.3a; *FSTY,* 6.4b; *HNZ,* 19.12b; *Liezi,* 5.7a; and *SY,* 8.5b–6a.

5. *DDLJ,* and *TPYL,* 38, read: "If you have not heard about the way of the ancient kings"; corruption of the original text to a common cliche.

6. *Hann* SF *han* 邗, the name of an ancient country and city absorbed during the Spring and Autumn period by Wu 吴, which subsequently came to be called Hann as well. The ancient state Hann, mentioned in *Zuo,* Ai 9, was located on the Han river, in modern Yangzhou prefecture, Jiangsu.

7. Yang Liang: the Yi and Mo were tribal people living in northeast China. *DDLJ* and *Liuzi jizheng* both read Rong 戎 and Yi, barbarians living, respectively, in the west and east of China.

8. *Shi,* Lesser Odes, "Xiao ming" 小明, Mao 207.

9. Xunzi quotes this Ode to admonish and encourage the gentleman to study. Yu Yue calls attention to the quotation of this same Ode in *Zuo,* Xiang 7, where Han Wuji 韓無忌 explains it: "A compassionate attendance to the business of the people is virtue (*de*). The rectification of one's own self is true rectitude (*zheng* 正). The straightening (*zheng* 正) of others' crookedness is real correctness (*zhi* 直). These three things in harmony constitute humaneness. To him who has such humaneness, the Spirits will listen, and they will send down great blessings to him. Would it not be well to appoint such a man to official position?" (Translated with Legge, 5:432.) Yu notes that the Mao commentary in paraphrasing part of this passage to explicate the Ode is based on Xunzi's teachings regarding it.

10. Yu Yue: "Spirits" and "blessings" have the same meaning as in the Ode cited. Gao Heng: "Spirits" should be understood in the sense of *Mengzi,* 7B.25: "To be great and be transformed by this greatness is called "sageness"; to be a sage and to be unknowable is called "spirit." On the concept of *shen* "spirit," see the Glossary.

11. *DDLJ* attributes this to Confucius; *SY,* to Zisi. Cf. *LY,* 15.30: "The Master said: 'I once spent a whole day without food and a whole night without sleep to think, but it was of no use. It is better to study.'"

12. The precise meaning here is not clear. In *Guliang,* Huan 14, Confucius remarks that "when you listen to sounds from afar, you can hear their *ji* 疾 but not their *shu* 舒. When you gaze at things in the far distance, you can be certain of their general appearance, but not the precise shape." *HFZ,* 34 "Waichu shui" II/A, 13.11a: "A teacher of music conforms to the tonic note (*gong* 宫); the *xu* (徐 synonymous with *shu*) sounds conform to the *zhi* note. If the *ji* sounds do not conform to the tonic note nor the *xu* sounds to the *zhi* note, then it cannot be called teaching." It is apparent that both *ji* and *shu* (or *xu*) refer to the contour

of a sound, some distinctive combination of volume, frequency, and timbre, with *ji* referring to the quality that sounds assume when they are rushed, uttered in urgency or haste, or staccato, and with *shu* meaning the quality of slow, stately, grave sounds, uttered in ease or deliberation, or legato.

13. A "thousand *li*," about 300 miles, is a standard expression for a great distance.

14. With Wang Niansun: emend *he* "river" to *hai* "seas" with *DDLJ*, *HNZ*, *SY*, and *Wenzi* to preserve the rhyme.

15. *DDLJ* reads: "The inborn nature of the gentleman is not different from that of other men." Wang Niansun thus emends "by birth" to "inborn nature." Yang Liang: saying "the gentleman by birth is not different" means that he is the same as ordinary men. Cf. *LY*, 17.2: "In inborn nature, men are close to one another; by repeated practice, they become quite different."

16. Yang Liang understands all these to illustrate how the self is cultivated through "borrowing." *LSCQ*, apud Kubo Ai: "Those who are adept in learning borrow the strengths of other people in order to overcome their own shortcomings."

17. On the basis of *SY*, 11.4b, Yang Liang identifies this as the tailor bird, a small yellowish-green bird with a long tail that stitches leaves together to make its nest. *Zhuangzi*, 1 "Xiaoyaoyou" 逍遙遊, 1.6a, says the bird builds its nests deep in the forests. The same illustration is used by a retainer persuading the Lord of Mengchang in *SY*, 1.4b: "Your servant has seen the tailor bird that builds its nest in the flowering tassel of reeds, weaving it out of hair so well that it can truly be called well made and solid. But when a great wind comes along, the tassel snaps, the eggs break, and the baby birds are killed. Why is this? It results from what is used for support." Yang Liang: the "stupidity" of the bird is like that of a man who is unaware of study and inquiry because what he makes use of to reform himself is fraught with dangers akin to those of attaching a nest to the top of an insubstantial reed.

18. *TPYL* quotes: "on the precipices of high mountains." The characters *yegan* 射干 are defined in the ancient sources either as a plant with leaves growing in clusters along one side in a horizontal row resembling the wing feathers of a crow, whence the name "crow's fan"; or as a plant with white flowers and a long trunk like the cane of a servant. The immediate context here requires that it be a tree since the point is the contrast between the dwarf size of the tree and the considerable view afforded it by its natural habitat. This is corroborated by *HFZ*, 28 "Gongming" 功名, 8.13a: "Accordingly, if a foot-long piece of something is placed on the top of a high mountain, it will look down into a valley a thousand fathoms deep. This is not because of its length, but because of where it is situated." One "inch" is a tenth of a Chinese foot, which equals about fourteen English inches. The height, if a real measurement is intended, would be about six inches—an unusually dwarfed tree.

19. This sentence does not appear in the present text, but is restored from quotations by Kubo Ai and Wang Niansun.

20. On the basis of the *DDLJ* parallel, reconstruct UR **lan zhi gen* 蘭之根,

huai zhi bao 懷之苞. Valerian is a plant whose dried rhizomes and roots were used for perfumes and incense. It was then the custom in China for beauties to wear garlands of pepper, russet, valerian, and other fragrant plants about the neck. (Cf. *HNZ*, 18.18a.)

21. Following the gloss apud the *SJ* parallel to the text. Vegetables were often soaked in the water used to wash rice to enhance their flavor. Apparently the idea is that soaking these exotic plants in a liquid that normally enhances produces in them a foul-smelling result. Yang Liang interprets this passage to refer to soaking them in urine, which obviously would make them offensive, but this does not seem to be the point of the passage.

22. Cf. *LY*, 4.1: "The Master said: 'It is humanity that gives a neighborhood its beauty. One who chooses freely not to reside in a neighborhood where there is humanity—can he be accorded the name wise?'"

23. Following *Yilin*, 1.12b, quotation. Present text reads: "decaying fish produce worms."

24. Cf. the *Yilin* quotation, "those whose character is proudly contemptuous will bring calamity and misfortune upon themselves," which appears to be conflated with a later sentence.

25. Wang Yinzhi: "The strong . . . broken; the weak . . . protected." Liu Shipei: " . . . bear up under stress; . . . to be bound." Karlgren: " . . . be hit; . . . to be protected."

26. Cf. the point of Shunyu Kun in a persuasion of King Xuan of Qi (*ZGC*, 4.10b): "If you search the great swamps for the dye plant and the catarrh herb, you may spend generations looking and never find one of them, but should you go to the north slopes of Mts. Baoshu and Liangfu, then it is simply a matter of filling your cart. Everything lives with its own kind."

27. Kubo Ai cites *Yijing*, "Xici," A 繫辭, 上, 7.17b–18a: "Words and actions are the pivotal axis of the gentleman. The manifestations of this pivotal axis is the master of glory and disgrace." Thus, the gentleman is cautious about where he is by observing ritual propriety.

28. The divine clarity of intelligence is characteristic of those whose vivid and sharp awareness enables them to discern the minute and subtle distinctions that others habitually miss. Such men naturally behave in a way that produces good fortune not only for themselves, but for others as well.

Wang Niansun understands this quite differently: "If you accumulate enough good to complete your inner power, the spirits will naturally be obtained and the sagelike mind will be perfected."

29. The contrast between the powerful thoroughbred Qiji and an ordinary old nag was common to the language of the time. Tian Guang 田光 explained his inability to destroy the First Emperor by saying: "I have heard that in the fullness of his prime Qiji could traverse a thousand *li* in a single day, but when he grew old and decrepit, a worn-out nag could outdistance him" (*SJ*, 86.25). Similarly Kuai Che 蒯徹 quotes as a proverb: "Better the leisurely paces of a worn-out nag than the hobblings of Qiji" (*SJ*, 92.33 [Kuai Tong of the *SJ* text is Han taboo avoidance of the personal name of Emperor Wu]).

30. The Yellow Springs, deep under the earth, were where the spirits of the dead went and so was another name for the underworld (*Zuo*, Yin 1).

31. The last phrase is added by Xunzi to a proverbial expression to tie it to its doctrine of the mind.

32. *DDLJ*: "If there is no ardor and enthusiasm in purpose." On the Yin-Yang symbolism Xunzi uses here, see the General Introduction.

33. Guo Pu 郭璞 apud the *Erya* definition explains that the *dengshe* 螣蛇 was a type of dragon that appeared sporting about in clouds and mists. The five talents of the flying squirrel are its abilities to fly, climb, swim, dig, and run. They are deficient in that though it can fly, it cannot fly well enough to get over a roof; though it can climb, it cannot get to the top of a tree; though it can swim, it cannot cross a gorge; though it can dig, it cannot build a safe shelter; and though it can run, it cannot outdistance a man. Thus, none of its talents amounts to real ability.

34. *Shi*, Airs of Cao, "Shijiu" 鳲鳩, Mao 152. Xunzi's interpretation of this Ode is rather different from that of modern scholars.

35. Cf. *LY*, 8.4.

36. The *HNZ* reads: "A team of four horses lifted their heads from their feed bags." Fujii Sen'ei: "six" refers to the six varieties of horses listed in the *Zhou li*: purebreds, half-breeds, nags, field horses, road horses, and war horses.

37. Gao You, apud *HNZ*, 16.1a: since jade is the Yin principle in the midst of the Yang principle of the mountain, it enables the trees and grasses to grow with a special sheen. Zuo Si 左思, "Prose Poem on the Capital of Wu" 吳都賦 (*WX*, 5.14b–15a): where there is jade, the trees take on a dark glossy color [indicating, according to the commentator Li Zhouhan 李周翰, that they are flourishing]. Gao You, apud *HNZ*, 16.1b: since pearls are the Yang principle in the midst of the Yin principle of water, they have a luster and iridescence that causes the banks not to become parched. Li Zhouhan, apud *WX*, 5.15a: it is the grasses along the banks that do not dry up.

38. The interpretation of this sentence is highly problematic. Some scholars believe that the present text is defective. Gong Guangshen, apud the *DDLJ*: "If you do good, but do not accumulate it, then you will never reach completion." Wang Niansun and others emend the text: "Do good and it will accumulate. How can this fail to be heard of?"

39. To "recite" means to intone in a rhythmic, high-pitched voice. It was considered appropriate for the Odes—the recitation of the words was called "poetry"—in contrast to singing, which was reserved for lyrical songs. Though it is clear that in earlier times the Odes were sung, by Han times they were "recited." By extension, to "recite" meant to have committed to memory through repetition and thus to have learned thoroughly. Cf. *LY*, 13.5. Yang Liang: "classics" here means the *Odes* and *Documents*; "rituals" refers to the whole corpus of ritual works. Lu Wenchao suggests emending the Yang Liang note to read "refers to the 'Quli' 曲禮," now the first book of the *Liji*. But since the "Quli" deals with minor matters of deportment, this seems inappropriate to the role Xunzi ascribes to ritual.

40. Cf. paragraphs 2.5 and 8.5 below.

41. The commentators dispute the meaning here: Kubo Ai: "to enter" means "to have gained it within yourself." Liang Qixiong: "to penetrate deeply into." Tao Hongqing: "to be a novice."

42. Cf. this sentence with the opening sentence of this book and with paragraph 21.9 below. Cf. the discussion of learning in *LY*, 8.7 and 8.17.

43. Yang Liang takes *shi* 詩 "odes" to refer to "musical sound patterns that regulate tones and notes, reaching exactly the right pitch, and allow nothing that is unbalanced or profligate." Hao Yixing rejects Yang's interpretation: (1) the Odes were never used as Yang says; (2) the immediate context of the passage militates against his understanding; and (3) the *Music* is mentioned later. The difficulty in assessing the meaning lies in determining whether the graph 樂 is here to be understood only as *le* "joy" or also as *yue* "music" and whether *sheng* 聲 here means merely "sounds in general" or more narrowly "musical tones." Translation does not permit the ambiguity possible in the original. Both Yang Liang and Wang Xianqian exploit this ambiguity in their interpretations of the text since the context requires that the graph be read *le* "joy" and not *yue* "music." There is, however, no need to involve music in the sentence since it is intelligible in terms of pronunciation: the rhymes give the key to pronunciation and establish the correct standard for each word.

44. With Liang Qixiong *zhu* 箸 LC *zhu* 貯, confirmed by *HSWZ* reading. The usual interpretation is "enters through the ear, appears in his mind (or heart)."

45. Yang Liang: this refers to the learning of the ancients, which later in the text is said to have been undertaken for the sake of self-improvement. This sentence would then mean that "it is committed to memory and not forgotten, giving one polish and a sense of decorum as well as the knowledge with which to manage one's personal conduct." The *HSWZ* versions reads: "A tradition says: 'When a gentleman hears of the Way, it enters through the ear and is stored in the mind.'"

46. Following Yang Liang based on variant readings of the same sentence in paragraph 13.7 below. The literal meaning is "words spoken with asthmatic breathing"; thus, words barely audible.

47. Following Yang Liang, confirmed by variant readings in *TPYL* and *Yilin* quotations.

48. *HSWZ* reads: "[The gentleman] examines [learning] with humanity, protects it with sincerity, practices it with morality, and expresses it with humility." Cf. *Zhongyong*, 29: "He acts and his age makes it a universal model; he speaks and his generation makes it a universal pattern."

49. Following Liu Taigong.

50. Yang Liang: this refers to the learning of people in recent times, which was undertaken for the sake of others. Cf. *LY*, 17.14. *HSWZ* reads: "When the petty man hears the Way, it enters his ears and comes out his mouth." "Seven feet" was considered the typical natural height of a man in ancient China.

51. *LY*, 14.24 attributes this sentence to Confucius. *BTSC*, 83.1b, quoting a

now-lost passage from the *Xinxu*, has the king of Qi ask Mozi about the differences between the way learning was pursued in the past and in the present. Mozi replies that whereas men of the past pursued learning in order to improve themselves, today men pursue learning only to please others.

52. According to *Liji*, 1 "Quli," "in matters of ceremonial offerings, the Son of Heaven presents herbed millet wine, the feudal lords jade tablets, the ministers lamb, grand officers wild geese, knights ringed pheasants, and commoners ducks" (*Liji zhengyi* 5.14a–15b). The purpose of such offerings was to attract the attention of a superior. Scholars used their learning as a means of attracting attention to themselves. Wang Xianqian understands that the nature of the petty man remains like that of beasts. Xunzi returns to the topic below in paragraph 14.1.

53. Cf. *LY*, 16.6: "To speak before being called on to do so is called forwardness." Others have interpreted this to mean "officiousness" or "boisterousness."

54. Cf. *Liji*, 1 "Quli" (*zhengyi* 1.6a): "It is a matter of ritual propriety not to engage in vain and foolish talk merely to give pleasure to others and not uselessly to waste words."

55. Following Yang Liang. Kubo Ai cites *Liji*, 11 "Jiaotexing" 郊特性 (*zhengyi* 36.9a), which expresses a similar idea: "Those who are accomplished at responding to questions are like a bell that has never been struck. When tapped with a light stroke, it will give off a light sound; when tapped with a strong stroke, it will give off a loud sound." There is, however, another reading, preserved in several editions and quoted by Wang Yinglin: "The gentleman knows the direction [of words and action]."

56. The commentators disagree over the reading of text *shuo* 說. Yang Liang: "do not contain *shuo* inconsequential doctrines." Yu Chang: "do not give *yue* (= 悅) pleasure." Yu Xingwu: GV *tuo* 脫 "are not careless."

57. Following Yang Liang. Yu Xingwu: *su* 速 LC *shu* 數 for "terse and not verbose"; Karlgren: "terse and not hastily formulated."

58. Zhong Tai takes "gentleman" to refer specifically to Confucius. The text of the sentence is corrupt, and this reading omits two characters, *zhi* 之 and *yi* 矣, as excrescent. An alternate reading that seems possible is "If you imitate the practices of a man of learning and the explanations of the gentleman, then you will be honored for your comprehensive and catholic understanding in your own generation."

59. With Wang Niansun, text *jing* 經 GV *jing* 徑; *zhi* 志 is an excrescent gloss entered into the text. Guo Songdao: "being near a man of learning" means "to make him your teacher" in the earlier passage and here "liking a man of learning" means to find pleasure in one's inner heart from sincerely serving him and becoming profoundly close and intimate with him. One uses ritual principles to restrain and regulate oneself on one's own.

60. Xunzi suggests that just as each of the innumerable hairs of a fur collar falls into its proper place when it is properly lifted, so, too, the comparably innumerable subjects of a state "fall into their proper place" when the ruler understands the way of the Ancient Kings.

61. Yang Liang: a *san* 散 Ru was one who paid no heed to self-development.

62. *HSWZ* reads: "Do not engage in discussion with a person who is in an argumentative mood."

63. Following the present text. Kanaya Osamu: emend *li* 禮 "ritual" to *ti* 體 "person" for "Thus, after he is respectful in his person, you can discuss the methods of the Way; after he is obedient in speech, you can discuss the principles of the Way; and after he is gracious in demeanor, you can discuss the attainment of the Way."

64. "Demeanor" means the outward expressions that show inner emotion and feeling. Cf. *LY*, 2.8, 11.19, 17.10.

65. Cf. paragraph 1.9 above.

66. Cf. *LY*, 17.8: "The Master said: 'Not to talk with those who could be talked to is to waste the man. To talk with those who cannot be talked to is to waste your words.'"

67. Cf. *LY*, 16.6: "Master Kong said: There are three mistakes made in waiting upon a gentleman. To speak when it is not yet one's turn to speak, which is termed 'forwardness.' Not to speak when it is one's turn, which is called 'secretiveness.' To speak not having first noticed the expression on his face, which is called 'blindness.'" Some editions emend the text from "demeanor and mood" to "expressions on his face" so that it will more closely resemble the *Analects*.

68. *HSWZ* reads: "Thus, the gentleman is not blind and speaks cautiously and circumspectly in his due order."

69. *Shi*, Lesser Odes, "Caishu" 采菽, Mao 222.

70. This reading is at variance with that of the Mao text and is assumed to reflect the Lu text of the *Odes*. The Mao text reads: "They associate without being remiss."

71. This is usually taken to mean the Five Natural Relationships of the Ru school: ruler and subject; father and son; husband and wife; older and younger brother; and between friends.

72. In the phrase *renyi* 仁義, *yi* transcends its usual meaning of the appropriateness between principle and act to mean principles of social conduct that incorporate a sense of humanity, or in short, justice.

73. Following Yang Liang.

74. Liu Taigong: although it is recited and enumerated, pondered over and reflected on, unless it is embodied in the person, it will lack the means to dwell within one. Guo Songdao: one should select the personal behavior of the ancients as the standard and obtain thereby the pattern by which they lived.

75. Yang Liang takes *fei shi* 非是 "not this" to refer in all these clauses to "learning." Yang quotes another opinion that takes *fei shi* to mean "not what is correct" referring to "the correct Way." Cf. *LY*, 12.1: "Do not look at anything that is contrary to ritual principles, do not hear anything contrary to them, do not speak of anything contrary to them, and do not lift hand or foot for anything contrary to them."

76. Yang Liang explains that the mind receives the benefits of possessing the blessings of the whole world. He quotes another opinion that asserts that "after

learning has been completed, the mind will receive so many riches that it can completely satiate its desires."

77. One who cannot be deflected from the pursuit of learning manifests a constancy and invariability that approaches that of the Way itself, and thus he is able to be resolute from his inner power.

78. "Firm of purpose" refers to what is within us, whereas "responsive" refers to what is external.

79. With Liu Taigong, text *guang* 光 LC *guang* 廣. Yang Liang understands this phrase as "the earth manifests itself in brightness," interpreting it to refer to the "luminosity of fire, the reflectiveness of water, and the luster of metal and jade." Wang Niansun: both characters mean "great; large"; thus, "Heaven manifests itself in its greatness; Earth manifests itself in its breadth." Thus, the inner power of the gentleman is prized for its completeness. Yu Yue emends: "Heaven is valued for its brilliance, Earth for its vast expanses, and the gentleman for his completeness."

BOOK 2

1. Xu Zhongshu, "Jinwen."

2. The expressions *nanlao* and *wusi* occur in early Eastern Zhou bronze inscriptions. Xu Zhongshu, "Chen Hou." The expression *nanlao* is found in *Guanzi*, 19.3b; *changsheng* in *Xunzi*, 4.7, *Mozi*, 1.2b, *Zhuangzi*, 4.18b *et passim*, *HFZ*, 6.6a *et passim*, and *LSCQ*, 1.7b; and *baoshen* in *HFZ*, 6.6a, and *Zhuangzi*, 1.1b. The terms *wusi* and *busi* are too common to catalogue.

3. See the excavation report, *Changsha Mawangdui*. The preliminary excavation reports of tombs nos. 2 and 3 indicate that the tomb of the marchioness (no. 1) postdates that of her son, which can be dated to 168 on the basis of an inscription. See *Wenwu* 1974, no. 7, and *Kaogu* 1975, no. 1.

4. Yang Bojun, "Lue tan," pp. 36–40.

5. On the *jing* 精 "seminal essence," see the Glossary under *shenming*.

6. Rickett, *Kuan-tzu*, p. 165, *n*55, assembles the evidence and examines the problems.

7. *Zhuangzi*, 15 "Keyi" 刻意, 6.1ab. Following Waley, *Three Ways of Thought*, p. 44.

8. Other terms are known from *HNZ*, 7.6b, including the pigeon bath, monkey dance, owl gaze, and tiger regard, which duplicates this passage. Among the manuscripts found at Mawangdui was a short treatise illustrating various gymnastic exercises that appear to have been connected with nurture of the bodily frame. Cf. *Wenwu* 1974, no. 7; 1975, no. 6., pp. 1–15.

9. This translation follows Karlgren, "Notes on Laotse." Waley, *Way and Its Power*, has a very different understanding of this passage.

10. *Zhuangzi*, 3.6a. The alchemical tradition said that he lived on cinnamon and magic mushrooms. With time his legend became quite elaborate. The commentaries provide a whole history: He was the grandson of the remote Di Ancestor Zhuanxu 顓頊. Because he was expert at nurturing his inner vitality and could blend the flavors of the cauldrons, when he brought some soup of ring

pheasant, Yao enfeoffed him with Peng. His behavior could be taken as a pattern for his descendants to emulate, thus he was called "patriarch." The *Shiben* makes him the clerk guarding the stores during the Zhou, attaining an age of more than 800 years. Another tradition identified him as Laozi. Yet another says that he became an immortal who never died. Such details were scholarly extrapolations from popular preconceptions.

11. *Mozi*, 19 "Fei gong" 非攻, III 下, 5.13ab. Mozi said: "You have not examined the logical distinctions contained in my teachings, nor have you understood the reasons for them. What they did was not what is called 'attack' but rather what is called 'punish.'"

12. Apud *Jinshu*, 64.6a.

13. On the *Gongsun Longzi*, see Graham, "'Hard and White' Disputations," p. 367.

14. Following Graham, *Chuang-tzu*, p. 283.

15. Zhong Tai argues that even though the extant work attributed to Deng Xi is a forgery, it must have used the original titles of his books. Since one of these is entitled "Dimension and Dimensionless," the paradox must be properly attributed to him.

16. Cf. *LY*, 4.17: "When you see a worthy man, consider how you can equal him; when you see an unworthy man, look within yourself."

17. With Ogyū Sorai and Liu Shipei: *zi* 茲 GV *zi* 緇, 淄 (= 茲).

18. Liu Shipei: *zei* 賊 GE *jian* 賤, for "but those who flatter me and toady after me are contemptible."

19. Cf. paragraph 1.8 above. In Chinese symbolism, the tiger represents ferocity and cruelty, and the wolf rapacity and savagery. Together they suggest avariciousness, brutality, cruelty, and insatiability. *Mengzi*, 4B.19, puts this even more strongly: "What differentiates man from the wild animals is but slight; the petty man loses this difference, whereas the gentleman preserves it."

20. Liang Qixiong: *zei* 賊 GE *jian* 賤, for "his complete loyalty becomes worthless."

21. *Shi*, Lesser Odes, "Xiao min" 小旻, Mao 195. According to the "Little Preface," this Ode condemns King You of Zhou 周幽王 (r. 781–771), whose reign ended with the royal house forced to abandon its capital to the barbarians and establish itself under the tutelage of the feudal lords at the eastern capital, Luoyang.

22. Following Karlgren, GL 574.

23. Following Karlgren, LC 1210. *HSWZ* reads: "The gentleman possesses the measure of discriminating what is good." Yang Liang construes this passage in the same way.

24. Text *hou* 後 can mean either "to come after" in the sense of "place second" or "next to," or in the sense "extend after," in this context, "outlive."

25. With Kubo Ai and Wang Yinzhi, on the basis of the *HSWZ* parallel, emend: *hou pengzu* 後彭祖 to *shen* 身 *hou pengzu*; *yi xiu shen zi ming* 以修身自名 to *yi xiu shen zi qiang* 强; and *ze pei yao yu* 則配堯禹 to *ze ming* 名 *pei yao yu*. Wang Yinzhi notes that Yang Liang's paraphrase presupposes the present reading of the text, showing that the damage to the text is ancient.

26. Following Wang Yinzhi. Yang Liang cites *Mengzi*, 7A.9: "If he is in impoverished circumstances, while alone he will ensure goodness in his own person; if he is advanced in office, he will extend ensuring goodness to the whole world." The *HSWZ* author seems to have had the *Mengzi* passage in mind in reworking the *Xunzi* text. Compare also *LY*, 1.15: "Zigong said: 'What do you think of the motto "poor yet not given to flattery; rich yet not given to pride"?' The Master said: "It will do, but it is not so good as "poor yet delighting in the Way; rich yet loving the rites." ' " And *LY*, 6.10: "The Master said: 'Worthy indeed was Hui! A handful of rice to eat, a gourdful of water to drink, living in a mean alley—others would have found that unendurably depressing, but Hui's happiness was not affected by it at all. Worthy indeed was Hui!' "

27. Text *bo* 勃 GV *bo* 悖; *man* 僈 GV *man* 慢; on *ti* 偍, see Karlgren LC 1658. Wang Xianqian believes that "unreasonable and disorderly" behavior results from an excess of strength in the blood humour and that "dilatory and negligent" behavior results from weakness of the blood humour.

28. *HSWZ*: "he will be aware of [their] measured quality."

29. "Rapid steps" were employed as a sign of respect, as when Confucius' son was hurrying past him (*LY*, 16.13) or when Confucius used such steps in approaching Robber Zhi (*Zhuangzi*, 29 "Dao Zhi" 盜跖, 9.18b).

30. Wang Yinzhi: *yigu* 夷固 GV *yiju* 夷倨 "to squat on the heels." It connotes a perverse disregard for acceptable behavior by arrogating to oneself dignities of a higher station, as when Yuan Rong remained squatting on his heels when he should have been standing for Confucius (*LY*, 14.43). Text *gu* 固 basically means "firm," by extension, "secure, fortified, established of old," and when applied to behavior, in a negative sense, "obstinate, mean, and rude." In the Ru tradition, it was particularly applied to anyone who refused to learn in the prescribed manner. *DDLJ* defines it as "not to know something and to fail to inquire about it" (4.5a) and notes that "a worthy man is ashamed that he does not know something and still does not inquire about it" (5.2a).

31. *Liji*, 28 "Zhongni yanju" 仲尼燕居, 50.9a: " 'Savagery' refers to respecting what does not coincide with the requirements of ritual principles."

32. The indented passage (rhymed in the original) is probably an older fragment that Xunzi is adapting to his purposes.

33. *Shi*, Lesser Odes, "Chu ci" 楚茨, Mao 209.

34. Cf. a similar series of definitions in *Zhuangzi*, 31 "Yufu" 漁父, 10.4b: "To echo the opinions of others and try to draw them out is called 'flattery.' To speak without separating the true from the false is called 'toadying.' To delight in talking about the failings of others is called 'slander.' To break up friendships and to set relatives at odds with each other is called 'malefaction.' "

35. Compare *HFZ*, 20 "Jie Lao," 6.4a: "What is called 'straightforwardness' properly consists in a sense of moral duty that necessarily makes public behavior upright and a frame of mind that is impartial and unbiased."

36. Cf. paragraph 2.2 above.

37. Literally, "leaky," the idea being that facts and things he should remember leak out of his mind as through a sieve.

38. This phrase stands apart from the remainder of the paragraph as though

it is a section title. Zhong Tai: this paragraph parallels 2.2, whereas 2.3 parallels 2.1.

39. Text *liang* 㐬 LC *liang* 諒 (corroborated by *HSWZ*); on *jian* 漸, see Karlgren, LC 1835. Xunzi refers to extrapolations such as those of Hui Shi on matters that are not yet clearly and precisely understood.

40. Hao Yixing prefers *HSWZ*: "If the impulse to be daring and bold is too strong and unyielding." Following Yu Yue: *shun* 順 GV *xun* 訓; *dao* 道 SF *dao* 導. The present text reads "stay it with obedience to the Way."

41. With Igai Hikohiro and Fujii Sen'ei: *chong chi* 重遟 is an excrescent gloss entered into the text. An alternate interpretation takes *beishi* 卑濕 to mean "lax," "inattentive to proper conduct."

42. Following Yang Liang.

43. Following Yu Xingwu. Cf. paragraph 1.5 above.

44. Cf. *LY*, 17.14: "In the past the simpleminded were at least straightforward, but today simplemindedness exists only as the artifice of the imposter."

45. Yu Yue notes that this sentence of five characters is unrelated to the previous sentence and is contrary to the style of the whole paragraph. Further, the *HSWZ* parallel omits them, and Yang Liang's commentary does not treat them. Accordingly he judges them to be an interpolation. Yu is certainly correct in judging that these five characters do not follow uninterruptedly from what precedes, but it seems more likely that the text has lost several characters that formed the first part of the sentence. I have translated accordingly.

46. Yang Liang takes *shen* 神 "divine" in the sense *shenming* 神明, on which see the Glossary. This interpretation derives from paragraph 8.11 below.

47. Such traditions were part of the large stock of maxims that Chinese writers quoted for literary and argumentative effect. Similar traditions occur in *Guanzi*, 49 "Neiye," 16.3a: "The gentleman manipulates external things, but is not manipulated by them." And *Zhuangzi*, 20 "Shanlin" 山林, 7.9a: "Treat things as things, but do not allow yourself to be treated as a thing."

48. The significance of this sentence has excited considerable controversy among the commentators. Gu Guangqi believes that the text is jumbled. Text *tong* 通 "successful" should be contrastive to *qiong* 窮 "impoverished" rather than to *shun* 順 "obedient," which is properly contrastive to *luan* 亂, here used in the special sense "insubordinate." Thus Gu reads: "Serving an insubordinate lord and being successful is inferior to serving an obedient lord and being impoverished." Wang Niansun accepts this interpretation.

Yu Yue points out that Gu misses Xunzi's point. Xunzi considered that service to a disorderly lord resulted in disobedience, whereas service to an impoverished lord resulted in lack of success. Nonetheless, Xunzi considered success in the service of a disorderly lord to be inferior to obedience in the service of an impoverished lord. Yu observes that understanding the sentence in this way makes its point similar to the preceding sentence. Wang Xianqian points out that being "successful" merely means finding employment, citing paragraph 7.4 below. Zhong Tai agrees and adds that "obedience" means acting in accord with the Way.

49. The parallel phrase in the third sentence reads *jing* 精 "essence" for *qing* 情

"feelings." Wang Yinzhi: *ren* 人 GV *ren* 仁. The present text reads: "your emotional disposition one of love for others."

50. Following Yang Liang and Zhu Junsheng. Others understand: "though you choose to live among the barbarians." The "Four Yi tribes" refers to the barbarians surrounding the Chinese "Middle Kingdom" and does not designate particular peoples. Compare *LY*, 13.19: "The Master said: 'In domestic matters be respectful; in public undertakings, be reverent; in relations with others, be loyal. Even among the Yi and Di tribes, these may not be abandoned.'"

51. Wang Yinzhi: *zhi* 執 GE *yi* 埶. With Liu Shipei reading *mo* 墨 as it stands. Yang Liang takes *mo* to refer to Mo Di and accordingly emends text *shun* 順 "accord with" to *shen* 慎, referring to Shen Dao. Yu Chang, who accepts Yang's emendation, takes text *shu* 術 "methods" as GV *shu* 述 "to carry forward, transmit to posterity," for "carry forward the doctrines of Shen Dao and Mo Di," which requires that the parallel passage in the first sentence read "carry forward ritual principles and justice."

52. Text *jing* 精 GV *qing* 情. Text *za* 雜 "heteronomy" means lacking any central principle or theme, thus given to uncertainty and confusion.

53. Liu Shipei: *er bu qu* 而不曲 GE for UR **ruan qu* 耎曲. Yang Liang understands the unemended text as "shrewd and not indirect."

54. Yang Liang: *bi* 辟 SF *pi* 僻. Other commentators understand this passage quite differently.

55. The idea is that the scholar does not fold his hands in the ritually prescribed fashion because he is worried lest he soil the long, flowing sleeves of his robes in the mud as he walks along. Rather he is concerned with proper respectfulness and reverence. Yang Liang: *ji* 冀 GE *yi* 翼 "reverent." Since this *yi* also means "wings," some commentators suggest that the scholar walks about with his arms outstretched like the wings of a bird so that the long sleeves of his robe will not touch the ground. This is based on *LY*, 10.3, which says that "he hastens forwards [in court receptions] with his arms like the wings of a bird" (so translates Legge; compare Lau). This interpretation has all the authority of Zhu Xi, but is mistaken. The correct meaning is understood by Waley: "As he advances with quickened steps, his attitude is one of majestic dignity."

56. Following Wang Niansun.

57. Cf. paragraph 1.6 above.

58. The idea is that the gentleman, because he sets limits to his inquiry, will not engage in argument where there can be no solution. Others have interpreted this to mean that the gentleman sets stopping places in such matters, as above. Wang Xianqian believes that the gentleman aims at a "final resting place" as in the *Daxue* phrase "he rests in the highest good." The gentleman, in his view, rests in the perfection of learning.

59. Yang Liang: *yi* 倚 GV *qi* 奇. Yang, Hao Yixing, and Kubo Ai: *kui* 魁 GV *gui* 瑰, 傀. Yang Liang: Xunzi refers to the behavior of eccentrics like Huang Liao 黃繚, who asked why Heaven and Earth did not collapse and crumble. In "Nothing Indecorous" (3.1), Xunzi describes as "difficult" the feat of Shentu Di, who took hold of a stone, jumped into a river, and drowned himself.

60. Momoi Hakuroku: *gu xue yue chi* 故學曰遲 reversal of UR **gu yue xue chi*.

61. Gao Heng: *lei* 累 SF *lei* 菓. Liang Qixiong: *chong* 崇 LC *zhong* 終. Cf. *DDJ*, 64: "A tower nine stories high rises up from baskets of earth; a journey of 1,000 *li* starts from beneath one's feet." *HNZ*, 17.13b, reads: "By accumulating earth basketful by basketful, you can complete a high mound."

62. The six horses probably refer to the famous team belonging to the Zhou king; see paragraph 1.7. The indented passage is a collection of traditional sayings that Xunzi adapts to his argument.

63. These three sentences are quoted in the *HSWZ* and are separated from the preceding paragraph in the *TZ* edition. Wang Xianqian and others make them the conclusion of paragraph 2.8.

64. Fang Bao, Hao Yixing, Wang Niansun, and Kubo Ai: *chu ru* 出入 GE *chu ren* 出人. Corroborated by *HSWZ* reading. The error is ancient since it is presupposed by the Yang commentary and is quoted in *WX*, 13.16a. The present text reads: "One who spends many days in idleness will not get far in his comings and goings." This Zhong Tai interprets: "Those who leave with one principle and return with another are men of the streets and alleys."

65. Cf. paragraph 1.8 above.

66. Following Kubo Ai.

67. Following Wang Yinzhi.

68. Chen Huan: *qu* 渠 LC *ju* 瞿. Cf. Karlgren, LC 854.

69. Following Wang Niansun.

70. Yang Liang: some take *li* 禮 GE *ti* 體, for: "Therefore one who is in the process of learning is one who learns to embody the model."

71. *Shi*, Greater Odes, "Huangyi" 皇矣, Mao 241. This sacrificial ode is the mandate from the Di Ancestor to King Wen to conquer various cities. King Wen acquires the mandate because of his outstanding qualities, which are praised in this Ode.

72. King Wen followed naturally the rules of the Di Ancestor without having to consider or think about them since his inner nature was good and was at peace with them. Yang Liang: Xunzi quotes this Ode to illustrate that the teacher and model accord with the Way without any prior or special knowledge, just as King Wen, though he was unaware, nonetheless obeyed the laws of Nature.

73. Omitting four characters 有鈞無上, which Yang Liang says some scholars considered excrescent. They bear no relation to the text and disturb the parallelism of this sentence with the remainder of the paragraph.

74. Cf. how *Mengzi*, 7A.22 (repeated 4A.13), describes what this involves: "Bo Yi fled from Zhou Xin and settled on the edge of the North Sea. The Grand Duke fled from Zhou Xin and settled on the edge of the East Sea. When they heard of the rise of King Wen, they stirred and said: 'Why not return home? I hear that the Earl of the West [King Wen] takes good care of the elderly.'" Mencius explains that King Wen "laid down the pattern for distribution of the land, taught men to plant trees and keep animals properly, and showed women how to care for the aged. A man needs silk for warmth at 50 and meat for sustenance at 70. To have neither warm clothes nor a full belly is to be cold and hungry. The people under King Wen had no old people who were cold or

hungry." Silk was not the ordinary clothing for the common people, who wore hemp. They ate mostly cereals and vegetables with very little meat.

75. Kubo Ai cites *LSCQ*: "The worthy ruler does not place hardships on those already having difficulties." Yu Yue: "those who have difficulties" are the unworthy in society; the "successful" are those who are worthy (based on the definition of Kong Zhao apud *Yi Zhou shu*).

76. Furuya Sekiyō and Yu Yue: *guo* 過 GV *huo* 禍. The idea is clearly expressed in *Mozi*, 6 "Ciguo" 辭過, 1.15b: "Hence, where Heaven has sent an inauspicious omen, it will cause his ruin and he will lose his country." A "greatly inauspicious omen" presages an impending, inevitable disaster.

77. Yu Xingwu: *sui* 遂 GV *zhui* 墜 via UR *SF 豕. Though an omen has occurred, Heaven will not cause his ruin. In his "Discourse on Nature," which was written after this book, Xunzi rejects the traditional notion that Heaven responds to men. This passage seems to take a position intermediate between the traditional view and that of his later philosophy.

78. Wang Niansun: *ku* 枯 GV *gu* 楛.

79. Cf. *Zuo*, Xi 23, where Chonger 重耳, the future duke of Jin, is described as "having wide aims, yet distinguished by moderation"; and *Zuo*, Wen 18, where the eight worthy sons of the Di Ancestor Gaoyang 高陽 are considered to have been "correct, sagacious, of wide comprehension, and deep." Cf. paragraph 20.1, where Xunzi makes a similar point in regard to listening to the *Odes* and *Hymns*. Because the gentleman exalts the principle of humanity, he keeps his sense of purpose fixed on the broader aims and goals it requires and is not reduced to the minute and petty concerns of the petty man.

80. Cf. *LY*, 4.5: "Wealth with honor is what all men desire, but if they can be obtained only at the expense of the Way, he will not dwell with them. Poverty and meanness are what all men hate, but if they are obtained through following his Way, he will let them come."

81. On *jian* 柬, see Karlgren LC 659 with GL 153 and GL 884. This follows Fang Bao and Zhong Tai. Other scholars read "restrained by" to mean "choose to follow." Some scholars emend *li* 理 "principle of natural order" to *li* 禮 "ritual principles." The "principles of natural order" are those that inhere in the basic structure and organization of a thing and that distinguish it from other things. These natural principles create a normal, homeostatic condition that is the optimum for the thing. The gentleman makes use of them in rest and he is not enfeebled, whereas those who do not follow natural principles atrophy from disuse.

82. With Wang Niansun, Kubo Ai, Wang Xianqian, and Zhang Heng: *jiao* 交 GE *wen* 文.

83. *Shu*, "Hongfan" 洪范, 12.14a. These lines are rhymed couplets.

BOOK 3

1. Waley, *Analects*, pp. 66, 248.

2. So in the *Zhuangzi yinyi*; Fu Qian, apud *HSBZ*, 51.15a; and Gao You, apud *HNZ*, 16.6a.

3. In the version of the legend contained in *HSWZ* and that in *Xinxu*, 7.13b–14a.

4. Yang Xiong, "Fei Qu Yuan" 非屈原, apud Yang Liang.

5. Sun Yirang, *Zhayi*, apud Liang Qixiong, p. 24.

6. See the essay on relativity in *Zhuangzi*, 17 "Qiushui," 6.5b–12a.

7. Hu, *Development*, pp. 113–17.

8. Chen Pan attempts to reconstruct a lost text of Zou Yan, which if his reconstruction is reliable, mentions volcanoes.

9. The explanation of Li Yi 李頤, which Yang quotes, adds no light: "The myriad things are without determined shape. The shape being indeterminate refers to the fact that at the top is the head and at the bottom is the tail."

10. The concept of *cheng* is philosophically important even in *Mengzi* (7A.4), which observes that "all things are within me. There is no greater joy than to find upon self-examination that I have been true to myself." Mencius stresses the relation of *cheng* to "goodness": "There is a Way to be true to one's self. If you do not understand goodness, you cannot be true to yourself. For this reason, being true to the way of Heaven and thinking about truth is the way of Man" (*Mengzi* 4A.12). Elsewhere in the *Mengzi* the term means "true" in the sense of genuine, as "genuine case of inability" (1A.7), "true man of Qi" (2A.1), or "truly right" (3A.5).

11. This passage is translated quite variously. Cf. Waley, *Way and Its Power*, p. 172; Chan, p. 141, and Karlgren, "Notes on Laotse," p. 5.

12. This translation differs from those by Legge, Watson, Lin Yu-t'ang, and Needham.

13. Graham, *Later Mohist Logic*, pp. 214, 295, 395–96; Tan Jiefu, *Mo Jing yijie*, Jing shang 44.

14. Graham, *Later Mohist Logic*, p. 214.

15. Yang Liang's interpretation is based on parallel language in *Zhongyong*, 2.4, but there foreknowledge is implied that is not appropriate to this passage in the *Xunzi*.

16. Cf. *HFZ*, 32 "Waichu shui," I/A, 11.5b; and *HNZ*, 13.15b.

17. Though the name is Shi Yu in the *Zhuangzi* and Shi Qiu in the *Xunzi*, we can be sure that the same person is involved since the characters with which the name is written are only orthographical variants of one another.

18. Yang Liang and Kubo Ai both understand "improper investigations" to mean "cleverness in examining problems." Yang Liang: "fitting" means what is concordant with ritual and moral principles.

19. Omit excrescent *huai* 懷. Liu Shipei: *huai* is a marginal note erroneously entered into the text. Confirmed by *TPYL*, 51.5a, quotation and by reading in paragraph 6.9 below.

20. Following Yang Liang, interpreting *zhong* 中 as the mean prescribed by ritual.

21. *Zhuangzi*, 33 "Tianxia," 10.20b, has paradoxes reading "Mountains are on a level with marshes" and "Heaven and Earth are both low."

22. Commentators generally agree that six characters of the present text—*ru*

hu er, chu hu kou, 入乎耳, 出乎口—are an emendation of an UR paradox that was not understood or of a damaged passage to the language of paragraph 1.9 above. Yang Liang quotes two emendations: (1) emend to *shan chu kou* 山出口, a paradox attributed to Hui Shi apud *Zhuangzi*, 33 "Tianxia," 10.22a; and (2) emend to *shan you* 有 *kou*, meaning that mountains can draw in and spit out clouds and mists.

23. Yu Yue: *gou* 鈎 LC *xu* 姁 "an old woman." Yang Liang noted that there was no Tang explanation for the paradox.

24. The text tradition and the meaning here are unclear. *SY* reads *xiong tan* 凶貪 "is cruel and avaricious" for text *yin kou* 吟口. Yang Liang: *yin kou* means that his praises have long been on everyone's tongue.

Hao Yixing and Liang Qixiong: follow *SY* reading. "Robber Zhi, though cruel and avaricious, had a reputation like that of the sun and moon."

Yu Yue: *yin* LC *qin* 黔 "black," referring to things that are like wild beasts of prey, thus equivalent to the *SY* reading. "Robber Zhi, though a black-mouthed beast of prey, had a reputation like that of the sun and moon."

Wang Xianqian: *yin kou* should be *kou yin* attested *Hou Hanshu jijie*, 34.9a, in the meaning "stammer and be tongue-tied." "Robber Zhi, though tongue-tied, had a reputation like that of the sun and moon."

Liu Shipei: *yin kou* GE for UR *tan* 貪 copied as 吟, and interpreted as SF *yin kou*. Text *ming sheng* 名聲, redundant with *sheng* excrescent for UR *盗跖貪名若 日明, with *tan ming* a binome glossed as *sheng*. Kanaya Osamu concurs. "Robber Zhi had a coveted reputation like that of the sun and moon."

Long Yuchun: *yin* LC *qin* 矜 "boastful" corroborated by *Zhuangzi*, 4.10a, description of a great thief. "Robber Zhi, with a boastful mouth, had a reputation like that of the sun and moon."

25. *Shi*, Lesser Odes, "Yuli" 魚麗, Mao 170.

26. This interpretation seems required by the context of Xunzi's quotation. Karlgren, "Odes," p. 111: "and yet they are correct." Legge, 4:270: "and all are in season."

27. An allusion to *Shi*, "Huanlan" 芄蘭, Mao 60. Following Yu Yue. *HSWZ* reads *he* 和 for text *zhi* 知, "easy to be on good terms with." Wang Niansun and Kubo Ai prefer the *HSWZ* reading.

28. Cf. *LY*, 2.14: "The gentleman is catholic and not partisan; the petty man is partisan and not catholic."

29. Text 言辯而不辭 is apparently defective. *HSWZ* reads *luan* 亂 for text *ci* 辭. Gongsun Long criticizes his opponent's arguments as *luan ci* "disordered formulations," which is the probable UR reading. Emend to *luan ci*. I take *bian* 辯 as "discrimination." The term *ci* "formulations" refers to any kind of compositions deliberately created for a ceremonial occasion or for persuasive effect, or cast in aesthetic or rhetorical form, or stated in a philosophical form. In this last sense, it means "proposition." *Mengzi*, 2A.2, criticizes four kinds of *ci*: those that are biased and one-sided, those that are immoderate and exceed due measure, those that are heterodox, and those that are evasive. Xunzi had something of this sort in mind.

Hao Yixing and Wang Niansun: follow *HSWZ*, for "in his speech he makes distinctions, but not to introduce confusion." Zhong Tai, Liang Qixiong, and Fujii Sen'ei: *ci* means "prolix," for "in his speech he makes distinctions, but is not prolix."

30. Following Yang Liang: *zun* 繜 GV *zun* 撙 (= *zun* 僔) [confirmed by *QSZY* quotation]; *zhu* 紃 GV *chu* 黜.

31. Following Yang Liang: text *ji* 激 means "rouse (to opposition)." Kubo Ai: *ji* GV *jiao* 徼 "cunning" as in *LY*, 17.22. Liu Shipei: *ji* GV *jiao* 繳 "tortuous, convoluted" as in *SJ*, 130.12.

32. Following Wang Niansun and Kubo Ai: emend text *gua li* 寡立, to *zhi li* 直立, for "upright position" instead of "singular position," the error arising from a nonstandard UR reading. (*Zhi li* is the reading employed in paragraph 4.2 below, but the emendation is unsupported by corroborative evidence. The quotation apud the Li Shan commentary to *WX*, 25.4b, shows that *gua li* is an ancient reading.) Yang Liang understands *sheng* 勝 as "triumph." Ogyū Sorai understands *sheng* as "overcome." Wang Niansun takes *sheng* to mean "be superior to" on the basis of Yu Fan (A.D. 164–233) gloss to *Yijing*, 5.31a, and the Mao commentary to *Shi*, Mao 192, for a parallel between "be superior to" and "haughty" in the next phrase. Substantially the same points are made in paragraph 4.2 in slightly different language. Xunzi is using the terminology of formal debate, though not in a narrow technical meaning, as is shown by the term *ji* "rouse (to opposition)."

33. *Shi*, Greater Odes, "Yi" 抑, Mao 256.

34. Following ZT reading in omitting excrescent *e* 惡. Qian Dian, "Kaoyi," notes that the Shu and Erzhe editions also omit *e*. *HSWZ* reads: "in rectifying his speech and straightening out conduct."

35. Following Hao Yixing: *qu shen* 屈伸 GV *qu xin* 詘信.

36. Following Yang Liang: *xin* 信 GV *shen* 伸.

37. Following Wang Xianqian. Long Yushen and Fujii Sen'ei: *yi* 義 LC *yi* 宜 "suitable, proper."

38. The commentators do not agree as to the meaning of *bian ying* 變應. Yu Yue: *bian* LC *bian* 徧 meaning "everywhere." Liu Shipei concurs in the emendation of Yu Yue, but with the meaning "manage, control."

39. *Shi*, Lesser Odes, "Shang shang zhe hua" 裳裳者華, Mao 214.

40. Xunzi understands "perfect fittingness" in the Ode to be the result of the gentleman's sense of what is morally right.

41. Following Lu Wenchao, Wang Niansun, and Kubo Ai: emend *tian er dao* 天而道 to *HSWZ* reading *jing* 敬 *tian er dao*. The Yang commentary is judged defective.

42. Following Yang Liang. Yu Xingwu: *zhi* 止 GE *zhi* 之 "to proceed"; *qi* 齊 LC *ci* 次 "halt," for "he proceeds to lead the way" . . . "he keeps back." Karlgren LC 1802 concurs.

43. Following Liu Taigong: *li* 理 Tang taboo avoidance UR *zhi* 治, confirmed by *HSWZ* reading. Wang Niansun, Wang Xianqian, and Liang Qixiong concur.

44. Text *li* 理 here means the natural pattern or grain that characterizes a thing uniquely. A similar idea is expressed in paragraph 7.2 below. Cf. *Yijing*, 1.21b: "When happy, he carries his principles into action; when dejected, he keeps them in retirement."

45. Following Hao Yixing and Kubo Ai: *jian* 漸 LC *qian* 潛, "clandestine, covert."

46. Following Yang Liang: *tui* 兌 SF *yue* 說 (= 悅). Wang Xianqian: *tui* SF *rui* 銳 "sharp" as in paragraph 2.6 above.

47. Cf. *LY*, 17.33: "The Master said: 'Women and ordinary people are difficult to nurture; if you are friendly with them, they become disobedient, and if you are remote, they are resentful.'"

48. Following Yang Liang. Yang notes another opinion: *xuan* 翾 GV *xuan* 儇 "smart-aleck." Liang Qixiong: *xuan* GV *xuan* 儇 "smart."

49. Following Yang Liang. Liu Shipei: *pian* 偏 GV *bian* 褊, for "filled with pride and is petty."

50. Following Hao Yixing. Yang Liang: *an* 偌 GV *shi* 濕, "depressed" after *HSWZ* reading *lei* 累 (SF 纍) "despondent."

51. This tradition is not elsewhere recorded.

52. Following Yu Yue: *xiu* 修 LC *di* 滌 "purify." The image is one of removing the impurities, as in clarifying spirits or purifying stagnant waters.

53. Following Lu Wenchao: emend *bian* 辯 to *shen* 身 on basis of *HSWZ* reading. Kubo Ai: *jie* 絜 SF *jie* 潔, following ZT edition.

54. On the basis of *HSWZ* parallel, add six characters: *niu wu er niu ying zhi* 牛鳴而牛應之.

55. The proverbs are also quoted in Qu Yuan's biography in *SJ*, 84.12–13. Wang Yinglin suggests that they are expressions native to Chu.

56. Following Yang Liang: *huo* 㦻 GV *huo* 惑 "deluded." The line occurs in the *Chuci* in a slightly different form usually interpreted as: "How should I be expected to endure soiling the unblemished purity of my own character with the mud and dirt of mere things." Gao Heng interprets the *Xunzi* like the *Chuci*.

57. Among the Mawangdui manuscripts, on the same scroll with the two versions of the *Daode jing*, is a previously unknown work called *Wu xing pian* 五行篇, which belongs to the eclectic Ru tradition of the third century. Its contents appear to be related to this passage, possibly derived in part from it. This suggests that there existed a tradition of philosophical argument concerning these issues and that the special vocabulary involves technical terms that are here incompletely rendered. But the parallel text and a close reading of the *Xunzi* suggest that Xunzi is commenting on previously existing texts. These are indicated by the indented passages. I am endebted to Jeffrey K. Riegel for calling my attention to the parallels with the *Wu xing*.

58. Following Wang Niansun and Kubo Ai: *tuo* 它 GV *tuo* 他, confirmed by ZT edition and *QSZY* quotation.

59. The "Hundred Clans" is a common term designating all the Chinese.

60. The idea is that the gentleman must be genuine in his inner private self even when he is alone, unlike the petty man, who will attempt any evil when he

is alone. The gentleman realizes that what is hidden is what is ultimately visible and what is minute is ultimately to be discovered. Attempts to hide the truth and put on an appearance of good are of no use since they can be seen as if in his very internal organs. The gentleman will not *gou* "make do" by depending on "fluke circumstances."

61. The "method" may refer to the "method of nourishing the mind" described in paragraph 2.4.

62. "All True Kings" refers to the sages of the past and to the methods they employed. "Later Kings" refers specifically to Kings Wen and Wu, together with the Duke of Zhou, whose methods are known in greater detail and whose example is thus more reliable. On this, see paragraph 5.5.

63. Wang Niansun: *bai* 拜 GE for UR **gong* 幵 (= 拱) "formal court salute."

64. Compare *DDJ*, 47: "Without leaving his door, he knows everything under heaven. Without looking out his window, he knows all the ways of heaven."

65. Text *bian* 辨 GV *ban* 辦 "manage, control."

66. Following Yang Liang: *ji* 疾 GV *ji* 嫉.

67. Following Wang Yinzhi: *bo* 悖 GV *bo* 勃.

68. Following Hao Yixing and Wang Niansun: *qing* 情 means "true circumstances"; *jie* 竭 GV *jie* 揭.

69. Following Gao Heng: *liu* 流 GE *yuan* 沇 LC *yan* 沿, "follow, imitate"; following Wang Niansun: *shen* 甚 GE *shi* 是.

70. Following Yang Liang and Zhong Tai. Contrast the description of the gentleman in paragraph 1.14.

71. This functions as a paragraph title analogous to that in paragraph 2.4. Gu Guangqi emends to: "Weighing the relative merits of choosing and refusing desires and aversions and what is beneficial and what harmful."

72. Following Lu Wenchao: add 人之所欲者，吾亦欲之, on the basis of parallelism and the Yang Liang commentary.

73. With Yu Yue: *qiu* 求 means "intent on"; *ren* 仁 "humane" is excrescent.

74. Following Yang Liang: *an* 奄 LC *an* 暗.

BOOK 4

1. Following the reading in *SJ*, 68.8, which preserves the rhyme; *Shangjun shu*, 1.1a, quoted with rhyme preserved in *TPYL*, 496.4ab.

2. *Guanzi*, 38 "Baixin," 13.10a See *n*19, to Chap. 4 of the General Introduction for the argument that Song Xing is the author of this book.

3. See below "Fei shier zi," 6.4, and "Zhenglun," 18.8. Cf. *Mengzi*, 4B.4.

4. *Mozi*, "Canons," 10.26a; Graham, *Later Mohist Logic*, A74.

5. *Mozi*, "Canons," 10.44a; Graham, *Later Mohist Logic*, B74.

6. *Zhuangzi*, 22 "Zhibeiyou" 知北遊, 7.25b; *Mengzi*, 3A.3, 4A.2.

7. See below "Ruxiao," 8.12, and "Fuguo," 10.1.

8. Text *jiao* 憍 GV *jiao* 驕; *xie* 泄, "excessive" contrastive to *jian* 儉, "frugal." Yang Liang: *xie* GV *xie* 媟, "disrespectful"; cf. Karlgren LC 1502. Kubo Ai: *xie* GE *yi* 益, "arrogance."

9. The five weapons are listed as spears, halberds, battle axes, shields, and bows and arrows by Fan Ning 范寧 apud *Guliang*, Zhuang 25 (*Fanshi jijie*, 6.7b); as knives, swords, spears, lances, and arrows by Wei Zhao 韋昭 apud *Guoyu*, 6.11b; and as spears, lances, double lances, chief's halberds, and barbarian halberds by Zheng Sinong 鄭司農 apud *Zhouli*, 32.5b.

10. Following Yu Xingwu: *bobo* 薄薄 GV *pupu* 溥溥.

11. With Kubo Ai, these two sentences appear to be defective either because of text lacunae or because of errors. The meaning is uncertain, and the translation accordingly tentative. Wang Niansun: *dai* 殆 LC *dai* 待 "wait," for "when the roadway is constricted, travelers must wait for the other columns to pass by in a single file." Yu Yue: *rang* 譲 GV *rang* 攘, in the special sense "embroiled, confused, disturbed," for "when the roadway is broad, travelers move along it in a confused mass and do not stop, but when it is constricted, the travelers, being few in number, feel imperiled and not tranquil."

12. Others understand this quite differently. Tao Hongqing: *kuai* 快 GV *kuai* 夬, "divisiveness"; Yang Liang and Wang Xianqian: "reckless"; Liang Qichao: "discontented."

13. Following Yang Liang. Cf. "Bugou," 3.3–4.

14. Liu Shipei suggests that Xunzi had in mind people like Gongsun Hong of the Han dynasty, who, despite personal probity, pandered after the wishes of Emperor Wu. Compare *Mengzi*, 7B.37: "He shares with others the practices of the day and is in harmony with the sordid world. He pursues such a policy and appears to be conscientious and faithful and to show integrity in his conduct" (Lau, *Mencius*, p. 203).

15. Following Yang Liang: *yu* 俞 SF *yu* 愈; Yu Chang: *kou* 口 LC *kou* 詬 "revile; slander." Compare *DDLJ*, 6.2b: "mouths produce slander." The *Xiaojing* (2.3a) notes: "What is contrary to the model [of the ancient Kings] is not to be spoken and what is contrary to their way is not to be done. The mouth has no part in the selection of words and the body no part in the selection of actions. Words can fill the entire world without reviling or excess; actions can fill the entire world without anger or hate."

16. Following Yang Liang: they associate with others with a view to obtaining such benefits as fattening foods, yet they still become emaciated.

17. Following Yang Liang. With Yang: *zhuan* 剸 GV *zhuan* 專, "alone," confirmed by *TPYL*, 492, quotation. Cf. "Bugou," 3.4, above.

18. Cf. the rhymed passage quoted by Confucius as though it were a well-known proverb (*LY*, 13.21): "The blind rage of a single morning caused him to be forgetful of his own person as well as of his relatives."

19. This reflects the contemporary Chinese practice of extending the punishment for a crime not only to the person committing the crime but also to his close relatives. Yang Liang cites a now-lost passage from the *Shizi* 尸子: "It is not the lord of men's use of armies that causes the people grief; it is rather the blind belligerency caused by a single incautious word."

20. Following the alternative explanation cited by Yang Liang: *you* 憂 GE *xia* 夏 LC *xia* 下. Wang Niansun and Liang Qixiong concur. The same emendation should be made in the two later recurrences of the phrase.

21. Following ZT reading *she* 赦 rather than Lü reading *she* 舍.

22. Following the Qian and ZT editions, with others cited in Qian Dian, *Kaoyi*. The Lü edition reads "a nursing sow will *not* charge a tiger." Following the Lü edition reading *ren ye* 人也. Qian Dian, *Kaoyi*: all other editions read *xiao ren* 小人, for "it is only the petty man." The reading of the Lü edition is preferable since the context is not the petty man, but mankind in general, especially the bellicose man. Xunzi intends to contrast the natural instinct of motherhood in animals, which makes a nursing bitch bite a tiger or a brooding hen attack a fox despite their inadequate strength, with men, who sacrifice everything. Pan Zhonggui calls attention to *Gongyang*, Zhuang 12, describing the death of Grand Officer Qiumu 仇牧: "Wan 宋萬 became furious, struck Duke Min 宋閔公, and broke his neck. When Qiumu heard that the ruler had been assassinated, he rushed to the scene, where he met Wan at the door. Qiumu grasped the sword and cursed him. Wan struck Qiumu with his hand and killed him, crushing his skull with such force that his teeth were stuck in the door panel. Of Qiumu it may be said that he 'did not fear the strong and refractory.'" The commentator He Xiu 何休 notes that the rash action of Qiumu may be compared to that "of a nursing bitch attacking a tiger or a brooding hen chasing a fox."

23. Following Hao Yixing: *zhu* 籥 GV *zhu* 斲, apud *Yupian* 玉篇. Liu Shipei: *shi* 矢 excrescent; confirmed *TPYL*, 353, quotation. The idea is that using such a high-quality weapon for an ordinary task is a kind of "overkill." Hufu was the name of an ancient city located in the state of Wu, near modern Dangshan in Zhejiang. Yang Liang says that Hufu was famous for the manufacture of lances. The *Guanzi*, 77 "Dishu" 地數, 23.2a, relates that Chiyou 蚩尤 fabricated metal that had come from springs in the hills of Yonghu into double lances. Chiyou was the minister who rebelled against Huang Di 黃帝 and is credited with the invention of weapons. Though Yang Liang believed that the double-lances of Yonghu and the lances of Hufu were the same, he is apparently wrong. Cao Pei 曹丕 (A.D. 188–227), who became Emperor Wen of the Wei dynasty 魏文帝, mentions both the double-lances of Yonghu and the lances of Hufu as "world-famous implements" in his *Jianan du xu* 建安諸序. An entirely different illustration is used in *SY*, 5.9ab, which explicitly quotes this passage: "This kind of man is what is called 'using a white fox to tend hairless dogs and sheep.' Such a person would smear them with dirt. What transgression could possibly be worse!"

24. Following Yang Liang. Since sage kings as well as the imperfect rulers of Xunzi's time condemned such behavior, it cannot be because of any delusion or illness on the part of contemporary rulers. Such men are not monsters; when we look at them, we see that they are men and that their likes and dislikes are no different from those of the sage. Only their fondness for belligerent actions makes such men different.

25. Following Yang Liang: *bi* 辟 SF *bi* 避.

26. With Wang Yinzhi and Kubo Ai: text *li* 利 excrescent, miscopied from parallel expression in next sentence.

27. Following Wang Yinzhi: *zhen* 振 GE *hen* 很, "with daring."

28. Kubo Ai notes that this sentence is substantially shorter than the others, indicating a lacuna. The descriptive sections of the four parallel sentences are 26,

24, 4, and 28 characters respectively, implying a lacuna of about 20 characters.

29. Yu Yue: read *er chi yi* 而持義 for *chi yi er*, confirmed by the Yang Liang paraphrase.

30. Compare "Quanxue," 1.14, and "Xiushen," 2.13.

31. The identity of the fish is uncertain as the character is a hapax legomenon. Hao Yixing: text 鮇 SF *li* 鱧, meaning "mullet" (Karlgren), "white-bellied shad" (*Shuowen*), or "snakefish" (*Erya*). Yang Liang: *fou yang* 浮陽 means "fond of floating about at the surface of the water." Liang Qixiong: *yang* 陽 GV *tang* 湯, "reckless" (attested in the *Jingdian shiwen*, 26.25a, s.v. placename). Text *yang* is glossed by Mao as "carefree," apud *Shi* 64 (Karlgren GL 199), for "dart about in a carefree way." Following Yu Yue: *qu* 胠 GV *qu* 弆, accepted by Wang Xianqian.

32. Following Wang Niansun and Kubo Ai: *zhi* 志 GE *zhi* 識, "knowledge" (derived from experience), confirmed by parallel phrase in "Faxing," 30.5. The idea is that they do not see that the way of Heaven is constant, raining on the rich and poor alike.

33. Lu Wenchao: this paragraph not distinguished in old editions of the text. It is, however, the probable original opening paragraph of the chapter. See Appendix B.

34. The idea is "success in office" and "reduced to poverty by not holding any official position."

35. Following Wang Zhong: *cai* 材 "talented" GE *po* 朴, (= *pu* 樸 [Wang Niansun]). This is the Daoist notion of an original simplicity and honesty uncorrupted by learning.

36. Calculated variously as 80 or 100 years and less than 30 years of age, respectively.

37. An allusion to *Shi*, Greater Odes, "Zhengmin" 烝民, Mao 260. Cf. *Mengzi*, 6A.6, treatment of the same Ode.

38. Following Yang Liang.

39. They do not call the peasants away from their fields during the planting and harvesting seasons to have them work on corvée projects, and they apply judicial power without bias and in the public interest rather than to further private advantage.

40. The *dafu* 大夫 grand officers and the *shi* knights were two aristocratic ranks below the ministers to the feudal lords. The *yi* 邑 were the smaller rural cities and towns over which *dafu* families ruled during the Spring and Autumn period. Such families were often known by the name of their ancestral home. "Fields" refers to the lands given in fief to knights for their own support and to provide them with an income sufficient to supply them with the equipment of war.

41. The petty officers in the lower echelons of the various bureaus of the government.

42. That *fa* 法 here means "laws" rather than "model" is indicative of a late date for this passage; *ze* 則 refers to the codes and rules, such as those of Prince Chan of Zheng and Deng Xi, inscribed on bronze tripods or written on bamboo.

43. Standardization of "weights and measures" was a program associated with Shang Yang and other Legalist thinkers. Xunzi apparently here means that by studying the weights and measures handed down from the past, one can accurately reconstruct those used by the sage kings.

44. Making maps was an important function of government. The *Zhouli* mentions that the director general of the masses prepared maps of the states with population statistics (10.1a) and that several different officials prepared maps of the topography of the states (15.13b, 30.12b, 33.9a), of the resources of the states (33.9a), and of minerals (16.14a). The *Zhanguo ce* (19.2b) mentions a map possessed by the state of Zhao that detailed the territory of the various states. *Guanzi*, 27 "Ditu" 地圖, 10.7a, describes the military use to which such maps were put. Maps containing population statistics for the region of the Han state around Changsha were found in Tomb 3 at Mawangdui. Riegel, "Mawangdui Tomb Three."

45. Yang Liang takes this to refer to the registers of the population, but the meaning here, as in *Shi*, Greater Odes, "Hanyi" 韓奕, Mao 261, is registers of the revenues derived from cultivation of fields.

46. That is, though they did not understand the rationale of the various regulations and procedures, they nonetheless followed them mechanically with the utmost accuracy and scrupulousness.

47. Following Kubo Ai and Liu Shipei. "King" refers to the Zhou king and not to the rulers of Xunzi's day, all of whom had usurped the title. "Duke" refers generally to the feudal lords whatever their title.

48. Cf. *Lüshi chunqiu*, 1/3 "Zhongji" 重己, 1.7b: "Everyone wishes for a long life and to see many days."

49. Following Hao Yixing and Kubo Ai: *yuan* 原 SF *yuan* 愿, confirmed by "Jundao," 12.11, reading. Following Yang Liang: *qu* 軥 GV *gou* 拘.

50. Text *bi* 比 GV *pi* 庀, "prepare; execute task" (attested *Zuo*, Xiang 5 and 9); *dun* 敦, defined *Erya* "make an earnest effort" (attested *Zuo*, Cheng 13).

51. Following Hao Yixing: *tao* 陶 LC *yao* 谣, "false reports." Wang Niansun: *tao* LC *tao* 慆, "false, insincere"; accepted by Zhang Heng and Liang Qixiong. Text *tao* is close in meaning to *dan* 誕 "boasting," both involving deceiving others concerning reality.

52. Following Yang Liang: *tang* 愓 GV *dang* 蕩; Hao Yixing: *jiao* 憍 GV *jiao* 驕.

53. Following Yu Yue.

54. Text *bian* 辯 GV *ban* 辦, "manage." An alternate interpretation, taking *bian* as it stands, is "is orderly in his discriminations."

55. With Wang Niansun: *cuo* 錯 GV *cuo* 措, "devise plans"; *zhu* 注 GV *zhu* 鈺, meaning with Yang Liang "concentrate on, be intent on."

56. Following Wang Yinzhi. The text actually reads "elegant," thus, the gentleman is contented with the cultured. Wang notes that *ya* 雅 "elegant" was sometimes used in the sense of Xia, referring to the Chinese as against the barbarians.

An alternate interpretation is to take this passage to refer to the way in which the language was pronounced. But there is not much doubt, says Waley, *Analects*,

p. 243, that *ya* "('refined,' 'standard,' 'correct' as applied to speech) is etymologically the same word as the ethnic term Xia." If one does take the passage to refer to pronunciation, then *ya* means, according to Liu Baonan (*Lunyu zhengyi*, under *LY*, 7.17), cultured High Chinese speech used to recite the *Odes* and *Documents* and in observance of the *Rituals* in contrast with the pronunciations employed in ordinary, dialectical usages. The passage then means: "though the native of Yue is content with the pronunciations of Yue and the native of Chu with those of Chu, the gentleman is content only with elegant standards of pronunciation."

57. Following Wang Xianqian.

58. Following Yang Liang: *man* 僈 GV *man* 漫, "reckless." Liang Qixiong: *wu* 汙 GV *xu* 訏 "boastful"; *man* GV *man* 謾, "deceive," for "being boastful and deceptive."

59. Following ZT edition; Lü edition omits *yue* 曰.

60. Text *dao* 道 SF *dao* 導. Yang Liang: *dao* means "discuss," for "the gentleman discusses the normal; the petty man the exceptional." Liu Shipei and Liang Qixiong: *dao* means "proceeds," for "the gentleman proceeds with the normal; the petty man with the exceptional."

61. Or, "as to their clarity or mutedness." The terms literally mean "clarity" referring to high-pitched, sharp, shrill sounds and "muddiness" referring to deep-pitched, heavy, flat sounds. Zheng Xuan (apud Yang Liang) says that "notes that are sonorous are noble whereas those that are shrill are base." The Preface of Lu Fayan to the *Qieyun* remarks: "In the regions of Wu and Chu the pronunciation is at times too light and shallow; in Yan and Zhao it is often too heavy and muted." Lu Deming, in the Preface to his *Jingdian shiwen*, says: "The greatest differences of dialect are those between the North and South. Some err in being too superficial and light, others in being too heavy and muted." See Zhou Zumo on the meaning of the terms as applied to pronunciation, in Malmquist, "Chou Tsu-mo," p. 36.

62. Yang Liang: these are the patterns of lines on the skin. It was thought that disease and irritations that cause itching alter the natural patterns on the skin.

63. With Kubo Ai and Wang Xianqian: text *chang* 常 excrescent.

64. Following Yu Xingwu. Kubo Ai and Wang Xianqian: text *shi* 埶 [= 勢] excrescent.

65. With Wang Niansun omitting 23 characters entered into the text through dittography.

66. Following Yu Yue: *li* 力 GE *duo* 多, the proper contrast to *gua* 寡 "few."

67. Following Furuya Sekiyō. With Yu Yue: *xiu zhi* 修之 excrescent. Text *wei* 爲 SF *wei* 僞, "conscious exertion." The idea is that their nature is left undeveloped and so remains in its rustic and uncultivated state. Yao and Yu differ from petty men because they developed their inborn talents, not because they were born with different talents.

68. Following Wang Xianqian.

69. Long Yuchun: *de* 得 GE *fu* 復, "repeat," for "use the chaotic to repeat the chaotic."

70. The text has been rearranged in the translation for smoother reading. Long Yuchun: *shi* 是 SF *shi* 寔 (= *shi* 實) "full."

71. Yang Liang: *yu* 隅 means "single corner," referring to a part of the Way. Wang Xianqian: *yu* means "a single corner" of the Way, which is *ji* 積 "thoroughly understood." Xunzi always uses "corner" of the Way in a pejorative sense, whereas the passage requires a positive meaning. Kubo Ai: *lian* 廉 and *yu* both mean "angle, corner."

Sometimes the meaning is negative as in *Liji*, 41 "Ruxing" 儒行, 59.6b, which says that a scholar must "acquaint himself with fine accomplishments and grind and smooth out the sharp angles" (i.e., imperfections) of his character. But the meaning can be positive as in *Shi*, Greater Odes, "Yi," Mao 256: "A composed and sober demeanor/is the *yu* angle of inner power." The Mao commentary defines *yu* by *lian*, the idea, according to Zheng Xuan, being the "smoothed angle," the refined appearance caused by inner power. Here *lian* means "to make angular," i.e., sharpen one's sense of shame, and *yu* to sharpen what one acquires through the process of accumulation. The idea is that both "angularities" suggest inner refinement.

72. "Pastured animals" refers to sheep and oxen, "grain-fed" to animals penned and fattened for slaughter, particularly dogs and pigs.

73. Text *xiu* 臭 SF *xiu* 嗅; Yang Liang: *qian* 嗛 GV *qian* 慊, "dissatisfied." Wang Niansun: *wu* 無 excrescent; *qian* read *qie* 慊, "satisfied."

74. Following Yang Liang.

75. Following Yang Liang: *ji* 幾 LC *qi* 豈, approved Karlgren LC 601. With Wang Shumin, omitting "rice and millet," which breaks the rhythm, as dittography.

76. Following Yu Yue: *li* GE *duo*, as in *n*66 above.

77. Wang Niansun: emend *ren* 人 to *ren* 仁, for "delights in proclaiming and manifesting humanity."

78. Following Gao Heng: *mi* 靡 LC *mo* 摩, "rub"; *xuan* 儇 GV *qiong* 翼 LC *ying* 鎣, "polish." Wang Yinzhi: *mi* means "heap up"; *xuan* GV *huan* 還 "accumulate," for "is heaped up and accumulated."

79. Following Yang Liang: *qian* 鉛 GV *yan* 沿.

80. Lu Wenchao: *xian* 僩 GV *xian* 嫻, "refined." Hao Yixing, Wang Niansun, Kubo Ai, and Chen Qiaocong 陳喬樅 concur. Yang Liang: *xian* GV *xian* 擱, in the sense of "fierce, valorous," attested in *Fangyan* for Jin and Wei. Alternate Tang opinion quoted by Yang: *xian* means "generous," attested in Mao gloss to *Shi*, Mao 55. Duan Yucai concurs in this opinion.

All these interpretations are based on the same *Shi* passage: the alternate opinion cited by Yang and concurred in by Duan is based on the Mao interpretation of the *Shi*; the opinion of Yang Liang on the Qi interpretation; and that of Lu Wenchao and others on the Han interpretation. Karlgren GL 153 examines the problem at length, concluding that "the only sense in which the character itself is attested in real texts (even though they are of Han date) is 'refined.'"

81. Yang Liang: emend *bu zhi bu zu* 不知不足 to *bu zhi zu*, for "will not know sufficiency."

82. Following Yang Liang: *yue* 約 means "parsimonious, miserly." Zhao Haijin ("*Xunzi* buyi"), Zhang Heng, and Karlgren concur.

83. With Wang Niansun, omitting excrescent *ji bu* 幾不 entered through contamination with reading below.

84. Yang Liang: some texts read *yu* 禦, "hinder, prevent" for text *yu* 御.

85. Following ZT reading. Lü edition omits *liang* 糧.

86. Wang Niansun: *ji* 瘠 "spine, showing the skeleton" LC *zi* 胔 "skeleton." Karlgren LC 1796: Wang LC "impossible," though meaning is correct.

87. *Fen* 分 is a technical term referring here to the patterns of life that characterize each of the classes into which the sages divided society. See the Glossary.

88. Following Wang Yinzhi: *cheng* 盛 GV *cheng* 成, "achievements." The metaphor is that of "warming up" the accumulated wisdom contained in these classics so that it can be applied to the present. Cf. *LY*, 2.10: "He who by re-animating the old can come to know the new is worthy of being a teacher."

89. This appears to be a proverb associated with Guan Zhong. In the *Zhuangzi*, 17 "Qiushui," 6.18b, Confucius quotes Guan Zhong: "You cannot use a small bag to hold something large, nor a short rope to draw water from a deep well." In *SY*, 7.2b, Guan Zhong replied to Duke Huan of Qi: "You cannot use a short rope to draw water from a deep well, and knowledge that is inadequate cannot be used in conversation with a sage." *HNZ*, 17.2b, repeats the first part of the sentence.

90. Wang Xianqian: *cong* 從 SF *zong* 縱.

91. Following Kubo Ai and Yu Yue: *que* 愨 GE *gu* 穀, "grain" (here used as a salary). Yang Liang explains that each person occupies his appropriate place in society, whether it be humble or exalted.

92. Following Yang Liang: *yu* 御 LC *ya* 迓. These positions were the humblest, typically being filled by cripples and those who had suffered mutilation as punishment for some crime.

93. This is quoted as a tradition in "Chendao," 13.9.

94. Following Liu Taigong and Wang Niansun: *zhan* 斬 LC *chan* 儳 "unequal," attested *Zuo*, Xi 23. Though ranks, privileges, and benefits are unequal, each class has what is appropriate to it, and thus they are equivalent. "Bent" refers to being disinclined by nature to follow the regulations of the Ancient Kings and the requirements of ritual principles. Yet in the society of the sages, each man was obedient to law and ritual because they were fair and fitting.

95. *Shi*, Ancestral Hymns of Shang, "Changfa" 長發, Mao 304.

96. Following Karlgren GL 1196. The *gong* was a fine-quality jade *bi* 璧 disc with a hole in the center. It was employed as an astronomical instrument and was part of the regalia of the Zhou king (*Shu*, 18.20a).

97. The meaning of this line has long baffled commentators. Following Karlgren GL 1194, 1197. Yang Liang follows Kong Yingda: "For the states under him, he was a great and generous ruler." Ma Ruichen: "He is the great protector of the states under him." Legge, 4:641, following Zhu Xi, translates: "He supported them as a strong steed."

98. Given the uncertain meaning of the poem itself, the meaning Xunzi saw in it is obscure.

BOOK 5

1. References to divination by the trigrams are frequently mentioned in the *Zuo zhuan* and *Guoyu* (see H. Wilhelm). The fragmentary Fuyang 阜陽 *Yijing* discovered in 1977, but as yet unpublished, appears to deal with individuals (*Wenwu* 1983, no. 2, pp. 21–23).

2. The "Jingtong" 精通 of the *LSCQ*, 9/5, is devoted entirely to such matters.

3. Cf. Eisler, p. 145.

4. H. Chatley, "Feng-Shui," in *Encyclopedia Sinica*.

5. Needham, 2:359. Loewe, pp. 123, 135, reviews the recently discovered physiognomical texts involving dogs and horses.

6. *Xunzi*, "Jundao," 12.8. Cf. *Zhuangzi*, 9 "Mati" 馬蹄, 4.6a; *LSCQ*, 9/5 "Jingtong," 9.9a, 24/2 "Zanneng" 贊能, 24.2b, 25/4 "Fenzhi" 分職, 25.5b; *HNZ*, 9.16a, 11.9b, 12.9a; *ZGC*, 5.44a, 9.8b; and *Lunheng*, 14.1b.

7. *HSWZ*, 9.9a; *SJ*, 47.42; *KZJY*, 5.11a. Details vary significantly among these versions. *HSWZ* says Wei; *SJ* and *KZJY* say that it occurred later, when Confucius was in Zheng.

8. So *HSWZ*; *KZJY* says that he "is nine feet six inches tall [in Chinese measurements, a normal man was seven feet tall], with eyes like the Yellow River and a prominent forehead. He has the head of a Yao, the neck of a Gaoyao, and the shoulders of a Prince Chan of Zheng. Below the waist he is just three inches shorter than Yu." The *SJ* version abridges the *KZJY* account. The technical terms of physiognomy are poorly understood, and the precise nature of the features identified and their significance is no longer evident.

9. The significance of this description is unclear. In the *SJ* and *KZJY* versions, Confucius laughingly accepts the description, but in the *HSWZ* version he vigorously disputes it, but the nature of his objection is obscure.

10. So *HSWZ*; *SJ* and *KZJY* omit. The term *wa* 洼, "sunken," is also applied to the chest of King Wen in *HNZ*, 16.16a.

11. So *SJ* and *KZJY*; *HSWZ* omits this.

12. *HFZ*, 49 "Wu du" 五蠹, 19.2ab; *HNZ*, 18.17b, and *Lunheng*, 10.4a, say 32 states.

13. Quoted in the *Zhengyi* commentary to *SJ*, 5.6–8.

14. *HNZ*, 18.19b. Cf. Needham, vol. 4, pt. 3, p. 271, for an evaluation of the importance of this achievement.

15. Cf. *LY*, 7.18, 13.18, and the comments of Creel, *Confucius and the Chinese Way*, pp. 46–47, 126, 135.

16. This division is attested in the *Zhuangzi*, *ZGC*, *LSCQ*, *HFZ*, *Guanzi*, and *Zhou li*.

17. With Wang Niansun and Kubo Ai following the ZT and Kong editions. Lü edition reads *xiang ren* 相人, "physiognomists."

18. According to a tradition recorded in *HSWZ* (9.9a) and *SJ* (47.22), in addition to having physiognomized Confucius in 495, Gubu was famous for having physiognomized the sons of Viscount Jian of Zhao 趙簡子 and prognosticating that his son Wuxu 毋卹 would have a great future. Wuxu succeeded his

father as Viscount Xiang 襄子 and, with the houses of Wei and Han, defeated the Earl of Zhi 知伯 in 453, resulting in the partition of the old state of Jin and the foundation of the state of Zhao.

19. Liang was an alternate name for the state of Wei after the capital was changed from Anyi to Daliang in 340.

20. Text *lun* 論, "evaluate," means to distinguish and arrange things by analysis to discover what is known and what not known, what is admissible in an argument or proof and what is inadmissible, what is a strength and what a weakness.

21. Compare "Xiushen," 2.4.

22. Chinese commentators have much disputed the identity of this Zigong. There are three theories. Wang Bi 王弼 (A.D. 226–49), quoted by Huang Kan 皇侃 (d. A.D. 545), *Lunyu yishu* 論語義疏, in Cheng Shude, p. 1114, identifies him with one Zhu Zhang 朱張, a recluse mentioned in *LY*, 18.8, among a group of men who lived before Confucius. Since the context implies that Zigong was after Confucius and was his disciple, this identification is unlikely. Further, there is doubt that Zhu Zhang is a person at all. Lu Deming clearly suspected that it is not a name but a corruption of part of the sentence. Zhang Shoujie 張守節, in his *Zhengyi* commentary to *SJ*, 67.39, identifies him with one Han Bi 馯臂, whose style name was Zigong 子弓. This theory was endorsed by Han Yu and is quoted by Yang Liang. Han Bi was a scholar of the *Yijing* and a disciple of the Confucian disciple Shang Ju 商瞿, styled Zimu 子木. He was thus a contemporary of Confucius' grandson Zisi, which makes the identification unlikely. Yang Liang identifies him with the Confucian disciple Ran Yong, whose style name was Zhonggong. This is generally accepted by scholars today. Yang Liang believed that Ran Yong was teacher of Xunzi, but, as Yu Yue notes, this is chronologically impossible.

23. Of Gongsun Lü nothing more is known.

24. Following Wang Shaolan: *yan* 焉 LC *e* 頞, "root of the nose." Gao Heng: *yan* LC *yan* 顔, "forehead," thus equals *e*, by which it is defined in the *Erya*. Liang Qixiong cites both theories with approval. Karlgren LC 2010 argues that since *yan* and *yan* were synonymous, cognate, and interchangeable, "the text probably originally had *yan* 顔 carelessly changed into its synonym by copyists; this *yan* is then a short form for *e*." Yu Chang: *yan* 焉 GE *tuan* 彖 SF *chui* 喙, defined by the *Shuowen* as "mouth," referring to the beak of a bird and the snout of a pig (*Zuo*, Zhao 4), and used in *Zhuangzi*, 8.16a, to describe people of unusual appearance. Yang Liang notes that some scholars consider the text defective and does not repeat the character *yan* in his paraphrase.

25. Following Yang Liang. Liu Shipei and Gao Heng: *ju* 具 SF *ju* 俱, "all together" with Gao adding *da* 大, "large," which he believes dropped out of the text; that is, all his features were exaggerated. An alternate interpretation of the passage would be: "whose body was seven feet tall, his face three feet wide and his beak of a nose three inches across, with his nostrils, eyes and ears all similarly exaggerated."

26. In his *Xiangren lun*, which seems to be based on the *Xunzi* and may reflect

an alternate reading, Cao Zhi (A.D. 192–232) says that "in Song there was a minister named Gongsun Lü, who was seven feet tall with a face three feet long and three inches across whose reputation shook the whole world."

27. Qisi is located in Gushi prefecture, Henan province. Yang Liang remarks that the phrase "small hamlet" implies that he was from the wilds. *Mengzi*, 6B.15, says that he was from the sea.

28. Following Yang Liang and Ogyū Sorai: *tutu* 突禿 means "short hair," the idea being that he was bald except for patches of short hair. Text *chang zuo* 長左 means that his left leg was longer. This passage is much disputed by commentators. Liu Shipei: *chang zuo* means that the hair on his left temple was long, whereas the remainder was short. Dubs notes that in China baldness was considered shameful. Text *xian* 軒, "carriage with poles that curve upwards at the end," and *jue* 較, "bars on the top sides of the carriage box that turn upwards in a hook shape in the front," suggest that he was so short that he could walk under the upward-turning part of carriage poles. Xunzi's point is that despite his physical peculiarities, by cultivating and refining his inner force and not exerting military force, he made the ruler of Chu lord-protector.

29. Following Furuya Sekiyō: *shan* 善 means "to bestow praise on."

30. With Kubo Ai, Liang Qixiong, and Fujii Sen'ei following the Lü reading *shi* 士 for ZT *shi* 事 preferred by Lu Wenchao and Wang Xianqian.

31. Following Yang Liang: *xie* 揳 GV *xie* 絜.

32. Following the Lü reading with *xin* 心 omitted in ZT edition. Cf. paragraph 5.1 above, where the mind is stressed as a reliable guide to a man's worth in contrast to his external form, which is unreliable.

33. Following ZT reading *yan* 焉 for Lü reading *ma* 馬, "horse." ZT reading corroborated by numerous quotations cited by Ruan Tingzhuo. Lu Wenchao, Wang Xianqian, and Kubo Ai follow Lü reading, meaning that he was so nearsighted that he had to look up to see a horse. Yang Liang notes the *Shizi* statement that King Yan of Xu had muscles and tendons but no bones. This fanciful statement is based, as Chavannes, 2:8, *n*2, observed, on interpreting his name Yan to mean that he was "bent down, inclined," and the theory that he was boneless was meant to justify the folk entomology.

34. Following Karlgren GL 712. The meaning is that Confucius' face was so immobile in preserving the correct ritual expressions that it seemed to be covered by a mask. Text *qi* 供 GV *qi* 頎, defined in *Shuowen* as "a hideous head used to expel pestilence," further explained *Zhou li*, 31.12a, as an "ugly and terrifying mask," which Zheng Xuan says resembled the Qi demon mask of his own day. Yang Liang cites a passage from the *Shenzi*: "Mao Qiang 毛嬙 and Xi Shi 西施 were the most beautiful women in the world, but were one to dress them in demon masks, everyone who saw them would run away." The mask mentioned here was made of bearskin and used to exorcize pestilence.

35. Following Hao Yixing. Unattributed quotations in Tang dictionaries and encyclopedia that may come from the *Xunzi* or from Cao Zhi, *Xiangren lun*, say that the Duke of Zhou was a hunchback.

36. Following Hao Yixing.

37. Legend current in Xunzi's day contended that the paralysis of Tang and the lameness of Yu proved them to be sages. See Granet, pp. 247–48.

38. Yang Liang *mou* 牟 SF *mou* 眸, "pupil of the eye"; *can* 參 meaning "double" on the basis of *SJ*, 7.75, statement that Shun had double pupils, confirmed by the *Shizi* cited by Pei Yin in his *Jijie* commentary on this passage. Kubo Ai cites as further evidence *HNZ*, 19.7a. Kubo Ai and Takegawa Kametarō (*SJ*) affirm that double pupils, though rare, are well attested. The obvious flaw in Yang's argument is that *can* means not "two" but "three." The legend that he had "double" pupils perhaps arose from his appellation Double Brilliance (重明). Text *can*, here read *cen*, has the meaning "uneven, irregular," attested *Shi*, Mao 1.

39. According to *SJ*, 3.26: "Zhou Xin was brilliantly quick in discernment with sharp senses and such superhuman strength that he could fight wild animals with his bare hands."

40. Following Yang Liang.

41. Following Yu Yue: *jun* 君 GE *min* 民, "people, subject."

42. Lu Wenchao: "Contra Physiognomy" originally ended here since the paragraphs that follow do not pertain to the subject, but rather resemble the content of Book 4, "Of Honor and Disgrace."

43. With Long Yuchun: text *ruo* 若 SF *nuo* 諾, "yeah, momentarily," with *bu* 不 *nuo*, "not saying 'yeah,'" equivalent to *wei* 唯 "yes" (formal), in support of which he adduces *Liji*, 30.11b: "When his father calls him to come, he respectfully says 'yes' and not 'yeah.'" It was a rule of Chinese etiquette that one used the formal *wei*, "yes sir," implying immediate attention and response, to one's superiors (*Mengzi*, 2B.2) and not the informal *nuo*, "yeah," which implied unresponsiveness and familiarity. Thus, "not saying 'yeah'" implies insincerity, deception, and hypocrisy.

44. Yang Liang: *xuan* 縣 SF *xuan* 懸; Wang Niansun: *you* 有 GV *you* 又.

45. Following Wang Niansun.

46. With Wang Yinzhi omitting an excrescent *san* 三, "three."

47. *Shi*, Lesser Odes, "Jue gong" 角弓, Mao 223. The text as quoted by Xunzi does not agree with the Mao, Han, or Lu readings.

48. Following Duan Yucai: *yan* 宴 LC *yan* 臙, "cloudless"; *ran* 然 SF *ran* 熯, "hot." Cf. Karlgren GL 723.

49. With Hao Yixing: *sui* 隓 GV *zhui* 墮, equivalent to Mao reading *yi* 遺, "be rejected, cast off." The idea is that unworthy officials are unwilling to lose their positions. With Karlgren GL 557: *lü* 厲, "empty" *Shuowen*; 居, "mode of living" as in *Guoyu*, 14.5a: "Fan Yang's mode of living was respectful since he did not presume to be easygoing or lax."

50. This repeats the definition given in "Rongru," 4.9.

51. The phrase also means "hairless," but since an ape is also described in the same language, the meaning must be "featherless."

52. This ape is described as having a yellowish brown fur with white ears. In the modern idiom, with pronunciation *xingxing*, it refers to the orangutan or to the chimpanzee.

53. The text here is defective. Yang Liang comments that the animal "could

laugh and talk," which is not apposite to the text. Yu Xingwu: *xiao* 笑 GE *xiao* 肖 (also attested in Dunhuang MS edition of *DDJ*, 76), for *xing* 形 *xiao*, "in appearance (resembling a man)." It appears that UR *形肖 was corrupted to 形笑 from careless copying. This not making sense, it was corrected by editors of the *YWLJ* (followed by *TPYL*) to *neng yan xiao* 能言笑, probably "corroborated" by folklore of the day concerning the animal. Texts dating from this period were probably similarly "corrected." When Yang Liang prepared his edition, he noted this alternate reading.

54. Emend *er mao* 而毛 to *wu* 無 *mao*, attested in quotations. *YWLJ* quotation reads *wei* 尾, "tailless." Some editor thought UR *wu mao*, understood as "hairless," was absurd for a type of monkey, so the text was corrected by *YWLJ* to *wu wei*, "tailless." This emendation was only rarely followed since Yang apparently did not note it. The emendation was unjustified since the real meaning of *mao* here, as in the conundrum "eggs have *mao*," was not understood. Yang, however, apparently understood the passage since he includes no annotation. A post-Yang editor, possibly Lü Xiaqing since ZT edition omits the character, again noting the "absurdity" corrected *wu* to *er*.

55. The reasoning here is obscure. Yang Liang: the gentleman will eat it because it is a lower animal that lacks the ability to draw boundaries. Dubs, *Works of Hsüntze*, finding this unacceptable, translates "but in contrast the superior man sips his soup and carves his slices of meat," adding that this means "he eats politely," but this is excluded by the grammar of the passage.

56. An alternate tradition preserved in quotations reads "but in his knowledge of ritual principles," which ill suits the context.

57. Boundaries such as those between high and low and between relatives and strangers lead to social distinctions and classes. Differences in social classes produce the need for ritual principles, which preserve class distinctions by making them visible in behavior and dress.

58. That is, of the many sage kings mentioned by the various conflicting schools, each possessing different characteristics, which provides the proper model?

59. With Wang Niansun: *xi* 息 GE *mie* 滅, which provides the proper rhyme, confirmed by the reading in paragraph 5.5. With Yang Liang: *zu* 族 LC *zou* 奏, "play, perform." Text *jie* 節 here means "pause" in contrast to *zou* "play," the idea being the rhythm of pauses and playing in music. Cf. Karlgren LC 1985. The idea is that over a long span of time inscriptions wear away from bronze and stone or are destroyed by rot in the case of bamboo.

60. With Yu Yue omitting excrescent *li* 禮.

61. Here, "Later Kings" refers specifically to Kings Wen and Wu along with the Duke of Zhou, but, as Zhong Tai notes, Xunzi also uses the term to refer to the Three Dynasties.

62. Following the ZT reading. The Lü text preferred by Lu Wenchao and Wang Xianqian reads "begin your enumeration with."

63. Meaning Confucius, Zigong, and Xunzi himself, who carried on their tradition.

64. With Wang Niansun following the *HSWZ* reading.

65. With Wang Niansun following the *HSWZ* reading.

66. This passage is interpreted as meaning "emotions" rather than "circumstances" by Yang Liang, but the use of the term in the opening sentence clearly means "circumstances" and the context requires the same construction here.

67. With Wang Niansun, omit excrescent *du* 度, "standard of measure."

68. This term indicates that this paragraph is earlier in date than the previous paragraph. The Ancient Kings were Yao, Shun, Yu, and Tang, together with Kings Wen and Wu.

69. Following Yang Liang.

70. With Wang Yinzhi: text *yan* 言 GE *shan* 善.

71. These sentences are repeated below in paragraph 5.9.

72. Taking the text as it stands, corroborated by early quotations. Wang Niansun: *guan* 觀 GV *quan* 勸, "encourage," attested in *YWLJ* and *TPYL* quotations, for "what man is encouraged to do through words is more beautiful than." To this sentence, these texts add another sentence not in the present text: "With words one can hurt a man more than by inflicting wounds with knives and lances," which appears to be related to the language of "Rongru," paragraph 4.1.

73. The text here lists four types of embroidered emblems that were used on the ceremonial court robes. One of them was an axe figure in white and black, another a notched stripe in azure and black, a third a stripe design in azure and crimson, and a fourth blazonry in white and crimson.

74. Xunzi alludes to the view of the ascetic pattern of life advocated by Mo Di and his followers, which, this passage suggests, is adopted by some misguided Ru.

75. Hexagram 2, 1.24b. The commentary interprets the "tied sack" to mean the mind with its knowledge and understanding stored within. If one expresses no thought, one will encounter no criticism for making errors, but neither will one accomplish anything worthy of praise.

76. Liang Qixiong: *shi* 世 SF *yi* 抴, "cite, adduce."

77. Yang Liang; canal ditches control water by determining the direction of its flow; the press-frame is the tool that controls wood by adjusting the curvature of its surface. The gentleman uses discussion to channel and direct. Xunzi uses the press-frame as an instrument of gentle pressure that the gentleman applies to others in contrast to the exactitude of the plumbline, which he applies to himself.

78. Han Yu, apud Yang Liang commentary: *yi* 抴 GV *yi* 枻 = 檠, "stand for bending a bow." The orthography for this word is quite varied in the literature. The bow-frame keeps the curvature of the bow true. The gentleman is thus like the plumbline that determines straightness or like the bow-frame that tests the curvature. *HNZ*, 16.16b, notes that "although the bow-frame itself is not true, it can be used to make the curvature of the bow true." The Mao commentary to *Shi*, Mao 223, observes that "if the bow is not kept in proper order on the frame and skillfully used, it will warp." The words "straight" and "curved" mean, by extension, respectively, "direct" as in "direct route" and "accommodating."

Xunzi exploits the metaphorical roots of the ideas here. An alternate Tang opinion: *yi* GV *yi* 枻, "oar," meaning that the gentleman is an "oar" that can be used to "push others" as an oar is used to push a boat.

79. Following Zhong Tai: *qiu* 求 SF *jiu* 救, "help."

80. *Shi*, Greater Odes, "Changwu" 常武, Mao 263.

81. Xunzi exploits two senses of the word *tong* 同, "to join with" and "to make the same." The idea he finds in the Ode is that the Zhou king did not merely conquer the region of Xu; he instructed its barbarian inhabitants so that they could be joined with the realm of the "civilized and cultivated."

82. This paragraph is quoted in *HSWZ*, 5.12b, where it is attributed to Confucius, and in *SY*, 11.1a, where it is correctly attributed to Xunzi.

83. With Wang Niansun following the reading of the *HSWZ* and *SY* parallels.

84. With Wang Niansun following the reading of the *HSWZ* and *SY* parallels.

85. Following the *SY* reading.

86. *SY* and *HSWZ* omit "this expresses my meaning" and add a citation from the *Shi*, Greater Odes, "Yi," Mao 256 (Karlgren, *Odes*, p. 218): "Do not let your tongue run away/do not say: 'I care not.'"

87. These sentences also occur in paragraph 5.6.

88. Yang Liang: *dao* 道 SF *dao* 導; *zheng* 正 SF *zheng* 政.

89. Following Wang Niansun: *mou* 謀 GE *jian* 諫.

90. This passage also occurs in slightly different language and order in paragraph 5.6

91. With Wang Yinzhi omitting excrescent *xian* 見.

92. Following Karlgren LC 1506 *zhi* 致 means "express." With Zhong Tai and Fujii Sen'ei: *dang* 黨 "partial."

93. ZT reads *zhi jun* 之均 (followed by Lu Wenchao and Kubo Ai); Lü edition reads *zhi yu* 之於 (followed by Hao Yixing). Qian Dian, *Kaoyi*, follows Lü but notes all other editions read with ZT. Following Gao Heng: ZT *jun*, Lü *yu* GE *li* 利 written UR *㓷, "clever, glib." Yu Yue: *zhi* = *ze* 則 as in following phrase; *jun* means "harmonious."

94. Yang Liang notes that this passage has never been adequately explained. Following Gao Heng: *wei* 唯 GV *hui* 譓 (for which no ancient character existed), "noisy, garrulity." With Ogyū Sorai *jie* 節 means "be in agreement with."

95. Following Yang Liang.

BOOK 6

1. *Mozi*, 38–39 "Fei Ru" 非儒, 9.16b–30b. Book 38 is missing from the present text.

2. Guo Moruo, *Qingtong shidai*, pp. 239–43; idem, *Shi pipan shu*, 172–74. Contrast Qian Mu, nos. 72, 75, 146. Guo proposes that Huan Yuan is the editor-author of the *Daode jing*. The views contained in this book do not coincide with Xunzi's descriptions of those of Tuo Xiao.

3. *SJ*, 47.90, probably based on *Kongcongzi*, 3.8b, where the book is said to

have comprised 49 bundles, indicating a far larger work than the present text.

4. It is possible that the *Mengzi* once contained the doctrines that Xunzi condemns here. The present text of the *Mengzi* was edited with a commentary by Zhao Qi (d. A.D. 201), who tells us that apart from the seven books of his text, the only extant *Mengzi*, there were four other "outer books" that he expunged because they "lack depth and breadth, bear no resemblance to the inner books, and are probably forged works from a later age." These expunged books no longer survive. Quotations from now-lost passages of the *Mengzi* offer little insight and cannot always be identified as from the "outer sections." In any case, the largest collection of such quotations, the 32 assembled by Ma Guohan are on the whole of little substance. We are thus unable to determine whether the outer books were rejected by Zhao Qi because they contained ideas of the sort Xunzi here criticizes.

5. Xunzi uses the term *wu xing* approvingly in this sense in his "Discourse on Music," 20.5, below. In the manuscripts found in the Mawangdui tombs, there are two versions of a book entitled *Wu xing pian* 五行篇 that refer to the Five Constants of the Confucians. See *Mawangdui Hanmu boshu*, 1:17–18.

6. Waley, *Three Ways of Thought*, pp. 204–5.

7. Liu Jie dates the text contemporaneous with the composition of this book, at the beginning of the Qin period, *GSB*, 5:388–403. Qu Wanli in contrast dates it to the beginning of the Warring States period or two centuries earlier, *Shangshu shiyi*, pp. 59–60. Chen Mengjia, "Xi Zhou tongqi VI," dates it generally to the Warring States period. At paragraph 2.14, Xunzi quotes a passage now occurring in the "Hongfan," indicating either that he found its content unobjectionable or that the work was compiled from pre-existing material at the beginning of the Qin period to advance the *wu xing* idea in the guise of Ru orthodoxy.

8. *HSBZ*, 27A.2ab; cf. Dubs, *History of the Former Han Dynasty*, 2:107–8.

9. On the translation of the term, see Major, "A Note"; Kunst; with Major's reply; and Major, "Myth."

10. On this conception, see Needham, 2:242–43.

11. Following the interpretation of Yu Yue, but see the interpretation of Karlgren, GL 1526, which follows Ma Rong.

12. Pankenier raises the possibility that *wu xing* ideas associated with astrology date back to the Shang dynasty.

13. See the *sheng xu* 生序 order given in the "Hongfan," as well as in *Zuo*, Zhao 9.

14. See the *xiang sheng* 相生 order given in the *Guanzi* and *Huainanzi*. On these orders and others as well, see Eberhard.

15. See the *xiang sheng* 相勝 order of Zou Yan apud *WX*, 59.9b.

16. Graham, *Later Mohist Logic*, B43; cf. Needham, 2:259.

17. *HSBZ*, 25A.17b, reporting that Han Gaozu established a temple to the Black Lord to increase the number of the Lords on High to five. Down to the end of the Former Han, palace attendants continued to wear black sables (*HSBZ*, 98.15a).

18. *SJ*, 10.32. Other scholars such as Jia Yi disputed Zhang'& theory. The issue came to a head when one Gongsun Chen 公孫臣 predicted that a yellow dragon would appear that would confirm that the prevailing power was Earth. In 165, a yellow dragon did appear, and Zhang was accordingly dismissed. Not until 104 did Emperor Wu officially recognize Earth as the ruling power and accordingly adopt yellow as the symbolic color of Han imperial institutions (*HSBZ*, 6.31b).

19. See *LY*, 2.23, 5.19, 11.20, 12.6, 12.10, 12.14, 12.20, 14.40, 15.6, 17.6, and 20.2.

20. Xunzi again mentions Zigong with Confucius in "Ruxiao," 8.9, below as transmitting the true doctrines of the Master.

21. Cf. *DDJ*, 71. The point is not modesty, as in Socrates professing to "know nothing."

22. Stories of such recluses are told in *Lunyu*, book 18.

23. Emending *yin* 晉 to *yi* 意 with Zhang Peilun and Guo Moruo; cf. Rickett, *Kuan-tzu*, pp. 158, *n*21, 159, *n*30.

24. This means the twilight years of the Warring States period, probably after 256.

25. "Treacherous doctrines" are defined in paragraph 5.6 as opinions inconsistent with the teachings of the Ancient Kings and not in accord with ritual and moral principles.

26. With Wang Niansun omitting four characters meaning "deceive and mislead the ignorant masses," which are in the Lü edition and *HSWZ* parallel, as an interpolation since they do not occur in the ZT and Gong editions and are not annotated by Yang Liang until their later occurrence in the text. Text *yu* 喬 with Yang Liang, SF *jue* 譎; text *yu* 宇 with Hao Yixing, "great, ostentatious"; and text *wei* 恑, also occurring at 8.9 and 18.6, with Karlgren, "conceited." Xunzi applies the word to figures who pretend to heroic greatness but are devoid of merit.

27. Xunzi defines the "emotional disposition" of man as embracing, among other things, the "likes and dislikes, delights and angers, griefs and joys."

28. This part of the sentence is repeated in "Man's Nature Is Evil" (23.1b), where Xunzi observes that "those who indulge their inborn nature and emotions, who are content with unrestrained passion and an overbearing manner, and whose conduct contravenes ritual principles and moral duty remain petty men." Li Si quotes a passage from Shen Buhai, which says that if the ruler who possesses the empire fails to indulge himself in every excess of passion, then he has allowed the empire to become a shackle on him (*SJ*, 87.28). Creel, *Shen Puhai*, p. 381, *n*9, argues that the original meaning of the term in the teachings of Shen Buhai was "unconstrained action, with no bad moral sense," a sense attested in *Zhuangzi*, 6 "Dazongshi" 大宗師, 3.13b, where it means "carefree."

29. The phrase *he wen* 和文 also occurs in 22.3e below, where it refers to discourse that conforms to proper patterns and social usages that conform to the requirements of ritual and moral principles. The phrase here has also been taken to mean "bring concord to civilization."

30. That is, they were able to offer facts in evidence to support their doctrines, could give them a foundation, observed the forms of argumentation of the day, used discriminations, and were skilled in debate.

31. For *Xunzi* Tuo Xiao, the *HSWZ* parallel reads Fan Sui. Tuo Xiao is unknown outside this passage. Guo Moruo, *Shi pipan shu*, p. 172, suggests that Tuo Xiao is GE Huan Yuan 環淵 (also written 玄淵, 娟嬛, 蜎蠉, 蜎淵, 便嬛, 便娟). UR *玄 confused 它 as surname; 淵 confused 罾. Guo suggests GE phonetic misreading of *玄 *g'iwan for *范 *b'iwam. Reading *范淵魏牟 miscopied 范魏牟 attested in the Yang Liang commentary.

32. The meaning of this phrase has long baffled commentators. With Hao Yixing, take text *qi* 綦 = *ji* 極, and with Kubo Ai and Yu Xingwu, text *qi* 谿 = *qi* 蹊. Taking text *li* 利 LC *li* 厲. Yang Liang understood "and keep apart from the world," but this has been refuted by Karlgren, who accepts the interpretation advanced by Yu Xingwu, "a profitable and intricate path." Alternate interpretation 利跂 variant of 離跂, which twice occurs in the *Zhuangzi* (11 "Zaiyou," 4.15b, 12 "Tiandi" 天地, 5.11b), where it is used to describe the Mohists standing on their tiptoes confronting the followers of Yang Zhu and the Ru in argumentation, but this seems not to have been the style of either Chen Zhong or Shi Qiu.

33. *HSWZ* reads "Tian Wen and Zhuang Zhou," a substitution of common names for rare ones, which indicates its derivative nature.

34. This refers to ritual principles. One "evaluates" each thing and then "designates" its proper use by ritual principles (11.9). The term "designates" refers particularly to the "modes of identification," which are used to distinguish rich and poor, insignificant and important (10.3). The sage can "evaluate" and "designate" for the whole world (18.8).

35. Text *man* 僈 GV *man* 嫚, common in the *Xunzi*.

36. Emend *xiu* 脩 to *xun* 循, common GE in *Xunzi*. The point is that they condemn adherence to the principle that "the gentleman is a follower and not a creator" (reported of the Ru in *Mozi* 25 "Fei ming 非命," I, 9.21a); like the Mohists, they are fond of innovation. Yu Xingwu emends *xia* 下 to *shang* 尚 for parallelism with the preceding phrase, for "who elevate the principle of 'following along' with the usages of the past but are fond of innovation." In Yu's understanding, they do not deprecate the principle, but rather feign adherence to it.

37. Following Wang Niansun. Yang Liang understands "when they are among the upper classes, they accommodate themselves to their views; when they are among the lower, they go along with their ideas." This understanding of the text is undoubtedly influenced by the statement in the *Zhuangzi*, 33 "Tianxia," 10.15b–16a, that Shen Dao "changed with the circumstances," "was concerned only with self-survival," and "went where he was pushed and followed where he was led."

38. Following the ZT edition, read *fan* 反 for Lü edition *ji* 及; text *xun* 訓 LC *xun* 巡.

39. With Yang Liang, text *qi* 埼 GV *qi* 奇. Cf. *Zhuangzi*, 33 "Tianxia,"

10.22b: "Hui Shi employed his knowledge to engage others in discriminations and propounded abstrusities for the debaters of the world."

40. With Wang Niansun emend *hui* 惠 GE *ji* 急.

41. Xunzi quoted examples of such propositions in paragraph 3.1.

42. *Zhuangzi*, 33 "Tianxia," 10.20a, remarks that Hui Shi was a man of many methods whose books would fill five carriages, but in the end, for all his many talents, he wandered about without achieving anything, to be known only as a skillful debater.

43. This paragraph has caused much of the opprobrium from which Xunzi has suffered since the canonization of Mencius in the Song period.

44. With Lu Wenchao following ZT edition *yu ran er* 猶然而 for Lü edition *ran er yu*.

45. Or, "their ambition great."

46. Text *pi* 僻 indicates an obliqueness that departs from orthodoxy or common sense; *wei* 違 suggests what departs from reasonable standards; *wu lei* 無類 implies that such theories lack the classifications and categories that are proper and necessary to logical truths.

47. Yang Liang takes *shuo* 說 in the common sense "explain, explicate," but the context requires a more philosophical meaning, "theorize; offer a theoretical basis." Text *bi* 閉 suggests that only the initiated can grasp the true nature of the doctrine; *jie* 解 means providing an exegesis in rational, factual terms.

48. The usual interpretation is that the direct quotation includes only the statement about "the gentleman of former times" (meaning Confucius) and that the statement about Zisi and Mencius is the direct observation of Xunzi. My interpretation requires that one take "provided a tune for them" (the words of the gentleman of former times) in the sense of "initiated" and "harmonized" in the sense of "expanded." The meaning of the passage is that such persons contended that Confucius began the doctrine (provided the words), Zisi elaborated upon it (provided the tune), and Mencius systematized (harmonized it). The use of "provided a tune" and "harmonized" is thus akin to that of "song" and "dance" in the Mohist logical chapters, where "song" means to present as a main thesis and "dance" to add a secondary thesis. (See Graham, "Later Mohist Treatises," pp. 152–53, 183.) Both sentences should be taken as a direct quotation of the claim Xunzi is rejecting and not as his own judgment. In paragraph 18.1, Xunzi observes that the ruler is the "singing master" who provides the lead to which the people respond.

49. With Yang Liang text *gou* 溝 LC *kou* 恂.

50. The text here reads Ziyou, which is anomalous since he is severely criticized in 6.13. Kubo Ai and Guo Songdao suggest that the text should read Zigong. Gao Heng suggests UR *弓 GV *汯 GE *you* 游.

51. In the other interpretation, this should read "this was the crime of Zisi and Mencius." Waley, *Three Ways of Thought*, p. 205, translates: "Such people have done a grave injustice" to Zisi and Mencius, citing the usage of *zui* 罪 in *Mengzi*, 6A.7.

52. The subject of this sentence, as often in Chinese, is unstated. Tradi-

tionally it has been assumed to be the sage ruler, but the context of the paragraph means that it applies not only to sage rulers such as Shun and Yu, but also to sages such as Confucius and Zigong who never ruled.

53. *HSWZ* reads "of the great Way," substituting a cliche for an unusual reading.

54. The allusion here is to the story that Sage Ancestor Shun simply sat in his room playing the lute and singing the "Song of the South Wind," yet the world was well ordered. Following Yang Liang on text *aoyao* 奧窔 meaning "southwest and southeast corners of a room." This presumably refers to the position of the person facing south; that is, assuming the position of a ruler or teacher, who always faced south (subjects or students faced north). This is the basis of the traditional view that the allusion is to a sage ruler. An alternate view is that he merely stays in his room, yet because he is a sage he understands everything.

55. The idea is that a true sage, by accumulating his inner power (*de*) and by assuming the ritually magical position of sitting facing south, causes everything about him to change through his sympathetic resonance, just as one musical instrument will cause others to sound or as the lodestone attracts particles to it. The presence of the sage's inner power manifests itself in external signs, which can be seen in the forms (*wen* 文) and outward signs that others recognize. The ritual objects of rulers were intended to display the excellence of their inner power. This could be seen in the ornaments of distinction on the ruler's robes, in the tinkling of the bells of his chariot, and in the heavenly bodies displayed on his flags and standards. See *LY*, 8.19, 5.12; *Zuo*, Huan 2.

56. Since this paragraph refers to Confucius and Zigong, some ancient interpreters of the text (quoted by Yang Liang) took this to mean that since his worthiness was not recognized, such a sage would be without a country, forced to wander from place to place as did Confucius.

57. The translation follows the reading of the edition of Gong Shihuo. The meaning and punctuation of this sentence is much disputed. This follows the interpretation of an anonymous commentator quoted by Yang Liang. The meaning seems to be that because the sage, though of humble origin, will so increase his reputation, all of the feudal lords will want to make him their minister.

58. With Yang Liang text *cai* 財 LC homophonous *cai* 裁 as often in *Xunzi*. The word connotes not only "regulation" but also "perfecting."

59. Following the reading of the Lü and Qian editions.

60. Yang Liang paraphrases: "wherever ships and carriages reach; wherever the strength of man penetrates." Cf. paragraph 8.2.

61. Cf. paragraph 5.4.

62. Yang Liang takes this to mean that the gentleman does not presume to propound original theories on his own authority but always abides by the corpus of the model received from the sages.

63. Emending the text to the reading of the parallel passage at 27.108 below. The image is that of one who so overflows with talk he loses sight of what is fundamental.

64. Yang Liang interprets this to refer to the four occupations mentioned in the literature of the period: scholar-knights, merchants, artists and craftsmen, and farmers. (*Guanzi*, 8 "Youguan" 幼官, 3.8b, and 17 "Bingfa" 兵法, 6.11b.)

65. Following Yu Yue: text *wei* 爲 SF *wei* 僞.

66. Text *hui* 惠 GE *ji* 急 as above (*n*40). Wang Niansun emends: "those who are useless but intelligently discriminating, those who concern themselves with matters of no urgency, but are precise in investigating them."

67. With Yang Liang, text *ze* 澤 "bounty" based on Mao gloss on *Shi*, Mao 133.

68. This list of prohibitions is related to a set promulgated by Confucius when he was director of crime in Lu ("Youzuo," 28.2).

69. Punctuating the text with Yu Yue; text *zhi* 之 GE *fa* 乏.

70. This is an allusion to Shentu Di carrying a stone on his back and drowning himself in a river (see "Bugou," 3.1).

71. As often in the *Xunzi*, this functions as a paragraph title.

72. With Wang Niansun emend *zheng* 爭 to *yi* 以 on basis of *HSWZ* and *SY* parallels. As it stands, the text reads "does not wrangle to gain precedence."

73. Text *xiu* 修 here has the special sense "to do one's best about"; attested in *Zuo*, Xiang 4, Zhao 13, 26; text *yi* 義 SF *yi* 儀.

74. The *HSWZ*. parallel ends here, adding "one who is like this gives comfort to the aged, cherishes the young, and shows good faith to his friends" (a paraphrase of *LY*, 5.25) and quoting a different Ode.

75. *Shi*, Greater Odes, "Dang" 蕩, Mao 255. This ode is traditionally associated with Duke Mu of Shao 召穆公, who used the demise of the Shang dynasty as a warning against the decay of the royal house of Zhou and the dissolute character of King Li 周厲王 (traditionally r. 877–842). The Ode is presented as a song by King Wen warning against the evils of Zhou Xin.

76. The main god of the Shang royal cult. He was conceived as above all the other ancestors who were the spirits of the departed kings of the dynasty.

77. The Zhou regularly used Yin, the name of the capital of the Shang dynasty during its last two centuries, as the name of the dynasty. The men, according to Zheng Xuan, are ministers like Yi Yin who had helped and advised Tang, who founded the dynasty. The Great Mandate is that of Heaven by which the royal house of Shang had ruled.

78. That is, a scholar who was willing to hold office. With Kubo Ai and Wang Niansun, emend 土仕 to 仕土.

79. Commentators have frequently suggested that the text here is defective and have proposed emending the text because Yang Liang says it means "he is fond of his Way." Zhong Tai rightly notes that Yang Liang is not explicating the passage but commenting on its significance. As Zhong Tai notes, in antiquity seeking after riches and honors as a part of one's service was not considered undesirable, but pandering after them at the expense of ethical principles was. The *Zhongyong* (17.2) says: "Hence possessing the greatest inner power, it could not but be that Shun should obtain the throne, that he should obtain the emoluments that went with it."

80. Following Zhong Tai. The gentleman, being ashamed of honors and riches, kept to himself alone, divided his salary with his relatives, and shared his good fortune with them.

81. Literally, "butting and shoving," that is, says Yang Liang, jockeying for positions of power and influence.

82. Yang Liang takes this to be reflexive, "but say they possess ability," adducing *Shenzi*: "If being strong, one causes harm to those who have ability, there will be chaos; if one is said to have ability and does harm to those who lack ability, there will be chaos."

83. Following the interpretation of Yang Liang and Karlgren, LC 1857.

84. Following Wang Niansun. Early editions place this sentence at the end of the previous paragraph, but it belongs with this paragraph in content.

85. *Shi*, Greater Odes, "Yi," Mao 256. This Ode is also quoted in paragraph 3.4.

86. This functions as a paragraph title. The ZT edition reads "desires" in place of "demeanor." The paragraph abounds in rare words of uncertain meaning.

87. Text *si* 肆 GE *dai* 佯 in the meaning "correct but easy" attested in *Zuo*, Xiang 31.

88. Cf. *LY*, 7.36: "The gentleman is calmly at ease."

89. Zhong Tai takes *jian* 僩 GV *lian* 斂 "composed."

90. Following the reading of the ZT edition. The Lü edition omits the Yang commentary and is defective. Text *zi* 紫 GE *zi* 孳 LC *zi* 孜 attested *Mengzi*, 7A.25, in the sense "constantly striving."

91. That is, in his actions the gentleman should be like a signal for others. Cf. *DDLJ*, 55 "Zengzi zhiyin," II, 5.5a: "Actions are tokens and signals to the whole world."

92. With Yang Liang, text *wen* 綎 LC *mian* 俛.

93. With Yang Liang, text *jin* 禁 LC *jin* 衿, meaning "sash-like," i.e., loose fitting.

94. Following Guo Xiang apud *Zhuangzi*, 9 "Mati," 4.7a, occurrence of the same phrase.

95. With Yang Liang, text *di* 狄 LC *ti* 趯.

96. With Karlgren, text *mo* 莫 SF *mo* 嘆. Text *gui* 䁘 GV *gui* 規; cf. *Zuo*, Zhao 26. An alternate understanding based on the same phrase apud *Zhuangzi*, 23 "Gengsang Chu" 庚桑楚, 8.4a, where Watson (p. 512) translates "confused and crestfallen" and Legge (p. 519) "frightened and amazed." The meaning in this passage is also unclear to the commentators. Li Yi says "lost your spirit"; another commentator quoted by Lu Deming says "concerned with minutiae" (adopted by Hao Yixing).

97. Text *ju* 瞿 is understood as in *Shi*, Mao 100; cf. Karlgren GL 252.

98. With Yu Yue, text *jin* 盡 GV *jin* 津 based on Lu Deming gloss apud *Zhuangzi*, 23 "Gengsang Chu," 8.4a, meaning "inner impurity" (cf. occurrence in *Zhou li*, 10.3a, where marsh dwellers are called "black and slimy").

99. Following Yang Liang, based on the *Shuowen* definition; cf. Karlgren GL 244.

100. Following Yang Liang; cf. Karlgren LC 1031. Liu Shipei: *ming* 瞑 LC *min* 泯 "confused, troubled." Yang understands text *ming* as "not carefully listening and looking" because of an excessive fondness for the performances, which causes them to ignore the details.

101. Text *zi* 訾 LC *zi* 恣 "unrestrained."

102. Text *ru* 儒 GV *ru* 懦; *wang* 罔 SF *wang* 惘, "dejected, irresolute."

103. The text tradition for the phrase *dituo* is unsettled. Liu Shipei suggests that text 弟佗/第佗/弟作 is *weituo* 委佗 itself GV 委蛇 used in *Shi*, Mao 18 and 47, where Mao, based on a gloss to the poem apud *Zuo*, Xiang 7, says the meaning is "obedient, compliant." *Wei* and *tuo/yi* mean "bending" and "serpentine" (cf. Karlgren GL 49).

104. The text as it stands seems corrupt. With Zhong Tai *dan* 覃 LC *dan* 澹 "undulating"; *zhong* 神 GV *chong* 沖 "billowing"; *ci* 辭 GE *yi* 裔.

105. Following Zhong Tai.

Bibliography

COMMENTATORS

An asterisk (*) indicates a commentary reprinted in Yan Lingfeng 嚴靈峰, *Xunzi jicheng* 荀子集成, 49 vols. (Taibei, 1979), a reprint of 83 Chinese and Japanese editions of, and commentaries on, the *Xunzi*, many difficult to locate. Works with no other indication of edition are known only from this collection.

*Asaka Gonsai 安積艮齋 (1817–61). *Junshi ryakusetsu* 荀子略說.
*Asakawa Kanae 朝川鼎 (1780–1848). *Junshi noberi* 荀子述.
Bao Zunxin 包遵信. "Du *Xunzi* zhaji" 讀荀子札記. *Wenshi* 文史 5 (1978), 205–24; 6 (1979), 217–36.
Beijing Daxue. *Xunzi xinzhu* 荀子新注. Beijing, 1979.
Chen Huan 陳奐 (1786–1863). Notes contained in Wang Xianqian.
Chen Qiaocong 陳喬樅 (1809–69). Notes contained in Wang Xianqian.
*Chen Zhu 陳柱. *Chan Xun* 闡荀.
Duan Yucai 段玉裁 (1735–1815). Notes contained in Wang Xianqian.
Fang Bao 方苞 (1688–1749). Notes contained in Wang Xianqian.
*Fang Guang 方光. *Xunzi "Fei shier zi" pian shi* 荀子非十二子篇釋. 1928.
*Feng Zhen 馮振. "*Xunzi* 'Jiebi' pian jiangji" 荀子解蔽篇講記. *Jida wenxueyuan jikan* 暨大文學院集刊 1 (1934).
*———. "*Xunzi* 'Xing'e' pian jiangji" 荀子性惡篇講記. *Xueyi zazhi* 學藝雜誌 1, no. 9 (1930), 37–52.
*———. "*Xunzi* 'Xing'e' pian pingyi" 荀子性惡篇評議. *Xueyi zazhi* 學藝雜誌 2, no. 8 (1931), 1–12.
Fujii Sen'ei 藤井專英. *Junshi* 荀子. Kyoto, 1966.
Furuya Sekiyō 古屋昔陽 (1734–1806). Notes contained in Kubo Ai.
*Gao Heng 高亨. *Zhuzi xinjian* 諸子新箋. Jinan, 1961.
*Gu Guangqi 顧廣圻 (1776–1835). *Xunzi jiaozheng* 荀子校正. 1883. Notes contained in Wang Xianqian.
Guo Songdao 郭嵩燾 (1818–91). Notes contained in Liang Qixiong.
*Hao Yixing 郝懿行 (1757–1825). *Xunzi buzhu* 荀子補注. 1865.
*Haoshi Banri 帆足萬里 (1778–1852). *Junshi hyōchū* 荀子標註.
*Hong Yixuan 洪頤煊 (1761–1837). *Xunzi conglu* 荀子叢錄. 1822.
*Hu Yuanyi 胡元儀 (19th century). *Xun Qing biezhuan* 郇卿別傳. Never published but quoted *in extenso* in Wang Xianqian.
*Hu Yunyu 胡韞玉. *Xunzi xueshuo* 荀子學說. 1923.

Igai Hikohiro 豬飼彥博 (1761–1845). *Junzi hoi* 荀子補遺. Tokyo reprint of 1911.

*Ji Lienkang 吉聯抗. *Xunzi "Yuelun"* 荀子樂論. 1977.

Jiang Zhongkui 姜忠奎. *Xunzi xingshan zheng* 荀子性善證. 1920.

Jin Dejian 金德建. Essays on *Xunzi* in *Guji congkao* 古籍叢考. Taibei, 1967.

*Jin Qiyuan 金其源. *Xunzi guanjian* 荀子管見. 1948.

Kanaya Osamu 金谷治. *Junshi* 荀子. Kyoto, 1962.

Katayama Kenzan 片山兼山 (1730–81). Notes in Kubo Ai.

Kubo Ai 久保愛 (1759–1832). *Junshi zōchū* 荀子增注. 1830 ed.

Liang Qixiong 梁啓雄. *Xunzi jianshi* 荀子簡釋. Taibei, 1965.

*Liu Nianqin 劉念親. "*Xunzi* 'Zhengming' pian gushi" 荀子正名篇詁釋. *Huaguo yuekan* 華國月刊 1(1924), 10–11; 2(1925), 1–9.

*Liu Shipei 劉師培 (1884–1919). *Xunzi jiaobu* 荀子斠補; *Xunzi bushi* 荀子補釋; *Xunzi ci li juyao* 荀子詞例舉要. In *Liu Shenshu xiansheng yishu* 劉申樹先生遺書. Taibei, 1965.

*Liu Taigong 劉台拱 (1751–1805). *Xunzi buzhu* 荀子補註. 1806.

Long Yuchun 龍宇純. "*Xunzi jijie* buzheng" 荀子集解補正. *DLZZ* 2, no. 8 (1955), 11–15; 2, no. 9, 22–26; 2, no. 10, 18–27.

Lu Wenchao 盧文弨 (1717–96). Notes contained in Xie Yong.

*Momoi Hakuroku 桃井日鹿 (1722–1801). Notes contained in Kubo Ai.

*Muraoka Reisai 村岡樂齋 (1845–1917). *Junshi senshaku* 荀子淺釋.

*Ogyū Sorai 荻生祖徠 (1666–1728). *Doku Junshi* 讀荀子. Notes in Kubo Ai.

Pan Zhonggui 潘重規. "Du Wang Xianqian *Xunzi jijie* zhaji" 讀王先謙荀子集解札記. *SFGW* 1(1956), 49–65.

Qian Dian 錢佃. *Xunzi jiao* 荀子校. Copied by Gu Guangqi and contained in Wang Xianqian.

*———. *Xunzi kaoyi* 荀子考異. Reprinted from manuscript copy in the Tieqin tongjian lou 鐵琴銅劍樓 by Miao Quansun 繆荃孫 in *Zhou Qin zhuzi jiaozhu shizhong* 周秦諸子斠注十種.

Ruan Tingzhuo 阮延卓. *Xunzi jiaozheng* 荀子斠證. Taibei, 1959.

*Sun Yirang 孫詒讓 (1848–1908). *Xunzi Yang Liang zhujiao* 荀子楊倞注校 in *Zhayi* 札迻. 1894.

Tao Hongqing 陶鴻慶 (1895–?). *Du zhuzi zhaji* 讀諸子札記. Beijing, 1959.

Tao Shicheng 陶師承. *Xunzi yanjiu* 荀子研究. 1926.

*Tsukada Taihō 冢用大峰 (1745–1832). *Junshi dan* 荀子斷.

*Uno Tetsuto 宇野哲人 (1875–?). *Junshi hochū* 荀子補注.

*Wang Mouhong 王懋竑 (1668–1741). *Xunzi cun jiao* 荀子存校. Fujian, 1873.

*Wang Niansun 王念孫 (1744–1832). *Dushu zazhi* 讀書雜志. 1832.

Wang Shaolan 王紹蘭 (1760–1835). Notes contained in Liang Qixiong.

Wang Shumin 王叔岷. "*Xunzi* jiaoli" 荀子斠理. *BIHP* 34(1962), 115–97.

*Wang Xianqian 王先謙 (1842–1918). *Xunzi jijie* 荀子集解. Changsha, 1891.

Wang Yinzhi 王引之 (1766–1834). Notes contained in Wang Niansun.

*Wang Zhong 汪中 (1745–94). Notes contained in Wang Xianqian.

*Xie Yong 謝墉 (1719–95). *Xunzi* 荀子. Reprinted in SBBY.

Xiong Gongzhe 熊公哲. *Xunzi jinzhu jinshi* 荀子今注今釋. Taibei, 1975.

*Yan Lingfeng 嚴靈峰. *Xunzi duji* 荀子讀記. Taibei, 1977.

*Yang Shuda 楊樹達 (1885–?) *Du Xunzi xiaojian* 讀荀子小箋. Notes contained in Liang Qixiong.

*Yu Chang 于鬯 (1850–1910). *Xiangcao xujiao shu* 香草續校書. 1897.

*Yu Xingwu 于省吾 (1896–?). *Shuangjianchi zhuzi xinzheng* 雙劍誃諸子新證. Beijing, 1940.

*Yu Yue 俞樾 (1821–1907). *Zhuzi pingyi* 諸子平議. 1870.

Zhang Heng 張亨. *Xunzi jiajiezi pu* 荀子假借字譜. Taibei, 1965.

*Zhang Shitong 章詩同. *Xunzi jianzhu* 荀子簡註. Shanghai, 1974.

*Zhong Tai 鍾泰. *Xunzi dingbu* 荀子訂補. Shanghai, 1936.

*Zhu Yidong 朱亦棟. *Xunzi zhaji* 荀子札記. 1878.

TRADITIONAL SINOLOGICAL WORKS

Beitang shuchao 北唐書鈔. Encyclopedia compiled by Yu Shinan 虞世南 (558–638). Taibei reprint.

Bielu 別錄. Liu Xiang 劉向 (77–6) and Liu Xin 劉歆 (d. A.D. 23) Reconstructed from quotations.

Boshi liutie 白氏六帖. Compiled by Bo Juyi 白居易 (772–846). Facsimile reprint of Song edition.

Chongwen zongmu fubuyi 崇文總目附補遺. Compiled by Wang Yaochen 王堯臣 (1001–56). Reconstruction by Qian Dongyuan 錢東垣 et al. Congshu jicheng edition.

Chuci 楚辭. Qu Yuan 屈原 (4th century B.C.) with poems by Han authors written in the style. SBBY. Tr. Hawkes.

Chunqiu jingzhuan yinde 春秋經傳引得. Taibei, 1966.

Chunqiu Zuo zhuan zhengyi 春秋左傳正義. Compilation traditionally attributed to Zuo Qiuming 左丘明 (5th century B.C.), with significant additions and changes in the 4th century B.C., possibly under Wu Qi 吳起, with later additions, principally corrections of dates, in the Han period, probably by Liu Xin 劉歆 (d. A.D. 23). Commentary by Kong Yingda 孔穎達 (574–648). SBBY and Shisanjing editions. Tr. Legge, *Chinese Classics*, V.

Chuxueji 初學記. Encyclopedia compiled by Xu Jian 許堅 (659–729) et al. Beijing, 1962.

Da Dai liji 大戴禮記. SBCK. Tr. Richard Wilhelm.

Daode jing. See under *Laozi.*

Dengxizi 登析子. Attributed to Deng Xi 登析 (6th century B.C.), but generally regarded with suspicion. SBBY.

Erya 爾雅. Author unknown. Compiled in the late Zhou with additions in the Han period. Commentary by Guo Pu 郭璞. SBBY.

Fangyan shuzheng 方言疏正. Dialectical dictionary compiled by Yang Xiong 楊雄 (53 B.C.–A.D. 18). Commentary by Guo Pu 郭璞. Modern commentary by Dai Zhen 戴震 (1722–77). SBBY.

Fengsu tongyi 風俗通義. Ying Shao 應昭 (d. A.D. 195). SBBY.

Gongsun Longzi 公孫龍子. Gongsun Long 公孫龍 (3d century B.C.). Several authentic works combined with forgeries reconstructed from Mohist fragments. SBBY.

Gongyang yishu 公羊義疏. Attributed to Gongyang Gao 公羊高, with later additions. Commentary by He Xiu 何休 (129–82). Modern commentary by Chen Li 陳澧 (1810–82). SBBY.

Guanzi 管子. Attributed to Guan Zhong 管仲 (7th century B.C.), with some sections perhaps accurately reflecting his views, but the majority of the book compiled from the writings of scholars at the Jixia Academy (4th–3d centuries B.C.), with possible additions from scholars at the court of Liu An 劉安 (d. 122 B.C.). SBBY. Modern edition, see Guo Moruo et al. Tr. Rickett.

Guliang buzhu 穀梁補注. Attributed to Guliang Chi 穀梁赤, with later additions. Commentary by Fan Ning 范寧 (d. A.D. 441). Modern commentary by Zhong Wenzheng 鍾文烝. SBBY.

Guoyu 國語. Compiled from 5th–3d century B.C. sources. Commentary by Wei Zhao 韋昭 (204–73). SBBY.

Hanfeizi 韓非子. Han Fei 韓非 (d. 233 B.C.) and his followers. SBBY. Modern edition, see Chen Qiyou. Tr. Liao.

Hanshi waizhuan 韓詩外傳. Han Ying 韓嬰 (2d century B.C.) SBCK. Tr. Hightower.

Hanshu buzhu 漢書補注. Ban Gu 班固 (d. A.D. 92). Commentary by Yan Shigu 顏師古 (579–645). Modern commentary by Wang Xianqian 王先謙. Yiwen reprint. Tr. Dubs.

Hou Hanshu jijie 後漢書集解. Fan Ye 范曄 (398–445), with monographs by Sima Biao 司馬彪 (240–305). Commentary by Li Xian 李賢 (d. A.D. 731). Modern commentary by Wang Xianqian 王先謙. Yiwen reprint.

Huainanzi 淮南子. Compiled by scholars at the court of Liu An 劉安 (d. 122 B.C.). SBBY. Modern edition, see Liu Wendian.

Jingdian shiwen 經典釋文. Compiled by Lu Deming 陸德明 (556–627). SBCK.

Jinshu 晉書. Compiled by Fang Xuanling 房玄齡 et al. in A.D. 635. Yiwen reprint.

Jiu Tangshu 舊唐書. Compiled by Liu Xu 劉昫 (887–946) et al. SBTK.

Kongcongzi 孔叢子. Kong Fu 孔鮒 (d. 210 B.C.?). SBBY.

Kongzi jiayu 孔子家語. Compiled by Wang Su 王肅 (d. A.D. 256) from ancient materials. SBBY. Tr. Kramers.

Laozi 老子. Alternate title *Daode jing*. Attributed to Laozi, identified as the sage who taught Confucius. Compiled from materials dating from 5th–4th centuries B.C. SBBY. Tr. Chan; Karlgren; Lau; Waley.

Lienu zhuan 列女傳. Compiled by Liu Xiang 劉向 (77–6). SBBY.

Liezi 列子. Compiled by Zhang Zhan 張湛 (4th century A.D.) from ancient materials. SBBY. Modern edition, see Yang Bojun. Tr. Graham.

Liji zhengyi 禮記正義. Compilation traditionally attributed to Dai De 戴德 and Dai Sheng 戴聖 during the 1st century B.C. from materials dating from several centuries earlier. A compendium of heterogeneous materials, dating from the time of Mo Di to first decades of the Han dynasty, some not of Ru origin nor compatible with pre-Qin Ru notions, reaching its present form only in the Later Han period. Commentaries by Zheng Xuan 鄭玄 (127–200) and Kong Yingda 孔穎達 (574–648), with phonological glosses by Lu Deming 陸德明 (556–627). SBBY. Tr. Legge.

Lunheng 論衡. Wang Chong 王充 (27–97). SBBY.

Lunyu zhengyi 論語正義. Confucius (551–479). Compiled by his disciples with some later interpolations. Commentaries by Zheng Xuan 鄭玄 (127–200) and Kong Yingda 孔穎達 (574–648). Modern commentary by Liu Baonan 劉寶楠 (1791–1855). SBBY. Tr. Lau; Legge, *Chinese Classics*, I; Waley.

Lüshi chunqiu 呂氏春秋. Compiled for Lü Buwei 呂不韋 in 239 B.C. SBBY. Modern editions, see Chen Qiyou or Xu Weiyu. Tr. R. Wilhelm.

Maoshi zhuan shu 毛詩傳疏. Chen Huan 陳奐 (1786–1863). In *Huang Qing jingjie xubian* 皇清經解續編.

Mengzi 孟子. Compiled by Mencius and his followers ca. 300 B.C. Commentaries by Zhao Qi 趙岐 (d. A.D. 201) and Sun Shi 孫奭 (962–1033). Modern commentary by Jiao Xun 焦循 (1763–1820). SBBY. Tr. Lau; Legge, *Chinese Classics*, II.

Mozi jiangu 墨子間詁. Mo Di 墨翟 and his disciples, dating 4th–3d centuries B.C. Modern commentary by Sun Yirang 孫詒讓. Taibei reprint. Tr. Mei; Graham.

Mu tianzi chuan 穆天子傳. SBBY.

Qianfu lun 潛夫論. Wang Fu 王符 (85–163). SBBY.

Qieyun 切韻. Compiled in A.D. 601 by Lu Fayan 陸法言.

Qilue 七略. Compiled by Liu Xin 劉歆 (d. A.D. 23). Shumu ed.

Qunshu zhiyao 群書治要. Compiled by Wei Zheng 魏徵 (580–643). Yiwen reprint.

Sanguo zhi 三國志. Chen Shou 陳壽 (233–97). SBBY.

Shangjun shu 商君書. Compiled by followers of Shang Yang 商鞅 (fl. 359–338). SBBY. Tr. Duyvendak.

Shenzi 申子. Shen Buhai 申不害. Reconstruction. Tr. Creel.

Shenzi 慎子. Shen Dao 慎到. Reconstruction. Tr. Thompson.

Shi jing 詩經. Text established by Mao Heng 毛亨 and Mao Chang 毛萇, with commentaries by Zheng Xuan 鄭玄 (127–200) and Kong Yingda 孔穎達 (574–648). Shisanjing edition. Tr. Karlgren; Legge, *Chinese Classics*, IV; Waley.

Shiben bazhong 世本八種. Reconstructed. Shanghai, 1957.

Shiji 史記. See *Shiki kaichū kōshō*.

Shiji jijie 史記集解. In *Shiki kaichū kōshō*.

Shiji zhiyi 史記志疑. Liang Yusheng 梁玉繩 (1745–1819). Taibei reprint.

Shiki kaichū kōshō 史記會注考證. Compiled by Sima Qian 司馬遷 (145–86?) and his father Sima Tan 談 (180?–110). *Jijie* 集解 commentary by Pei Yin 裴駰 (5th century A.D.); *Suoyin* 索隱 by Sima Zhen 司馬貞 (8th century A.D.); and *Zhengyi* 正義. Zhang Shoujie 張守節 (8th century A.D.). Modern commentary by Takegawa Kametarō 瀧川龜太郎. Taibei reprint.

Shu jing 書經. The New Script 今文 version transmitted by Fu Sheng 伏勝; the Old Script 古文 version did not survive the Han dynasty, and the present Old Text *Documents* are artful forgeries probably by Mei Ze 梅賾. Preferred readings for New Script version established by Karlgren, "The Book of Documents." The readings for the Old Script adopted from Legge, *Chinese Classics*, III.

Shuowen tongxun dingsheng 說文通訓定聲. Zhu Junsheng 朱駿聲 (1788–1858). Taibei reprint.

Shuoyuan 說苑. Liu Xiang 劉向 (77–6). SBBY.

Siku quanshu zongmu 四庫全書總目. Completed under imperial auspices in A.D. 1782. Taibei reprint of Datong edition.

Siku tiyao bianzheng 四庫提要辨證. Yu Jiaxi 余嘉錫. Taibei reprint.

Suishu 隋書. Compiled by Wei Zheng 魏徵 (580–643) et al. SBCK.

Suishu jingjizhi 隋書經籍志. Taibei, 1963.

Sun Bin bingfa 孫臏兵法. Han copy of lost text recovered at Linyi xian. Beijing, 1975.

Sunzi 孫子. Attributed to Sun Wu 孫吳 (5th century B.C.). SBBY. Tr. Giles; Griffith.

Taiping yulan 太平御覽. Compiled by Li Fang 李昉 et al. in A.D. 983. Taibei reprint.

Tang huiyao 唐會要. Compilation by Wang Pu 王溥 (922–84). Beijing, 1971.

Tangshu jingji yiwen hezhi 唐書經籍藝文合志. Taibei, 1963.

Wenxuan 文選. Xiao Tong 蕭統 (501–31). SBBY.

Wenzi 文子. Attributed to a Xin Jin 辛鈃 (Zhou dynasty). Compilation of uncertain date containing some ancient materials. SBBY.

Wu Yue chunqiu 吳越春秋. Compiled from ancient sources by Zhao Ye 趙曄 (fl. A.D. 40). Shijie reprint.

Xiaojing 孝經. Attributed to Zeng Shen 曾參. SBBY.

Xinshu 新書. Jia Yi 賈誼 (201–169). SBBY.

Xin Tangshu 新唐書. Compiled by Ouyang Xiu 歐陽修 (1007–72) and Song Qi 宋祁 (988–1061). SBCK.

Xinxu 新序. Liu Xiang 劉向 (77–6). SBCK.

Xuelin 學林. Wang Guanguo 王觀國 (Song dynasty). Congshu jizheng edition.

Yanshi jiaxun huizhu 顏氏家訓滙注. Yan Zhitui 顏之推 (531–95). SBBY.

Yantie lun 鹽鐵論. Huan Kuan 桓寬 (fl. 81–73). SBBY.

Yanzi chunqiu 晏子春秋. Attributed to Yan Ying 晏嬰 (6th century B.C.). Compiled by Liu Xiang 劉向 (77–6). SBBY.

Yi jing 易經. Early Zhou divination text with philosophical appendixes added as late as Han times. Commentaries by Wang Bi 王弼 (fl. 226–49) and Kong Yingda 孔穎達 (574–648). Shisanjing edition.

Yilin 意林. Quotations excerpted from ancient texts by Ma Zong 馬總 (10th century A.D.). SBBY.

Yinwenzi 尹文子. Attributed to Yin Wen 尹文 (4th–3d centuries). SBBY.

Yiwen leiju 藝文類聚. Compiled by Ouyang Xun 歐陽詢 (547–641). Beijing, 1965.

Yi Zhou shu 逸周書. Collection of early documents, some authentic, found in tomb in A.D. 281. Shijie reprint.

Yuhai 玉海. Wang Yinglin 王應麟 (1223–96). Taibei reprint of 1883 edition.

Zhanguo ce 戰國策. Compiled by Liu Xiang 劉向 (77–6). SBCK. Tr. Crump.

Zhonglun 中論. Xu Gan 徐幹 (3d century A.D.). Shijie reprint.

Zhongyong 中庸. Attributed to Zisi 子思 (5th century B.C.). SBBY. Tr. Legge, *Chinese Classics*, I.

Zhou li 周禮. Zhou compilation of uncertain date. Commentaries by Zheng Xuan 鄭玄 (127–200) and Jia Gongyan 賈公彥 (fl. 650–55). Shisanjing edition.

Zhuangzi 莊子. Compiled by the followers of Zhuang Zhou 莊周 with materials from related schools of thought, 4th–2d centuries B.C. Commentary by Guo Xiang 郭象 (d. A.D. 312) with phonetic glosses added from Lu Deming 陸德明 (556–627). *Zhuangzi yinyi* 莊子音義. SBBY. Tr. Graham; Legge; Lin; Watson.

Zuo Zhuan 左傳. See under *Chunqiu Zuo zhuan zhengyi.*

CHINESE AND JAPANESE WORKS

Changsha Mawangdui yihao Hanmu 長沙馬王堆一號漢墓. Beijing, 1972.

Chao Gongwu 晁公武 (d. A.D. 1171). *Junzhai dushu zhi* 郡齋讀書志. Shumu reprint.

Chen Daqi 陳大齊. "Meng Xun xueshuo suoyi yi qu di yice" 孟荀學說所以異趣的臆測. *Kong Meng xuebao* 孔孟學報 2(1961), 1–20.

―――. *Mengzi xing shan shuo yu Xunzi xing'e shuo di bijao yanjiu* 孟子性善說與荀子性惡說的比較研究. Taibei, 1953.

―――. "Xunzi di xinli xueshuo" 荀子的心理學說. *DLZZ* 7, no. 8(1953), 1–4; 7, no. 9(1953), 17–22.

―――. "Xunzi mingxue fafan chugao" 荀子名學發凡初稿. *Wen shi zhe xuebao* 文史哲學報 2(1951), 1–66.

*――――. *Xunzi xueshuo* 荀子學說. Taibei, 1954.

Chen Dengyuan 陳登元. *Xunzi zhexue* 荀子哲學. Shanghai, 1928.

Chen Duxiu 陳獨秀. "*Xunzi* yunbiao ji kaoshi" 荀子韻表及考釋. *Dongfang zazhi* 東方雜志 34, no. 2(1937), 67–72.

Chen Mengjia 陳夢家. *Shangshu tonglun* 尚書通論. Shanghai, 1957.

―――. "Xi Zhou tongqi duandai, VI" 西周銅器斷代. *Kaogu xuebao* 考古學報 1956, no. 4, 85–122.

Chen Pan 陳槃. "Chanwei su yuan" 讖緯溯源. *BIHP* 11(1946), 317–35.

Chen Qian 陳謙. "Xunzi shiji" 荀子事輯. *Guoxue zhuankan* 國學專刊 1(1926), 2–3.

Chen Qiyou 陳奇猷. *Hanfeizi jishi* 韓非子集釋. Beijing, 1958.

―――. *Lüshi chunqiu jiaoshi* 呂氏春秋校釋. Shanghai, 1984.

Chen Shaopei 陳召培. "Xunzi zhexue ji qi fangfa lun" 荀子哲學及其方法論. *Renai yuekan* 仁愛月刊 1(1935), 6–8.

Chen Yuan 陳垣. "Shi hui juli" 史諱舉例. *Yanjing xuebao* 燕京學報 4(1928), 537–651. Reprinted: *Shi hui juli.* Beijing, 1962.

Chen Zhensun 陳振孫 (fl. A.D. 1234). *Zhizhai shulu jieti* 直齋書錄解題. Shumu reprint.

Cheng Shude 程樹德. *Lunyu jishi* 論語集釋. Taibei, 1965.

Cui Shu 崔述. *Lunyu yushuo* 論語餘說. In *Cui Dongbi yishu* 崔東壁遺書, vol. 6. Ed. Gu Jiegang 顧頡剛. Taibei, 1963.

Deng Jiaming 登夏鳴. "*Xunzi* zhaji" 荀子札記. *Guozhuan yuekan* 國專月刊 2, no. 1 (1936); 2, no. 2(1936).

Ding Bing 丁丙 (1832–99). *Shanben shushi cangshu zhi* 善本書室藏書志. 1901. Shumu reprint.

Du Guoxiang 杜國庠. *Du Guoxiang wenji* 杜國庠文集. Beijing, 1962.

―――. *Xian Qin zhuzi di ruogan yanjiu.* 先秦諸子的若干研究. Beijing, 1955.

―――. *Xian Qin zhuzi sixiang gaiyao* 先秦諸子思想概要. Beijing, 1955.

Fang Shouchu 方授楚. *Moxue yuanliu* 墨學源流. Taibei, 1957.

Fang Xiaobo 方孝伯. *Xunzi xuanzhu* 荀子選注. Beijing, 1954.

Feng Youlan 馮友蘭. *Zhongguo zhexue shi xinbian* 中國哲學史新編. Beijing, 1962.

Fujikawa Masakazu 藤川正數. *Junshi chūshaku shijō ni okeru bojū no katsudō* 荀子注釋史上における邦儒の活動. Kyoto, 1980.

Gong Lequn 龔樂群. *Meng Xun yitong* 孟荀異同. Taibei, 1968.

Gu Yanwu 顧炎武 (1613–82). *Rizhilu jishi* 日知錄集釋. SBBY.

Gui Fu 桂馥 (1736–1805). *Zhapu* 札樸. Taibei, 1964.

Guo Moruo 郭沫若. *Qingtong shidai* 青銅時代. Beijing, 1962.

———. *Shi pipan shu* 十批判書. Shanghai, 1950.

Guo Moruo 郭沫若, Wen Yiduo 聞一多, and Xu Weiyu 許維遹. *Guanzi jijiao* 管子集校. Beijing, 1956.

Hattori Shirō 服部四郎 and Tōdō Akiyasu 藤堂明保. *Chūgen on'in no kenkyū* 中原音韻の研究. Tokyo, 1958.

Hong Ye 洪業 et al. *Liji yinde* 禮記引得. Beijing, 1937.

———. *Xunzi yinde* 荀子引得. Beijing, 1950.

Hou Wailu 侯外廬. *Zhongguo sixiang tongshi* 中国思想通史. 3 vols. Beijing, 1957.

Hu Shi 胡適. *Zhongguo zhexue shi dagang* 中国哲學史大綱. Shanghai, 1919.

Huang Peilie 黃丕烈 (1763–1825). *Raopu cangshu tizhi xulu* 蕘圃藏書題識續錄. Shumu reprint.

Jiang Shangxian 姜尚賢. *Xunzi sixiang tixi* 荀子思想體系. Taibei, 1966.

Jin Dejian 金德建. "Sima Qian suo jian shukao xulun" 司馬遷所見書考續論. *Shixue nianbao* 史學年報 1, no. 5(1933), 35–52.

Jin Shoushen 金受申. *Jixiapai zhi yanjiu* 稷下派之研究. Shanghai, 1930.

Jin Yaoji 金耀基. "Xunzi zhengzhi zhexue zhongzhan" 荀子政治哲學重佔. *DLZZ* 18, no. 1(1959), 11–16.

Kimiya Yasuhiko 木宮泰彥. *Nihon koinsatsu bunkashi* 日本古印刷文化史. Tokyo, 1932.

Kimura Eichi 木村英一. "Doku Junshi nisoku: Shoshigakuteki sakki" 讀荀子二則：書誌學的箚記. *Kanda hakushi kanreki kinen shoshigaku ronshū* 神田博士還曆記念書誌學論集. Kyoto, 1957.

Kong Fan 孔繁. *Xun Kuang* 荀況. Xian, 1975.

Li Deyong 李德永. *Xunzi* 荀子. Shanghai, 1959.

———. "Xunzi di sixiang" 荀子的思想. *Wenshizhe* 文史哲 1(1957), 72–96.

Li Duqing 李獨清. "Liu Xiang *Bielu* kaoshi" 劉向別錄考釋. *Guida xuebao* 貴大學報 1(1946), 77–110.

Li Fengding 李風鼎. "Xunzi zhuan jing bian" 荀子傳經辨. In *GSB* 4:136–40.

Li Jingchi 李鏡池. "Zhou Yi guaming kaoshi" 周易卦名考釋. *Lingnan xuebao* 嶺南學報 9, no. 1(1948), 197–303.

Liang Qichao 梁啓超. "Xun Qing ji *Xunzi*" 荀卿及荀子. In *GSB* 4:104–14.

*———. *Xunzi ping zhuzi yuhui shi* 荀子評諸子語彙釋. Beijing, 1936.

*———. *Xunzi "Zhengming" pian* 荀子正名篇. Beijing, 1936.

———. *Yaoji jieti ji qi dufa* 要籍解題及其讀法. Taibei, 1965.

Liu Jie 劉節. "'Hongfan' shuzheng" 洪範疏證. In *GSB*, 5:388–403.

Liu Jie 劉節 et al. *Gushi kaocun* 古史考存. Beijing, 1958.

Liu Shipei 劉師培. *Liu Xiang "Sun Qing shulu" jiaobu* 劉向孫卿書錄校補. Shanghai, 1936.

Liu Wendian 劉文典. *Huainan honglie jijie* 淮南鴻烈集解. Shanghai, 1933.

Liu Zhenghao 劉正浩. *Zhou Qin zhuzi shu Zuo zhuan kao* 周秦諸子述左傳考. Taibei, 1966.

Liu Zijing 劉子靜. *Xunzi zhexue gangyao* 荀子哲學綱要. Taibei, 1965.

Lu Xinyuan 陸心源 (1834–94). *Bi Song lou cangshu zhi* 皕宋樓藏書志. Shumu reprint.

———. *Yigutang xuba* 儀顧堂續跋. Shumu reprint.

Luo Genze 羅根澤. *Zhuzi kaosuo* 諸子考索. Beijing, 1958.

Ma Guohan 馬國翰 (1794–1857). *Yuhan shanfang jiyishu* 玉函山房輯佚書. Reconstructions of ancient books compiled from quotations in ancient sources. Taibei reprint.

Machida Saburō 町田三郎. "*Kanshi* shi hen ni tsuite" 管子四篇について. *Bunka* 文化 25(1961), 75–102.

Mawangdui Hanmu boshu 馬王堆漢墓帛書. Beijing, 1980.

Miao Quansun 繆荃孫 (1844–1919). *Yifeng cangshu ji* 藝風藏書記. Shumu reprint.

Mo Baiji 莫伯驥. *Wushiwan juan loucang shumu chubian* 五十萬卷樓藏書目初編. Shumu reprint.

Mori Takiyuchi 森立之等 (19th century). *Jingji fanggu zhi* 經籍訪古志. Shumu reprint.

Moriya Mitsuo 守屋美都雄. "Shin no gunkō hōshōsei ni okeru jinteki shihai no mondai ni tsuite" 秦の軍功褒賞制における人的支配の問題について. *Shakai keizai shigaku* 社會經濟史學 23(1957), 1–20.

Pan Zongzhou 潘宗周. *Baolitang Songben shulu* 寶禮堂宋本書錄. Wenhai reprint.

Qian Daxin 錢大昕 (1728–1804). *Ershier shi kaoyi* 二十二史考異. SBBY.

Qian Mu 錢穆. *Xian Qin zhuzi xinian* 先秦諸子繫年. Hong Kong, 1956.

Qian Zeng 錢曾 (1629–99?). *Dushu minqiu ji jiaozheng* 讀書敏求記校證. Shumu reprint.

Qu Wanli 屈萬里. *Shangshu shiyi* 尚書釋義. Taibei, 1956.

Qu Yong 瞿鏞 (19th century). *Tieqin tongjian lou cangshu mulu* 鐵琴銅劍樓藏書目錄. Shumu reprint.

Rao Zongyi 饒宗頤. "Tianshen guan yu daode sixiang" 天神觀與道德思想. *BIHP* 49, no. 1(1978), 77–100.

Ruan Tingzhuo 阮延卓. "Song ben *Xunzi* kaolue" 宋本荀子考略. *Minzhu pinglun* 民主評論 22, no. 11(1961), 12–13.

———. "*Xunzi* 'Dalue' pian kaoyuan" 荀子大略篇考原. *DLZZ* 30, no. 5, (1965), 19–24.

———. "*Xunzi* shulu" 荀子書錄. *SFGW* 5(1961), 405–37.

———. "*Xunzi* tongkao" 荀子通考. *DLZZ* 34(1967), 241–48.

Sun Deqian 孫德謙. "Xunzi tongyi" 荀子通誼. *Xuehai* 學海 1, no. 1(1955), 47–55; 1, no. 2, 52–61; 1, no. 5, 57–60; 2, no. 2(1956), 30–36.

Sun Yue 孫曜. *Chunqiu shidai zhi shizu* 春秋史代之世族. Shanghai, 1936.

Tan Jiefu 譚戒甫. *Mo Jing yijie* 墨經易解. Shanghai, 1935.

———. "*Xunzi* 'Zhengming' pian jiangji" 荀子正名篇講記. *Dongfang zazhi* 東方雜志 32, no. 7(1935), 157–166.

Tang Junyi 唐君毅. "Meng Mo Zhuang Xun zhi yan xin shen yi" 孟墨莊荀之言心申義. *Xinya xuebao* 新亞學報 1, no. 2(1956), 29–81.

————. "Xunzi zhengming yu xian Qin mingxue san zong" 荀子正名與先秦名學三宗. *Xinya xuebao* 新亞學報 5, no. 2(1963), 1–22.

Tang Lan 唐蘭. "Mawangdui chutu *Laozi* Yi ben juanqian guyi shu di yanjiu" 馬王堆出土老子乙本卷前古佚書的研究. *Kaogui xuebao* 考古學報 1975, no. 1, 7–38.

Tao Shicheng 陶師承. *Xunzi yanjiu* 荀子研究. Shanghai, 1926.

Wang Guowei 王國維. *Guben Zhushu jinian jijiao* 古本竹書紀年輯校. Taibei, 1963.

Wang Liqi 王利器. *Yantie lun jiaozhu* 鹽鐵論校注. Taibei, 1965.

Wang Shumin 王叔岷. "*Shiji* Mengzi Xun Qing liezhuan jiaozheng 史記孟子荀卿列傳斠證. *Kong Meng xuebao* 孔孟學報 13(1967), 71–141.

Wang Wenjin 王文進. *Wenlu tang fangshu ji* 文錄堂訪書記. Shumu reprint.

Wang Yinglin 王應麟 (1223–96). *Kunxue jiwen* 困學紀聞. SBBY.

Wei Zhengtong 韋正通. *Xunzi yu gudai zhexue* 荀子與古代哲學. Taibei, 1966.

Wu Feibai 伍非百. *Zhongguo gu mingjia yan* 中國古名家言. 2 vols. Beijing, 1983.

Wu Wen 吳文. "Xunzi shi Zhongguo fengjianzhuyi sixiang di kai shanzhe ma" 荀子是中國封建主義思想的開山者嗎. *Zhexue yanjiu* 哲學研究 4(1957), 136–45.

Xia Zhentao 夏甄陶. *Lun Xunzi di zhexue sixiang* 論荀子的哲學思想. Shanghai, 1979.

Xiao Gongquan 蕭公權. *Zhongguo zhengzhi sixiang shi* 中國政治思想史. 2 vols. Chongqing, 1945–46.

Xiong Gongzhe 熊公哲. *Xun Qing xuean* 荀卿學案. Shanghai, 1936.

Xu Weiyu 許維遹. *Lüshi chunqiu jishi* 呂氏春秋集釋. Beijing, 1955.

Xu Zhongshu 徐中舒. "Chen Hou si qi kaoshi" 陳侯四器考釋. *BIHP* 3(1934), 478–506.

————. "Jinwen jiaci shili" 金文假辭釋例. *BIHP* 6(1936), 1–44.

Yan Kejun 嚴可均 (1762–1843). *Quan shanggu sandai wen* 全上古三代文. Beijing, 1958.

Yang Bojun 楊伯峻. *Chunqiu Zuo zhuan zhu* 春秋左傳注. Beijing, 1981.

————. *Liezi jishi* 列子集釋. Shanghai, 1958.

————. "Lue tan woguo shiji shang guanyu shi ti fangfudi jizai he Mawangdui yihao Hanmu muzhu wenti" 略談我國史籍上關於屍體防腐的記載和馬王堆一號漢墓墓注問題. *Wenwu* 文物 1972, no. 9, 36–40.

Yang Daying 楊大膺. *Xunzi xueshuo yanjiu* 荀子學說研究. Shanghai, 1936.

Yang Shaohe 楊紹和 (1831–76). *Yingshu yulu* 楹書隅錄. Shumu reprint.

Yang Shoujing 楊守敬 (1839–1915). *Riben fangshu zhi* 日本訪書志. Shumu reprint.

Yang Xiangkui 楊向奎. "Xunzi di sixiang" 荀子的思想. *Wenshizhe* 文史哲 10(1957), 1–10.

Yang Yunru 楊筠如. "Guanyu *Xunzi* benshu di kaozheng" 關於荀子本書的考證. In *GSB* 6:120–46.

————. *Xunzi yanjiu* 荀子研究. Shanghai, 1936.

You Guoen 游國恩. "Xun Qing kao" 荀子考. In *GSB* 4:94–103.

Zhang Binglin 張炳麟 (1868–1936). *Guogu lunheng* 國故論衡. In *Zhangshi congshu* 張氏叢書. Shanghai, 1936.

Zhang Changgong 張長弓. "Xun Qing di yunwen" 荀子的韻文. *Lingnan xuebao* 嶺南學報 3, no. 2(1934), 145–67.

Zhang Heng 張亨. "Du *Xunzi* zhaji" 讀荀子札記. *DLZZ* 22, no. 8(1961), 11–16; 22, no. 9(1961), 21–26.

———. "Xunzi yu hui yanjiu" 荀子與彙研究. *Zhongguo xueshu niankan* 中國學術年刊 1(1962), 271–377.

Zhang Jinwu 張金吾 (1787–1829). *Airi jinglu cangshu zhi* 愛日精廬藏書志. 1826.

Zhang Senjie 張森楷. *Shiji xin jiaozhu* 史記新校注. Taibei, 1962.

Zhang Weixiang 張惟驤. *Jiahui kao* 家諱考. Shanghai, 1932.

Zhang Xincheng 張心澂. *Weishu tongkao* 偽書通考. Changsha, 1939.

Zhang Xitang 張西堂. "*Xunzi* 'Quanxue' pian yuan ci" 荀子勸學篇冤詞. In *GSB*, 6:147–61.

———. "*Xunzi* zhen wei kao" 荀子眞偽考. *Shixue jikan* 史學集刊 3(1936), 165–236.

Zhao Haijin 趙海金. "*Xunzi* buyi" 荀子補遺. *DLZZ* 24, no. 7(1962), 17.

———. "*Xunzi* 'Fuguo' pian wei hu xingfa wei cuojian shuo" 荀子富國篇威乎刑罰爲錯簡說. *DLZZ* 32, no. 11(1966), 22.

———. "*Xunzi* jiaobu" 荀子校補. *DLZZ* 21, no. 3(1960), 25.

———. "*Xunzi* jiaoshi" 荀子校釋. *DLZZ* 23, no. 2(1961), 217.

———. "*Xunzi* 'Jiebi' pian 'gu you yong wei zhi dao li yi' zhi dao dang zhong du shuo" 荀子解蔽篇故由用謂之道利矣之道當重讀說. *DLZZ* 32, no. 10(1966), 11.

———. "*Xunzi* 'Rongru' pian 'an zhi lian chi yu ji' dang zuo 'an zhi lian chi, an zhi long ji' zhi shuo" 荀子榮辱篇安知廉恥隅積當作安知廉恥安知隆積之說. *DLZZ* 32, no. 10(1966), 26.

———. "*Xunzi* 'Tianlun' pian zi 'gu dao zhi suo shan' zhi 'ni ze da huo' wei cuo jian shuo" 荀子天論篇自故道之所善至匿則大惑爲錯簡說. *DLZZ* 32, no. 9(1966), 10.

Zhao Yue 趙鉞 and Lao Ge 勞格. *Tang Shangshusheng langguan shizhu timingkao* 唐尚書省郎官石柱題名考. Kyoto, 1978.

Zheng Liangshu 鄭良樹. *Zhujian Boshu lun wenji* 竹簡帛書論文集. Beijing, 1982.

Zhou Fagao 周法高. "*Xunzi* 'Zhongni' pian zhaji er ze" 荀子仲尼篇札記二則. *DLZZ* 10, no. 7(1955), 25.

Zhou Hulin 周虎林. "Xunzi xueshu yuanyuan ji qi liuyan" 荀子學術淵源及其流衍. *SFGW* 8(1964), 459–522.

Zhu Shizhe 朱師轍. "*Xunzi* 'Chengxiang' pian yundu bushi" 荀子成相篇韻讀補釋. *Zhongshan daxue xuebao* 中山大學學報 3(1957), 42–47.

Zhu Xuan 朱玄. "Meng Xun shu shi kao ji Meng Xun liezhuan shuzheng" 孟荀書十考及孟荀列傳疏證. *SFGW* 10(1966), 69–216.

WORKS IN WESTERN LANGUAGES

Bodde, Derk. *China's First Unifier: A Study of the Ch'in Dynasty as Seen in the Life of Li Ssu (280?-208 B.C.)*. Hong Kong, 1967.

———. *Essays on Chinese Civilization*. Princeton, 1981.

———. *Statesman, Patriot, and General in Ancient China*. New Haven, 1940.

Broman, Sven. "Studies on the *Chou Li*." *BMFEA* 33(1961), 1–89.

Chan, Wing-tsit. *The Way of Lao Tzu*. New York, 1963.

Chavannes, E. *Les Mémoires historiques de Se-ma Ts'ien*. 5 vols. Paris, 1895–1905.

Creel, H. G. "Confucius and Hsün-tzu." *JAOS* 51(1931), 23–32.

———. *Confucius and the Chinese Way*. New York, 1960.

————. *The Origins of Statecraft in China*, vol. 1, *The Western Chou Empire*. Chicago, 1970.

————. *Shen Pu-hai, A Chinese Political Philosopher of the Fourth Century B.C.* Chicago, 1974.

————. *What is Taoism?* Chicago, 1970.

Creel, H. G., T. C. Chang, and R. C. Rudolph. *Literary Chinese by the Inductive Method*. Vol. 2. Chicago, 1939.

Crump, J. I. *Chan-Kuo Ts'e*. Oxford, 1970.

————. *Intrigues: Studies of the Chan-kuo Ts'e*. Ann Arbor, 1964.

Dobson, W.A.C.H. "Linguistic Evidence and the Dating of the *Book of Songs*." *TP* 51(1960), 322–34.

————. "The Origin and Development of Prosody in Early Chinese Poetry." *TP* 54(1968), 231–50.

Dubs, Homer H. *The History of the Former Han Dynasty*. 3 vols. Baltimore, 1938–55.

————. *Hsüntze: The Moulder of Ancient Confucianism*. London, 1927.

————. "Mencius and Sun-dz on Human Nature." *Philosophy East and West* 6(1956), 213–22.

————. *The Works of Hsüntze*. London, 1928.

Duyvendak, J.J.L. *The Book of Lord Shang*. London, 1928.

————. "The Chronology of Hsüntzu." *TP* 26(1929), 73–95.

————. "Hsün-tzu on the Rectification of Names." *TP* 23(1924), 221–54.

————. "Notes on Dubs' translation of *Hsün-tzu*." *TP* 29(1932), 1–42.

Eberhard, Wolfram. "Beiträge zur kosmologischen Spekulation Chinas in der Han Zeit." *Baessler Archiv* 16(1933), 1–100.

Eisler, Rudolf. *Wörterbuch der philosophischen Begriffe*. 3 vols. Berlin, 1929.

Forke, A. *The World-Conception of the Chinese*. London, 1925.

Giles, L. *Sun Tzu on the Art of War*. London, 1910.

Graham, A. C. "The Background of the Mencian Theory of Human Nature." *Tsing Hua Journal of Chinese Studies* 6(1967), 215–74.

————. "'Being' in Western Philosophy Compared with Shih/Fei and Yu/Wu in Chinese Philosophy." *Asia Major*, N.S. 7(1959), 79–112.

————. *The Book of Liehtzu*. London, 1960.

————. *Chuang-tzu: The Inner Chapters*. London, 1983.

————. "The Composition of the *Gongsuen Long tzyy*." *Asia Major*, N.S. 5(1957), 147–83.

————. "The Concepts of Necessity and 'A Priori' in Later Mohist Disputation." *Asia Major*, N.S. 19(1972), 163–90.

————. "The Date and Composition of *Liehtzyy*." *Asia Major*, N.S. 8(1961), 139–98.

————. "The Dialogue Between Yang Ju and Chyntzyy." *Bulletin of the School of Oriental and African Studies* 22(1959), 191–299.

————. "The 'Hard and White' Disputations of the Chinese Sophists." *Bulletin of the School of Oriental and African Studies* 30(1967), 358–68.

————. "Kung-sun Lung's Essay on Meaning and Things." *Journal of Oriental Studies*, 2(1955), 282–301.

————. *Later Mohist Logic, Ethics, and Science*. London, 1978.

————. "Later Mohist Treatises on Ethics and Logic Reconstructed from the Ta-ch'ü Chapter of *Mo-tzu*." *Asia Major*, N.S. 17(1972), 137–89.

————. "The Logic of the Mohist Hsiao-ch'ü." *TP* 51(1964), 1–54.

————. "Two Dialogues in the *Kung-sun Lung tzu*." *Asia Major*, N.S. 11(1965), 128–52.

Granet, Marcel. *Etudes sociologiques sur la Chine*. Paris, 1953.

Griffith, S. B. *Sun Tzu: The Art of War*. New York, 1963.

Haloun, Gustav. "Legalist Fragments. Part 1: *Kuan-tsï* 55 and Related Texts." *Asia Major*, N.S. 2(1951), 85–120.

————. "Das Ti-tsï-tsï, Frühkonfuzianische Fragmente II." *Asia Major* 9(1933), 467–502.

Hawkes, David. *Ch'u Tz'u: The Songs of the South*. Oxford, 1959.

Hightower, James. *Han Shih Wai Chuan*. Cambridge, Mass., 1952.

————. "The *Han-shih Wai-chuan* and the *San Chia Shih*." *Harvard Journal of Asiatic Studies* 11(1948), 241–310.

Hsiao, Kung-chuan. *A History of Chinese Political Thought*, vol. 1, *From the Beginnings to the Sixth Century A.D.* Tr. F. W. Mote. Princeton 1979.

Hu Shih. *Development of the Logical Method in Ancient China*. Shanghai, 1922.

Hulsewé, A.F.P. *Remnants of Han Law*. Leiden, 1955.

Kane, Virginia C. "Aspects of Western Chou Appointment Inscriptions." *Early China* 8(1982–83), 14–28.

Karlgren, Bernhard. "The Authenticity of Early Chinese Texts." *BMFEA* 1(1929), 165–83.

————. "The Book of Documents." *BMFEA* 22(1950), 1–81.

————. *The Book of Odes*. Stockholm, 1950.

————. "Early History of the *Chou Li* and *Tso Chuan* Texts." *BMFEA* 3(1931), 1–59.

————. "Glosses on the *Book of Documents*." *BMFEA* 20(1948); 21(1949).

————. "Glosses on the *Book of Odes*." *BMFEA* 14(1942); 16(1944); 18(1946).

————. "Glosses on the *Li Ki*." *BMFEA* 43(1971), 1–65.

————. "Glosses on the *Tso Chuan*." *BMFEA* 41(1969), 1–158.

————. *Grammata Serica Recensa*. Stockholm, 1957.

————. "Legends and Cults in Ancient China." *BMFEA* 18(1946), 199–365.

————. "Loan Characters in Pre-Han Chinese." *BMFEA* 35(1963), 1–128; 36(1964), 1–105; 37(1965), 1–136; 38(1966), 1–82; 39(1967), 1–51.

————. "Notes on Laotse." *BMFEA* 47(1975), 1–19.

————. *On the Authenticity and Nature of the Tso Chuan*. Göteborg, 1926.

Knoblock, John. "The Chronology of Xunzi's Works." *Early China* 8(1982–83), 28–52.

Köster, Hermann. "Ein chinesischer Beamterspiegel aus den 3 Jahrhundert v. Chr. *Hsün-tzu*, Abschnitt 13." *Oriens Extremus* 3(1956), 18–27.

————. *Hsün-tzu*. Kaldenkirchen, 1967.

————. "Nichts ungebührlich". *Sinologica* 4(1956), 233–49.

Kramers, R. P. *K'ung Tzu Chia Yü: The School Sayings of Confucius*. Leiden, 1950.

Kunst, Richard A. "More on *Xiu* 宿 and *Wuxing* 五行, with an Addendum on the Use of Archaic Reconstructions." *Early China* 3 (1977), 67–69.

Lau, D. C. *Confucius: The Analects.* New York, 1979.

———. *Lao Tzu Tao Te Ching.* Baltimore, 1963.

———. *Mencius.* New York, 1970.

———. "Theories of Human Nature in Mencius and Shyuntzyy." *Bulletin of the School of Oriental and African Studies* 15 (1953), 541–65.

Legge, James. *The Chinese Classics,* 5 vols. Hong Kong reprint.

———. *The Li Ki.* In *Sacred Books of the East,* vols. 27–28. Dover reprint.

———. *The Texts of Taoism.* In *Sacred Books of the East,* vols. 39–40. Dover reprint. [Contains translations of the *Zhuangzi* and the *Daode jing.*]

Liao, W. K. *The Complete Works of Han Fei Tzu.* 2 vols. London, 1959.

Lin Yutang. *The Wisdom of Lao Tzu.* New York, 1948.

Loewe, Michael. "Manuscripts Found Recently in China: A Preliminary Survey." *TP* 63 (1977), 99–135.

Major, John. "Myth, Cosmology, and the Origins of Chinese Science." *Journal of Chinese Philosophy* 5 (1978), 1–20.

———. "A Note on the Translation of Two Technical Terms in Chinese Science: *Wu-hsing* 五行 and *Hsiu* 宿." *Early China* 2 (1976), 1–3.

———. "Reply to Richard Kunst's Comments on *Hsiu* and *Wu Hsing.*" *Early China* 3 (1977), 69–70.

Malmquist, Göran. "Chou Tsu-mo on the *Ch'ieh-yün.*" *BMFEA* 40 (1968), 33–78.

———. "Studies on the *Gongyang* and *Guuliang Commentaries,* II." *BMFEA* 47 (1975), 19–69.

Maspero, Henri. *China in Antiquity.* Tr. Frank A. Kierman, Jr. Amherst, 1978.

———. "La chronologie des rois de Ts'i au IVᵉ siècle avant ère." *TP* 2 (1927), 367–86.

———. "Le mot ming 明." *Journal asiatique* 223 (1933), 249–56.

Mei, Y. P. *The Ethical and Political Works of Motse.* London, 1929.

———. "Hsün-tzu on Terminology." *Philosophy East and West* 1 (1951), 51–66.

———. "Hsün-tzu's Theory of Education." *Qinghua xuebao* 2 (1961), 361–79.

———. "Hsün-tzu's Theory of Government." *Qinghua xuebao* 7 (1970), 36–83.

———. *Mo-tze: The Neglected Rival of Confucius.* London, 1934.

Needham, Joseph. *Science and Civilization in China.* 7 vols. Cambridge, Eng., 1954– .

Nivison, David. "Royal 'Virtue' in Shang Oracle Inscriptions." *Early China* 4 (1978–79), 52–55.

Pankenier, David. "Astronomical Dates in Shang and Western Zhou." *Early China* 7 (1981–82), 2–52.

Parker, E. H. "Liu Hsiang and Ts-ien Ta-hien on Süntsz." *New China Review* 4 (1922), 443–49.

———. "The Philosopher Süntsz." *New China Review* 4 (1922), 360–71.

Pelliot, Paul, "Le Chou King en caractères anciens et le Chang chou che wen." *Mémoires concernant l'Asie orientale* 2 (1916), 123–77.

Rickett, W. Allyn. *Guanzi.* 3 vols. Princeton, N.J., 1985– .

————. *Kuan-tzu: A Repository of Early Chinese Thought.* Hong Kong. 1965.

Riegel, Jeffrey K. "Mawangdui Tomb Three: Documents." *Early China* 2 (1976), 68–72.

————. "A Summary of Some Recent *Wenwu* and *Kaogu* Articles on Mawang-dui Tombs Two and Three." *Early China* 1(1975), 10–15.

Rubin, V. A. "Tzu-chan and the City-state of Ancient China." *TP* 52(1965), 16–30.

Sargent, Galen Eugene. "Le débat entre Meng-tseu et Siun-tseu sur 'la nature humaine.'" *Oriens Extremus* 3(1956), 1–17.

Shih, Vincent Y. C. "Hsüntzu's Positivism." *Qinghua xuebao* 4(1963), 152–74.

Thompson, Paul. *The Shen-Tzu Fragments.* London, 1975.

Tsuda Sokichi. "On the Dates When the *Ta-tai Li Chi* and the *Li Chi* Were Edited." *Memoirs of the Research Department of the Toyo Bunko* 6(1932), 77–112.

Waley, Arthur. *The Analects of Confucius.* London, 1938.

————. *The Book of Songs.* London, 1937.

————. *Three Ways of Thought in Ancient China.* London, 1939.

————. *The Way and Its Power.* London, 1934.

Walker, Richard Louis. *The Multi-state System of Ancient China.* Hamden, Conn., 1953.

Watson, Burton, *The Complete Works of Chuang Tzu.* New York, 1968.

————. *Early Chinese Literature.* New York, 1962.

————. *Hsün Tzu: Basic Writings.* New York: 1963.

————. *Records of the Grand Historian of China.* New York, 1961.

Wilhelm, Helmut. "The *I Ching* Oracles in the *Tso Chuan* and the *Kuo-yü.*" *JAOS* 79(1959), 175–80.

Wilhelm, Richard. *Frühling und Herbst des Lü Bu We.* Jena, 1928.

————. *Li Gi: Das Buch der Sitte der älteren und jüngeren Dai.* Jena, 1930.

Yang, Hsien-yi, and Gladys Yang. *Records of the Historian.* Hong Kong, 1974.

Zhang Yachu 張亞初 and Liu Yu 劉雨. "Some Observations About Milfoil Divination Based on Shang and Zhou *Bagua* 八卦 Numerical Symbols." *Kaogu* 考古 1981, no. 2, 155–63. Tr. Edward L. Shaughnessy, *Early China* 7(1981–82), 46–55.

Index

In this index an "f" after a number indicates a separate reference on the next page, and an "ff" indicates separate references on the next two pages. A continuous discussion over two or more pages is indicated by a span of page numbers, e.g., "pp. 57–58." *Passim* is used for a cluster of references in close but not consecutive sequence.

Library of Congress Cataloging-in-Publication Data

Hsün-tzu, 340–245 B.C.
　[Works. English. 1988]
　A translation and study of the complete works/John Knoblock.
　　p.　cm.
　Bibliography: p.
　Includes index.
　ISBN 0-8047-1451-7 (v. 1 : alk. paper)
　I. Knoblock, John.　II. Title.
B128.H66E5　1988
181'.09512—dc 19　　　　　　　　　　　　　　　　87-33578
　　　　　　　　　　　　　　　　　　　　　　　　　　　CIP